AN INTRODUCTION TO

# ACCOUNTING and MANAGERIAL FINANCE

A Merger of Equals

AN INTRODUCTION TO

# ACCOUNTING and MANAGERIAL FINANCE

A Merger of Equals

Harold Bierman, Jr.

*Cornell University, USA*

 **World Scientific**

NEW JERSEY · LONDON · SINGAPORE · BEIJING · SHANGHAI · HONG KONG · TAIPEI · CHENNAI

*Published by*

World Scientific Publishing Co. Pte. Ltd.

5 Toh Tuck Link, Singapore 596224

*USA office:* 27 Warren Street, Suite 401-402, Hackensack, NJ 07601

*UK office:* 57 Shelton Street, Covent Garden, London WC2H 9HE

**Library of Congress Cataloging-in-Publication Data**
Bierman, Harold.
    An introduction to accounting and managerial finance : a merger of equals /
by Harold Bierman.
      p. cm.
    Includes index.
    ISBN-13: 978-9814273824 (hardcover)
    ISBN-10: 9814273821 (hardcover)
  1. Corporations--Accounting.  2. Corporations--Finance.  I. Title.
    HF5636.B54 2009
    657--dc22
                                 2009034159

**British Library Cataloguing-in-Publication Data**
A catalogue record for this book is available from the British Library.

Typeset by Stallion Press
Email: enquiries@stallionpress.com

Printed in Singapore by B & Jo Enterprise Pte Ltd

# Preface

Introductory accounting and finance have traditionally been taught as two separate courses, even though the importance of a basic knowledge of finance in learning accounting and a knowledge of accounting in learning finance have been widely acknowledged. One important historical reason for having two separate courses was that, in the past, few professors could teach both courses well. This lack of competent instructors has disappeared, and there are now many professors who can well integrate the basic elements of accounting and finance.

Accounting is an ever-evolving art. Understanding accounting is necessary to understand financial reporting by business organizations and the uses of financial reports by decision makers, both internal managers and financial analysts.

The structure of accounting is an important educational tool. The basic logic of the debit-credit process is elegant and logically consistent. The use of debits and credits emphasizes the relationships between accounts and simplifies the explanation of a wide range of financial transactions.

This book is also an introduction to corporate financial management, building on the basic capital budgeting framework and the time value of money. The objective is to stress the theoretical formulations that are most useful in making managerial financial decisions. A working knowledge of the time value of money is essential to having a complete liberal education.

The terms *net present value*, *internal rate of return*, and *capital asset pricing model* are today widely used by managers. A few years ago, the persons in important managerial positions might have said that they made the firm's big decisions on the basis of their experience, judgment, and intuition. Now, top managers insist more and more on having financial information properly analyzed before they exercise their judgments.

Many of the financial models are simplifications of the real world. If they were to be applied without thought, it is likely that some of the models would lead to undesirable decisions. However, if used correctly, such models will give insights into the weaknesses of other, more simplified and erroneous decision-making techniques. This book emphasizes that the correct application of financial techniques in business situations improves the likelihood of making good decisions. However, exact answers and correct decisions are not always guaranteed in a complex and uncertain world.

This book is based on a number of fundamental principles. First, the time value of money is used as the basic foundation for a large amount of the analysis. Second, decisions are approached on an after-tax basis. Third, we have avoided relatively complex models that are more appropriate for a more advanced finance course. Fourth, we emphasize decision making. We emphasize the models and methods of analysis that are most useful and practical rather than discussing theory for theory's sake. Finally, once the reader understands the basic concepts and methods, we think it is important to introduce various real-world constraints and complexities.

I acknowledge the invaluable contributions of my co-authors on other writing projects, Sy Smidt, Jerry Hass, and Bob Swieringa. While these friends and colleagues cannot be held responsible for any mistakes (misstatements), they did help contribute significantly to my understanding of the topics covered in this book.

**Harold Bierman, Jr.**
Cornell University

# Contents

*Chapter 1*

# Finance, Accounting and Corporate Objectives

## Corporate Objectives

The motivation for buying the common stock of a corporation is the expectation of making a larger risk-adjusted return than can be earned elsewhere. The managers of a corporation have the responsibility of administering the affairs of the firm in a manner consistent with the expectation of returning the investors' original capital plus the required return on their capital. The common stockholders are the residual owners, and they earn a return only after the investors in the more senior securities (debt and preferred stock) have received their contractual claims. We will assume that the objective of the firm is to maximize its common stockholders' wealth position.

Stockholders invest in a corporation with the expectation of making a net gain on their investment consistent with the investment's risk. The managers and the board of directors of a corporation have the responsibility of administering the affairs of the firm in a manner consistent with the interests of the stockholders. Thus, one of management's primary goals should be the maximization of stockholders' wealth. Although corporations might have other objectives (such as fulfilling their social responsibilities or treating their workers fairly), we will focus our attention on the more narrow corporate goal of stockholder wealth maximization.

But even this narrow definition is apt to give rise to misunderstanding and conflict. It is very likely that situations will arise where one group of stockholders will prefer one financial decision while another group of stockholders will prefer another decision. For example, imagine a situation where a business undertakes an investment that is deemed to be desirable by management, but the immediate effect of the investment will be to depress earnings and the common stock price today. In the future, the market may realize that the investment is desirable, and at that

1

time the stock price will reflect the enhanced value. But the stockholders expecting to sell their stock in the near future would prefer that the investment be rejected, while stockholders holding for the long run would prefer that the investment be undertaken.

A statement such as "profit maximization" does not adequately describe the appropriate objective of the firm, since profits are conventionally computed and do not effectively reflect the cost of the stockholders' capital that is tied up in the investment. Total sales or share of product market are also inadequate normative descriptions of corporate goals, although these goals may also lead to maximization of the shareholders' wealth position by their positive effect on profits.

Since the managers of a corporation are acting on behalf of the stockholders, there is a fiduciary relationship between the managers (and the board of directors) and the stockholders. The stockholders, the suppliers of the risk capital, have entrusted a part of their wealth position to the firm's management. Thus, the success of the firm and the appropriateness of management's decisions must be evaluated in terms of how well this fiduciary responsibility has been met. The accounting reports measure (at their best) how well management is meeting this goal.

## Managerial Finance

The study of managerial finance is concerned with the financial decisions of a firm (as distinct from the study of the structure of markets for obtaining capital). We break the firm's decisions down into three basic types:

1. Investment decisions or, more generally, the allocation of funds among different types of assets or activities.
2. The obtaining of capital in the appropriate mixture of debt and common stock or other securities.
3. The dividend or distribution decision (giving of funds back to common stock investors in return for the use of the capital).

We shall find that there are analytical methods of analyzing all of these decisions. In some cases, we can reach fairly definite judgments as to correct and incorrect decisions; in others, we can only identify the relevant quantitative and qualitative considerations.

Business organizations are continually faced with the problem of deciding whether the commitments of resources — time or money — are worthwhile in terms of the expected benefits. If the benefits are likely to accrue reasonably soon after the expenditure is made, and if both the expenditure and the benefits can be measured in dollars, the solution to such a problem is relatively simple.

If the expected benefits are likely to accrue over several years, the solution is more complex.

We shall use the term *investment* to refer to commitments of resources made in the hope of realizing benefits that are expected to occur over a reasonably long period of time in the future. Capital budgeting is a many-sided activity that includes searching for new and more profitable investment proposals, investigating engineering and marketing considerations to predict the consequences of accepting the investment, and making economic analyses to determine the profit potential of each investment proposal.

## The Finance Managers

Finance managers (financial vice-presidents, controllers, treasurers, etc.) are responsible for a wide range of decisions made in a corporation. The accounts that appear on a balance sheet can be used to describe the tasks of a finance manager. On the asset side, there is the administration of current assets (managing cash, investing in short-term securities, and determining and administering a credit policy) and long-term assets (i.e., making capital budgeting decisions that commit the company to investments in long-lived assets). Shifting to the equity (liabilities and stockholders' equity) side of the balance sheet, the finance manager is responsible for offering advice as to the best financial structure (determining the relative use of debt, preferred stock, or common stock) and the characteristics of the firm's securities and then implementing the decisions that are made.

Decisions described in this book can be related to decisions that involve one or more of the accounts on a balance sheet. This book will offer suggestions on how to improve the likelihood of making the correct decision, although frequently it will be seen that absolutely correct choices cannot be made.

To study problems of a manageable size, we shall generally assume that a specific decision does not affect other decisions. This naïve assumption may not be valid because of the interrelationships of decisions, but it does enable us to gain understanding. After this understanding is achieved, the complexities can be introduced. We shall learn to walk before we try to run.

## Time, Risk, and the Risk-Return Trade-off

Two primary factors that make finance an interesting and complex subject are the elements of *time* and *risk*. Because decisions today often affect cash flow for many future time periods and we are not certain as to the outcomes of our actions, we have to formulate decision rules that take risk and time value into consideration in a systematic fashion. These two problems are as intellectually challenging as any problem that one is likely to encounter in the world of economic activity.

Frequently, the existence of uncertainty means that the decision maker faces alternatives that involve trade-offs of less return and less risk or more return and more risk. A large part of the study of finance has to do with learning how to approach this type of risk-return trade-off choice.

## Three Basic Generalizations

We offer three generalizations that are useful in the types of financial decisions that are to be discussed. The first generalization is that investors prefer more return (cash) to less, all other things being equal. Investors who think that the returns are excessively high could distribute the excess in such a manner that the results would meet their criterion of fairness.

The second generalization is that investors prefer less risk (a possibility of loss) to more risk and have to be paid to undertake risky endeavors. This generalization is contrary to common observations such as the existence of race tracks and gambling casinos (where the customers of such establishments are willing to pay for the privilege of undertaking risky investments), but the generalization is useful even if there are some exceptions.

The third generalization is that everyone prefers cash to be received today rather than for the same amount to be received in the future. This only requires the reasonable assumption that the funds received today can be invested to earn some positive return. Since this is the situation in the real world, the generalization is reasonable.

These three generalizations are used implicitly and explicitly throughout the book.

## Relevance of Cash Flows

Given the objective of stockholder wealth maximization, how should individual financial decisions be evaluated? For the publicly traded firm, it is convenient to assume that the market value of the stock is a reasonable measure of wealth. The market's assessment of the firm's future is manifest in today's stock price, but unfortunately this assessment is not always accurate. For the privately held firm, where there is no market value, the wealth position is even more difficult to assess.

Theoretically, alternative actions should be evaluated based on the extent to which they will improve the market value of the stock, and the action leading to a maximization of value should be chosen. Unfortunately, while this evaluation scheme is correct, it is sometimes not operational, for the chain of relationships between a decision and its ultimate impact on the value of equity is long and complicated. As stated above, the decision time horizon may affect the choice of decision.

There is, however, an approach that can be used to evaluate all decisions. The decision maker should focus on the cash flows resulting from the decision. Any decision that is expected to alter the anticipated cash flows of the firm is likely to alter the value of the firm's common stock. Cash is the common element in all financial decisions: investments require it, creditors are paid with it, and stockholders expect to receive it in the form of dividends or capital gains. Thus, most financial decisions can be characterized by the incremental cash flows that their acceptance is expected to cause.

## Cash Flows versus Earnings

A decision may be characterized by its effect on accounting earnings as well as by its incremental cash flows. The earnings and cash flows would lead to consistent decisions if it were not for the fact that earnings are affected by many accounting conventions, such as expense versus capitalization decisions and the choice of a depreciation method. Thus, following Generally Accepted Accounting Principles, an investment might generate substantial cash flows in its late years but adversely affect profits during the early years if the initial investment depreciates rapidly. Assuming the firm has sufficient cash inflows with which to meet its cash obligations, the investment may be desirable regardless of the lack of short-run profitability. Of course, long-run profitability is a necessary condition. If all the expenses cannot be covered over all the years of the life of the decision, then the effect of the decision on the stockholders' wealth position will be negative. Profitability is a sufficient condition for a successful decision if the profits are correctly measured. But the correct measure of profits is a difficult task, and not always perfectly executed by the accounting profession.

Since cash flows are easily measured, when properly discounted for time and adjusted for risk they are a good proxy for profits. We consider cash flows to be a relevant measure of the impact of a decision on the firm, and will use cash flows as the primary input in the financial decisions to be analyzed.

## A Merger of Equals

In the parlance of finance, a merger of equals occurs when a merger is executed with the stockholders of both the firm being acquired and the firm doing the acquiring receiving the same value after the merger as they did before the merger. In the title of this book, the reference to a merger of equals implies that both accounting and knowledge of finance contribute to making good financial decisions.

There follows an example of a merger-of-equals value calculation.

Example: Parent firm wants to acquire Target firm.

| Company | Stock Price | Shares Outstanding | Market Capitalization |
|---------|-------------|--------------------|-----------------------|
| Parent | $ 50 | 500 | $25,000 |
| Target | 100 | 40 | 4,000 |
|  |  | Total | $29,000 |

Assume Parent shareholders retain their 500 shares worth $50 each. Target must receive $N$ shares with a value per share of $P$. Target's shares must have a total value of $4,000.

$$NP = 4{,}000 \quad \text{or} \quad P = \frac{4{,}000}{N}.$$

In addition, the total value of merged firms must equal $29,000.

$$29{,}000 = P(N + 500)$$

or

$$29{,}000 = \frac{4{,}000}{N}(N + 500)$$
$$29{,}000N = 4{,}000\,N + 4{,}000(500)$$
$$25{,}000N = 4{,}000(500)$$
$$25N = 4(500)$$
$$N = 4(20) = 80 \quad \text{and} \quad P = \$50.$$

Give Target 80 shares (two for each outstanding share) with a total value of $4,000. With a new stock value of $50, we have for the merged firm value:

$$50(500 + 80) = \$29{,}000.$$

## The Capital Market

Corporations at some stage in their life are likely to go to the capital market to obtain funds. The market that supplies financial resources is called the capital market and it consists of all savers (banks, insurance companies, pension funds, people, etc.). The capital market gathers resources from the savers of society (people who consume less than they earn) and rations these savings out to the organizations that have a need for new capital and that can pay the price that the capital market defines for capital.

The availability of funds (the supply) and the demand for funds determine the cost of funds to the organizations obtaining new capital and the return to be earned by the suppliers of capital. The measure of the cost of new capital becomes very important to a business firm in the process of making decisions involving the use of capital. We shall have occasion to use the market cost of funds (the interest rate) frequently in our analyses, and you should be aware of the relevance of capital market considerations to the decisions of the firm.

Actually, there is not one market cost of funds; rather, there is a series of different but related costs depending on the specific terms on which the capital is obtained and the amount of risk associated with the security. One of the important objectives of this book is to develop an awareness of the cost of the different forms of capital (common stock, preferred stock, debt, retained earnings, etc.) and of the factors that determine these costs. This is a complex matter, since the cost of a specific form of capital for one firm will depend on the returns investors can obtain from other firms, on the characteristics of the assets of the firm that is attempting to raise additional capital, and on the capital structure of the firm. We can expect that the larger the risk, the higher the return that will be needed to attract investors.

## Tactical and Strategic Decisions

Investment decisions may be tactical or strategic. A tactical investment decision generally involves a relatively small amount of funds and does not constitute a major departure from what the firm has been doing in the past. The consideration of a new machine tool by a motor manufacturing company is a tactical decision, as is a buy-or-lease decision made by an oil company.

Strategic investment decisions involve large sums of money and may also result in a major departure from what the company has been doing in the past. Strategic decisions directly affect the basic course of the company. Acceptance of a strategic investment will involve a significant change in the company's expected profits and in the risks to which these profits will be subject. These changes are likely to lead stockholders and creditors to revise their evaluation of the company. If a private corporation undertook the development of a supersonic commercial transport (costing over \$20 billion), this would be a strategic decision. If the company failed in its attempt to develop the commercial plane, the very existence of the company would be jeopardized. Frequently, strategic decisions are based on intuition rather than on detailed quantitative analysis.

The investment strategy of a firm is a statement of the formal criteria it applies in searching for and evaluating investment opportunities. Strategic planning guides the search for projects by identifying promising product lines or geographic areas in which to search for good investment projects. One firm may seek opportunities for rapid growth in emerging high-technology businesses; another may seek opportunities to become the low-cost producer of commodities with well-established technologies and no unusual market problems; a third firm may look for opportunities to exploit its special knowledge of a particular family of chemicals. A strategy should reflect both the special skill and abilities of the firm (its comparative advantage) and the opportunities that are available as a result of dynamic changes in the world economy.

Strategic planning leads to a choice of the "forest" — tactical analysis studies — and makes a choice between individual "trees." The two activities should complement and reinforce each other. Project analysis may provide a feedback loop to verify the accuracy of the strategic plan. If there are good opportunities where the strategic plan says they should be found, and few promising opportunities in lines of business that the strategy identifies as unattractive, confidence in the strategic plan increases. Alternatively, if attractive projects are not found where the plan had expected them, or if desirable projects appear in lines of business that the strategic plan had identified as unattractive, a reassessment of both the project studies and the strategic plan may be in order.

## Scope of Financial Management

Many financial decisions have a time dimension: not all relevant events occur immediately. Adjusting for the timing of cash flows and choosing between certain alternative cash flow patterns are discussed in Chapter 2.

## Conclusions

The study of accounting and finance should be an exciting and stimulating experience, since it is an opportunity to eliminate a large number of common misunderstandings and to add to your own understanding of financial instruments and decisions. You will be better able to manage your own personal financial affairs as well as the affairs of a business entity.

The basic building blocks of this book are three generalizations that are introduced in this chapter:

1. Investors prefer more expected return to less.
2. Investors prefer less risk to more risk.
3. Investors prefer an amount of cash to be received earlier than the same amount to be received later.

All modern finance is built on these generalizations. Some investors accept or seek risk, but they normally do so with the hope of some monetary gain. They expect to be compensated for the risk they undertake.

Corporations, or more exactly, the managers running the corporations, have many different goals. We have simplified the complex set of objectives that exist to one basic objective, the maximization of the value of the stockholders' ownership rights in the firm. Though a simplification, it enables us to make specific recommendations as to how corporate financial decisions should be made.

We shall find that while some financial decisions may be solved exactly, more frequently we shall only be able to define and analyze the problem. We may not always be able to identify the optimum decision with certainty, but we shall generally be able to describe some errors in analysis to avoid. In most cases in corporate finance, useful insights for improved decision making can be obtained by applying modern finance theory and using good accounting information.

## Questions and Problems

1. Can a firm have income without having a positive cash flow? Explain.
2. If a firm currently earning $1 million can increase its accounting income to $1.1 million (an action consistent with profit maximization), is this always a desirable move? Explain.
3. A sales force is proud of having doubled sales in the past four years. What questions should be asked before praising them?
4. A president of an automobile manufacturing firm has the opportunity to double the firm's profits in the next year. To accomplish this profit increase, the quality of the product (currently the prestige car of the world market) must be reduced. No additional investment is required. What do you recommend?
5. Name an "economic cost" that is omitted from the accounting income statements that should be of interest to management.
6. The ABC Company can undertake an investment that is economically desirable. It will adversely affect current earnings, but in management's judgment will

benefit future earnings. Management fears that the stock market will interpret the decrease in earnings as a sign of weakness and the common stock price will immediately go down as the lower earnings are reported. Management plans to describe the characteristics of the investment in the annual report and in meetings with security analysts. The company's primary goal is to maximize the well-being of its stockholders.

   a. What would a decrease in stock price as a result of the investment imply about the stock market?

   b. What does the decrease in income as a result of the investment imply about the accounting measures?

   c. Should the company undertake the investment?

7. The ABC Company has to make a choice between two strategies:

*Strategy 1*: Is expected to result in a market price now of $100 per share of common stock and a price of $120 five years from now.

*Strategy 2*: Is expected to result in a market price now of $80 and a price of $140 five years from now.

What do you recommend? Assume that all other things are unaffected by the decision being considered.

8. It has been said that few stockholders would think favorably of a project that promised its first cash flow in 100 years, no matter how large this return. Comment on this position.

9. Each of the following is sometimes listed as a reasonable objective for a firm: (a) maximize profit (accounting income), (b) maximize sales (or share of the market), (c) maximize the value of a share of common stock $t$ time periods from now, (d) ensure continuity of existence, (e) maximize the rate of growth, (f) maximize future dividends. Discuss each item and the extent of its relevance to the making of investment decisions.

# References

A number of excellent introductory and intermediate financial management texts are available to be used in conjunction with this book to provide a parallel description of many of the decisions we discuss and to fill the reader in on institutional material. Among them are the following:

Brealey, R. and S. Myers (2000). *Principles of Corporate Finance*. New York: McGraw-Hill Book Company.

Copeland, T. E. and J. F. Weston (2004). *Financial Theory and Corporate Policy*, 4th Edition. Reading, MA: Addison-Wesley Publishing Company.

Van Horne, J. C. (2001). *Financial Management and Policy*, 12th Edition. Englewood Cliffs, NJ: Prentice-Hall, Inc.

*Chapter 2*

# The Time Value of Money

## Time Discounting

One of the basic concepts of business economics and managerial decision making is that the value of an amount of money to be received in the future depends on the time of receipt or disbursement of the cash. A dollar received today is more valuable than a dollar to be received in the future. The only requirement for this concept to be valid is that there be a positive rate of interest at which funds can be invested.

The time value of money affects a wide range of business decisions, and a knowledge of how to incorporate time value considerations systematically into a decision is essential to an understanding of finance. This chapter is devoted to describing the mathematical models of compound interest. The objective is to develop skills in finding the present equivalent of a future amount and the future equivalent of a present amount.

## The Interest Rate

A dollar available today is more valuable than a dollar available one period from now if desirable investment opportunities exist. There are two primary reasons why real investments can generate an interest return:

1. Some types of capital increase in value through time because of changes in physical characteristics, for example, cattle, wine, and trees.
2. There are many work processes where roundabout methods of production are desirable, leading to increased productivity. If you are going to cut down a large tree, it may be worth investing some time to sharpen your axe. A sharp axe may result in less time being spent cutting down trees (including sharpening time) than working with a dull axe. If you are going to dig a hole, you might want to

build or buy a shovel, or even spend the time to manufacture a backhoe if it is a big hole. The investment increases productivity sufficiently compared to the alternative methods of production without capital so that the new asset can earn a return for the investor.

These characteristics of capital lead to a situation in which business entities can pay interest for the use of money. If you invest $1 in an industrial firm, the firm may be able to pay you $1 plus interest if your investment enabled the firm to use some roundabout method of production or to delay the sale of an item while it increased in value.

## Future Value

Assume that you have $1.00 now and can invest it to earn $r$ interest. After one period, you will have the $1.00 plus the interest earned on the $1. Let $FV$ be the future value and $r$ be the annual interest rate. Then,

$$FV = 1 + r.$$

Repeating the process, at time 2 you will have

$$FV = (1 + r) + r(1 + r) = (1 + r)^2$$

and the future value of $1.00 invested for $n$ periods is

$$FV = (1 + r)^n.$$

If $r = 0.10$ and $n = 2$, we have

$$FV = (1 + r)^n = (\$1.10)^2 = \$1.21.$$

If instead of starting with $1 we start with a present value, $PV$, of $50, the value at time 2 is

$$FV = PV(1 + r)^n \qquad (2.1)$$
$$FV = 50(1.10)^2 = \$60.50.$$

With a 0.10 interest rate, the $50 grows to $55 at time 1. The $55 grows to $60.50 at time 2. Equation (2.1) is the standard compound interest formula. The term $(1 + r)^n$ is called the accumulation factor.

The power of compounding (earning interest on interest) is dramatic. It can be illustrated by computing how long it takes to double the value of an investment. Table 2.1 shows these periods for different values of $r$.

**Table 2.1.** The Power of Compounding.

| Interest Rate ($r$) | Time Until Initial Value Is Doubled |
|:---:|:---:|
| 0.02 | 35.0 years |
| 0.05 | 14.2 |
| 0.10 | 7.3 |
| 0.15 | 5.0 |
| 0.20 | 3.8 |

A useful rule of thumb in finance is the "double-to-72" rule, where for wide ranges of interest rates, $r$, the approximate doubling time is $0.72/r$. Note how closely the rule approximates the values in Table 2.1. With a 0.10 time value factor, an investment will double in value every 7.3 years. The rule of thumb gives 7.2 years.

Frequently, to make business decisions, instead of computing future values we will want to work with present values.

## Time Indifference: Present Value

Today, close to 100 percent of large corporations use some form of discounted cash flow (DCF) techniques in their capital budgeting (investment decision making). To perform a DCF analysis, we must find the present value equivalents of future sums of money. For example, if the firm will receive $100 one year from now as a result of a decision, we want to find the present value equivalent of the $100.00. Assuming that the money is worth (can be borrowed or lent at) 0.10 per year, the $100.00 is worth $90.91 now. The indifference can be shown by noting that $90.91 invested to earn 0.10 will earn $9.09 interest in one year; thus, the investor starting with $90.91 will have $100.00 at the end of the year. If the investor can both borrow and lend funds at 0.10, the investor would be indifferent to receiving $100.00 at the end of the year or $90.91 at the beginning of the year.

If the 0.10 interest rate applies for two periods, the investor would be indifferent to receiving $82.64 today or $100 two years from today. If the $82.64 is invested to earn 0.10 per year, the investor will have $90.91 after one year and $100 at the end of two years.

The unit of time can be different from a year, but the unit of time for which the interest rate is measured must be the same as the unit of time for measuring the timing of the cash flows. For example, the 0.10 used in the example is defined as the interest rate per year and is applied to a period of one year.

Starting with equation (2.1), we have

$$FV = PV(1 + r)^n. \tag{2.1}$$

Dividing both sides of equation (2.1) by $(1 + r)^n$, we obtain

$$PV = \frac{FV}{(1 + r)^n}. \tag{2.2}$$

Using $C_n$ to denote the cash flow at the end of period $n$ and $r$ to denote the time value of money, we find that the present value, $PV$, of $C_n$ is

$$PV = \frac{C_n}{(1 + r)^n} \tag{2.3}$$

or, equivalently,

$$PV = C_n(1 + r)^{-n}, \tag{2.4}$$

where $(1 + r)^{-n}$ is the present value of $\$1$ to be received at the end of period $n$ when the time value of money is $r$. The term $(1 + r)^{-n}$ is called the present value factor, and its value for various combinations of time periods and interest rates is found in Table A of the Appendix to the book. Any hand calculator with the capability to compute $y^x$ can be used to compute present value factors directly. If $y^x$ is used, then $y = 1 + r$ and $x = n$. First, $y^x$ is found, and then the reciprocal is taken to determine the present value factor. For example, to find the present value factor for $r = 0.10$, $n = 5$ using a typical calculator, we would place 1.10 in the calculator, press the $y^x$ button, insert 5, press the "equals" button, and then the reciprocal to find 0.62092.

## *Example 2.1*

What is the present value of $\$1.00$ to be received three time periods from now if the time value of money is 0.10 per period?

In Table A at the end of the book, the 0.10 column and the line opposite $n$ equal to 3 gives 0.7513. If you invest $\$0.7513$ to earn 0.10 per year, after three years you will have $\$1.00$. Thus, $(1.10)^{-3} = 0.7513$.

What is the present value of $\$100.00$ to be received three time periods from now if the time value of money is 0.10? Since $(1.10)^{-3} = 0.7513$, the present value of $100 is

$$PV = \$100(0.7513) = \$75.13.$$

If $75.13 is invested at time 0, the following interest growth takes place with a 0.10 interest rate.

| Time | Investment at Beginning of Period | Interest | Investment at End of Period |
|---|---|---|---|
| 0 | $75.13 | $7.513 | $ 82.643 |
| 1 | 82.643 | 8.264 | 90.907 |
| 2 | 90.907 | 9.091 | 100.000 |

If investors can earn 0.10 per period and can borrow at 0.10, then they are indifferent to $75.13 received at time 0 or $100 at time 3.

The present value of a series of cash flows is the sum of the present values of each of the components.

## *Example 2.2*

What is the present value of two cash flows, $100.00 and $200.00, to be received at the end of one and two periods from now, respectively, if the time value of money is 0.10?

| Period $t$ | Cash Flow $X_t$ | Present Value Factors $PVF\,(t, 0.10)$ | Present Value $PV$ |
|---|---|---|---|
| 1 | $100 | 0.9091 | $ 90.91 |
| 2 | 200 | 0.8264 | 165.28 |
| | | Total present value using $0.10 = \$256.19$ | |

## Present Value of an Annuity

Frequently, the evaluation of alternatives will involve a series of equal payments spaced equally through time. Such a series is called an annuity. The present value of an annuity of $1 per period for $n$ periods with the first payment one period from now is the sum of the present values of each dollar to be received:

$$B(n, r) = \frac{1}{(1+r)} + \frac{1}{(1+r)^2} + \frac{1}{(1+r)^3} + \cdots + \frac{1}{(1+r)^n}, \qquad (2.5)$$

where $B(n, r)$ is the symbolic representation for an annuity of $n$ periods and an interest rate of $r$ (first cash flow one period from now). It can be shown (see

Appendix 2.1) at the end of this chapter that

$$B(n, r) = \frac{1 - (1 + r)^{-n}}{r}. \tag{2.6}$$

Equation (2.6) is for an annuity in arrears. Appendix Table B at the end of the book gives the present values of annuities of $1 per period for different values of $r$ and $n$. The present value of an annuity can also be computed directly using many hand calculators, or a personal computer.

If $C$ dollars are received each period instead of $1, we can multiply equation (2.6) by $C$ to obtain the present value of $C$ dollars per period. That is, for an annuity for $C$ dollars per period, the present value is

$$PV = C \times B(n, r). \tag{2.7}$$

## Example 2.3

The ABC Company is to receive $1 a period for three periods, the first payment to be received one period from now. The time value factor is 0.10. Compute the present value of the annuity.

There are three equivalent solutions:

a. From Appendix Table B,

$$B(3, 0.10) = 2.4869.$$

b. Using equation (2.6) and Appendix Table A,

$$B(3, 0.10) = \frac{1 - (1 + r)^{-n}}{r} = \frac{1 - 0.7513}{0.10} = \frac{0.2487}{0.10} = 2.487.$$

c. Adding the first three entries in the 0.10 column in Appendix Table A,

$$(1.10)^{-1} = 0.9091$$
$$(1.10)^{-2} = 0.8264$$
$$(1.10)^{-3} = \underline{0.7513}$$
$$B(3, 0.10) = 2.4868.$$

If, instead of $1 per period, the amount is $100.00, then using equation (2.7), we would multiply $2.487 by $100.00 and obtain $248.70.

## An Annuity

When the first payment is at time 1, we have an annuity in arrears (also called an ordinary annuity). When the payment occurs at the beginning of each period, we have an annuity due (also called an annuity in advance). Equation (2.6) gives the present value of an annuity in arrears:

$$B(n, r) = \frac{1 - (1 + r)^{-n}}{r}. \tag{2.6}$$

If we have $(n + 1)$ payments of $1 each period with the first payment taking place immediately, we would merely add $1 to the value of equation (2.6). Thus, if $B(3, 0.10)$ equals $2.4868, a four-payment annuity with the first payment at time 0 would have a present value of $3.4868. An $n$ period annuity due is nothing more than an $(n - 1)$ period annuity in arrears plus the initial payment.

## Present Value of a Perpetuity

A perpetuity is an annuity that goes on forever (an infinite sequence). If we let $n$ of equation (2.6) go to infinity, so that the annuity becomes a perpetuity, then the $(1 + r)^{-n}$ term goes to zero, and the present value of the perpetuity using equation (2.6) becomes

$$B(\infty, r) = \frac{1}{r}. \tag{2.8}$$

Thus, if $r = 0.10$ and the series of cash receipts of $1.00 per period is infinitely long, investors would pay $10.00 for the infinite series. They would not pay $11.00, since they could invest that $11.00 elsewhere and earn $1.10 per period at the going rate of interest, which is better than $1.00 per period. Investors would like to obtain the investment for $9.00, but no rational issuer of the security would commit to pay $1.00 per period in return for $9.00 when $10.00 could be obtained from other lenders for the same commitment.

Although perpetuities are seldom a part of real-life problems, they are useful, since they allow us to determine the value of extreme cases. For example, if $r = 0.10$, we may not know the present value of $1 per period for 50 time periods, but we do know that it is only a small amount less than $10 since the present value of a perpetuity of $1 per period is $10 and 50 years is close enough to being a perpetuity for us to use $10 as an approximate present value:

$$B(\infty, r) = \frac{1}{r} = \frac{1}{0.10} = \$10.$$

## A Flexible Tool

We now have the tools to solve a wide range of time value problems that have not been described. While we could introduce other formulas, we prefer to adapt the three basic formulas that have been introduced.

For example, if a $60-per-year annuity for 20 years were to have its first payment at time 10 and if the interest rate is 0.10, the present value is

$$PV = CB(n, r)(1 + r)^{-t} = 60B(20, 0.10)(1.10)^{-9}$$

$$= 60 \ (8.5136)(0.4241) = \$216.64.$$

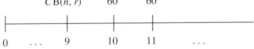

Note that if the first annuity payment is at time 10, we only have to discount the annuity for nine years to find the present value since $B(10, r)$ gives the annuity present value as of time 9 and the first payment at time 10.

We want to determine how much we would have at time 29 if we saved $60 per year for 20 years, with the first amount saved starting at time 10. Above we obtained $216.64 for the present value of $60 per year. The future value (time 29) of $216.64 is

$$\text{Future value} = \$216.64(1.10)^{29} = \$216.64(15.8631) = \$3,437.$$

Now assume the $60 annuity starting at time 10 is a perpetuity. The present value at time 9 is $60/0.10 = $600. The present value of the $600 at time 0 is

$$PV = \$600(1.10)^{-9} = \$600(0.4241) = \$254.46.$$

Another approach to solving for the present value of the annuity is to compute the present value of a perpetuity and subtract the present value of a nine-period annuity:

$$PV = \$600 - \$60B(9, 0.10) = \$600 - \$60(5.7590) = \$254.46.$$

The basic time-discounting tools are very flexible.

## Annual Equivalent Amounts

In many situations we want to determine the annual equivalent of a given sum. For example, what is the annual equivalent over 20 years of $100,000 received today if the time value of money is 10 percent?

Solve equation (2.7) for the annual cash flow:

$$C = \frac{PV}{B(n, r)}. \tag{2.9}$$

That is, to find the annual equivalent, $C$, of a present sum, $PV$, that sum is divided by the annuity factor, $B(n, r)$, where $r$ is the time value of money and $n$ is the number of years over which the annual equivalent is to be determined.

Calculations of this type are particularly useful in the management of financial institutions such as insurance companies or banks, where customers make periodic payments over an extended time period in return for a lump-sum immediate loan.

## *Example 2.4*

The ABC Company wishes to borrow $10,000 from the City Bank, repayable in three annual installments (the first one due one year from now). If the bank charges 0.10 interest, what will be the annual payments?

From equation (2.9),

$$C = \frac{\$10,000}{B(3, 0.10)}$$

$$= \frac{\$10,000}{2.4869} = \$4,021$$

and the loan amortization schedule is

| (1) Time | (2) Beginning Balance | (3) Interest 0.10 of (2) | (4) Payment | (5) = (2) + (3) − (4) Ending Balance |
|---|---|---|---|---|
| 0 | $10,000 | $1,000 | $4,021 | $6,979 |
| 1 | 6,979 | 698 | 4,021 | 3,656 |
| 2 | 3,656 | 366 | 4,021 | 0 |

The loan amortization schedule starts with the initial amount owed. Column 3 shows the interest on the amount owed at the beginning of the period (column 2). Column 4 is the payment to pay the debt and column 5 shows the ending debt balance. The ending debt balance is equal to the beginning debt balance plus the period's interest less the debt payment.

The process is repeated for the life of the debt. If the present value of the debt payments is equal to the initial beginning balance (as it will be using the effective cost of debt to compute the present value), the ending balance after the last debt payment will be equal to zero.

## Conclusions

Most investment analyses performed by a company are made on the basis of annual cash flows. Finer divisions of time are usually unwarranted in light of the approximate nature of the cash flow estimates. Some firms use present value tables that assume the cash flows are distributed evenly over the year or occur at the midpoint of the year in question rather than at the end of the year, as do the present value tables at the end of this book. Such refinements add little to the substance of discounted cash flow analysis and are not likely to alter materially any investment decision obtained from using the "end-of-year" assumption.

Most financial decision making can be reduced to evaluating incremental or alternative cash flows. There are three steps in the analysis. First, the relevant incremental cash flows must be estimated. Second, there must be some means of dealing with uncertainty if the cash flows are uncertain. Third, there must be some way to take into consideration the time value of money. The material in this chapter is essential for dealing with the time value of money to determine the present and future values of sums of money to be received or paid at various times.

## Review Problems

### Review Problem 2.1

Exactly 15 years from now, Jones will start receiving a pension of $20,000 a year. The payments will continue forever. How much is the pension worth now, assuming that the appropriate discount rate is 0.10 per year?

**Solution to Review Problem 2.1**

The present value at time 14 is $200,000.

The present value at time 0 is

$$\$200,000(1.10)^{-14} = \$200,000(0.26333)$$

$$= \$52,666.$$

## Review Problem 2.2

(a) Twelve rental payments of $1,000 will be paid monthly at the end of each month. The monthly interest rate is 0.01. What is the present value of the payments?

(b) If the payments are at the beginning of each month, what is the present value?

**Solution to Review Problem 2.2**

(a) $\$1,000B(12, 0.01) = \$1,000(11.2551) = \$11,255.$

(b) $\$1,000[B(11, 0.01) + 1] = \$1,000(10.3676 + 1) = \$11,368$
or $\$11,255(1.01) = \$11,368.$

## Questions and Problems

1. Assume a 0.05-per-year time value of money. Compute the value of $100 (a) received 1 year from now; (b) received immediately; (c) received at the end of 5 years; (d) received at the beginning of the sixth year; (e) received at the end of 50 years; (f) received at the end of 50 years, but with an interest rate of 0.10.

2. Assume that the interest rate is 0.10. Compute the present value of $1 per year for four years (first payment one year from now) using three different methods (Appendix Table A, Appendix Table B, and an equation).

3. Assume a 0.05 time value of money. Compute the value of the following series of payments of $100 a year received for (a) five years, the first payment received one year from now; (b) four years, the first of five payments received immediately; (c) ten years, the first payment received one year from now; (d) nine years, the first of ten payments received immediately.

4. Assume a 0.05 time value of money. The sum of $100 received immediately is equivalent to what quantity received in 10 equal annual payments, the first to be received one year from now? What would be the annual amount if the first of 10 payments were received immediately?

5. Assume a 0.05 time value of money. We have a debt to pay and are given a choice of paying $1,000 now or some amount X five years from now. What is the maximum amount that X can be for us to be willing to defer payment for five years?

6. We can make an immediate payment now of $10,000 or pay equal amounts of $R$ for the next five years (first payment due one year from now). With a time value of money of 0.05, what is the maximum value of $R$ that we would be willing to accept?

7. If the interest rate per month is 0.05, compounded quarterly, what is the annual equivalent rate?

8. If a firm borrowed $100,000 for one year and paid back $9,455.96 per month, what is the cost of the debt?

9. A firm can save $10,000 per year for 15 years. If the time value of money is 0.10, how much better off will the firm be after the 15 years if it accomplishes the saving?

10. If the time value of money is 0.10, how much do you have to save per year for 20 years to have $50,000 per year for perpetuity? Assume that the first deposit is immediate and that the first payment will be at the beginning of the twenty-first year.

11. If $100 earns 0.08 per year, how much will the investor have at the end of 10 years? What is the present value of $100 due in 10 years if money is worth 0.08?

12. What is the present value of $20 per year for perpetuity if money is worth 0.10?

13. Refer to Problem 12. If the first payment is to be received in 11 years, what is the series of payments worth today?

14. You are the loan officer of a bank. The ABC Company wants to borrow $100,000 and repay it with four equal annual payments (first payment due one year from now). You decide that the ABC Company should pay 0.10 per year on the loan.

   a. What is the annual payment?
   b. Complete the following debt amortization table:

| Period | Amount Owed (beginning of year) | Interest | Principal | Amount Owed (end of year) |
|---|---|---|---|---|
| 1 | $100,000 | | | |
| 2 | | | | |
| 3 | | | | |
| 4 | | | | |

c. What would be the annual payment if the first of four equal payments is due immediately?

15. a. If the interest rate per month is 0.02, compounded monthly, what is the annual effective equivalent rate?

b. How much do you have to save per year for 20 years in order to have $50,000 per year for perpetuity? $r = 0.10$. The first $50,000 payment will be received at time 21.

c. If $100 will grow into $120 in one year, what is the continuous rate of growth?

16. Assume a 0.10 interest rate. How much is a perpetuity of $1,000 per year worth?

17. Assume a 0.10 interest rate (you can borrow and lend at that rate). Specify which you would prefer:

a. $10,000 in cash or $1,000 per year for perpetuity (first payment received at the end of the first period).

b. $10,000 in cash or $1,100 per year for perpetuity (first payment received at the end of the first period).

c. $10,000 in cash or $900 per year for perpetuity (first payment received at the beginning of the first period).

18. a. What would be the annual payments on an 8% per annum installment loan of $1,000 from a credit union with repayment over three years?

b. Write out the amortization schedule for the loan.

c. Now suppose that the payments are to be made on a semiannual basis; what would the semiannual payments be? Assume the 0.08 is a nominal rate.

d. Is the total paid in case (c) less or more than in the former case? Why?

19. a. How much do you have to save per year (at the end of each year) for 40 years in order to have $10,000 per year for perpetuity, first receipt starting in year 41? Use 0.10 as the time value factor.

b. If the interest rate being earned is 0.04 per quarter, compounded quarterly, what is the annual equivalent rate?

20. a. We can make an immediate payment now of $10,000 or pay equal amounts of $R$ for the next four years (first payment due one year from now). With a time value of money of 0.10, what is the maximum value of payment that we would be willing to make?

b. Now assume that the first of the *five* payments is *immediate*. What is the maximum value of payment we would be willing to make?

21. The XYZ Company has borrowed $100,000. Payments will be made over a four-year period (first payment at the end of the first year). The bank charges interest of 0.20 per year.

a. The annual payment will be _____.

b. The debt amortization schedule is:

| Amount Owed (Beginning of Period) | Interest | Principal |
|---|---|---|
| 1. $100,000 | | |
| 2. | | |
| 3. | | |
| 4. | | |

c. If there are five payments with the first payment made at the moment of borrowing, the annual payment will be _____.

22. The XYZ Company has borrowed $40,000. Equal payments will be made over a three-year period (first payment at the end of the first year). The bank charges interest of 0.15 per year.

a. The annual payment will be _____.

b. The debt amortization schedule is:

| Amount Owed (Beginning of Period) | Interest | Principal |
|---|---|---|
| 1. $40,000 | | |
| 2. | | |
| 3. | | |
| 4. | | |

c. If there are four payments with the first payment made at the moment of borrowing, the annual payment will be _____.

## Appendix 2.1: The Derivation of an Annuity Formula

Let

$r$ = the time value of money per period

$n$ = the number of time periods

$B(n, r)$ = the present value of an annuity for $n$ periods, $r$ interest rate, with the first payment one year from time zero.

In the following table, each entry in column (1) gives the present value of $1 received at the end of the period indicated in the column headed "Time". The sum of the items in this column is $B(n, r)$. Each entry in column (2) of this table gives the item in that row of column 1 multiplied by $(1 + r)$. The sum of the items in this column is $(1 + r)B(n, r)$. Note that $(1 + r)^0 = 1$ and that all except two of the amounts are in both columns. Taking the difference between the sum of the two columns and solving for $B(n, r)$ gives the formula we wish to derive.

| Time | (1) | (2) |
|---|---|---|
| 1 | $(1+r)^{-1}$ | $(1+r)^0$ |
| 2 | $(1+r)^{-2}$ | $(1+r)^{-1}$ |
| 3 | $(1+r)^{-3}$ | $(1+r)^{-2}$ |
| . | . | . |
| . | . | . |
| . | . | . |
| $n-1$ | $(1+r)^{-n+1}$ | $(1+r)^{-n+2}$ |
| $n$ | $(1+r)^{-n}$ | $(1+r)^{-n+1}$ |
| | $B(n, r)$ | $(1+r)B(n, r)$ |

Column (2) minus column (1) yields

$$(1+r)B(n, r) - B(n, r) = 1 - (1+r)^{-n}.$$

Simplifying the left-hand side,

$$rB(n, r) = 1 - (1+r)^{-n}$$

and, dividing by $r$,

$$B(n, r) = \frac{1 - (1+r)^{-n}}{r}.$$

Appendix Table B of this book gives the values of $B(n, r)$, the present value of an annuity of \$1 per period. If the annuity is for \$$R$, we multiply the value obtained from the table by $R$.

If $n$ is very large (let $n$ approach infinity), we have the present value for a perpetuity of \$1 per period:

$$B(\infty, r) = \frac{1}{r}.$$

## Chapter 3

# An Introduction to Financial Reporting

Accounting is a formal system of record keeping and reporting that should be designed to be useful in making economic decisions for a business organization. An individual could operate a small business with a minimum of record keeping. The information required to operate the business can be observed and recalled as needed. Formal records would improve the quality of the information available to the owner, but the owner may be able to make reasonably good decisions on the basis of less precise information.

With increases in the size and complexity of a business organization, the need for organized quantitative information also increases. The manager of a large business organization with far-flung plants, a diversified product line, and thousands of employees cannot depend on firsthand observation in managing the organization's affairs. Adequate records must be kept. These records help managers at various levels and locations to make and evaluate decisions that meet the organization's policy objectives.

In most large business organizations, ownership and management functions are separated. This separation makes it necessary for the managers to communicate the economic progress of the organization to its owners. For example, although the shareholders are the owners of a corporation, they do not know how well the corporation is performing unless management provides information to them. The responsibility of reporting the results of management's administration of the organization's resources to the owners is referred to as the **stewardship function of accounting**.

A second important function of accounting is to present useful information for making managerial decisions. Accounting reports should reflect the effectiveness and efficiency with which the resources have been used by the firm. They should also reflect how well the complex objectives of an organization are met. One goal of a business organization is to use the resources profitably in the interests of its owners. Accounting information is widely used by investors to determine the merits of investment opportunities.

In summary, accounting is concerned with presenting information useful for making managerial and investment decisions. Accounting information can help managers make decisions about the day-to-day operations of the company. Accounting information can also help keep investors informed about a business organization's financial progress.

## Financial Statements

One focus of accounting is on *financial information* that is measured in dollars or other currency units. Accounting cannot provide all the information that is required or useful for every decision. However, it can provide a profile of two basic financial aspects or dimensions of a business organization:

*Financial position*: the current financial strength of the organization at a particular point in time as indicated by the resources it owns and the obligations it owes;

*Operating results*: the results of an organization's operations — whether it earned or lost resources from operations — over a specific period of time.

These results are presented in formal documents called **financial statements**. The financial statement that provides information about a business organization's financial position is called a **balance sheet**. The primary financial statement that provides information about a business organization's operating results is called an **income statement**.

### *Uses of Financial Statements*

Knowing about the financial position of a business organization and the results of its operations can be important to a wide range of interested parties. *Managers* are likely to make day-to-day operating decisions affecting the organization. They must know the impact of their decisions on the organization's financial well-being. *Taxing authorities* need to know whether income-based taxes are properly calculated.

In large corporations, the **shareholders**, who are the owners of the corporation, are dependent on published financial statements to provide the information they require for decisions. Shareholders may elect a board of directors, which is responsible for guiding the management of a corporation. However, the principal decisions made by shareholders are whether to hold their stock, sell it, or purchase additional shares. It is important for financial statements to provide the informational requirements of shareholders and other purchasers of securities.

**Creditors** are other individuals or organizations to whom a business organization owes money. Creditors are also interested in the financial position and operating results of a business organization. Direct lenders, such as banks, can insist on receiving whatever financial information they require to support their decisions. However, large corporations do much of their borrowing through the issuance of financial securities sold to the public. Purchasers of these securities are dependent on financial statements to provide the information they require for their decisions.

## Accounting Professions

A **private accountant** may be employed by the organization to prepare the records and reports. A **public accountant** is an independent professional engaged by an organization to verify the accuracy and acceptability of the organization's reports. Independent professional accountants who have been certified to practice by their states are known as **Certified Public Accountants (CPAs)**.

The uses of accounting information go beyond business enterprises. Accountants are useful in providing financial information about governments, hospitals, schools, churches, etc. Virtually any kind of organization that engages in economic activity maintains accounting records and provides accounting reports.

## The Discipline of Accounting

**Accounting** is a term used to describe a wide range of techniques and fields of study. We will broadly define it as *the identifying, measuring, recording, and communicating of financial information associated with economic events*. The tasks of accountants cover diverse areas, such as measuring economic changes and conditions, recording financial transactions, reporting the results of financial transactions, preparing reports for government agencies (including the income tax return), and establishing systems for record keeping and reporting. Many of the things that accountants do are dictated by the rules of government. An example is preparing income tax returns. However, accountants primarily present information for use by decision makers.

### *The Accounting Process*

Accountants observe or are informed of some *economic event*. An example would be the purchase of equipment. Accountants then determine if the event qualifies for *accounting treatment*. If it does qualify, they must measure the economic changes that took place. Then, an *accounting entry* that updates the set of records to reflect this event is composed. Once the new information is reported, it may be the basis for a decision that sets off a new set of economic changes.

Accountants must know what information decision makers need. Also, they must be able to measure the events and their effects on the economic position of the organization. These requirements imply that accountants must be knowledgeable in finance and managerial economics. In addition, the accounting reports become the basis for decisions and judgments of individuals and groups.

## Financial and Managerial Accounting

The terms *financial accounting* and *managerial accounting* reflect different uses of accounting information. **Financial accounting** pertains to the financial statements prepared for and used by individuals internal or external to the business organization. These individuals may not be actively engaged in or responsible for the day-to-day operations of the organization, but they do have an interest in knowing about its economic progress. **Managerial accounting** pertains to the financial statements that are used by management for making economic decisions within the business organization.

Basically, this book is concerned with financial accounting and financial decision making.

## Income Taxes and Financial Accounting

The taxation of income by the federal government and various state governments has had an impact on the record-keeping process. Taxes are based on a figure that is defined to be taxable income. The rules and regulations pertaining to taxable income are not necessarily designed to reflect the economic progress of a business organization, but to reflect the public policy objectives of Congress and other governmental bodies. As a result, there are many instances in which the income tax treatment of an event or transaction differs from its financial accounting treatment.

Management strategy must take into account the tax consequences of any decision. Some accountants believe that financial accounting procedures should be forced to coincide with the income tax requirements. But there is no reason to believe that the treatment prescribed by income tax requirements would be the same as the treatment suggested by a desire to measure and record economic events in a reasonable manner.

## Business Organizations

Among business organizations, there are three basic forms of organization: the *individual proprietorship*, the *partnership*, and the *corporation*. Most small retail establishments, farms, and professional practices (such as law, medicine, and accounting) are organized as individual proprietorships or partnerships. The distinction between a partnership and an individual proprietorship is based on the number of individuals involved in the ownership of the organization. An **individual proprietorship** has only one owner, whereas a **partnership** has more than one owner.

In terms of economic importance, the **corporation** is the primary form of business organization. The advantages of the corporate form include limited liability for the stockholders, continuity of existence, and relative ease of raising large sums of money and transferring ownership rights. As a result, practically all large businesses are organized as corporations. This book will focus on the accounting problems of corporations, but virtually all of the accounting principles applicable to corporations also apply to other types of business organizations. The specialized details of accounting for proprietorships and partnerships are outside the scope of this book.

## Assets, Liabilities, and Stock Equities

The financial position of a corporation can be described at any point in time in terms of the amount of resources it owns and the claims or interests of various parties in those resources. The resources owned by a company are called *assets*, and the interests of various claimants in the assets are called *liabilities and stock equities*.

## The Accounting Equation

The total of resources (assets) owned by a corporation must always be equal to the sources of those resources. We can also state that the total sources of assets (equities) must be equal to the total assets. The relationship of assets and sources may be expressed in the form of an equation:

$$\text{Assets} = \text{Liabilities} + \text{Stockholders' Equity}. \qquad (3.1)$$

The balance sheet of a corporation shows measures of the assets of the corporation, the debts owed, and the interests of the owners. The interests of owners, termed *stockholders' equity*, together with the debts owed (*liabilities*) constitute the total asset sources of the corporation.

The interests of the owners (stockholders' equity) may also be described as being equal to the difference between the total assets and the total liabilities. This manner of viewing the basic components of the balance sheet results in the equation:

$$\text{Assets} - \text{Liabilities} = \text{Stockholders' Equity.} \tag{3.2}$$

These relationships are, in fact, identities — that is, the equalities hold for all values of assets and equities for all corporations at all times. We have, therefore, one basic accounting identity (or accounting equation) and two variations of it:

$$\text{Assets} = \text{Liabilities} + \text{Stockholders' Equity} \tag{3.1}$$

$$\text{Assets} - \text{Liabilities} = \text{Stockholders' Equity.} \tag{3.2}$$

Each change in total assets must be accompanied by an equal change in the sources. For example, if the stockholders of a corporation invest $8,000, the total assets of the corporation are increased by $8,000, as are the claims of the stockholders. If a corporation borrows $3,000 from a financial institution, the total assets would be increased by $3,000. The source of the asset is the financial institution from whom the amount was borrowed. We could also say that the rights of this financial institution represent a $3,000 liability. Assets are increased by $3,000, and liabilities are increased by the same amount. This equality of assets and sources can never be upset, except by making an error.

## Form of the Balance Sheet

The balance sheet reports the dollar amounts of assets and equities of the corporation as recorded in the accounting records. There are several variations in the form of the balance sheet, but it is most often presented as a balanced array, with assets on the left side and sources on the right. This is a convention that has been adopted by accountants to facilitate understanding. In some countries, the order of presentation is reversed with no loss of information.

## *Example*

A corporation has cash of $5,000, owns merchandise that cost $6,000, and owes $3,000. The stockholders originally invested $8,000 in the corporation. The balance sheet in its simplest form would appear as follows:

**Company X**
**Balance Sheet as of December 31, 20XX**

| Assets | | Liabilities and Stockholders' Equity | |
|---|---|---|---|
| Cash | $ 5,000 | Liabilities | $ 3,000 |
| Merchandise | 6,000 | Stockholders' Equity | 8,000 |
| Total Assets | $11,000 | Total Equities | $11,000 |

The balance sheet has a heading containing three items: the name of the company, the name of the report, and the date for which this statement is applicable. Note that this statement is "as of December 31, 20XX." The statement is for a particular moment in time, namely the close of business on the date indicated. A balance sheet may be prepared as of any date, so specifying the date is important.

Notice that the body of the statement has two main sections, the Assets and the Liabilities and Stockholders Equity. Because the total assets must equal the total sources, the stockholders' equity value of $8,000 could have been computed by subtracting the total liabilities from the total assets: $11,000 − $3,000 = $8,000. However, in actual accounting practice, the stockholders' equity is not computed in this manner but rather is obtained directly from the accounting records, as will be seen in a later section. The equality definition acts as a check rather than as a means of obtaining the amount of stockholder equity.

## Accounting for Assets

The term **asset** may have differing connotations depending on whether it is being used by an economist or an accountant. We will define the term as used in accounting practice as follows: *Assets are the resources of a business organization that were acquired in a market transaction and that will provide future economic benefits to the organization.* Examples of accounting assets are:

**Nonphysical resources**: cash, marketable securities, accounts receivable.
**Physical resources**: land, buildings, equipment, merchandise.
**Intangible resources**: patents, goodwill, copyrights, trademarks.
**Cost factors applicable to future periods**: rent and insurance premiums paid in advance for the following year.

## *Economic and Accounting Assets*

It is important to understand the distinction between assets that are recorded and those that are not. The definition of assets above reflects two criteria: they (1) were acquired in a market transaction, and (2) will provide future economic benefits to the corporation.

Accountants typically rely heavily on a clearly defined market transaction as the basis for recording assets. The market price reflected in a transaction between two independent parties provides objective evidence of the cost of assets acquired or the market value of assets sold.

It is useful for accountants to rely on objective evidence of economic value other than a long-ago actual market transaction. In the past, accountants have chosen to rely on actual market transactions. This reliance tended to bring about uniformity in how assets are recorded, but resulted in less useful information in those situations where a purchase cost may bear little relation to the economic value of the asset acquired. For example, the costs of drilling an oil well are not related to the value of the well as measured by the amount of oil in it. Recording the costs of drilling the well is less useful than recording the economic value of the oil. Similarly, the cost of Manhattan may have been $24, but its current economic value far exceeds $24.

Requiring actual market transactions also results in some assets not being recorded. Items such as copyrights and trademarks are usually recorded as assets only if they have been purchased by a corporation for a specific price. When such items have been created or invented by the corporation, they were historically not recorded as assets, regardless of their economic value to the corporation. Similarly, high-quality employees of a corporation may have a large economic value, but accountants typically do not record such a value. For example, accountants for a professional football team might record the multimillion-dollar cost of a star quarterback obtained from another team as an asset, but an equally fine quarterback obtained without explicit cost (except for a year's wages) from a college campus would not appear in the accounting records as an asset.

Economic assets provide future economic benefits to the corporation. All accounting assets are economic assets, but not all economic assets are accounting assets. Accounting assets are a subset of economic assets. Unless an item has future economic benefits to the corporation, it is not an economic asset and thus not an accounting asset. An item (e.g., an employee) can have future economic benefits to the corporation and therefore be an economic asset, but it is not recorded as an accounting asset if it was not acquired in a market transaction.

At the time an asset is acquired, an attempt will be made to record its economic value as reflected by the amount actually paid for the asset. However, this amount may not adequately measure the asset's economic value to the purchaser but rather the minimum value, and this fact must be kept in mind when making decisions using recorded amounts. With the passage of time, there is little chance that the amount paid to acquire an asset will be an exact estimate of its economic value, and so the accountant must consider using fair value.

## Financial Accounting Standards No. 157

This standard is dated September 2006 and is titled "Fair Value Measurements." It is an extensive study of fair value and its uses. "This statement defines fair value, establishes a framework for measuring fair value, and expands disclosures about fair value measurements" (paragraph 1).

It recognizes that there are "practicability exceptions to fair value measurements … " (paragraph 2b). But fair value, in general, is the basic method of measuring assets and liabilities. The definition of fair value is: "Fair value is the price that would be received to sell an asset or paid to transfer a liability in an orderly transaction between market participants at the measurement date" (paragraph 5).

The *Standard* as published by the FASB is 145 pages long plus a five-page summary. It is an important accounting document since it defines the use of fair value as the basis of accounting measurements replacing the nearly universal cost-based accounting rule.

## Current and Noncurrent Assets

The asset section of the balance sheet is normally divided into two basic components: *current assets* and *noncurrent assets*. **Current assets** are cash and those other assets that will normally be converted into cash within a period of one year (or one operating cycle, if it is longer than a year). **Noncurrent assets** are those assets that are not likely to be converted into cash in the normal operating cycle.

Current assets include items such as cash on hand or in the bank; amounts due from customers (accounts receivable); materials, supplies, or goods on hand (inventories); readily marketable securities that are expected to be sold within one year; and advance payments for insurance, rent, and the like (prepaid items).

The listing of prepaid items as a current asset is justified if the advance payment will be used during the next operating period. If the prepayment is for a period longer than a year, only the portion applicable to the next year would be included as a current asset. When items are prepaid, they reduce the outlay of cash that might otherwise be required in future years.

Noncurrent assets are also referred to as **fixed assets** or **long-lived assets**. This category includes such items as land, buildings, and equipment. These items are normally expected to last more than one year and cannot be sold (converted into cash) without disrupting the normal business operations.

The distinction between current and noncurrent assets is made on the basis of intention or normal expectation rather than the ability to convert to cash. Thus, inventories of materials are classified as current because they would normally be disposed of within one year. A building that might be disposed of is just as easily treated as noncurrent if it would not be sold within a year of a normal business cycle.

Identical assets may be classified differently when it is clear that they are being held for different purposes. Automobiles used in a business that are expected to be used for several years would be classified as a noncurrent asset. Similar automobiles held for sale by a dealer or manufacturer would be considered current assets (inventories).

Marketable securities are securities held for temporary purposes for which there is a ready market. These are considered to be a current asset, as it is normally expected that they will be sold within one year. If similar securities were being held for control purposes and therefore not likely to be sold, they would be referred to as investments and classified as a noncurrent asset. An asset held as a noncurrent investment becomes a current marketable security when the corporation intends to dispose of its holding in the next year.

Inconsistencies occasionally arise in the classification between current and noncurrent assets. For example, buildings and equipment are not usually reclassified even when it becomes clear that they will be disposed of within a year. Slow-moving inventory items are not reclassified as noncurrent even when it is likely to take more than a year to dispose of them. These inconsistencies have one desirable effect in that they give stability to the classification procedure. It would be troublesome if assets were continually reclassified according to changes in the stated intentions of management.

## *Tangible and Intangible Assets*

A distinction is often made between *tangible* and *intangible* assets. This distinction is based on the usual physical characteristics of the items. Buildings, equipment, and merchandise are considered to be **tangible assets** because these items have physical substance. Patents, trademarks, and copyrights are considered to be **intangible assets** because they do not possess physical substance (they may be represented by pieces of paper).

## Accounting for Liabilities and Stock Equity

The sources section of the balance sheet has two main sections and several subsections. The basic division is between *liabilities* and *stockholders' equity*.

**Liabilities** are the obligations of the organization. The terms of these obligations are generally fixed by legal contract and have definite due dates. **Stockholders' equity** refers to the ownership interest in a corporation. The amount of the stockholders' interests is not fixed by contract, and does not have due dates.

The liability section can be further divided on the basis of due dates between *current liabilities* and *noncurrent liabilities*. The distinction is essentially the same as that applied to assets: **current liabilities** are those obligations that are to be paid within one year, whereas **noncurrent (or long-term) liabilities** are those coming due in more than one year. This distinction is important, because the solvency of an organization rests on its ability to meet payment obligations when due.

Current liabilities usually include amounts owed to trade creditors (accounts payable), workers (wages payable), government (taxes payable), investors (interest or dividends payable), and customers (advances from customers). All of these items are current liabilities if they are due within a year (or within the operating cycle of the organization).

Noncurrent liabilities often include bonds, mortgages, and notes. If part of these items is due within 12 months, that amount should be classified as a current liability. It is the due date, not the title, that determines whether an obligation is classified as current or noncurrent.

In some cases, the exact amount to be paid is not known. For example, a corporation can estimate its income tax liability and show it as such on a balance sheet, even though the amount is not certain and will not be certain until detailed computations are made (and reviewed by the Internal Revenue Service). Although the amount must be estimated, an obligation to pay on or before a specific date exists, and the expected liability should be recognized by the accountant.

The stockholders' equity section of the balance sheet may be divided into the amount originally paid to a corporation by stockholders, often referred to as *common stock* or *capital received from stockholders*, and the amount retained from past earnings, often referred to as *retained earnings*. There are also several variations of titles and different classifications that are used in practice. These will be discussed in later chapters.

The common stockholders are the residual owners. The economic value of these interests varies, depending on the fortunes of the corporation. The earnings of the corporation accrue to this ownership group, but, unlike debt-like obligations, the corporation is not considered insolvent if it fails to make payments to these investors.

An ownership interest of some type and amount must exist as long as the corporation exists. If the corporation is liquidated, the stockholders are entitled to the resources remaining after all other claims have been satisfied. Their amount may be more or less than the accounting measures of these interests.

The earnings of the corporation may be either retained by the corporation or distributed to stockholders. These distributions normally take the form of cash payments that are called **dividends** or **share repurchases**. Barring complexities, the retained earnings balance is equal to the sum of the past earnings of the corporation reduced by any distributions to shareholders that have been made. A negative balance in retained earnings is referred to as a **deficit**. This occurs when the corporation sustains cumulative losses in its operations or has made larger cash distributions than it has earned.

The classification of accounts is based on the legal nature of the item and not on the nature of the individuals holding the claim. Thus, if a dividend of a definite amount has been declared payable as of a definite date, the obligation to pay the dividend is a liability of the corporation. Even though the sum is payable only to stockholders, it would be considered a liability of the corporation and not a part of stockholders' equity.

## Sample Balance Sheet

The first balance sheet illustrated below is not complete in all details, but it does show a basic arrangement. More detailed balance sheets are found in practice, but the basic format is not changed.

Note that the current assets are listed in order of liquidity, or how close they are to being cash. The most liquid assets are listed first. The fixed assets are listed with the longest-lived assets presented first. That is, land is followed by buildings and equipment. There is no order specified for current liabilities. In preparing a balance sheet, the arrangement of the items and the appearance of the statement are important. The reader will expect to find items in specific locations. The person preparing the report should either conform to current practice or warn the reader of differences in presentation.

The balance sheet may be prepared in **vertical form** as shown here, with assets on top and equities on the bottom, or it is prepared as a **balanced array**, with assets on the left and liabilities and stockholders' equities on the right. Either form is acceptable, as well as several other variations of these basic arrangements.

For example, another method of presentation is the **step format**, in which current liabilities are subtracted from current asset balances to obtain net current assets. This form has the advantage of highlighting the relationship of the current assets to the current liabilities and of showing the difference between the two. It has the disadvantage of not explicitly showing the total assets or total liabilities.

These totals can be derived from the balance sheet regardless of the format, but they are more difficult to find when the step presentation is used. An example of a balance sheet using this format is also shown below.

**Sample Company**

**Balance Sheet as of December 31, 20XX**

**Assets**

**Current Assets**

| | | |
|---|---|---|
| Cash on Hand | $ 2,000 | |
| Cash in Bank | 30,000 | |
| Marketable Securities | 8,000 | |
| Accounts Receivable | 60,000 | |
| Inventories | 50,000 | |
| Prepaid Expenses | 2,000 | |
| **Total Current Assets** | | $152,000 |

**Long-Lived Assets**

| | | |
|---|---|---|
| Land | $ 15,000 | |
| Buildings | 53,000 | |
| Equipment | 60,000 | |
| **Total Long-Lived Assets** | | 128,000 |
| **Total Assets** | | $280,000 |

**Liabilities and Stockholders' Equity**

**Current Liabilities**

| | | |
|---|---|---|
| Accounts Payable | $30,000 | |
| Taxes Payable | 70,000 | |
| **Total Current Liabilities** | | $100,000 |

**Long-Term Liabilities**

| | | |
|---|---|---|
| Bonds Payable | 80,000 | |
| **Total Liabilities** | | $180,000 |

**Stockholders' Equity**

| | | |
|---|---|---|
| Common Stock | $ 90,000 | |
| Retained Earnings | 10,000 | |
| **Total Stockholders' Equity** | | 100,000 |
| **Total Liabilities and Stockholders' Equity** | | $280,000 |

**Sample Company**
**Balance Sheet as of December 31, 20XX**

**Current Assets**

| | |
|---|---|
| Cash on Hand | $  2,000 |
| Cash in Bank | 30,000 |
| Marketable Securities | 8,000 |
| Accounts Receivable | 60,000 |
| Inventories | 50,000 |
| Prepaid Expenses | 2,000 |
| | $152,000 |

**Deduct: Current Liabilities**

| | |
|---|---|
| Accounts Payable | $ 30,000 |
| Taxes Payable | 70,000 |
| | $100,000 |

| | |
|---|---|
| **Net Current Assets** | $ 52,000 |

**Noncurrent Assets**

| | |
|---|---|
| Land | $ 15,000 |
| Buildings | 53,000 |
| Equipment | 60,000 |
| **Total Assets less Current Liabilities** | $180,000 |

**Deduct: Long-Term Debt**

| | |
|---|---|
| Bonds Payable | $ 80,000 |
| **Net Assets** | $100,000 |

**Ownership**

| | |
|---|---|
| Common Stock | $ 90,000 |
| Retained Earnings | 10,000 |
| | $100,000 |

## Managerial Uses of the Balance Sheet

The primary function of a balance sheet is to indicate the financial position of an organization. The statement may provide useful information in determining the degree of financial risk. For example, a bank considering a short-term loan to a corporation would want to know the financial position of the business organization as of the date of the loan (or as close to that date as possible). Its primary internal use is as a means of measuring the soundness of the financial position of the organization.

By looking at an organization's balance sheets for successive periods, managers can observe changes in specific items. If the direction and amount of the change are undesirable, managers may be able to take action to correct the situation. For example, an increase in accounts receivable (the amounts owed by the customers to the company) may indicate inefficiency in the operation of the collection department. Although individual items such as accounts receivable will be the subject of separate reports, it is helpful to have all assets displayed in one report so that the various items may be readily compared with each other.

Balance sheets prepared for management should be designed especially for the requirements of the executives who are using them. Executives have no need for statements showing pennies; in fact, very large organizations round off balances to the nearest hundred thousand or million dollars. Reports may also be simplified by combining similar items. Thus, the single title Prepaid Expenses may include prepaid rent, insurance, and taxes. The aim of these simplifications is to save time when executives review the statement and avoid overwhelming them with too extensive an array of numbers.

In using a balance sheet for managerial purposes, it is important to keep in mind that this statement is not prepared primarily for the use of managers. Traditional financial statements intended to serve the public at large may not be optimal for managerial decision making. This means that a conventional balance sheet may have to be adjusted or modified to increase its helpfulness to management for use by a financial analyst (or a potential investor).

## Nature of Accounts

A separate **account** is maintained for each item in the balance sheet. Transactions may be recorded by entering the amount by which each item is affected into the respective account.

## T-Accounts

The **T-account**, named for its shape, is a convenient way of representing an account on a piece of paper. The T, with the account name entered at the top, permits transaction information to be entered on either side of the vertical line. To record transactions, we must be able to record additions to as well as subtractions from accounts. This is easily handled in T-accounts by designating that additions are to be recorded on one side of the vertical line and subtractions on the other.

By convention, assets are increased by entries on the left side of the account and are decreased by entries on the right side of the account. Entries to liability and stockholders' equity accounts are handled in the reverse manner. They are increased by entries on the right side and are decreased by entries on the left side. These rules may be summarized as follows:

Assets are increased by entries on the left side.
Assets are decreased by entries on the right side.
Liabilities and Stockholders' Equity are increased by entries on the right side.
Liabilities and Stockholders' Equity are decreased by entries on the left side.

|  **Any Asset Account**  |  |  **Any Liability or Stockholders' Equity Account**  |  |
| --- | --- | --- | --- |
| Increases | Decreases | Decreases | Increases |

All one has to remember is that increases for assets are reported on the left side of the account and are the opposite of increases for liabilities and stockholders' equities, and that decreases for any account are the opposite of increases for that account.

The process of recording transactions consists of determining what accounts are affected, whether they are asset or liability and equity accounts, and whether they are to be increased or decreased. With this information, any transaction can be recorded.

## Example

To illustrate the use of accounts, we will record a transaction. Suppose that stockholders invest $10,000 in cash to organize a corporation. The Cash account increases by $10,000 and the Common Stock account increases by the same amount.

To record the increase in cash, we can draw a T-account with the heading Cash and write 10,000 on the left side of the account:

| **Cash** | |
| --- | --- |
| 10,000 | |

This entry of $10,000 on the left side of the account is interpreted as indicating that the amount of cash has increased by $10,000. Thus, the information is preserved and can be used to prepare a balance sheet at a later time.

We can never make an entry to one account without also making an entry to at least one other account. The receipt of cash resulted in a corresponding increase in common stock. Therefore, an entry must be made to the account, Common Stock, to indicate an increase of $10,000.

Following the convention used for cash, it might seem logical to record the increase in common stock by writing the amount on the left side of the T-account. This would be the case if the rule were to record all increases on the left side. However, the increases in equity accounts are recorded by entries to the *right* side. Thus, the increase in common stock would be recorded by writing $10,000 on the right side of an account with the heading Common Stock:

| Common Stock | |
|---|---|
| | 10,000 |

## Debits and Credits

It is awkward to speak of entries "to the left side of an account" and entries "to the right side of an account." This difficulty is eliminated by the use of specialized terminology. Thus, instead of entries to the left side of an account, the accountant speaks of **debits** (abbreviated Dr.); instead of entries to the right side of an account, the accountant speaks of **credits** (abbreviated Cr.). These are the primary definitions of debits and credits. One is likely to run into confusion attempting to infer any other meaning for these terms. The most useful definition is that *a debit is an entry to the left side of an account.* It follows that *a credit is an entry to the right side of an account.*

It has been shown previously that an entry to the left side of an asset account increases that account. If an asset account is increased by debits, it must be decreased by the opposite entry — credits. Liability or stockholders' equity accounts have the opposite characteristics of asset accounts. Therefore, they are increased by credits and decreased by debits.

| Any Asset Account | | Any Liability or Stockholders' Equity Account | |
|---|---|---|---|
| Debit (increase) | Credit (decrease) | Debit (decrease) | Credit (increase) |

The term **charge** is often used interchangeably with debit. A charge to an account is a debit.

## Keying Transactions

When several transactions are involved, it is convenient to place a number identifying each transaction in the T-account near the dollar amount. This procedure is called **keying** the transaction. Keying facilitates cross-references and aids in checking the recording process. Transactions should always be keyed.

## Example

We will now continue the illustration. Determine the accounts affected by each transaction, whether they are assets or equities, and whether they are increased or decreased. This determines whether the entries are to be made on the left or right side of the accounts. For each transaction, the left-side entries (debits) must be equal to the right-side entries (credits).

Transactions:

1. Stockholders invest $10,000 in cash (increase an asset; increase an equity).
2. The company buys $5,000 of merchandise on account (increase an asset; increase a liability).
3. At the end of the year the company buys a building for $20,000, pays $4,000 cash, and issues $16,000 of bonds (increase an asset; decrease another asset; increase a liability).
4. The merchandise (see Transaction 2) is paid for (decrease an asset; decrease a liability).

| Cash | | | Common Stock | |
|---|---|---|---|---|
| (1) 10,000 | (3) 4,000 | | | (1) 10,000 |
| | (4) 5,000 | | | |

| Merchandise | | | Accounts Payable | |
|---|---|---|---|---|
| (2) 5,000 | | | (4) 5,000 | (2) 5,000 |

| Building | | | Bonds Payable | |
|---|---|---|---|---|
| (3) 20,000 | | | | (3) 16,000 |

## Equality of Entries

Notice that it is *not* necessarily the case that the number of increases will equal the number of decreases for any transaction. It is possible to have valid entries with two increases (e.g., increase an asset, increase a stockholder's equity) or two decreases (decrease an asset, decrease a liability) as well as entries with equal increases and decreases (increase an asset, decrease another asset). Relating increases to decreases is not a useful check. The equality of left-side and right-side (debit and credit) entries is an important control device.

## Recording Accounting Transactions

In any accounting entry, the debits must equal the credits. This is synonymous with the statement that entries to the left side of accounts must equal entries to the right side of accounts. Entries may take many forms, for there is a variety of transactions that may be recorded with debits and credits.

It is not possible to be correct and make an entry that increases one asset and also increases another asset (two debits and no credits). Nor is it possible to be correct and make an entry that increases liabilities and stockholders' equity but does not affect another account (two credits and no debits).

The procedure for deciding on the entries to be made in recording a financial transaction consists of the three steps suggested by the following three sets of questions:

1. What accounts are affected? What was given or received in the transaction?
2. What accounts should be debited or credited?
3. What amounts should be debited and credited?

Assume that $500 of accounts payable are paid. What accounts are affected? Cash and Accounts Payable are the two accounts affected. What accounts should be debited or credited? Which accounts are increased or decreased by the transaction? Cash is decreased and Accounts Payable is decreased. To decrease an asset, it is necessary to credit it; and to decrease a liability, it is necessary to debit it. What amounts should be debited and credited? Both accounts are decreased by $500. This transaction is recorded by debiting Accounts Payable for $500 and crediting Cash for $500. This type of systematic analysis is useful in recording transactions.

## Account Balances

For many purposes, it is necessary to determine the balance in an account. This is accomplished by adding the debits, adding the credits, and determining the difference between the two sums.

An account is said to have a **debit balance** if the sum of the debit entries to that account exceeds the sum of the credit entries. Conversely, an account has a **credit balance** if the sum of the credit entries exceeds the sum of the debit entries. In the example illustrated earlier in this chapter, the cash account appeared as follows:

| Cash | |
|---|---|
| (1) 10,000 | (3) 4,000 |
| | (4) 5,000 |

The debits total $10,000 and the credits total $9,000; the debits exceed the credits by $1,000.

Asset accounts normally have debit balances inasmuch as these accounts are increased by debiting. An asset account with a credit balance is no longer an asset. For example, suppose the Accounts Receivable account had a credit balance. This would indicate that the company owed money to its customers, and thus it is properly classified as a liability. Liability and stockholders' equity accounts normally have credit balances because these accounts are increased by crediting.

It is not possible to tell whether an account is an asset or a stockholder's equity by merely observing its balance. For example, accounts with credit balances may represent deductions from assets rather than stockholders' equities. Accounts with debit balances may represent deductions from liabilities rather than assets.

The fact that total debits were equal to total credits in the illustrations is not due merely to chance or to the contrived nature of the examples. This equality must always exist if the recording process is to be carried out correctly. Whenever the total debits are not equal to total credits, it is certain that an error has been made. Testing the equality of the debit and credit entries serves as a convenient device to detect mistakes.

Although the inequality of debits and credits always signals the presence of an error, the equality of debits and credits does not assure the accuracy of the records. The range of errors that might be disclosed by the equality test is quite broad. However, it discloses neither the omission of an entry nor an entry to the wrong account.

It is impossible to conceive of a transaction whereby an asset would be increased and a liability decreased with no other changes. Any time that debits do not equal credits, it follows that an error has been made.

The choice to increase stockholders' equity accounts with credits given that asset accounts are increased with debits was not an arbitrary whim. The convention was adopted to result in the equality of debits and credits for each transaction, a desirable control feature.

## Journal Entries

Up to this point we have made entries in T-accounts, which are very useful for learning how to record accounting entries. In concept, the T-account is related to an important component of the recording system used in accounting practice — the ledger. The **ledger** is a collection of accounts that is used to summarize the results of transactions so that the balance of each account may be readily determined.

When many transactions are involved, it might become rather cumbersome to record each of them directly in the ledger. The ledger would soon become cluttered with numerous entries, and it would be difficult to trace the effects of individual transactions even when the ledger entries are keyed.

As a matter of convenience, it is often desirable to record transactions in **journal entry form**. In this form, the titles of accounts to be debited or credited are listed along with the amounts involved. The accounts to be debited are listed first. The accounts to be credited are listed next and are distinguished by indenting. An explanation may be added where it is desirable.

In most cases, the journal entries contain the same information as would have been presented if the transactions had been recorded in T-account form. If the **journal entry form** is used rather than T-accounts to record transactions, we would have the following format:

|  | **Dr.** | **Cr.** |
|---|---|---|
| Cash . . . . . . . . . . . . . . . . . . . . . . . . . . . . . . . . . . . . . . . . . . . | 1,000,000 | |
| Common stock . . . . . . . . . . . . . . . . . . . . . . . . . . . . . . . . . | | 1,000,000 |
| To record the issuance of $1,000,000 of common stock. | | |
| Building . . . . . . . . . . . . . . . . . . . . . . . . . . . . . . . . . . . . . . . . . | 500,000 | |
| Cash . . . . . . . . . . . . . . . . . . . . . . . . . . . . . . . . . . . . . . . . . . | | 500,000 |
| To record the purchase of a building for $500,000 cash. | | |

The **journal entry format** is also related to a recording procedure used in practice. A **journal**, or **book of original entry**, is used to record transactions in chronological order. Entries are normally recorded first in a journal and then transferred to the ledger.

## Summary

We have defined the equation:

$$\text{Assets} = \text{Liabilities} + \text{Stockholders' Equity.}$$

This equality always holds. The formal expansion of this equality leads to the important financial statement, the balance sheet.

The primary function of financial accounting is to report the results of operations and the financial position of the enterprise. These reports are important to management and other users of the statements, since they reflect the results of past decisions and the execution of these decisions. Also, management knows that the present decisions will be similarly evaluated. However, when managers make decisions, they generally supplement conventional financial statements with information prepared especially for the decisions being made. Thus, the primary accounting concern of this book is financial reporting of a score-keeping nature. Knowing where you are (the balance sheet) and how you got there (the income statement) is important to decision makers.

Accounts are used to record increases and decreases in assets, liabilities, and stockholders' equity. Assets are increased by entries to the left-hand side of T-accounts (debits) and are decreased by entries to the right-hand side of T-accounts (credits). Liabilities and stockholders' equity are decreased by entries to the left-hand side of T-accounts (debits) and are increased by entries to the right-hand side of T-accounts (credits).

The accounting convention of increasing asset accounts with debits and increasing liability or equity accounts with credits provides a system in which, for each entry, the debits must equal the credits. Thus, for the total of all entries, the sum of the debits must equal the sum of the credits.

It is not important that we defined a debit to increase assets; we could just as reasonably have defined it as a decrease. It is important that, having defined a debit as an increase in an asset account, a debit should have the opposite effect on a liability or stockholders' equity account. The changes in assets must equal the changes in sources of assets. Also, the debits must equal the credits for each transaction.

## Review Problems

### *Review Problem 3.1*

The following facts apply to the ABC Company in the year 20XX.

1. Stockholders invest $1,000,000.
2. The company buys land for $20,000 and a building for $380,000 in cash.
3. The company borrows $100,000 from the bank. The five-year note bears 14 percent interest per year.
4. The company purchases $300,000 of merchandise, pays for $200,000 of it, and reflects the remainder as an account payable.
5. Sales of $800,000 are made on account, and there is $50,000 of merchandise remaining at the end of the year. Wages and other expenses for the year are $370,000. Interest of $3,000 is paid on the bank debt. The income is $177,000.
6. Dividends of $100,000 are paid to stockholders.
7. Accounts receivable has an ending balance of $500,000.

Set up T-accounts and record the above transactions. Key all entries. Prepare a balance sheet as of December 31, 20XX, that reflects the foregoing transactions.

## Solution to Review Problem 3.1

**Cash**

| | | | |
|---|---|---|---|
| (1) | 1,000,000 | (2) | 20,000 |
| (3) | 100,000 | (2) | 380,000 |
| (7) | 300,000 | (4) | 200,000 |
| | | (5) | 373,000 |
| | | (6) | 100,000 |
| | | √ | 327,000 |
| | 1,400,000 | | 1,400,000 |
| √ | 327,000 | | |

**Common Stock**

| | | | |
|---|---|---|---|
| √ | 1,000,000 | (1) | 1,000,000 |
| | 1,000,000 | | 1,000,000 |
| | | √ | 1,000,000 |

**Merchandise**

| | | | |
|---|---|---|---|
| (4) | 300,000 | (5) | 250,000 |
| | | √ | 50,000 |
| | 300,000 | | 300,000 |
| √ | 50,000 | | |

**Retained Earnings**

| | | | |
|---|---|---|---|
| (6) | 100,000 | (5) | 177,000 |
| √ | 77,000 | | |
| | 177,000 | | 177,000 |
| | | √ | 77,000 |

**Land**

| | | | |
|---|---|---|---|
| (2) | 20,000 | √ | 20,000 |
| | 20,000 | | 200,000 |
| √ | 20,000 | | |

**Accounts Payable**

| | | | |
|---|---|---|---|
| √ | 100,000 | (4) | 100,000 |
| | 100,000 | | 100,000 |
| | | √ | 100,000 |

**Building**

| | | | |
|---|---|---|---|
| (2) | 380,000 | √ | 380,000 |
| | 380,000 | | 380,000 |
| √ | 380,000 | | |

**Notes Payable**

| | | | |
|---|---|---|---|
| √ | 100,000 | (3) | 100,000 |
| | 100,000 | | 100,000 |
| | | √ | 100,000 |

**Accounts Receivable**

| | | | |
|---|---|---|---|
| (5) | 800,000 | (7) | 300,000 |
| | | √ | 500,000 |
| | 800,000 | | 800,000 |
| √ | 500,000 | | |

## The ABC Company
### Balance Sheet as of December 31, 20XX

| Assets | | Liabilities and Stockholders' Equity | |
|---|---|---|---|
| **Current Assets** | | **Current Liabilities** | |
| Cash | $ 327,000 | Accounts Payable | $ 100,000 |
| Accounts Receivable | 500,000 | | |
| Merchandise | 50,000 | **Long-Term Liabilities** | |
| | | Notes Payable | 100,000 |
| Total Current Assets | $ 877,000 | Total Liabilities | $ 200,000 |
| **Long-Lived Assets** | | **Stockholders' Equity** | |
| Land | 20,000 | Common Stock | 1,000,000 |
| Building | 380,000 | Retained Earnings | 77,000 |
| **Total Assets** | $1,277,000 | **Total Liabilities and** | $1,277,000 |
| | | **Stockholders' Equity** | |

## Questions and Problems

1. Define the term *accounting*. What are some of the tasks that accountants perform?
2. Should financial accounting principles be based upon income tax regulations?
3. What form of business organization would you expect the following industries to take? Why?

   a. Steel industry.
   b. Law.
   c. Retailing.
   d. Farming.

4. What are two principal financial statements? What is the function of each?
5. The XYZ Company has listed on one of its financial reports (balance sheet), "Buildings, $451,000." Describe the usefulness of this measure for decision making.
6. Accounting is one type of information system. Name several other systems supplying information to business managers. Name several other sources of financial information available to investors.
7. Compare the need for financial information of a bank loan officer, an investor in common stock, and the financial analyst of an insurance company investing in long-term corporate debt.
8. It is sometimes stated that the asset side of a balance sheet should include the rights in property, both tangible and intangible, of a business enterprise. Accepting this statement, discuss whether the following items should be included among the assets:

   a. Investment in government bonds.
   b. Investment in corporate bonds.
   c. Prepaid expenses.
   d. Costs of drilling for oil (assuming oil was found).
   e. Advertising costs connected with a new product (not yet offered for sale).
   f. Costs of organizing a new corporation.
   g. Costs connected with issuing bonds.
   h. Costs of installing a piece of equipment.
   i. Costs of drilling for oil (assuming oil was not found).

9. Indicate which of the following items might be expected to be found on a balance sheet prepared in accordance with Generally Accepted Accounting Principles (the basic framework of accounting):

   a. The value of the managerial organization, which had been developed through the years.

b. The cost incurred in organizing the firm.

c. The value of oil, which had been discovered under a corporate parking lot (there are no drilling costs).

d. The value of the goodwill of customers toward the firm (the goodwill had been built up through the years by good service).

e. The excess of the price paid for an enterprise that had been purchased over the value of the tangible assets acquired (consider tangible assets to refer to the value of inventories, plant, and equipment).

10. A major stockholder of a corporation is concerned about the management of her firm, since the company has land with a value of $8,000,000 being used for parking lots. The controller is aware of the "stewardship function" of accounting and checks the invoices. He finds that the cost of the land was $400,000 and there was no possibility of dishonesty. The controller reports this finding back to the stockholder.

Comment on the information presented to the stockholder.

11. It has been suggested by reputable economists that firms should be allowed for tax purposes to consider the cost of equipment as a reduction of income at the time of acquisition, since the equipment was paid for at that time (other reasons are also offered).

If the above proposal were to be accepted, do you think this procedure should be followed for financial reporting purposes? Explain.

12. Assume there is an unknown "true" value. Consider two measurement procedures. One procedure (A) will provide a measure that is less than the true value, and all measurers will present the same measure. The second procedure (B) will provide, on average, a measure equal to the true amount, but it can be either larger or smaller on a random basis. Which measurement procedure do you prefer, assuming your decision will be based on the information obtained?

13. Assume that in the hiring process a firm spends $4,000 per university graduate that it hires. Should the firm consider the entire $4,000 to be an expense in the period in which the person is hired or should portions of it be considered an expense each year for the duration of employment?

14. A dividend of $10,000 will decrease _____ if it has been paid.

15. Determine the accounting income of a company for which the following information is available for the month of June:

| | |
|---|---|
| Dividends Paid to Stockholders | $10,000 |
| Employee Salaries for June | 30,000 |
| Interest Paid on Bank Loan for June | 5,000 |
| June Rent Paid to Landlord | 25,000 |
| Sales to Customers in June | 80,000 |

16. The assets of a corporation total $10,000; the liabilities, $4,000. The claims of the owners are _____.

17. The Aesop Company has total assets of $1,000,000 and total liabilities of $600,000. The common stockholders have explicitly invested $100,000 in the firm. Since organization, the firm has paid cash dividends of $800,000.

    a. What have the total earnings been since organization?

    b. If the stockholders had explicitly invested $700,000 but if all other facts were unchanged, what would be the total earnings since organization?

18. From the following information, presented as of December 31, 20XX, prepare a balance sheet for the Arley Corporation in good form.

| | |
|---|---|
| Liabilities | $8,000 |
| Cash | 4,000 |
| Materials | 2,000 |
| Buildings | 7,000 |
| Owners' Equities | ? |

19. From the following information, obtained as of December 31, 20XX, prepare a balance sheet for the Adams Corporation in good form.

| | | | |
|---|---|---|---|
| Accounts Payable | $ 12,000 | Land | $ 25,000 |
| Dividends Payable | 5,000 | Equipment | 75,000 |
| Cash | 45,000 | Accounts Receivable | 15,000 |
| Marketable Securities | 10,000 | Interest Payable | 2,000 |
| Investments | 40,000 | Merchandise | 25,000 |
| Bonds Payable | 100,000 | Supplies | 2,000 |
| Common Stock | 150,000 | Buildings | 100,000 |
| | | Retained Earnings | ? |

20. From the following information, obtained as of December 31, 20XX, prepare a balance sheet for the Adler Corporation in good form.

| | | | |
|---|---|---|---|
| Accounts Payable | $ 10,000 | Land | $10,000 |
| Dividends Payable | 4,000 | Equipment | 60,000 |
| Cash | 20,000 | Accounts Receivable | 15,000 |
| Marketable Securities | 10,000 | Interest Payable | 1,000 |
| Investments | 40,000 | Merchandise | 18,000 |
| Bonds Payable | 50,000 | Supplies | 2,000 |
| Common Stock | 100,000 | Buildings | 50,000 |
| | | Retained Earnings | ? |

21. Certain accounts are increased by entries to the left side of the account, others by entries to the right side of the account. For each of the following items, indicate whether the amount should be entered on the right or left side of the account.

   **Increase Cash**
   **Increase Wages Payable**
   **Decrease Bonds Payable**
   **Increase Retained Earnings**
   **Decrease Cash**
   **Increase Common Stock**

22. For each of the following transactions, indicate the two (or more) accounts that are affected and how they are affected (increase or decrease). Indicate whether the accounts are debited or credited.

   a. Cash is invested by the stockholders.
   b. Merchandise is purchased on account.
   c. The merchandise is paid for.
   d. Insurance is purchased and paid for.
   e. Merchandise is sold on account.
   f. Dividends are paid to the stockholders.

23. For each of the following transactions, indicate what accounts are likely to be affected and whether the accounts are likely to be debited or credited.

   a. Money is received from stockholders.
   b. Merchandise is purchased on account.
   c. A building is purchased. Payment is made by cash and by taking out a mortgage.
   d. A piece of equipment is sold for cash.

24. a. Set up T-accounts and record the following transactions of the Barker Corporation for the month of March.

   (1) Stockholders invest $100,000.
   (2) The company buys $19,000 of merchandise on account.
   (3) The company pays $11,000 of the amount owed for the merchandise.
   (4) One year's rent is paid, $4,800. The rent applies to the year beginning March 1.
   (5) Sales for March, the first month of operations, total $13,300. All sales are for cash. The merchandise sold costs $7,900. Salaries paid in cash to employees during the month are $1,000, and the company owes an additional $300 of wages as of the end of the month.

    (6) Dividends of $500 are paid to stockholders.

  b. Prepare a balance sheet as of March 31, 20XX.

25. a. Set up T-accounts and record the following transactions; key all entries.

    (1) Stockholders invest $100,000.

    (2) The company buys $12,000 of merchandise on account.

    (3) The company buys a building, paying $2,000 cash and assuming a $28,000 mortgage for the remainder of the purchase price of $30,000.

    (4) The merchandise (see Transaction 2) is paid for.

    (5) Sales of $9,000 are made. Of these sales, $7,000 are for cash and the remainder on account. The cost of the merchandise sold is $6,000. Wages earned and paid during this period total $1,200.

    (6) An amount of $800 is paid to the mortgagee. Of this amount, $560 is interest and the remainder represents a reduction of the principal balance.

    (7) Dividends of $400 are paid to stockholders.

  b. Prepare a balance sheet as of December 31, 20XX, giving effect to all the foregoing transactions.

*Chapter 4*

# Capital Budgeting

A capital budgeting decision is characterized by costs and benefits (cash flows) that are spread out over several time periods. This leads to a requirement that the time value of money be considered in order to evaluate the alternatives correctly. Although in actual practice we must consider risk as well as time value, in this chapter we restrict the discussion to situations in which the costs and benefits (in terms of cash) are known with certainty. There are sufficient difficulties in just taking the time value of money into consideration without also incorporating risk factors. Moreover, when the cash flows are finally allowed to be uncertain, we shall suggest the use of a procedure that is based on the initial recommendations made with the certainty assumption, so nothing is lost by making the initial assumption of certainty.

In this chapter, we shall describe four of the more commonly used procedures for making capital budgeting decisions. We shall not attempt to describe all the variations that are possible or all the procedures used that are faulty. If you understand the basic elements of a correct procedure, you will be able to distinguish between correct and incorrect procedures. The two basic correct capital budgeting techniques presented in this chapter are applicable to a wide range of decisions found throughout the economy both in the profit and not-for-profit sectors.

## Rate of Discount

We shall use the term *time value of money* to describe the discount rate. One possibility is to use the rate of interest associated with default-free securities. This rate does not include an adjustment for the risk of default; thus risk, if present, would be handled separately from the time discounting. In some situations, it is convenient to use the firm's borrowing rate (the marginal cost of borrowing funds). The objective of the discounting process is to take the time value of money into consideration. We want to find the present equivalent of future sums, neglecting risk considerations. Later, we shall introduce several techniques to adjust for the risk of the investment.

Although the firm's weighted average cost of capital is an important concept that should be understood by all managers and is useful in deciding on the financing mix, we do not advocate its general use in evaluating all investments.

## Classification of Cash Flows

We shall define conventional investments as those having one or more periods of outlays followed by one or more periods of cash proceeds. Borrowing money is a kind of "negative investment" or "loan type of cash flow" in which one or more periods of cash proceeds are followed by one or more periods in which there are cash outlays. Loan-type investments have positive cash flows (cash inflows) followed by periods of negative cash flows (cash outlays). There are also nonconventional investments, or investments that have one or more periods of outlays interspersed with periods of proceeds. With nonconventional investments, there is more than one sign change in the sequence of the cash flow. With a conventional investment or loan, there is one sign change. The possibilities may be illustrated as follows:

|  | **Sign of Flow for Period** | | | |
| --- | :---: | :---: | :---: | :---: |
|  | **0** | **1** | **2** | **3** |
| Conventional investment | − | + | + | + |
| Loan type of flows | + | − | − | − |
| Nonconventional investment | − | + | + | − |
| Nonconventional investment | + | − | − | + |

## Dependent and Independent Investments

In evaluating the investment proposals presented to management, it is important to be aware of the possible interrelationships between pairs of investment proposals. A given investment proposal may be economically independent of, or dependent on, another investment proposal. An investment proposal is said to be *economically independent* of a second investment if the cash flows (or the costs and benefits) expected from the first investment are the same regardless of whether the second investment is accepted or rejected. If the cash flows associated with the first investment are affected by the decision to accept or reject the second investment, the first investment is said to be *economically dependent* on the second. It should be clear that when one investment is dependent on another, some attention must be given to the question of whether decisions about the first investment can or should be made separately from decisions about the second.

## Economically Independent Investments

In order for investment A to be economically independent of investment B, two conditions must be satisfied. First, it must be technically possible to undertake investment A whether or not investment B is accepted. For example, it is *not* possible to build a school and a shopping center on the same site; therefore, the proposal to build the one is not independent of a proposal to build the other. Second, the net benefits to be expected from the first investment must not be affected by the acceptance or rejection of the second. If the estimates of the cash outlays and the cash inflows for investment A are not the same when B is either accepted or rejected, the two investments are not independent. Thus, it is technically possible to build a toll bridge and operate a ferry across adjacent points on a river, but the two investments are not independent because the proceeds from one will be affected by the existence of the other. The two investments would not be economically independent in the sense of which we are using the term, even if the traffic across the river at this point were sufficient to profitably operate both the bridge and the ferry.

Sometimes two investments cannot both be accepted because the firm does not have enough cash to finance both. This situation could occur if the amount of cash available for investments were strictly limited by management rather than by the capital market, or if increments of funds obtained from the capital market cost more than previous increments. In such a situation, the acceptance of one investment may cause the rejection of the other. But we will not consider the two investments to be economically dependent. To classify this type of investment as dependent would make all investments for such a firm dependent, and this is not a useful definition for our purposes.

## Economically Dependent Investments

The dependency relationship can be classified further. If a decision to undertake the second investment will increase the benefits expected from the first (or decrease the costs of undertaking the first without changing the benefits), the second investment is said to be a *complement* of the first. If the decision to undertake the second investment will decrease the benefits expected from the first (or increase the costs of undertaking the first without changing the benefits), the second is said to be a *substitute* for the first. In the extreme case where the potential benefits

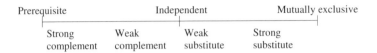

**Fig. 4.1.**   Investment Relationships.

to be derived from the first investment will completely disappear if the second investment is accepted, or where it is technically impossible to undertake the first when the second has been accepted, the two investments are said to be *mutually exclusive*.

It may be helpful to think of the possible relationships between investments as being arrayed along a line segment (see Fig. 4.1). At the extreme left, investment A is a prerequisite to investment B. In the center of the line, investment A is independent of investment B. At the extreme right-hand end of the line, investment A is mutually exclusive with respect to investment B. As we move to the right from the left-hand side of the line, we have varying degrees of complementariness, decreasing to the right. Similarly, the right-hand side of the line represents varying degrees of substitutability, increasing to the right.

## Statistical Dependence

It is possible for two or more investments to be economically independent but statistically dependent. Statistical dependence is said to be present if the cash flows from two or more investments would be affected by some external event or happening whose occurrence is uncertain. For example, a firm could produce high-priced yachts and expensive cars. The investment decisions affecting these two product lines are economically independent. However, the fortunes of both activities are closely associated with high business activity and a large amount of discretionary income for the "rich" people. This statistical dependence may affect the risk of investments in these product lines, because the swings of profitability of a firm with these two product lines will be wider than those of a firm with two product lines having less statistical dependence.

## Measures of Investment Worth

In this chapter, we introduce four methods of evaluating the worth of investments that are in common use or have been frequently recommended as being desirable. If we take a group of investment proposals and rank them by each of these methods, we shall find that each method will frequently give a different ranking to the same set of investment proposals. In fact, it can be said that the different measures will only accidentally give identical rankings to a set of investment proposals. Although we shall not be able to rank economically independent investments in a useful manner, we shall normally be able to make decisions without such rankings.

Various executives faced with the same set of investment possibilities, but using different measures of investment worth, will tend to make dissimilar investment decisions. Clearly, all the measures that will be described here cannot be equally valid. We shall attempt to determine which of the measures have some legitimate reason for use and to isolate the circumstances under which they will tend to give satisfactory results.

In current business practice, each of the methods selected has its advocates, and frequently they are used in combination with each other. Because investment proposals are rarely accepted by top management solely on the basis of such analyses, it may be argued that the choice of method is of little significance because the investment decision is likely to be influenced by many different factors. Insofar as the executives making the final decision are aware of the risks involved, are intimately familiar with the proposals, know the possible technical or operating problems that may be encountered, and realize the potential erosion of earnings resulting from competitive action or changing technology, this criticism may very well be valid. In most large organizations, however, it is impossible for the top management officials, who must finally approve or disapprove investment proposals, to be intimately familiar with the details of each and every proposal presented to them. To the extent that this intimate knowledge is impossible or impractical, these executives must rely upon the economic evaluations prepared by their subordinates. To make reasonable choices in weighing alternative investments, it is increasingly necessary that various proposals be evaluated as nearly as possible on some uniform, comparable basis. In such circumstances, although the measure of economic worth of an investment should never be the sole factor considered in making a final decision, it should play an important part in the evaluation of the investments under consideration by the firm.

The fact that various measures give different rankings and indicate different accept-or-reject decisions to identical sets of investment proposals is a matter of concern. Substantial improvements in efficiency and income may result if more adequate measures can be discovered and widely adopted. Any such progress requires first a more general agreement about the desirable characteristics to be possessed by a good index of the economic worth of an investment. We assume that the objective is to maximize the well-being of the common stockholders.

## Incremental Cash Flow

Investments should be analyzed using after-tax incremental cash flows. Although we shall initially assume zero taxes so that we can concentrate on the technique of analysis, it should be remembered that the only relevant cash flows of a period are after all tax effects have been taken into account.

The definition of incremental cash flows is relatively straightforward: if the transaction changes the bank account or cash balance, there is a cash flow. This definition includes opportunity costs (the value of alternative uses). For example, if a warehouse is used for a new product and the alternative is to rent the space, the lost rentals should be counted as an opportunity cost in computing the incremental cash flows.

It is generally advisable to exclude financial types of cash flows from the investment analysis. One common error in cash flow calculations is to include interest payments on debt in the cash flows and then apply the time-discounting formulas. This results in double-counting the time value of money. The time discounting takes interest into consideration. It is not correct to also deduct the interest expense of an investment in computing cash flows.

## Special Assumptions

The computations of this chapter make several assumptions that are convenient, but are not essential. They simplify the analysis. The assumptions are:

1. Capital can be borrowed and lent at the same rate.
2. The cash inflows and outflows occur at the beginning or end of each period rather than continuously during the periods.
3. The cash flows are certain, and no risk adjustment is necessary.

In addition, in choosing the methods of analysis and implementation, it is assumed that the objective is to maximize the well-being of stockholders, and more wealth is better than less.

## The Elements of a Cash Flow Projection

To arrive at the set of projected incremental cash flows used in evaluating any investment, it is usually necessary to project the impact of the investment on the revenues and expenses of the company. Some investments will affect only the expense components (i.e., cost-saving investments), whereas others will affect revenues as well as costs. Projecting how various expense and revenue items will be affected if the investment is undertaken is not an easy task, for incremental impacts are often difficult to assess. In some cases, such as the impact of a new product on the sales of an existing product that is considered a substitute, the problem is the uncertain extent of the erosion. In other cases, such as with overhead items (e.g., accounting services, plant security, a regional warehouse system), the problem arises because there is not a well-defined cash flow relationship between the incremental action contemplated and these costs. No exact solution exists to these knotty problems.

An investment in plant or equipment to produce a new product will probably also require an investment in current assets less current liabilities (working capital). There may be an increase in raw material, work-in-process, and finished goods inventories. Also, if there are sales on credit rather than cash, accounts receivable will increase; that is, sales per the income statement will be collected with a lag, and there will be an increase in accounts receivable. Finally, not all payables will be paid immediately, and this lag will manifest itself in an increase in current liabilities (reducing the need for other financing). Thus, a working capital investment (a negative cash flow and a need for capital) usually accompanies the direct investment in plant and equipment.

One can assume that the working capital investment is fully turned into cash at the hypothesized end of the project. That is, it is assumed that inventories are depleted, receivables are collected, and payables are paid. Hence, over the life of the project, the sum of the working capital changes should be zero if this assumption is accepted. However, the commitment of resources to working capital has a cost (the time value of money) even if those resources are ultimately freed.

## Two Discounted Cash Flow Methods

We shall first introduce the two primary discounted cash flow investment evaluation procedures, net present value (NPV) and internal rate of return (IRR). After a brief discussion of these two measures of investment worth, we shall describe a series of four hypothetical investments. The four hypothetical investments have been designed such that for two selected pairs it is possible to decide that one investment is clearly preferable to the other. If a measure of investment worth indicates that one investment is better when the other investment is actually better, then clearly there is a danger in using that measure. We shall find that some measures can easily be eliminated as general decision rules because in some situations they give obvious wrong answers whereas another measure gives the "right" answer. We shall conclude that the net present value method is better than the other possible methods.

## *Net Present Value*

We offer two proposed measures of investment worth that as a group could be called the discounted cash flow, or DCF, measures. Before proceeding to analyze them, it is desirable to explain again the concept of the present value of a future sum because in one way or another this concept is utilized in both these measures.

The present value of $100 payable in two years can be defined as that quantity of money necessary to invest today at compound interest in order to have $100 in two years. The rate of interest at which the money will grow and the frequency at which it will be compounded will determine the present value. We shall assume that interest is compounded annually. The manner in which a rate of interest is chosen will be discussed later. For the present, assume that we are given a 0.10 annual rate of interest. Let us examine how the present value of a future sum can be computed by using that rate of interest.

Suppose that an investment promises to return a total of $100 at the end of two years. Because $1.00 invested today at 10 percent compounded annually would grow to $1.21 in two years, we can find the present value at 10 percent of $100 in two years by dividing $100 by 1.21 or by multiplying by the present value factor, 0.8264. This gives a present value of $82.64. Therefore, a sum of $82.64 that earns 10 percent interest compounded annually will be worth $100 at the end of two years. By repeated applications of this method, we can convert any series of current or future cash payments (or outlays) into an equivalent present value. Because tables, hand calculators, and computers are available that give the appropriate conversion factors for various rates of interest, the calculations involved are relatively simple.

The net present value method is a direct application of the present value concept. Its computation requires the following steps: (1) choose an appropriate rate of discount, (2) compute the present value of the cash proceeds expected from the investment, (3) compute the present value of the cash outlays required by the investment, and (4) add the present value equivalents to obtain the investment's net present value.

The sum of the present value of the proceeds minus the present value of the outlays is the net present value of the investment. The recommended accept-or-reject criterion is to accept all independent investments whose net present value is greater than or equal to zero, and to reject all investments whose net present value is less than zero.

*With zero taxes, the net present value of an investment may be described as the maximum amount a firm could pay for the opportunity of making the investment without being financially worse off.* With such a payment, the investor would be indifferent to undertaking or not undertaking the investment. Because usually no such payment must be made, the expected net present value is an unrealized capital gain from the investment, over and above the cost of the investment used in the calculation. The capital gain will be realized if the expected cash proceeds materialize. Assume an investment that costs $10,000 and returns $12,100 a year later. If the rate of discount is 10 percent, a company could make a maximum immediate outlay of $11,000 in the expectation of receiving the $12,100 a year later. If it can receive the $12,100 with an actual outlay of only $10,000, the net present value of the investment would be $1,000. The $1,000 represents the difference between the actual outlay of $10,000 and the present value of the proceeds $11,000. The company would have been willing to spend a maximum of $11,000 to receive $12,100 a year later.

The following example illustrates the basic computations for discounting cash flows, that is, adjusting future cash flows for the time value of money, using the net present value method.

Assume that there is an investment opportunity with the following cash flows:

|  | Period | | |
|---|---|---|---|
|  | **0** | **1** | **2** |
| Cash flow | −$12,337 | $10,000 | $5,000 |

We want first to compute the net present value of this investment using 0.10 as the discount rate. Table A in the Appendix of the book gives the present value of $1 due *n* periods from now. The present value of

$1 due 0 periods from now discounted at any interest rate is 1.000.
$1 due 1 period from now discounted at 0.10 is 0.9091.
$1 due 2 periods from now discounted at 0.10 is 0.8264.

The net present value of the investment is the algebraic sum of the three present values of the cash flows:

| Period | (1)<br>**Cash Flow** | (2)<br>**Present Value Factor** | (3)<br>**Present Value**<br>**(col. 1 × col. 2)** |
|---|---|---|---|
| 0 | −$12,337 | 1.0000 | −$12,337 |
| 1 | $10,000 | 0.9091 | $ 9,091 |
| 2 | 5,000 | 0.8264 | 4,132 |
|  |  | Net present value = | $    886 |

The net present value is positive, indicating that the investment is acceptable. Any investment with a net present value equal to or greater than zero is acceptable using this single criterion. Since the net present value is $886, the firm could pay an amount of $886 in excess of the cost of $12,337 and still break even economically by undertaking the investment. The net present value calculation is a reliable method for evaluating investments.

## *Internal Rate of Return*

Many different terms are used to define the internal rate of return concept. Among these terms are yield, interest rate of return, rate of return, return on investment, present value return on investment, discounted cash flow, investor's method, time-adjusted rate of return, and marginal efficiency of capital. In this book, IRR and internal rate of return are used interchangeably.

The internal rate of return method utilizes present value concepts. The procedure is to find a rate of discount that will make the present value of the cash proceeds expected from an investment equal to the present value of the cash outlays required by the investment. Such a rate of discount may be found by trial and error. For example, with a conventional investment, if we know the cash proceeds and the cash outlays in each future year, we can start with any rate of discount and find for that rate the present value of the cash proceeds and the present value of the outlays. If the net present value of the cash flows is positive, then using some higher rate of discount would make them equal. By a process of trial and error, the correct approximate rate of discount can be determined. This rate of discount is referred to as the internal rate of return of the investment, or its IRR.

The IRR method is commonly used in security markets in evaluating bonds and other debt instruments. The yield to maturity of a bond is the rate of discount that makes the present value of the payments promised to the bondholder equal to the market price of the bond. The yield to maturity on a $1,000 bond having a coupon rate of 10 percent will be equal to 10 percent only if the current market value of the bond is $1,000. If the current market value is greater than $1,000, the IRR to maturity will be something less than the coupon rate; if the current market value is less than $1,000, the IRR will be greater than the coupon rate.

The internal rate of return may also be described as the rate of growth of an investment. This is more easily seen for an investment with one present outlay and one future benefit. For example, assume that an investment with an outlay of $1,000 today will return $1,331 three years from now.

This is a 0.10 internal rate of return, and it is also a 0.10 growth rate per year:

| Time | Beginning-of-Period Investment | Growth of Period | Growth Divided by Beginning-of-Period Investment |
|---|---|---|---|
| 0 | $1,000 | $100 | $100/$1,000 = 0.10 |
| 1 | 1,100 | 110 | $110/$1,100 = 0.10 |
| 2 | 1,210 | 121 | $121/$1,210 = 0.10 |
| 3 | 1,331 | — | |

The internal rate of return of a conventional investment has an interesting interpretation. It represents the highest rate of interest an investor could afford to pay, without losing money, if all the funds to finance the investment were borrowed and the loan (principal and accrued interest) was repaid by application of the cash proceeds from the investment as they were earned.

We shall illustrate the internal rate of return calculation using the example of the previous section where the investment had a net present value of $886 using 0.10 as the discount rate.

We want to find the rate of discount that causes the sum of the present values of the cash flows to be equal to zero. Assume that our first choice (an arbitrary guess) is 0.10. In the preceding situation, we found that the net present value using 0.10 is a positive $886. We want to change the discount rate so that the present value is zero. Should we increase or decrease the rate of discount for our second estimate? Since the cash flows are conventional (negative followed by positive), to decrease the present value of the future cash flows, we should increase the rate of discount (thus causing the present value of the future cash flows that are positive to be smaller).

Let us try 0.20 as the rate of discount:

| Period | Cash Flow | Present Value Factor | Present Value |
|---|---|---|---|
| 0 | −$12,337 | 1.0000 | −$12,337 |
| 1 | $10,000 | 0.8333 | $ 8,333 |
| 2 | 5,000 | 0.6944 | 3,472 |
| | | Net present value = | $ 532 |

The net present value is negative, indicating that the 0.20 rate of discount is too large. We shall try a value between 0.10 and 0.20 for our next estimate. Assume that we try 0.16:

| Period | Cash Flow | Present Value Factor | Present Value |
|--------|-----------|----------------------|---------------|
| 0 | −$12,337 | 1.0000 | −$12,337 |
| 1 | $10,000 | 0.8621 | $ 8,621 |
| 2 | 5,000 | 0.7432 | 3,716 |
| | | Net present value = | $     0 |

The net present value is zero using 0.16 as the rate of discount, which by definition means that 0.16 is the internal rate of return of the investment.

Although tables give only present value factors for select interest rates, calculators and computers can be used for any interest rate.

## Net Present Value Profile

The net present value profile is one of the more useful devices for summarizing the profitability characteristics of an investment. On the horizontal axis, we measure different discount rates; and on the vertical axis, we measure the net present value of the investment. The net present value of the investment is plotted for all discount rates from zero to some reasonably large rate. The plot of net present values will cross the horizontal axis (have zero net present value) at the rate of discount that is called the internal rate of return of the investment.

Figure 4.2 shows the net present value profile for the investment discussed in the previous two sections. If we add the cash flows, assuming a zero rate of discount, we obtain

$$-\$12,337 + \$10,000 + \$5,000 = \$2,663.$$

The $2,663 is the intersection of the graph with the $Y$-axis. We know that the graph has a height of $886 at a 0.10 rate of discount and crosses the $X$-axis at 0.16, since 0.16 is the internal rate of return of the investment. For interest rates greater than 0.16, the net present value is negative.

Note that for a conventional investment (minus cash flows followed by positive cash flows), the net present value profile slopes downward to the right.

The net present value profile graph can be used to estimate the internal rate of return by plotting one negative value and one positive value and connecting the two points with a straight line. The intercept with the $X$-axis will give a sensible estimate (not the exact value) of the internal rate of return.

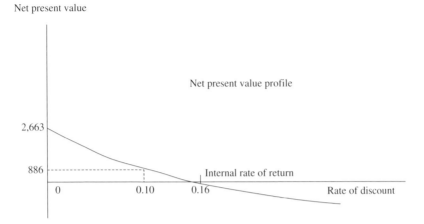

**Fig. 4.2.** Net Present Value Profile for the Investment.

We shall now consider four different investment opportunities and will apply four different investment criteria to these investments.

## Four Investments

In Table 4.1, four hypothetical investments are described in terms of the initial cost of each and the net proceeds expected during each year of life. The salvage value or terminal value of each investment is assumed to be zero. We shall illustrate the ranking that may be given to these investments by each measure of investment worth under consideration.

To avoid complexities, we will assume that there are zero taxes and no uncertainty. An evaluation of the risk or uncertainty associated with an investment is a crucial part of the investment decision process. Also, all investments must be

**Table 4.1.** Cash Flows of Hypothetical Investments.

| Investment | Initial Cost | Net Cash Proceeds per Year | |
| --- | --- | --- | --- |
| | | Year 1 | Year 2 |
| A | $10,000 | $10,000 | |
| B | 10,000 | 10,000 | $1,100 |
| C | 10,000 | 3,762 | 7,762 |
| D | 10,000 | 5,762 | 5,762 |

placed on an after-tax basis. The concepts of risk or uncertainty and taxation are complex, however, and these problems are avoided here.

## *Ranking by Inspection*

It is possible in certain limited cases to determine by inspection which of two or more investments is more desirable. Two situations in which this is true are the following:

1. Two investments have identical cash flows each year through the final year of the short-lived investment, but one continues to earn cash proceeds in subsequent years. The investment with the longer life would be more desirable. Thus, investment B is better than investment A, because all factors are equal except that B continues to earn proceeds after A has been retired.
2. Two investments have the same initial outlay and the same earning life and earn the same total proceeds. If at the end of every year (during their earning life) the total net proceeds of one investment are at least as great as, and for at least one year are greater than, the total for the other investment, then the first investment will always be more profitable. Thus, investment D is more desirable than investment C, because D earns $2,000 more in year 1 than investment C does; investment C does not earn this $2,000 until year 2. The earning of $2,000 more in the earlier year leads to the conclusion that investment D is more desirable than investment C.

## *Payback Period*

The payback period is one of the simplest and most frequently used methods of measuring the economic value of an investment. The *payback period* is defined as the length of time required for the stream of cash proceeds produced by an investment to equal the original cash outlay required by the investment. If an investment is expected to produce a stream of cash proceeds that is constant from year to year, the payback period can be determined by dividing the total original cash outlay by the amount of the annual cash proceeds expected. Thus, if an investment required an original outlay of $300 and was expected to produce a stream of cash proceeds of $100 a year for five years, the payback period would be $300 divided by $100, or three years. If the stream of expected proceeds is not constant from year to year, the payback period must be determined by adding up the proceeds expected in successive years until the total is equal to the original outlay.

Ordinarily, the administrator sets some maximum payback period and rejects all investment proposals for which the payback period is greater than this maximum. Investigators have reported that maximum payback periods of two, three, four, or five years are frequently used by industrial concerns. The relatively short periods mentioned suggest that different maximum payback periods are required for different types of investments because some kinds of investments (construction, for example) can seldom be expected to have a payback period as short as five years.

Assume that the payback period is also used to rank investment alternatives, with those having the shortest payback periods being given the highest ranking. The investments described in Table 4.1 are ranked by this method in Table 4.2.

Let us check the reasonableness of the ranking given to the investments by the cash payback approach. Investments A and B are both ranked as 1 because they both have shorter payback periods than any of the other investments, namely, one year. But investment A earns total proceeds of $10,000, and this amount merely equals the cost of the investment. Investment B, which has the same rank as A, will earn not only $10,000 in the first year but also $1,100 in the next year. Obviously, investment B is superior to A. Any ranking procedure, such as the payback period, that fails to disclose this fact is deficient.

Consider investments C and D modified so as to cost $11,524. Both would be given identical rankings because both would return their original outlay by the end of the second year. The two investments are in fact similar, with the single exception that out of identical total returns, more proceeds are received in the first year and less in the second year from investment D than is the case with C. To the extent that earnings can be increased by having $2,000 available for reinvestment one year earlier, D is superior to investment C, but both would be given the same ranking by the payback period measure.

Thus, the cash payback period measure has two weaknesses: (1) it fails to give any consideration to cash proceeds earned after the payback date, and (2) it fails

**Table 4.2.** Ranking of Investments.

| Investment | Payback Period (years) | Ranking | Calculations of Payback |
|---|---|---|---|
| A | 1.0 | 1 | |
| B | 1.0 | 1 | |
| C | 1.8 | 4 | $1 + \frac{\$6,238}{\$7,762} = 1.803$ |
| D | 1.7 | 3 | $1 + \frac{\$4,238}{\$5,762} = 1.736$ |

to take into account the differences in the timing of proceeds earned prior to the payback date. These weaknesses disqualify the cash payback measure as a general method of ranking investments. Payback is useful as a general measure of risk (all things being equal, a 2-year payback is less risky than a 10-year payback).

## Return on Investment

The methods described in this section are commonly referred to as rate of return analysis or return on investment (ROI) analysis. Terminology is a problem because both these terms are also used to describe other procedures. We shall consistently use internal rate of return only when we refer to a discounted cash flow calculation, and return on investment to refer to an income divided by investment calculation.

To get a measure of efficiency, analysts frequently use the ratio of the firm's income to the book value of its assets. Some companies also use this measure as a means of choosing among various proposed internal investments. When this measure is used, the average income is computed after depreciation. If the denominator in the ratio is the book value of the investment, the value of both the numerator and the denominator will depend on the depreciation method used. An alternative procedure is to divide the average income by the cost of the investment (the accrued depreciation is not subtracted).

The ratio of income to book value is a common and useful measure of performance, but it is less useful as a device for ranking investments. Table 4.3 shows that the same ranking of one is given to investments C and D, although D is preferable to C. This procedure fails to rank these investments correctly because it does not take into consideration the timing of the proceeds.

**Table 4.3.** Average Income on Book Value.

| Investment | Average Proceeds | Average Depreciation[a] | Average Income (proceeds less depreciation) | Average Book Value[b] | Income on Book Value (%) | Ranking |
|---|---|---|---|---|---|---|
| A | $10,000 | $10,000 | $ 0 | $5,000 | 0 | 4 |
| B | 5,550 | 5,000 | 550 | 5,000 | 11 | 3 |
| C | 5,762 | 5,000 | 762 | 5,000 | 15 | 1 |
| D | 5,762 | 5,000 | 762 | 5,000 | 15 | 1 |

[a]Assuming straight-line depreciation.
[b]Investment divided by 2.

**Table 4.4.** Average Income on Cost.

| Investment | Cost | Average Income | Average Income on Cost (%) | Ranking |
|---|---|---|---|---|
| A | $10,000 | $ 0 | 0 | 4 |
| B | 10,000 | 550 | 5.5 | 3 |
| C | 10,000 | 762 | 7.6 | 1 |
| D | 10,000 | 762 | 7.6 | 1 |

An alternative procedure (see Table 4.4) is to divide income by the cost of the investment (accumulated depreciation not being subtracted). For purposes of measuring performance and computing return on investment, the use of undepreciated cost will give lower measures than will the use of book value. Both measures illustrated fail to take into consideration the timing of cash proceeds. It is this failing that leads to incorrect decisions from the use of either of the two methods.

## Discounted Cash Flow Methods

We have considered payback and return on investment as methods for measuring the value of an investment. Payback indicated that B is as desirable as A. ROI indicated that C is tied with D. But B is clearly better than A, and D is better than C. On the basis of such an example, we have been able to reject payback and ROI as general methods of evaluating investments.

These two measures failed to consider the timing of cash proceeds from the investments. The payback period represents one extreme in this regard because all the proceeds received before the payback period are counted and treated as equal, and all the proceeds received after the payback period are ignored completely. With the return on investment, the proceeds were related by simple averaging techniques to such things as the original cost of the investment or its book value. Neither of these methods succeeded in bringing the timing of cash proceeds into the analysis.

We have seen that the measures of investment worth that were previously considered may give obvious incorrect results because they fail either to consider the entire life of the investment or to adequately consider the timing of future cash proceeds. The discounted cash flow concept provides a method of taking into account the timing of cash proceeds and outlays over the entire life of the investment. We now return to the two measures of investment worth already introduced that incorporate present value concepts.

**Table 4.5.** Internal Rate of Return of the Investments.

| Investment | IRR (%) | Ranking |
|---|---|---|
| A | 0 | 4 |
| B | 10 | 1 |
| C | 9[a] | 3 |
| D | 10 | 1 |

[a]Approximate measure.

## Internal Rate of Return

In Table 4.5, we show the internal rate of return for each of the investments listed in Table 4.1 and the ranking of investments that would result if this method were used.

Examine the rankings given by this method applicable to each pair of investments in this list for which we were earlier able to determine the more desirable investment of each pair. We previously compared two pairs of investments and decided that investment B was preferable to A, and D to C. In each case, if preference had been determined by using the internal rate of return of an investment method, the pairs would be given the correct ranking. This is the first method that we have used that gives the correct rankings of both pairs:

$$A, \quad 0\% \quad C, \quad 9\%$$
$$B, \quad 10\% \quad D, \quad 10\%$$

## Net Present Value

Note the rankings that will be given to the hypothetical investments of Table 4.1 by the net present value method, using two sample rates of discount. In Table 4.6,

**Table 4.6.** Net Present Values of the Investment — Rate of Discount is 6 Percent.

| Investment | Present Value of Cash Flow | Present Value of Outlay | Net Present Value | Ranking |
|---|---|---|---|---|
| A | $ 9,430 | $10,000 | −$570 | 4 |
| B | 10,413 | 10,000 | +$413 | 3 |
| C | 10,457 | 10,000 | +$457 | 2 |
| D | 10,564 | 10,000 | +$564 | 1 |

**Table 4.7.** Net Present Values of the Investment — Rate of Discount is 30 Percent.

| Investment | Present Value of Proceeds | Present Value of Outlay | Net Present Value | Ranking |
|---|---|---|---|---|
| A | $7,692 | $10,000 | −$2,308 | 3 |
| B | 8,343 | 10,000 | −$1,657 | 1 |
| C | 7,487 | 10,000 | −$2,513 | 4 |
| D | 7,842 | 10,000 | −$2,158 | 2 |

we present the results of using the net present value method and a 6 percent rate of discount.

In discussing the measures of investment worth that do not use the discounted cash flow method, we pointed out that the relative ranking of certain pairs of these four investments was obvious. That is, it is obvious from examining the cash flows that investment B is preferable to A and that D is preferable to C. In each case, the net present value method using a 6 percent rate of discount ranks these investment pairs in the correct relative order.

In Table 4.7, the same investments are ranked by the net present value method using a 30 percent rate of discount instead of 6 percent. The relative ranking of investments C and D does not change with the change in the rate of discount. Investment C, which was ranked second when a 6 percent rate of discount was used, is ranked fourth when the 30 percent discount rate is used. The ranking of investment D is changed from first to second by the change in the rate of discount. The higher rate of discount results in the proceeds of the later years being worth less relative to the proceeds of the early years; thus, the ranking of B goes from 3 to 1, but D is still ranked ahead of C.

Even with a 30 percent rate of interest, the present value method maintains the correct ordering of each of the two pairs of investments for which an obvious preference can be determined. Thus, we still find investment B preferred to A, and D preferred to C. Whenever it is possible to determine obvious preferences between pairs of investments in the correct order, no matter what rate of discount is used to compute the present value, as long as the same rate of discount is used to determine the present value of both the investments, the ranking given by the present value method will be correct.

## *Summary of Rankings*

The rankings given by each measure of investment worth for each of the hypothetical investments described in Table 4.1 are summarized in Table 4.8.

**Table 4.8.**   Summary of Rankings.

| Measure of Investment Worth | Investment | | | |
|---|---|---|---|---|
| | A | B | C | D |
| Payback period | 1[a] | 1[a] | 4 | 3 |
| Average income on book value or cost | 4 | 3 | 1[a] | 1[a] |
| Internal rate of return | 4 | 1[a] | 3 | 1[a] |
| Net present value | | | | |
| At 6% | 4 | 3 | 2 | 1 |
| At 30% | 3 | 1 | 4 | 2 |

[a]Indicates a tie between two investments.

The most striking conclusion to be drawn from Table 4.8 is the tendency for each measure of investment worth to give a different ranking to the identical set of investments. This emphasizes the need to give careful consideration to the choice of measures used to evaluate proposed investments. All four methods cannot be equally valid. By considering specific pairs of investments, we have shown that the measures of investment worth that do not involve the use of the discounted cash flow method can give rankings of investments that are obviously incorrect. For this reason, these measures will be excluded from further consideration.

The rankings given to the investments by the net present value measures are not identical to that given by the internal rate of return of an investment measure. Neither of these rankings can be eliminated as being obviously incorrect; yet, because they are different, they could lead to contradictory conclusions in certain situations.

## Limitation of Investment Rankings

In this chapter, we discussed the ranking of four investments and showed that, given a carefully defined set of investments, we can make definite statements about the relative desirability of two or more investments. If the investments are not restricted to this set, we would find our ability to rank investments very limited.

We shall not aim for a "ranking" of investments; instead, we shall:

1. Make accept-or-reject decisions for investments that are independent (i.e., if we undertake one investment, the cash flows of undertaking the other investment are not affected).

2. Choose the best of a set of mutually exclusive investments (i.e., if we undertake one, either we would not want to undertake the other or we would not be able to because of the characteristics of the investments).

Although the objectives are somewhat more modest than the objective of ranking investments, we shall still encounter difficulties. There is nothing in our recommendations, however, that will preclude a manager from applying qualitative criteria to the investments being considered to obtain a ranking. The ranking that is so obtained is likely to be difficult to defend. Fortunately, for a wide range of decision situations, a manager can make decisions without a ranking of investments.

## The Rollback Method

Using a simple hand calculator (one where there is no present value button), it is sometimes convenient to use a rollback method of calculation to compute the net present value of an investment. One advantage of this procedure is that the present values at different moments in time are obtained. Consider the following investment:

| Time | Cash Flow |
|------|-----------|
| 0 | −$7,000 |
| 1 | $5,000 |
| 2 | 2,300 |
| 3 | 1,100 |

Assume that the discount rate is 0.10.

The first step is to place the cash flow of period 3 ($1,100) in the calculator and divide by 1.10 to obtain $1,000, the value at time 2. Add $2,300 and divide the sum by 1.10 to obtain $3,000, the value at time 1. Add $5,000 and divide by 1.10 to obtain $7,273, the value of time 0. Subtract $7,000 to obtain the net present value of $273.

## Where We Are

There are many different ways of evaluating investments. In some situations, several of the methods will lead to identical decisions. We shall consistently recommend the net present value method as the primary means of evaluating investments.

The net present value method ensures that future cash flows are brought back to a common moment in time called *time 0*. For each future cash flow, a present value equivalent is found. These present value equivalents are summed to obtain a net present value. If the net present value is positive, the investment is acceptable.

The transformation of future flows back to the present is accomplished using the mathematical relationship $(1 + r)^{-n}$, which we shall call the present value factor for $r$ rate of interest and $n$ time periods.

In cases of uncertainty, additional complexities must be considered, but the basic framework of analysis will remain the net present value method.

Today, almost all large corporations use one or more discounted cash flow methods. NPV and IRR are two of the more widely used methods.

However, ROI (without time discounting) is also used, though it is not recommended in this book as a method of evaluating prospective investments. It has use as a means of evaluating performance once the investment has been made, if it is used carefully.

## Conclusions

An effective understanding of present value concepts is of great assistance in the understanding of a wide range of areas of business decision making. The concepts are especially important in financial decision making, since many decisions reached today affect the firm's cash flows over future time periods.

It should be stressed that this chapter has only discussed how to take the timing of the cash flows into consideration. This limitation in objective should be kept in mind. Risk and taxes must still be considered before the real-world decision maker has a tool that can be effectively applied. In addition, there may be qualitative factors that management wants to consider before accepting or rejecting an investment.

It is sometimes stated that refinements in capital budgeting techniques are a waste of effort because the basic information being used is so unreliable. It is claimed that the estimates of cash proceeds are only guesses and that to use anything except the simplest capital budgeting procedures is as futile as using complicated formulas or observations of past market levels to determine which way the stock market is going to move next.

It is true that in many situations reliable estimates of cash proceeds are difficult to make. Fortunately, there are a large number of investment decisions in which cash proceeds can be predicted with a fair degree of certainty. But even with an accurate, reliable estimate of cash proceeds, the wrong decision is frequently made because incorrect methods are used in evaluating this information.

When it is not possible to make a single estimate of cash proceeds that is certain to occur, it does not follow that incorrect methods of analysis are justified. If the investment is large, the use of a careful and comprehensive analysis is justified, even if this means that the analysis will be more complicated and costly. With small tactical investments, somewhat less involved methods might be used, but again, there is no need to use inferior methods that decrease the likelihood of making correct investment decisions.

When all the calculations are completed, judgmental insights may be included in the analysis to decide whether to accept or reject a project.

## Review Problems

### Review Problem 4.1

Assume that a firm has a cost of money of 0.15. It is considering an investment with the following cash flows:

| Time | Cash Flow |
|------|-----------|
| 0 | −$27,000,000 |
| 1 | +$12,000,000 |
| 2 | +$11,520,000 |
| 3 | +$15,552,000 |

Should the investment be accepted?

**Solution to Review Problem 4.1**

The net present value using 0.15 as the discount rate is:

| Time | Cash Flow | Present Value Factor | Present Value |
|------|-----------|----------------------|---------------|
| 0 | −$27,000,000 | $1.15^{-0}$ | −$27,000,000 |
| 1 | +$12,000,000 | $1.15^{-1}$ | $10,435,000 |
| 2 | +$11,520,000 | $1.15^{-2}$ | 8,711,000 |
| 3 | +$15,552,000 | $1.15^{-3}$ | 10,226,000 |
| | | Net present value = | $ 2,372,000 |

The net present value is positive and the investment is acceptable. The internal rate of return is 0.20.

## Questions and Problems

1. Compute the net present value for each of the following cash flows. Assume a cost of money of 10 percent.

| Investment | Period | | | | | |
|---|---|---|---|---|---|---|
| | 0 | 1 | 2 | 3 | 4 | 5 |
| A | $(1,000) | $100 | $100 | $100 | $100 | $1,100 |
| B | (1,000) | 264 | 264 | 264 | 264 | 264 |
| C | (1,000) | | | | | 1,611 |

2. Compute the internal rate of return for each of the cash flows in Problem 1.
3. Compute the payback for each of the cash flows in Problem 1. If the maximum acceptable payback period is four years, which (if any) of the cash flows would be accepted as a desirable investment?
4. Assume a cost of money of 5 percent. Compute the net present values of the cash flows in Problem 1.
5. Assume a cost of money of 15 percent. Compute the net present values of the cash flows in Problem 1. Compare with the results obtained from Problems 1 and 4.
6. The Arrow Company is considering the purchase of equipment that will return cash proceeds as follows:

| End of Period | Proceeds |
|---|---|
| 1 | $5,000 |
| 2 | 3,000 |
| 3 | 2,000 |
| 4 | 1,000 |
| 5 | 500 |

Assume a cost of money of 10 percent.

What is the maximum amount the company could pay for the machine and still be financially no worse off than if it did not buy the machine?

7. a. An investment with an internal rate of return of 0.25 has the following cash flows:

| Time | Cash Flow |
|------|-----------|
| 0 | $C_0$ |
| 1 | +$ 8,000 |
| 2 | +$10,000 |

The value of $C_0$ is _____.

b. If the firm financed the investment in (a) with debt costing 0.25, the debt amortization table (using the funds generated by the investment to repay the loan) would be:

| Time | Amount Owed | Interest | Principal Payment |
|------|-------------|----------|-------------------|
| 0 | | | |
| 1 | | | |
| 2 | | | |

8. Compute the net present value (use a cost of money of 0.15) and the internal rate of return for each of the following investments:

| Investment | 0 | Period 1 | 2 |
|------------|---|----------|---|
| A | $(1,000) | | $1,322 |
| B | (1,000) | $ 615 | 615 |
| C | (1,000) | 1,150 | |

9. Recompute the net present values using (a) a cost of money of 0.20 and (b) a cost of money of 0.05 for each of the investments in Problem 8.

10. Prepare a schedule showing that, with a rate of growth of 0.15 per year, $1,000 will grow to $1,322 in two years.

11. Determine the internal rate of return of the following investment:

| Time | Cash Flow |
|------|-----------|
| 0 | −$12,800 |
| 1 | +$ 8,000 |
| 2 | +$10,000 |

12. How much could you pay in excess of the indicated cost for the investment in Problem 11 if the cost of money were 0.10?

13. Assume that you can only invest in one of the three investments in Problem 8.

   a. Using the internal rates of return on the three investments, which is preferred?
   b. Using the net present value method and a cost of money of 0.05, which is preferred?

14. A company uses a 10 percent discount rate. Assume equal annual cash proceeds.

   What should be the maximum acceptable payback period for equipment whose life is 5 years? What are the maximum acceptable paybacks for lives of 10, 20, and 40 years and infinite life?

15. Assume that the discount rate is 5 percent and answer Problem 14.

16. Assume that $r = 0.06$. A new machine that costs $7,000 has equal annual cash proceeds over its entire life and a payback period of 7.0 years.

   What is the minimum number of full years of life it must have to be acceptable?

17. Compute the internal rate of return of the following investments:

| | | Period | | |
|------------|-----------|---------|---------|----------|
| Investment | 0 | 1 | 2 | 3 |
| A | −$10,000 | $4,747 | $4,747 | $ 4,747 |
| B | −$10,000 | | | 17,280 |

Compare the two investments.

   Which do you prefer? Are you making any assumption about the reinvestment of the cash flows?

18. Determine the internal rate of return of the following investment:

| Period | Cash Flow |
|--------|-----------|
| 0 | −$15,094 |
| 1 | $10,000 |
| 2 | 10,000 |
| 3 | 1,000 |

19. The Super Company used a ROFE (return on funds employed) method of evaluating investments. The income of each period is divided by the average assets used during the period. This is done for each period and then an average ROFE is computed of all the ROFEs.

The controller of the Super Company defends the procedure since it is consistent with the performance evaluation procedures that are used after the investment is acquired.

The company is currently evaluating two investments (A and B).

|   | 0 | 1 | 2 |
|---|---|---|---|
| A | −$20,000 | +$11,000 | +$12,100 |
| B | −$20,000 | +$12,100 | +$11,000 |

|   | A | | B | |
|---|--------|--------|--------|--------|
|   | Year 1 | Year 2 | Year 1 | Year 2 |
| Revenue | $11,000 | $12,100 | $12,100 | $11,000 |
| Depreciation | 10,000 | 10,000 | 10,000 | 10,000 |
| Income | $ 1,000 | $ 2,100 | $ 2,100 | $ 1,000 |
| Average investment | 15,000 | 5,000 | 15,000 | 5,000 |
| ROFE | 0.067 | 0.420 | 0.140 | 0.200 |
| Average ROFE | 0.24 | | 0.17 | |

The firm requires a 0.20 return for an investment to be acceptable. The firm acquired investment A.

Which investment is more desirable?

20. The ABC Company has determined that its cost of money is 0.12. However, because of a series of necessary nonproductive (not generating cash flows)

investments, it has found that on the average a discretionary investment must earn 0.15 in order for the firm to break even.

The firm has a chance to undertake an investment that has an internal rate of return of 0.14 and no risk. This investment will also not affect the amount of nonproductive investments needed.

Should the investment be accepted?

*Chapter 5*

# The Income Statement

The measurement of income is one of the most important functions of financial accounting. Investors, managers, bankers, and others are interested in knowing how well the corporation is doing. In this chapter, we will discuss the procedures for recording transactions for income determination and the basic assumptions relating to income measurement.

## The Revenue Transaction

The sale of goods or services to customers is called a **revenue transaction**. A revenue transaction usually involves an increase in an asset, such as cash or accounts receivable, to recognize the amount received or due from customers because of a sale of goods or services.

Stockholders do not benefit to the full extent of the sales amount. Expenses related to the sale must be recognized as reducing or offsetting the impact of revenue transactions on stockholders' equity. For example, an expense for the cost of the merchandise delivered to customers is subtracted from revenue to calculate the net benefit to stockholders.

To illustrate a revenue transaction, assume that merchandise costing $30,000 is sold on a customer's account for $50,000 in January. Also assume that wages of $5,000 were earned and paid to employees during January.

As a result of these transactions, the following changes would occur in balance sheet accounts. A Receivables account would increase by $50,000, the amount owed to the company by a customer. The Cash account would decrease by $5,000, the amount paid to employees. The Merchandise account would decrease by $30,000, and the Retained Earnings account would increase by $15,000, the net benefit to stockholders of the sale. The two sides of the balance sheet would still be in balance, as may be seen from the following summary of changes:

| Assets | | Stockholders' Equities | |
|---|---|---|---|
| Receivable | +$50,000 | Retained Earnings | +$50,000 |
| Merchandise | −$30,000 | Retained Earnings | −$30,000 |
| Cash | −$ 5,000 | Retained Earnings | −$ 5,000 |
| Net Change | +$15,000 | Net Change | +$15,000 |

**Revenues** are measured by the monetary value of the assets received (or reduction of liabilities) in return for goods and services that are sold. The decreases in the assets associated with obtaining the revenues (e.g., the cost of the merchandise sold and the cost of wages during the period) are called **expenses**. The difference between the revenues of a period and the expenses associated with earning those revenues is called **income** if the revenues exceed the expenses, or **loss** if the expenses exceed the revenues. The terms "revenues" and "income" should not be used interchangeably.

If there are no distributions of income to the stockholders during a period, the Retained Earnings balance will increase by the amount of the income. In the foregoing example, the income was $15,000 and the Retained Earnings balance increased by the same amount. If there had been a loss during the period (i.e., expenses exceeded revenues), the Retained Earnings balance would have decreased. A negative balance in the Retained Earnings account is called a *deficit*.

## Accrual Accounting

In the previous example, a receivable was recorded to show that amounts were owed to the enterprise for the merchandise sold. Recording this receivable permits the recognition of revenues when they have been earned (because the sale occurred), without regard to whether cash payments are received.

Now, suppose that in the previous example the wages had not actually been paid to employees in January, even though they had earned $5,000 for the services they performed. In this case, an expense and a liability would be recorded to show that amounts were owed to the employees. Expenses are recognized when they have been incurred (because the services were performed), without regard to when payments are made.

The recognition of revenues when they have been earned and expenses when they have been incurred is referred to as **accrual accounting**. The use of accrual accounting results in recording receivables and liabilities, with no immediate effect on cash.

The use of accrual accounting can also result in the recognition of expenses when assets expire or are used up (or consumed) during a period. For example, if annual rent of $36,000 is paid on January 1, this amount could initially be recorded as an asset, prepaid rent. However, by the end of January, one-twelfth of the prepaid rent has expired. As a result, the Prepaid Rent account balance should be credited by $3,000 and rent expense should be debited by $3,000.

Assets with longer lives are treated in a similar manner. For example, if a company purchases a truck for $24,000 that is expected to be used for five years, the initial cost of the truck would be recorded as an asset. As the truck is used, however, we may assume that one-sixtieth of the initial cost, or $400, expires each month and thus becomes an expense. Recognition of the costs of long-lived assets that expire in a period is referred to as **depreciation accounting**. Depreciation is an expense that reduces the accounting measure of the asset being depreciated and reduces income.

To illustrate the recognition of expenses by accrual accounting, let us extend the preceding example. Suppose that in addition to the facts presented previously (merchandise costing $30,000 was sold on customer account for $50,000 and payments for wages totaled $5,000), we are given the following information. Rent on the store building, $36,000 for the year, was paid on January 1. A truck used to make deliveries had originally cost $24,000 and was expected to last for five years. In addition to the work for which they were paid, employees performed services during the month for which they will be paid $2,500 next month.

To reflect this information, we would decrease the asset, prepaid rent, by $3,000 ($36,000/12 months); decrease the asset, delivery truck, by $400 ($24,000/60 months); and increase the liability, wages payable, by $2,500. These changes would be accompanied by a decrease in retained earnings. The balance sheet would be affected as shown in the following summary of changes:

| Assets | | Liabilities and Stockholder Equity | |
|---|---|---|---|
| Receivable | +$50,000 | Retained Earnings | +$50,000 |
| Merchandise | −$30,000 | Retained Earnings | −$30,000 |
| Cash | −$ 5,000 | Retained Earnings | −$ 5,000 |
| Prepaid Rent | −$ 3,000 | Retained Earnings | −$ 3,000 |
| Delivery Truck | −$ 400 | Retained Earnings | −$ 400 |
| | | Wages Payable | +$ 2,500 |
| | | Retained Earnings | −$ 2,500 |
| Net Change | +$11,600 | Net Change | +$11,600 |

The net income of $9,100, shown in the summary income statement for January, is equal to the change in retained earnings for the month. The stockholders' interests were increased by the net difference between the sales revenues and the expenses recognized during the month.

## Recording Revenue Transactions Using Temporary Accounts

Up to this point, the revenues and expenses have been recorded using only asset and equity accounts. New accounts are now introduced in which the revenues and expenses are recorded and accumulated separately. The accounts are called *temporary* because they do not appear on the balance sheet. Thus, they must be eliminated whenever a balance sheet is prepared.

Revenue and expense accounts come into being because of practical consider-ations. Imagine the nuisance if every time we recorded a sale we had to record the expense of making that sale. The difficulty is avoided by using temporary accounts to record the revenues and expenses rather than computing the income of each individual sale. Sales may be grouped together and the results of the operations of a time period (month, quarter, year, and so forth) determined. In special situations where the sales consist of items with a large dollar value per unit, the profit of the individual sale may be determined, but these are exceptional cases.

Expense accounts are also useful in analyzing efficiency and controlling costs. They perform the function of accumulating information about the amount of the costs that have expired in the production of the revenues. An expense may or may not be accompanied by an expenditure of cash. The sales effort connected with making a sale becomes an expense even though the salesperson has not yet been paid. The same is true of electricity, rent, supplies, and other similar items.

### *Example*

Assume that the opening balances of the following T-accounts reflect the financial position of the Sample Company (the balances are indicated by checks $\sqrt{}$). The transaction numbered (1) records the sale for cash of $100 of merchandise that cost the company $60. The only other expense is the expiration of $15 of prepaid rent. Entries (2) and (3) record the expenses. First, the transaction will be recorded using only asset and equity accounts.

| Cash | | | | Common Stock | | |
|---|---|---|---|---|---|---|
| $\sqrt{}$ | 300 | | | | $\sqrt{}$ | 200 |
| (1) | 100 | | | | | |

| Merchandise | | | | Retained Earnings | | |
|---|---|---|---|---|---|---|
| $\sqrt{}$ | 150 | (2) | 60 | (2) | 60 | $\sqrt{}$  295 |
| | | | | (3) | 15 | (1)  100 |

| Prepaid Rent | | | |
|---|---|---|---|
| $\sqrt{}$ | 45 | (3) | 15 |

This is the way in which we have been recording revenue transactions until now. Entering the amounts of revenues and expenses directly in the Retained Earnings account enables us to determine the amount of stockholders' equity as of any specific time, but it destroys some very valuable information. Since we want to know the various components of revenue and expense for each accounting period, it is important to maintain records of these amounts in the accounting system.

## Temporary Accounts

This information can be preserved during a specific accounting period by setting up temporary accounts to keep track of revenues and expenses. We can regard these temporary accounts as being a temporary subdivision of the Retained Earnings account. We will create *revenue* accounts to record each item of revenue: sales, interest revenue, rent revenue, and so forth. As revenues have the effect of increasing retained earnings, these accounts are increased in the same way as retained earnings — they are increased by credits, and they are decreased by debits.

| Revenue Accounts | |
|---|---|
| Decrease | Increase |

Similarly, we will create *expense* accounts to record each item of expense: wages expense, rent expense, merchandise cost of goods sold, and so on. As expenses have the effect of decreasing retained earnings, these accounts are increased by debits and decreased by credits.

| Expense Accounts | |
|---|---|
| Increase | Decrease |

## Periodic Adjustments

In previous illustrations, we have demonstrated some of the accounting entries that would be used to adjust the accounts at the end of an accounting period. For example, the adjustment of prepaid rent to reflect the remaining balance at the end of the year was shown. This adjustment not only provides for the proper balance in the asset account, but also results in the proper measure of rent expense for the year. Similarly, entries would be made for the proper statement of the asset balance of merchandise inventory and also for the determination of cost of goods sold.

These entries, which are made to bring asset and equity accounts, as well as revenue and expense accounts, into agreement with the facts as of the date of an accounting report, are called adjusting entries. At the end of each accounting period, there will be some accounts for which the balances require adjustment. Although there may be no explicit transaction at the time, the accountant nevertheless will record an entry to adjust the accounts to their proper balances, so that the financial statements prepared at that time will provide a fair presentation.

## The Income Statement

The income statement shows the results of operations for a period of time. Whereas the balance sheet is "as of" a particular moment, the income statement is "for the period ending...." The period of time may be a year or any fraction of a year, but it is a period of time rather than a moment in time. It is essential that the income statement disclose the exact period covered, because the length of the period is a basic element of the interpretation of income. For example, a given income for one month would have a far different significance than the same income for a year.

The income statement compares the revenues of the period with the expenses that were incurred to gain those revenues. The difference between the revenues and expenses is generally defined as the income for the period:

$$\text{Revenues} - \text{Expenses} = \text{Income}.$$

## Revenue Recognition

The accountant determines income by subtracting expenses from revenues. As simple as this may seem, there are many complexities that arise when trying to implement this concept. For example, there are many activities and events that must take place to generate revenues. The accountant adopts the procedure of recognizing revenues at the time a certain **critical event** takes place. But which event is important enough to justify the recognition of revenue? Depending on the situation, there are several acceptable methods of revenue recognition, but only three will be discussed here.

**Production basis** — recognize revenue at time of production.
**Sales (or accrual) basis** — recognize revenue at time of sale.
**Cash receipts basis** — recognize revenue at time cash is received.

### *Production Basis*

Production is the critical event for companies that produce or construct assets under long-term production or construction contracts. Boeing Aerospace did not build the Boeing 747 and 767 aircrafts to open stock. Instead, these aircrafts are built to customer specifications under production contracts. These contracts specify who the customer is and the amounts and timings of cash flows. As a result, the contracts reduce the uncertainty of the sale and cash receipts events. Companies that produce to order under production or construction contracts often attempt to spread prospective revenues, related costs, and resulting net income over the life of the contract in proportion to the work accomplished. The method used to accomplish this spreading of revenues, costs, and income is called the percentage-of-completion or production method.

## Sales Basis

The sales (or accrual) basis is the most widely used method for recognizing revenues. Revenues are assumed to be earned at the time the sale is made, even though the cash may not have been collected from customers. For companies that produce to open stock, the sale is the critical event for revenue recognition. Even though value is added to goods through the production process, these companies face considerable uncertainty about who the customer will be and about the amount and timing of the sale. It is necessary to have an **arm's length transaction**, in which the customer is legally obligated to pay for the merchandise or service. Such factors as the signing of a sales contract and the delivery of the product provide evidence that the sale has been made. At the time of the sale, revenue is recognized and the amount due from the customer is reflected as an asset such as accounts receivable.

However, some uncertainty still remains about cash receipt. Companies that use the sales method must also be able to estimate bad debts or doubtful accounts at the time of the sale so that the sales amounts and accounts receivable balances can be adjusted to reflect the expected cash receipts.

## Cash Receipts Basis

In some cases, the receipt of cash is considered to be the critical event for revenue recognition. There are three reasons for using the cash receipts basis. First, for some taxpayers, the use of the cash receipt basis is allowable for computing taxable income and may result in some postponement of tax payments. Second, when collection from customers is regarded as very uncertain, the cash receipts basis may be the best indication of actual revenues. Finally, the cash receipts basis is more conservative than the sales basis. It is important to realize that when the cash receipts basis of revenue recognition is used, the product must also have been delivered to customers before revenue is recognized. Thus, if cash is received in advance (such as with magazine subscriptions), the receipt of cash would not be considered sufficient evidence for recognizing revenue.

## Expense Recognition — The Matching Concept

Either the production, sales, or cash receipts method can be used to assign revenues to periods of time. Expense recognition involves assigning or matching expenses to periods of time. Some expenses are closely related to the revenues assigned to periods of time. For example, the costs of goods sold during a period reflect the costs of materials, labor, and manufacturing overhead incurred to produce units of product that were sold. These costs are called product expenses. Other expenses are closely related to the periods of time to which revenues are assigned. For example, costs are incurred to maintain a sales and marketing organization, a research and development capability, and a general administrative organization. These costs are called period expenses, because they are closely related to the periods during which these organizations and capabilities exist.

When to recognize costs as expenses is one of the most perplexing problems the accountant faces. It is easier to describe what should not be done than to describe what should be done. For example, whether the costs have been paid for with a disbursement of cash has little to do with the determination of whether they should be recognized as expenses. Thus, the electricity consumed in lighting a store is an expense of the period in which the electricity is used, even though the electric bill has not yet been paid. That is, the electricity expense is a period expense. If the electricity is used to run a machine in producing a product, then the cost of the electricity becomes a part of the cost of the product and is not considered an expense until the product is sold. That is, the electricity cost is a cost of product, which becomes a product expense when the product is sold.

Labor costs in a *manufacturing situation* are considered to be an asset until the product that was produced is sold. They become part of the cost of inventory and are only regarded as part of the cost of goods sold when the product is sold (product expense). However, labor costs in a *merchandising situation* are generally considered to be expenses at the time they are incurred (period expenses), and the step of first recognizing these costs as assets is bypassed. This is not harmful, because the labor costs of a merchandising company would only rarely be considered unexpired at the end of the period.

The guiding rule is that expenses should be matched with the revenues that they help to earn or generate. Costs become expenses when their future service potential expires, and this normally occurs as the revenues are earned. For example, the cost of a building is charged to expense over its useful life. The expense associated with allocating the original cost of buildings and equipment to the periods in which they are used is called depreciation expense.

Occasionally, an asset loses value without having produced any revenue. Examples of this type of event include the destruction of a building by fire or the theft of cash. Situations of this nature are described as *losses*. A loss occurs when an asset loses all or part of its value without providing compensating economic benefits. Any insurance proceeds would reduce the amounts of these losses.

Frequently, the accountant will not take note of the fact that an item is an asset before recognizing that it is an expense. Where the asset loses value and becomes an expense in the same period in which the company acquires it, no error results and it does save some bookkeeping effort. In other cases, where the cost of an item is small (such as pencils or small tools), the cost may be treated as an expense even though it does not expire in the current period. Although this may not seem proper from a theoretical viewpoint, the costs of keeping detailed records about small items and amounts may justify this treatment. This departure reflects the materiality assumption.

There is a difference of opinion in the accounting profession as to whether or not matching is a valid concept. Accepted or not by the profession, it is useful to keep the matching objective in mind.

## Recognition Criteria

As described previously, many functions must be performed to earn revenue. A sales order is obtained, the product is manufactured and then delivered to the customer, cash is collected, and perhaps services are required by guarantees provided for a period of time after delivery of the product. With the need for financial statements covering specific periods of time, the accountant must make assumptions about the exact point in time at which revenue is to be recognized. Before the manufactured goods are sold, there may be a great deal of uncertainty about the amount of revenue to be received and expenses to be incurred. The need for objective, verifiable evidence prevails at this level, and revenue is not usually recognized while goods are still being manufactured. When the goods are delivered to customers, there is objective and verifiable evidence of the amount that the customer has agreed to pay. Even though the full amount might not ultimately be collected, accountants normally recognize revenue at this point. In some instances, accountants prefer to wait until the cash proceeds are collected before recognizing revenue. This, however, is generally an overly conservative procedure.

The accountant does not usually recognize revenue until it is considered to have been realized. The **realization of revenue** is assumed to take place when there is a market transaction, such as a sale, and a well-defined asset is received in exchange for the asset or service that has been provided. Although the accountant requires realization before recognizing revenue (or a gain), the same requirement does *not* carry over to losses or other decreases in value. Accountants will generally record a *decrease* in value even though a market transaction has not occurred, whereas they would not use the same type of evidence as the basis for recording an *increase* in value. This procedure is considered to be conservative and is viewed as desirable by most accountants, although it is inconsistent because comparable gains are not recognized.

Regardless of the assumptions or criteria used in recognizing revenues, expenses should be recognized on a comparable basis. Therefore, if the accountant recognizes a certain level of revenues because of a revenue recognition assumption or criterion, the expenses to be used in determining income should be the costs that expired in earning those particular revenues. It would be incorrect to recognize revenues on all goods delivered to customers, but show as expenses only the costs attributable to goods on which collections have been made.

## Form of Income Statement

As with the balance sheet, there is no uniform agreement among accountants concerning the form of an income statement. Varied formats are used in practice. As long as the statement conveys the essential information in a manner that allows the reader to interpret it without confusion or ambiguity, the form may be considered acceptable.

The form presented in Exhibit 4.1 is a single-step *income statement*. There are no income subtotals above the net income figure. Some accountants prefer to take various subtotals, such as Gross Profit, Net Income before Depreciation, and Net Income before Taxes. The average reader of a financial report is likely to

**Exhibit 4.1.**　Single-Step Income Statement.

**ABC Company**
**Income Statement for Year Ending December 31, 19xx**

| | | |
|---|---:|---:|
| Revenue | | |
| 　Sales Revenue | $19,600 | |
| 　Interest Revenue | 900 | |
| 　Rent Revenue | 1,100 | $21,600 |
| Expenses | | |
| 　Cost of Goods Sold | $10,000 | |
| 　Wages | 3,000 | |
| 　Rent Expense | 1,000 | |
| 　Utilities | 200 | |
| 　Interest Charges | 100 | |
| 　Income Taxes | 2,000 | 16,300 |
| Net Income | | $ 5,300 |

be confused rather than assisted by the numerous subtotals, not knowing which income figure is significant. The single-step income statement has the virtue of being simple.

The single-step income statement has increased in popularity in recent years, but many corporations prefer to use some variant of the multi-step income statement.

## Discontinued Operations

If a major portion of a company's business has been discontinued, comparisons of operating results among years could become distorted. Readers of the income statement who are interested in projecting trends of earnings might want to exclude income attributable to these operations. Yet, the income statement must show the actual operating results for the year.

To accomplish both of these purposes, a separate item for income from discontinued operations is included in the determination of net income. In this way, users of financial statements who wish to ignore the results of discontinued operations may make their own calculations of earnings by adjusting for this item.

In current practice, the special treatment of discontinued operations applies only to the disposal of a division or other operating unit whose activities represent a separate major line of business or class of customer. Any gain or loss arising from the disposal of such an operating unit would also be included in the income from discontinued operations.

## Earnings per Share

The stockholders of a company are likely to be very interested in the amount of the company's earnings per share of common stock. This is an indication of how the results of the period affected their interests, and this figure often has a direct bearing on the market value of the shares.

Although the concept of earnings per share is rather simple, there are many complexities that arise in attempting to make the computation in practice. Separate earnings-per-share figures are shown to indicate the effects of extraordinary items or discontinued operations. Items such as mergers, issuance of new shares, and convertible securities also may affect the computation.

## Summary

Although we could record transactions using only asset and equity accounts, the use of revenue and expense accounts simplifies the recording of revenue transactions and allows the accumulation of more information. These temporary accounts are used in practice.

The accountant determines the revenues and expenses of the period. Income is defined as the difference between the revenues recognized during the period and the expenses matched against the revenues. This is an operational definition consistent with the way in which the accountant measures income.

The income statement reports the results of operations for a period of time. Several methods can be used to assign revenues to periods of time, and various income statement formats can be used to compare the revenues with the expenses that were incurred to generate those revenues.

Net income and earnings per share are important measures of performance, but these measures can be affected by such special events as extraordinary items and the treatment of discontinued operations. Accounting for these and other special events requires judgment. Users of financial statements should be aware of areas where judgment enters (or should enter), and thus be better able to assess and use the information provided.

## Questions and Problems

1. Why are revenues increased by credits and expenses increased by debits?
2. When a purchase is made, would you expect the item purchased to be recorded in an asset account or an expenses account? Explain.
3. At what step should the cost of oil be considered an expense?

   a. Oil is ordered.
   b. The oil is received.
   c. The oil is paid for by check.
   d. The oil is burned in a boiler to make steam that is used to run a generator that produces electricity that powers a machine that manufactures gadgets.
   e. A gadget is shipped to a wholesaler, and the wholesaler is billed.
   f. The cash is received from the wholesaler.

4. Some cost factors are conventionally treated as expenses as they are required. Which of the following items could be expenses immediately on acquisition without adversely affecting the information provided by the accounting system?

   a. Salesperson's commissions.
   b. Automobile assembly line worker's wages.
   c. Cost of heating department store.
   d. Cost of heating factory building.

5. For each of the following events, indicate whether the item would qualify as an extraordinary item in the determination of income as applied in current practice.

   a. A major company plant is destroyed by an unexpected earthquake.
   b. Company citrus groves are completely destroyed by frost. A frost of this magnitude occurs about once in five years.
   c. Sales of the company's product have been reduced because of the introduction of a superior product by a competitor.
   d. The company sells land that it held for many years, recognizing a large gain. The company is in the manufacturing business, and this was the company's only investment in land.
   e. The company's current income taxes are reduced because of the carryforward of losses from previous years.

6. A construction firm has a contract to build an office building that is expected to take three years to complete. Would it be desirable for the construction firm to wait until the building is completed before recognizing any revenue? What other methods of revenue recognition might be appropriate in this case?

7. For each account that follows, (a) list its normal balance (debit or credit); (b) identify it as a balance sheet or temporary account; and (c) classify it as a current asset, noncurrent asset, current liability, long-term liability, owners' equity, revenue, or expense account.

   Accounts Payable
   Bonds Payable (due in 20 years)
   Buildings
   Cash
   Common Stock
   Cost of Goods Sold
   Heat and Power
   Labor
   Merchandise Inventory
   Prepaid Rent
   Rent
   Retained Earnings
   Sales
   Taxes Payable
   Wages Payable

8. Record the following transactions, using T-accounts. Use temporary accounts. When is the merchandise recognized as an expense?

   a. Merchandise costing $23,000 is purchased on account.
   b. Merchandise that cost $1,900 is sold for $4,700 cash.
   c. Of the amount owed to trade creditors, $17,000 is paid.

9. Record the following transactions, using T-accounts. Use temporary accounts. When is the merchandise recognized as an expense?

   a. Merchandise costing $19,000 is purchased on account.
   b. Merchandise that cost $2,100 is sold for $4,500 cash.
   c. Of the amount owed to trade creditors, $12,000 is paid.

10. For each of the following situations, record the entries necessary to adjust the accounts at the end of the year. Use T-accounts.

    a. Wages of $700 have not yet been recorded. This is for labor services performed during the last three days of the year, for which payment will be made on the first payday of next year.
    b. The Prepaid Insurance account has a balance of $800. An analysis of the insurance contracts indicates that the amount of premiums applicable to future years is $500 as of December 31.
    c. Six months' interest on $100,000 of 14 percent bonds outstanding (a liability) has not yet been recognized.
    d. Six months' interest of $80,000 on government securities held as an investment has not yet been recognized.
    e. The Prepaid Rent account has a balance of $1,000 before making adjusting entries. Analysis indicates that rent of $200 is owed as of the date of closing.

11. For each of the following situations, record the entries necessary to adjust the accounts at the end of the year. Use T-accounts.

    a. Wages of $1,100 have not yet been recorded. This is for labor services performed during the last three days of the year, for which payment will be made on the first payday of next year.
    b. The Prepaid Insurance account has a balance of $1,200. An analysis of the insurance contracts indicates that the amount of premiums applicable to future years is $750 as of December 31.
    c. Six months' interest on $200,000 of 12 percent bonds outstanding (a liability) has not yet been recognized.

d. Six months' interest of $8,000 on government securities held as an investment has not yet been recognized.

e. The Prepaid Rent account has a balance of $1,500 before making adjusting entries. Analysis indicates that rent of $300 is owed as of the date of closing.

12. Record the following transactions for the year 20x1, using T-accounts (open any accounts you may need). The Burnside Company uses the periodic inventory procedure.

a. Sales of $150,000 were made, of which $90,000 were made on account.

b. Collections during the period from customers were $95,000.

c. Merchandise purchased on account during the period was $80,000.

d. The merchandise inventory on December 31, 20x1, was $45,000.

e. Payments to trade creditors for merchandise and supplies purchased were $85,000.

f. Supplies purchased on account during the period were $5,500.

g. On December 15, 20x1, the rent for 20x2 was paid, $5,000. The rent for the year 20x1 was $4,000.

h. As of December 31, 20x1, the company owed its employees wages totaling $5,000. During the year, employees were paid $70,000.

i. Supplies on hand as of December 31, 20x1, were $900.

The account balances before the transactions were as follows:

| | December 31, 20x0 | |
| | Debits | Credits |
| --- | --- | --- |
| Cash | $ 90,000 | |
| Accounts Receivable | 59,500 | |
| Merchandise | 60,000 | |
| Supplies | 1,500 | |
| Rent (Prepaid) | 4,000 | |
| Wages Expense | — | |
| Cost of Goods Sold | — | |
| Supplies Expense | — | |
| Rent Expense | — | |
| Accounts Payable | | $ 16,000 |
| Wages Payable | | 24,000 |
| Sales | | — |
| Common Stock | | 100,000 |
| Retained Earnings | | 75,000 |
| | $215,000 | $215,000 |

13. The accountant of the Burt Company makes use of expense and revenue accounts. All sales are for cash.

   a. Stockholders invest $100,000 on January 1, 20xx.

   b. Rent of $4,800 is paid. This is rent for a 12-month period beginning February 1.

   c. Merchandise that cost $25,000 is purchased on account.

   d. Supplies are purchased for $6,000 cash on February 1.

   e. The Burt Company starts operations on February 1. Sales for the first week are $5,000.

   Record the foregoing transactions using T-accounts.

14. The following transactions affecting the Curtis Corporation took place in the year 20xx.

   a. On January 1, 20xx, stockholders paid $100,000 to the corporation for 10,000 shares of common stock.

   b. The following items were purchased on account:

       Merchandise    $85,000
       Supplies         6,000

   c. An amount of $6,500 was paid to the landlord. This included rent of $500 for January of the next year.

   d. Sales of $117,000 were made.

       Cash Sales       $57,000
       Sales on Account    60,000

   e. Collection of accounts receivable was $47,000.

   f. Payment of accounts payable was $82,000.

   g. Wages paid during the year were $25,000. Wages payable as of December 31 were $500.

   h. Insurance premiums paid during the year were $3,000. Prepaid insurance as of December 31 was $1,800.

   i. Supplies used during the period were $4,200.

   j. The merchandise inventory as of December 31 was $15,000.

   k. Bonds were issued on July 1. The par value of the bonds is $50,000, and this amount was received from the investors. The bonds have a 7 percent rate of interest.

   l. Income taxes for the year are $1,837. No income taxes were paid in the current year.

   Record the foregoing transactions, including adjusting entries, in T-accounts.

## Chapter 6

# Comparing the Use of Cash Flows and Incomes

Chapter 4 stressed the usefulness of cash flows in evaluating and valuing investment alternatives. Chapter 5 explained the calculation of the corporate income measure. Some students of business will argue the relative merits of the two measures. The position put forth in this book is that they are both useful measures. It is important to understand how to correctly use both measures.

## The Use of Cash Flows

We will use a simple example to illustrate the use of cash flows to value an investment. Assume an alternative has the following cash flows:

| Time | Cash Flows |
|------|-----------|
| 1 | $1,300 |
| 2 | 1,200 |
| 3 | 1,100 |

The appropriate discount rate is 0.10. The present value (PV) of the investment's benefits at time zero is $3,000.

$$PV = \frac{1,300}{1.10} + \frac{1,200}{(1.10)^2} + \frac{1,100}{(1.10)^3} = \$3,000.$$

The calculation is simple to make and to understand.

## Use of Earnings

Assume there is a $3,000 investment with the above set of cash flows for three years. The projected income statements for the three years of the investment's life are:

|  | Year 1 | Year 2 | Year 3 |
|---|---|---|---|
| Revenue | $1,300 | $1,200 | $1,100 |
| Depreciation Expense | 1,000 | 1,000 | 1,000 |
| Net Income | $ 300 | $ 200 | $ 100 |

To use the income measures for valuation, there has to be a capital charge for the stock equity capital being used. Assume there is a 0.10 annual capital charge. We have for each year:

|  | Year 1 | Year 2 | Year 3 |
|---|---|---|---|
| Amount of Capital[1] | $3,000 | $2,000 | $1,000 |
| Annual Capital Charge | 0.10 | 0.10 | 0.10 |
| Capital Charge for Year | $ 300 | $ 200 | $ 100 |

We then deduct the capital charge for the year from the net income to obtain the economic income.

|  | Year 1 | Year 2 | Year 3 |
|---|---|---|---|
| Net Income | $300 | $200 | $100 |
| Capital Charge | 300 | 200 | 100 |
| Economic Income | $ 0 | $ 0 | $ 0 |

The present value of the economic incomes (zero) is added to the book value to obtain the asset's value of $3,000. This is the same value as we obtained using the cash flow measures.

We need to make the example somewhat more complex to illustrate the more complete calculations.

## The Use of Cash Flows: A More Complex Example

Now assume the same set of cash flows, but the discount rate is 0.05. Computing the present value of cash flows, we obtain ($V_i$ is the investment's value at

---

[1] Reduced each year by the amount of depreciation expense.

time $i$):

|  | Time | | | |
|---|---|---|---|---|
|  | **0** | **1** | **2** | **3** |
| Cash Flow |  | $1,300 | $1,200 | $1,100 |
| $V_0$ | $3,276.75 |  |  |  |
| $V_1$ |  | 2,140.59 |  |  |
| $V_2$ |  |  | 1,047.62 |  |
| $V_3$ |  |  |  | 0 |

The present value of the three cash flows at time zero is now $3,276.752 using 0.05 as the discount rate (the present value was $3,000 using 0.10 as the discount rate).

Assume the resale value at time 3 is $576.75 with a present value of $498.218. The present value of the asset's cash flows including the resale value of $498.218 is:

$$PV \text{ of Cash Flows} = 3,276.752 + 498.218 = \$3,774.970.$$

## Use of Earnings: A More Complex Example

We will now assume the asset cost of $3,276.75, but the annual depreciation expense is again $1,000. At the end of year 3, the asset's book value is $276.75 and the resale value is $576.75 (resale value minus book value is $300).

The income statements for the three years are:

|  | **Year 1** | **Year 2** | **Year 3** |
|---|---|---|---|
| Revenue | $1,300 | $1,200 | $1,100 |
| Depreciation Expense | 1,000 | 1,000 | 1,000 |
| Net Income | $ 300 | $ 200 | $ 100 |
| Capital Charge* | 163.838 | 113.838 | 63.838 |
| Economic Income | $ 136.162 | $ 86.162 | $ 36.162 |

*Capital Charges: $(0.05)(3,276.75) = \$163.838$ for year 1
$(0.05)(2,276.75) = \$113.838$ for year 2
$(0.05)(1,276.75) = \$ 63.838$ for year 3.

The present value of the economic incomes is $239.068. The present value of the resale value minus book value at time 3 is $300(1.05)^{-3} = \$259.151$. The value of the asset is:

$$Value \text{ of Asset} = 3,276.75 + 239.068 + 259.151$$
$$= \$3,774.97,$$

where

$3,276.75 is the book value of the asset

$239.068 is the present value of the economic incomes

$259.151 is the present value of the $576.75 resale value minus the $276.75 remaining book value.

Using the incomes rather than the cash flows, we obtain exactly the same value for the asset if we use the economic incomes and adjust for the initial book value, resale value and ending book value.

$$\text{Value of Asset} = \text{Initial Book Value}$$
$$+ \text{Present Value of Economic Incomes}$$
$$+ \text{Present Value of Resale Value}$$
$$- \text{Present Value of Remaining Book Value}.$$

This relationship is not only complex, but it is likely also to be misleading to a casual reader. It looks like the value of the asset is a function of the book value, but it is not.

## Changing the Book Value

Now assume that instead of $3,276.75, the book value is $4,276.75 and the remaining book value at time 3 is $1,276.75.

The present value of the cash flows is not changed from $3,774.97 since the cash flow assumptions are not changed. However, many of the calculations using earnings are now changed. The new calculations of economic incomes are:

|  | Year 1 | Year 2 | Year 3 |
|---|---|---|---|
| Revenue | $1,300 | $1,200 | $1,100 |
| Depreciation Expense | 1,000 | 1,000 | 1,000 |
| Net Income | $ 300 | $ 200 | $ 100 |
| Capital Charge |  |  |  |
| 0.05(4,276.75) | 213.838 |  |  |
| 0.05(3,276.75) |  | 163.838 |  |
| 0.05(2,276.75) |  |  | 113.838 |
| Economic Income | $ 86.162 | $ 36.162 | −$ 13.838 |

PV of Economic Incomes = $102.91

PV of Resale Value = $(1.05)^{-3}(576.75) = \$498.22$

PV of Book Value at Time 3 = $(1.05)^{-3}(1,276.75) = \$1,102.90$

PV of Asset = 4,276.75 + 102.91 + 498.22 − 1,102.90

= $3,774.98.

Aside from a rounding error, the present value of the asset using earnings is unchanged from when the initial book value was $3,276.75 instead of $4,276.75. The following conclusions are important. The asset's value is not affected by:

a. the initial book value
b. the depreciation method being used.

The value is affected by the cash flows and their timing. It is also affected by the resale value and the economic incomes and their timing (and this is affected by the timing of the cash flows).

While the book value and the accounting depreciation method do not affect the asset value, they do influence important measures used by management and thus should not be considered completely irrelevant.

## The Book Value Washes Out

We need to illustrate why the amount of book value does not affect the asset's value. Let us continue the example where the initial book value is $4,276.75.

We have:

| | | |
|---|---|---|
| Initial Book Value = | | $4,276.75 |
| PV of Depreciation Expenses | | |
| 1,000 B(3, 0.05) | | −$2,723.25 |
| PV of Capital Charges | | −$ 450.58 |

| | PV | |
|---|---|---|
| $213.838 | $203.655 | |
| 163.838 | 148.606 | |
| 113.838 | 98.338 | |
| | $450.58 | |
| Ending Book Value 1,276.75 with PV of | | −$1,102.91 |
| Subtotal | | −$4,276.74 |
| Net | | $    0.01 |

The $4,276.75 initial cost is added to determine the value; but the present value of depreciation expenses, interest, and ending book value are all subtracted, and their present value is equal to the initial book value. If the initial book value changes, enough of the other measures change and the equality is maintained. If the method of calculating depreciation expense is changed, the capital charges and the ending book value are all changed and (if no mistakes are made) the equality is maintained.

This analysis should agree with your intuition that if the actual receipt and disbursement of cash flows are not changed, the value of the asset is not changed by a change in the accounting method.

## Revenue Recognition and Finance

Mr. Alex (a fictitious name) was in the process of selling his business (a firm selling computer software and servicing the software). He and the buyers had agreed on the price when the public accounting firm (which had audited the corporation for ten years) decided that an error had been made in the audits of the revenue recognition method used. The firm had recognized 60% of the first year's revenue at the signing of the contract, 30% on receipt of the first cash receipts, and 10% on receipt of the remainder of the first year's receipts. The accountants thought 60% was too large.

Mr. Alex did not question the merits of the proposed revenue schedule and the recomputation of the monthly and yearly incomes. He did, however, point out to the buyers that they had valued the firm using the historical cash flow numbers, and these numbers were not changed by the proposed accounting changes.

The timing of forecasted cash flows might be changed because of the calculation method being used, but logically forecasted cash collection should not be affected by the method (or details) of revenue recognition used by the accountants.

With the sale of a public corporation, the market price of the firm's stock could be affected by the revenue recognition (and the periodic earnings) and our conclusion could be different than with the sale of a private firm.

## Conclusions

The basic method of valuation advocated in this book is the discounted cash flow (DCF) method, but other methods are used in practice. This chapter shows that the use of accounting earnings can give exactly the same value as the DCF method, but the accounting earnings have to be adjusted for a capital charge to arrive at economic income.

There are several methods of valuation used which recognize the difficulty of forecasting the future and use simplified calculations. For example, the following methods are widely used:

a. Price earnings multiple — Earnings times an assumed P/E multiple.
b. EBIT multiple — Earnings before interest and taxes (EBIT) times an assumed EBIT multiple (smaller than the P/E multiple).
c. EBITDA multiple — Earnings before interest, taxes, depreciation and amortization (EBITDA) times an EBITDA multiple (smaller than the EBIT multiple).

## Questions and Problems

1. Assume an investment of $4,000 has the following projected income statements. There are zero taxes. The cost of equity is 0.10.

|  | 1 | 2 | 3 | 4 |
|---|---|---|---|---|
| Revenue | $1,800 | $1,600 | $1,400 | $1,200 |
| Depreciation | 1,000 | 1,000 | 1,000 | 1,000 |
| Income | $ 800 | $ 600 | $ 400 | $ 200 |

   a. Compute the NPV using the cash flows.
   b. Compute the economic incomes of each year.
      Compute the NPV using economic incomes.
   c. Compue the investment's internal rate of return.

2. (continue 1) Assume the depreciation schedule is:

| Year | Depreciation |
|---|---|
| 1 | $1,600 |
| 2 | 1,200 |
| 3 | 800 |
| 4 | 400 |

   Compute the economic incomes of each year and the investment's NPV using the economic incomes.

3. (continue 1) Instead of an investment of $4,000, assume the book value is $9,000 and the terminal value at time 4 is $1,756.92.

   a. Compute the NPV using the cash flows.
   b. Compute the economic incomes of each year.
   c. Compute the NPV using economic incomes and other relevant information.

4. Assume an asset with a book value of $4,000 has the following projected income statements. There are zero taxes. The cost of equity is 0.10. The expected residual value at time 3 is $1,331.

|  | 1 | 2 | 3 |
|---|---|---|---|
| Revenue (Cash) | $1,600 | $1,400 | $1,200 |
| Depreciation | 1,000 | 1,000 | 1,000 |
| Income | $ 600 | $ 400 | $ 200 |

   a. Compute the PV using the cash flows.
   b. Compute the economic incomes of each year.
   c. Compute the PV using economic incomes.

5. (continue 4) Assume the initial book value is $8,000. All other facts are the same.

    a. Compute the PV using the cash flows.

    b. Compute the PV using economic incomes.

6. Assume a firm with a book value of $8,000 has the following cash flows:

| Time | Cash Flows |
|:---:|:---:|
| 1 | $1,200 |
| 2 | 1,440 |
| 3 | 1,728 |

The investment has a 0.20 internal rate of return. There are zero taxes and the firm uses straight-line depreciation of $1,000 per year. At the end of year 3, the value of the firm is expected to be $11,979.

    The CFO thinks 0.10 is the correct risk-adjusted discount rate for the investment.

    a. Compute economic income of each year.

| Year | Cash Flow | Depreciation Expense | Capital Cost (Interest) | Economic Income |
|:---:|:---:|:---:|:---:|:---:|
| 1 | $1,200 | $1,000 | | |
| 2 | 1,440 | 1,000 | | |
| 3 | 1,728 | 1,000 | | |

    b. Compute the firm's present value using 0.10 and the firm's cash flows.

    c. Compute the firm's present value using 0.10 and the economic incomes and any other relevant information.

    d. Are your answers to parts (b) and (c) likely to be correct? Why?

7. Assume a $3,000 investment has the following cash flows:

| Time | Cash Flows |
|:---:|:---:|
| 1 | $1,200 |
| 2 | 1,440 |
| 3 | 1,728 |

The investment has a 0.20 internal rate of return. There are zero taxes and the firm uses straight-line depreciation.

    The CFO thinks 0.10 is the correct risk-adjusted discount rate for the investment.

a. Compute economic income of each year.

| Year | Cash Flow | Depreciation Expense | Capital Cost (Interest) | Economic Income |
|------|-----------|----------------------|-------------------------|-----------------|
| 1 | $1,200 | $1,000 | | |
| 2 | 1,440 | 1,000 | | |
| 3 | 1,728 | 1,000 | | |

b. Compute the investment's net present value using 0.10 and the cash flows.
c. Compute the investment's net present value using 0.10 and the economic incomes.

*Chapter 7*

# Depreciation Expense

The matching of costs and revenues in determining income requires a system for assigning the cost of assets with terminable lives to specific time periods. Buildings and equipment are *depreciated*, natural resources are *depleted*, and patents and leaseholds are *amortized* over their useful lives. The credits for depreciation, depletion, and amortization are usually made to contra asset accounts, reducing the net book value of the related assets.

**Depreciation accounting** may be defined as a systematic procedure for allocating the cost of a long-lived asset over its useful life. The depreciation expense is the cost of using an asset, and it is assigned as either a cost of production or an expense of earning the revenues of the period.

As an alternative, we could define depreciation as the decrease in the economic value of a long-lived asset. In practice, however, depreciation has little relationship with the measurement of the change in economic value. The depreciation cost is computed for the period based on the original cost of the asset, and the decrease in the economic value of an asset is not considered in the depreciation calculations made by the accountant.

An essential feature of the accounting measurement of income is that a deduction from revenue is made for the expense of using the long-lived assets. A more precise measurement of income could be made if we waited until the long-lived assets were retired (we could then determine more exactly the total expense of their utilization). Because of the need for periodic reports of a company's progress, however, estimates must be made of the expense of using long-lived assets during relatively short periods of time — hence, the necessity for estimating the depreciation expense.

The initial cost of an asset, minus the portion of this cost that has been previously charged to depreciation, is called the **book value** of the asset. It should be remembered that depreciation accounting in practice is a procedure for cost allocation and not a process of valuation. The book value of an asset is not necessarily a reasonable estimate of its economic value. It cannot be used as the basis for decisions without adjustment into a value measure.

## Elements of Depreciation Computation

The determination of the depreciation expense of a period depends on three basic elements. These are:

1. The depreciation base: the cost less residual value of the long-lived asset;
2. The useful life of the asset; and
3. The systematic procedure chosen for allocating the cost over the asset's life.

### *Depreciation Base*

The cost to be allocated over the period of use is known as the **depreciation base**. This consists of the initial purchase cost of the asset minus any salvage value expected at the time of retirement plus the anticipated costs of removing the asset when it is retired (we will assume the removal is not discretionary).

The cost of using an asset during its life is reduced by any salvage value recoverable at the end of the period and is increased by costs of removal. These elements of the depreciation base are often extremely difficult to measure. When it is anticipated that a substantial residual value will be recovered, an estimate of this value should be included in the determination of the depreciation base.

### *Example*

Establish the bases for the computation of depreciation, given the following facts:

a. A building is purchased for an immediate payment of $10,000. The forecasted salvage is $500, and the forecasted removal cost is $200.

**Answer to (a)**

| | | |
|---|---:|---:|
| Cost of Building | | $10,000 |
| Salvage | $500 | |
| Removal Cost | 200 | |
| Net Salvage | | 300 |
| Base for Depreciation Computation | | $ 9,700 |

b. Equipment is purchased for $9,000. The forecasted salvage is $400, and the forecasted removal cost is $600.

**Answer to (b)**

| | | |
|---|---:|---:|
| Cost of Equipment | | $9,000 |
| Removal Cost | $600 | |
| Salvage | 400 | |
| Net Removal Cost | | 200 |
| Base for Depreciation Computation | | $9,200 |

In example (b), the depreciation base is greater than the cost of the asset. This is not allowed for tax purposes. It is reasonable that the logic of the situation leads to a depreciable base of $9,200, inasmuch as this will spread all the costs, including the removal costs, over the periods in which the revenues are earned. It is equally reasonable for the Internal Revenue Service to suggest that the depreciable base cannot exceed the cost of the asset.

## Useful Life

The *useful life* of a fixed asset is a function not only of the physical wear and exhaustion to which the asset is subjected, but also of technological change and innovation. Thus, a particular machine might be expected to last for ten years on the basis of physical endurance alone, but the development of new and better machines might reduce our expectation of its economic usefulness to four years.

Both obsolescence and physical endurance must be considered in estimating useful life. In general, the useful life to be used for depreciation purposes will be the shorter of the lives estimated on the two bases. An asset that is physically exhausted can be expected to be replaced, even though it is not yet obsolete. On the other hand, an asset that is obsolete should also be replaced even though it is not physically worn out.

## Procedures for Computing Depreciation

The objective of depreciation accounting is to assign to expense systematically the cost of a long-lived asset over the asset's useful life. There are, however, many procedures for accomplishing this task. Although there are numerous depreciation procedures used in practice, our discussion will be limited to procedures that are most widely used.

## *Straight-Line Depreciation*

When using the **straight-line procedure** for computing depreciation, the annual depreciation charge is obtained by dividing the depreciation base by the number of years of useful life forecasted.

## Example:

A machine is purchased for $10,000. The forecasted salvage is $456, and the forecasted removal cost is $200. The expected useful life of the machine is four years. Compute the annual depreciation charge using the straight-line procedure. (These figures will also be used for other methods discussed in this chapter.)

$$\text{Annual Depreciation} = \frac{(\text{Initial Cost} - \text{Salvage} + \text{Removal Cost})}{\text{Useful Life}}$$

$$= \frac{\$10,000 - \$456 + \$200}{4} = \frac{\$9,744}{4} = \$2,436.$$

$$(7.1)$$

Using the straight-line procedure for the four-year period produces the following results:

| Year | Book Value Beginning of Year | Depreciation Charge | Total Accumulated Depreciation | Book Value End of Year |
|------|------|------|------|------|
| 1 | $10,000 | $2,436 | $2,436 | $7,564 |
| 2 | 7,564 | 2,436 | 4,872 | 5,128 |
| 3 | 5,128 | 2,436 | 7,308 | 2,692 |
| 4 | 2,692 | 2,436 | 9,744 | 256 |

Note that the depreciation charge is the same every year, and the book value (initial cost minus accumulated depreciation) at the end of year 4 is equal to the anticipated salvage less removal cost.

The main advantages of the straight-line procedure are its simplicity and the fact that revenues of successive years are charged with equal amounts of depreciation. The main disadvantage is that, given the assumptions of constant revenue and constant maintenance costs, the return on investment of the asset (income divided by the investment) will increase as the asset becomes older and the net book value decreases.

The basic simplicity of the straight-line procedure has caused it to be the most widely used depreciation procedure for accounting purposes.

## Decreasing Charge (Accelerated Depreciation) Methods

The **decreasing charge** or **accelerated methods** of computing depreciation have become popular because the tax law allows their use. A firm will generally benefit by taking as much depreciation for tax purposes as possible in the early years of the asset's life. The method of accounting for tax purposes has a tendency also to influence the financial accounting, although there is no requirement that the same depreciation procedures must be used for both purposes.

By definition, with a decreasing charge method of accruing depreciation, the depreciation in the beginning years is greater than the depreciation in the later years. Over the life span of an asset, the total depreciation charges should be approximately equal regardless of the procedure used.

When we consider the computation of depreciation for purposes of determining taxable income, the timing of the depreciation charges becomes important from the point of view of conserving cash. If we assume the present tax rates will continue or decline in the future, a firm will want to deduct depreciation as early as possible to reduce its current tax payments. Thus, the accelerated methods of depreciation have become very popular for tax purposes.

## Declining Balance Procedure

The **declining balance procedure** involves the application of a constant depreciation rate to the decreasing book value of the asset. With the straight-line procedure, a constant rate was applied to a constant depreciation base. With the declining balance method, the use of book value instead of the constant base results in diminishing charges over the life span of the asset.

Conventionally, salvage value and removal costs are both ignored under the declining balance procedure. It is impossible to reduce the book value to zero by continually applying a constant rate to the book value. The residual value remaining after the application of this procedure throughout an asset's life might be considered to be an approximation of salvage. Although the two figures are not likely to be the same, they might be close enough for practical purposes.

With the declining balance procedure any depreciation rate could conceivably be used, but the rate is generally expressed as a function of the straight-line rate. If a rate equal to twice the straight-line rate is used, the method is called the **double declining balance method** of depreciation.

## Example:

Assuming the same figures as those used to illustrate the straight-line procedure, compute depreciation on a declining balance basis using a rate equal to twice the straight-line rate. The straight-line depreciation rate was 25 percent, and twice this rate is 50 percent. The rate is to be applied to the book value at the beginning of each year. Depreciation for each of the four years will be as follows:

| Year | Book Value Beginning of Year | Rate (%) | Depreciation Charge | Total Accumulated Depreciation | Book Value End of Year |
|------|------|------|------|------|------|
| 1 | $10,000 | 50 | $5,000 | $5,000 | $5,000 |
| 2 | 5,000 | 50 | 2,500 | 7,500 | 2,500 |
| 3 | 2,500 | 50 | 1,250 | 8,750 | 1,250 |
| 4 | 1,250 | 50 | 625 | 9,375 | 625 |

Note that the book value remaining at the end of year 4 is $625, which is somewhat higher than the expected net salvage value. The total depreciation charges for the four-year period were $9,375, which is less than the amount accrued by using the straight-line procedure ($9,744).

The Internal Revenue Code allows a firm to switch from declining balance to straight-line depreciation during the life of an asset. In this case, the straight-line depreciation is obtained by dividing the remaining amount to be depreciated by the remaining life. The total amount of depreciation cannot exceed the cost less the expected salvage. In the examples just cited, at the end of the third year the company could switch to the straight-line procedure and charge $994 to depreciation in the fourth year (book value of $1,250 less the $256 salvage equals $994). Because a firm desires to charge as much to expense for tax purposes as it is legally allowed to charge, the switch to the straight-line method may be desirable from an economic standpoint (that is, it may delay the payment of income taxes until subsequent periods). The present tax code allows the ignoring of salvage value if the expected salvage is less than 10 percent of cost.

## Sum-of-the-Years' Digits Procedure

The **sum-of-the-years' digits procedure** is a device for obtaining a pattern of depreciation that starts out high and decreases over the years.

Essentially, this procedure uses a constant depreciation base — the same as the straight-line base — but applies a constantly reducing rate to it to obtain a decreasing charge. The rate is determined by a fraction having as its denominator the sum of the digits from one through the useful life, in years. The numerators are the individual year numbers in descending order each year (equivalently, the number of years of life remaining at the beginning of the year).

## Example:

We will use the information from the previous example, where the useful life was four years. The denominator of each year's rate will be the sum of the digits from 1 through 4:

$$
\begin{array}{r}
1 \\
2 \\
3 \\
\underline{4} \\
\text{Sum of digits} = \quad 10
\end{array}
$$

The numerators for the depreciation rate will be the numbers in descending order: 4, 3, 2, 1. Thus, the rate for the first year will be 4/10, the second year 3/10, and so forth. Using the depreciation base of $9,744 (initial cost minus salvage plus removal cost), the following depreciation charges are obtained:

| Year | Book Value Beginning of Year | Depreciation Base | Rate | Depreciation Charge | Total Accumulated Depreciation | Book Value End of Year |
|------|------|------|------|------|------|------|
| 1 | $10,000.00 | $9,744 | 4/10 | $3,897.60 | $3,897.60 | $6,102.40 |
| 2 | 6,102.40 | 9,744 | 3/10 | 2,923.20 | 6,820.80 | 3,179.20 |
| 3 | 3,179.20 | 9,744 | 2/10 | 1,948.80 | 8,769.60 | 1,230.40 |
| 4 | 1,230.40 | 9,744 | 1/10 | 974.40 | 9,744.00 | 256.00 |

Over the four-year life, the total depreciation charges and the ending book value balance are identical with the straight-line procedure. It is the pattern of charges over the years that distinguishes the two methods. The sum-of-the-years' digits method results in substantially higher charges in the early years, which are offset by lower charges in later years.

The use of one of the decreasing charge procedures may be justified logically for accounting and managerial purposes if the productive output of the asset being analyzed is expected to diminish rapidly with age. If the services provided by a machine will be significantly greater in the first year of life than in the later years, it is reasonable to charge more of the depreciation cost to the earlier years. Also, as machines grow older they may require more maintenance, so the use of decreasing charge methods might result in total costs (including maintenance) that are about equal in each period.

## Accelerated Cost Recovery System (ACRS)

In 1981 a tax act was passed that introduced the **Accelerated Cost Recovery System (ACRS)**. The details of the act were changed by the 1982, 1984, and 1986 tax acts. While ACRS survived these reforms, it is likely to be modified in the future.

ACRS changed and increased the alternatives available to corporations. It tends to be a more generous method of writing off an asset than the previously approved accelerated depreciation methods. New assets were originally placed into five classes:

| **Class** | |
| --- | --- |
| 3-year class: | Tangible property with a life of no more than four years (includes tools, research and development equipment, light trucks and autos). |
| 5-year class: | Practically all machinery and equipment, as well as public utility property with lives between 4.5 and 18 years. |
| 10-year class: | Selected equipment and public utility property with lives between 18.5 and 25 years. |
| 15-year class: | Public utility property with lives greater than 25 years. |
| Real estate: | 18 years using 200 percent declining balance (for low-income housing) or 175 percent declining balance with a switch to straight-line (for other real estate). |

The 1986 act added other classes. Corporations must use a classification scheme for the determination of the asset's depreciation expense, unless straight-line depreciation is used for all assets acquired in the year for the given class. Real estate exceptions are also possible.

## Depreciation and Activity

Up to this point, procedures have been considered by which costs are allocated as a function of time. There are some types of fixed assets whose lives are more a function of activity (use) than of time. An example of a fixed asset of this type is an airplane engine. The life of the engine may well be a function of flight hours rather than age. The rate of obsolescence as well as the physical deterioration tends to determine whether the depreciation accrual should be based on activity or time.

## Example

a. An airplane engine that cost $5,000 has a life of 10,000 hours of flying time. What is the first year's depreciation, if the plane is flown a total of 2,000 hours?

Answer:

The rate of depreciation is $0.50 per hour of flying time. The depreciation expense for 2,000 hours would be $1,000.

b. If the engine were flown only 500 hours, and if the expected useful life were only five years (because of technological change), what would be the depreciation charge for the year?

Answer:

On an activity basis the depreciation would be

$$\$0.50 \times 500 = \$250,$$

but the useful life of the asset is only five years; thus, the minimum depreciation on a straight-line basis would be

$$\frac{\$5,000}{5} = \$1,000.$$

The depreciation cost for the year should be $1,000. If there is reason to suspect the usage of the engine in the next four years to be more than 2,000 hours per year, there may be justification for considering the depreciation of the first year to be $250 (or $0.50 per hour).

## Units of Production Procedure

The **units of production procedure** also assumes that depreciation is a function of use or activity. The life of the asset is measured in terms of its expected units of output or the expected number of service or machine hours available.

## Example

Assume that the machine purchased for $10,000 that has a forecasted salvage value of $456 and a forecasted removal cost of $200 is expected to have a productive life of 4,060 units. The depreciation rate per unit is calculated as follows:

$$\text{Depreciation Rate per Unit} = \frac{(\text{Initial Cost} - \text{Salvage} + \text{Removal Cost})}{\text{Expected Total Units}}$$

$$= \frac{\$10,000 - \$456 + \$200}{4,060} = \$2.40. \qquad (7.2)$$

If 985 units are produced in the first year, 1,060 units are produced in the second year, 1,115 units are produced in the third year, and 900 units are produced in the fourth year, depreciation for each of the four years will be as follows using the units of production procedure:

| Year | Units | Rate | Depreciation Charge | Total Accumulated Depreciation | Book Value at End |
|------|-------|------|---------------------|-------------------------------|-------------------|
| 1 | 985 | $2.40 | $2,364 | $2,364 | $7,636 |
| 2 | 1,060 | 2.40 | 2,544 | 4,908 | 5,092 |
| 3 | 1,115 | 2.40 | 2,676 | 7,584 | 2,416 |
| 4 | 900 | 2.40 | 2,160 | 9,744 | 256 |

## Accounting Entries

The accounts involved in recognizing depreciation are frequently misunderstood. In order to understand the entries that are conventionally made, it is useful to review their purpose. The accountant is attempting to allocate the cost of an asset over its useful life and to measure the cost of using the asset in each accounting period. The basic journal entry to record depreciation increases a cost or expense account (by debiting it) and decreases an asset account (or a contra account by crediting it).

## *Example*

A building is purchased on January 1 for $10,000. It has an expected useful life of ten years. Salvage value is expected to equal removal cost. Assume that depreciation is calculated by the straight-line procedure.

| | | | |
|---|---|---|---|
| Jan. 1 | Building.............................. | 10,000 | |
| | Cash............................. | | 10,000 |
| | To record the purchase of the building. | | |
| Dec. 31 | Depreciation Expense.................. | 1,000 | |
| | Building......................... | | 1,000 |
| | To record the depreciation cost for the year and the decrease in the Building account. | | |

The entries given represent a sound accounting treatment of depreciation, but note that the Building account will have a balance of $9,000 after the $1,000 has been credited to the Building account. The original cost of the fixed asset is no longer equal to the balance of the Building account. This procedure makes it more difficult to obtain a bit of relevant information. A reader of financial reports may want to know how much was paid for the assets and to what extent they have been depreciated. This information cannot be readily obtained if the former procedure is followed. In practice, the accountant does not credit the Building account directly, as was done in the example, but rather credits a contra account to the Building account (an account that is a subtraction from the Building account). This contra account has various titles. Among the most widely used are Allowance for Depreciation and Accumulated Depreciation. The entry made on December 31 to accrue the depreciation cost and the decrease in the Building account would then be

Depreciation Expense............................ 1,000
    Building, Accumulated Depreciation ............     1,000

This is the generally accepted entry for recognizing depreciation. The credit is not made directly to the fixed asset account, but to a contra asset account. The balance in this contra account, no matter what its title, is *a subtraction from the fixed asset account*.

## Depreciation and Cash Flow

The accounting depreciation expense entry does not affect the cash flow of a business organization, but the depreciation expense for taxes does affect cash flow. Assume a situation in which the following facts apply — cash sales total $100, accounting and tax depreciation expense is $20, and the tax rate is 0.40.

The first step is to compute the taxable income.

| | |
|---|---|
| Cash Sales | $100 |
| Depreciation Expense | 20 |
| Taxable Income | $ 80 |

Given taxable income of $80 and a tax rate of 0.40, the income tax provision is $0.40($80) = $32$. The income statement for the period is

| | | |
|---|---|---|
| Cash Sales | | $100 |
| Depreciation Expense | $20 | |
| Tax Expense | 32 | 52 |
| Income | | $ 48 |

The enterprise's income is $48. However, its cash flow from operations is $68.

| | |
|---|---|
| Cash Sales | $100 |
| Tax Expense | 32 |
| Cash Flow from Operations | $ 68 |

The enterprise's cash flow from operations can also be obtained by adding the depreciation expense back to income:

$$\text{Income} + \text{Depreciation Expense} = \$48 + \$20 = \$68. \qquad (7.3)$$

By deducting depreciation expense of $20 from the cash sales, the enterprise saved $8 of taxes. In general, the tax savings from depreciation expense is equal to the tax rate times the depreciation expense allowed for taxes:

$$\text{Tax Rate} \times \text{Depreciation Expense} = 0.40 \times \$20 = \$8. \qquad (7.4)$$

Equivalently, we can state that the cash flow effect of deducting depreciation expense of $20 is to increase the after-tax cash flows by $0.40(\$20) = \$8$. Note that we multiply the tax depreciation by the tax rate to obtain the cash flow increase. Each $1 of depreciation expense reduces taxable income by $1 and saves $0.40 of taxes.

## Interpretation of Gain or Loss

The gain or loss recognized at the time of retirement of a long-lived asset will depend on three factors: the book value at time of retirement, the proceeds of salvage or sale, and the costs of removal. These factors can rarely be known with certainty at the time of acquiring an asset, so there will invariably be gains or losses on retirement. In current practice, the gain or loss on retirement is regarded as affecting current income.

The amounts of the retirement gains or losses are affected by the choice of the method of depreciation. As shown in the preceding section, there are several acceptable procedures for determining the depreciation charges. The use of different procedures will result in differing book values at retirement and thus affect the gain or loss recognized.

## *Example*

To illustrate this point, consider a machine that cost $10,000 and is being depreciated on the basis of a four-year useful life with no removal cost or salvage value expected. At the end of the third year of use, the machine is retired with net salvage value of $1,000. Compute the amount of gain or loss that would be recognized assuming that the asset is being depreciated by use of straight-line depreciation.

## *Solution*

Using straight-line depreciation, the depreciation deduction is $2,500 per year. The accumulated depreciation at the end of year 3 would be $7,500. Book value at the end of year 3 would be

| | |
|---|---|
| Asset Cost | $10,000 |
| *Less:* Accumulated Depreciation | 7,500 |
| Book Value | $ 2,500 |
| **Calculation of Loss:** | |
| Book Value | $ 2,500 |
| Net Salvage | 1,000 |
| Loss on Retirement | $ 1,500 |

## Recording of Natural Resources

Consider the drilling of an oil well and the accounting for events that take place. Is the cost of the oil that is found the cost of the successful wells or the cost of drilling *all* the wells, dry and successful? If the latter, over what time frame and covering what geographical area? Is cost relevant at all, or would the users of financial statements rather be informed of the value of the resources that the company owns?

These questions have been pondered by accountants for many years. The "successful efforts" method of reporting for oil exploration activities has become accepted practice by many accountants. This means that the cost of the oil owned by an oil company will reflect the cost of finding the oil. The recorded cost includes the cost of nearby dry wells, but not the cost of dry wells that are totally unconnected with the areas where the oil was found.

## Depletion of Natural Resources

The previous discussion dealt with the problems of allocating the cost of assets whose lives extend over several accounting periods. The lives of these assets were determined by either physical deterioration or obsolescence, and the costs of using the assets were charged either to production cost or immediately to expense.

In certain extractive industries — coal mining, petroleum production, ore refining, and so forth — an analogous problem exists. Ordinarily a single sum is paid to acquire a quantity of natural resources, but the process of extracting these resources will extend over many accounting periods. The problem of allocating the cost of such items to production is analogous to the problem of depreciation, except that in this case the asset becomes physically embodied in the product being manufactured. The procedure for allocating such costs is called **depletion accounting**.

The useful life of a natural resource depends on the physical quantity of the resource and the rate of usage. Every ton of coal or iron ore extracted from a mine results in one less ton remaining in the mine. Thus, instead of years or machine hours, depletion accounting assigns costs based on physical quantities of product that are expected to be extracted.

The precise quantity of a resource still in the ground may be very difficult to evaluate. However, geologists and other knowledgeable persons may be called upon to take samples and estimate the quantities of minerals or other resources existing in a particular operation. Once such an estimate is available, the depletion calculations are made in a fashion similar to depreciation. Although procedures involving decreasing charges could be used, the depletion procedures are generally based on a straight-line assumption about the physical quantities. The depletion cost of a year will depend upon the quantities extracted in that period. Part of the cost will be assigned to inventory and part to the expense of the period.

The accounting entries for depletion are similar to those used in accounting for depreciable assets, although usually the long-lived asset account is credited directly rather than reduced through use of a contra asset account.

## Intangible Assets

Intangible assets are items that the firm purchased but that lack physical substance. Their value to the firm is often dependent on other business factors and is subject to considerable uncertainty. In many instances, such assets have value only in the context of a particular business and therefore cannot be transferred to another organization. Because of the uncertainty surrounding the value of these items, they are frequently recognized at only a nominal amount in the financial statements or expensed at time of acquisition. Yet intangibles *could* represent a significant amount of the economic resources of a company. Assets classified as intangible by accountants include patents, trademarks, copyrights, goodwill, and organization costs.

Intangible resources may be purchased from others or developed internally by a company. Although purchased intangibles are generally recorded as assets, self-developed intangibles are not. Thus, a patent purchased from another company would be shown at its cost as an asset on the balance sheet, whereas a similar patent developed through the company's own research and development efforts would not.

Because purchased intangibles are included as assets while nonpurchased intangibles usually are not, a double standard for asset recognition exists, making comparisons among firms difficult. Suppose, for example, that Company A has developed a patent as a result of its own research efforts. The patent would not be shown as an asset in the accounting statements of Company A. However, if Company A were to sell the patent to Company B for $100,000 cash, Company B would recognize the patent initially at its cost to that company, $100,000. Even though the patent remains unchanged, its transfer from the original owner to a new owner for an objectively determinable price gives rise to the recognition of an asset that had not been recognized before by the originating firm.

## *Research and Development Costs*

The costs of research and development present a difficult problem for the accountant. In the past, these costs were frequently capitalized and regarded as an intangible asset. But because there is an uncertain relationship between research spending and subsequent benefits, the Financial Accounting Standards Board (FASB) in Financial Accounting Standard 2 decided that all research and development costs should be expensed. Thus, accountants must now charge all research costs to current expenses. It should be realized, however, that research costs are usually incurred with the expectation of benefiting future periods rather than the present period. Theoretically, such costs are assets, even if they are expensed for purposes of conforming to the reporting requirements of the FASB.

The cost deferral concept emphasizes income determination and is directly related to the accepted definition of accounting income. The determination of accounting income is based on the process of matching costs with the revenues to which they relate. When costs that are expected to benefit revenues of future periods are incurred, they may be deferred until the time when they may be "matched" with the related revenues to determine income. The asset classification of the balance sheet may be viewed following this theory as including costs awaiting final disposition through periodic charges against revenues.

Two corporations may be identical in all respects, and then one of the two may declare and pay a $10,000,000 dividend to its stockholders while the other spends $10,000,000 on research. The balance sheets of these two corporations after these transactions would be exactly the same. In the year of the transactions, the second firm would report lower income, since the research expenditure is treated as an expense of the period. Actually, the second firm has accumulated knowledge as a result of its expenditure of $10,000,000, but this knowledge would not be recognized as an asset according to current generally accepted accounting practice.

## *Amortization of Intangibles*

The costs of intangibles that have been recognized as assets should be allocated to income over their estimated useful lives. This process is analogous to depreciation of tangible assets, but it is usually referred to as **amortization** when used with intangibles.

Determining the useful life of an intangible asset is extremely difficult. There is no physical wear and exhaustion to consider, only obsolescence or decline in economic value.

Many intangibles have a maximum life prescribed by law. A patent, for example, is granted for a period of 17 years and may not be renewed. Copyrights are issued for a period of 28 years with the possibility of renewal for another 28-year period at expiration, giving a total of 56 years. From an economic standpoint, however, it is rare that an intangible asset would maintain its full value during the entire period of its legal existence. For example, a patent may be made obsolete by a new development that supersedes it. A copyrighted work may not provide any revenues after the first few years of its existence. For these reasons, the useful life of an intangible asset should be regarded as the shorter of the legal or economic life.

Some intangibles with indeterminate lives, such as goodwill, were once regarded as having perpetual lives and thus were not amortized. In current practice, however, all newly acquired intangibles are regarded as having a *maximum* useful life of 40 years, and they must be amortized over that or a shorter period.

Once the amortization period has been established, the cost of an intangible asset may be amortized over this period by any reasonable systematic method, although the straight-line method tends to be used most often in current practice. Unlike the situation in depreciation of tangible assets, there is no salvage value or removal cost to consider. The main asset account is usually credited directly rather than crediting a contra account. The debit is to an Amortization Expense account.

## *Goodwill and Organization Costs*

**Goodwill** may be defined as the present value of future earnings in excess of what might normally be expected to be earned on the identifiable assets used in the enterprise. Thus, goodwill arises because of the expectation of exceptional earnings. There are many reasons why a company might have earnings that are higher than could normally be expected. Among these reasons are an established reputation, customer acceptance, a unique product or process leading to a monopolistic position, and astute management.

If goodwill arises because of the presence of exceptional earnings, does that mean that the accountant should record goodwill whenever earnings are expected in excess of normal? In practice, the accountant records goodwill only when it is purchased. This is usually interpreted to mean the purchase of one business entity by another business entity. Thus, if Firm A purchases Firm B for $1,000,000, and the value of the identifiable assets less liabilities of Firm B is only $750,000, then Firm A has paid $250,000 for something of an intangible nature. The accountant calls this something *goodwill*.

Should goodwill be recorded when purchased, and should it then be amortized? Purchased goodwill reflects the expectation of future earnings, where the expectation is verified by a willingness of the purchaser to pay for these future earnings. The goodwill is amortized if the recent events indicate that the goodwill has lost value.

The maintenance of goodwill usually depends on the continuance of expenditures for items such as advertising and public relations. The cessation of such spending could cause the life of goodwill to become terminable. Goodwill is also often closely attached to a company and might not be easily transferred to another firm. Any conditions that might limit the life of a company could also limit the life of its goodwill.

The problem of valuing an entire industrial organization is usually too complex to permit this valuation to be the basis of recording income and financial position. Goodwill is not recorded unless it is explicitly purchased.

When the accountant records as assets those items that have no sale value (in the terminology of the economist, their opportunity cost is zero), then the balance sheet does not present the liquidation value of the business entity. The statement does present a picture of the financial position assuming the firm continues as a going concern.

## Deferred Benefits

Conventional depreciation accounting combined with the uses of ROI is at its worst when the benefits produced by the asset are expected to increase through time or when the benefits are constant. The early years are greatly penalized by conventional accounting, with the managers having an incentive to avoid such investments so that their performance evaluations do not suffer.

For example, assume an investment costing $3,000 is expected to have the following benefit stream:

| Period | Cash Flow |
|--------|-----------|
| 1      | $1,100    |
| 2      | 1,210     |
| 3      | 1,331     |

The firm's cost of money is 0.10 and is equal to the investment's discounted cash flow internal rate of return. The results using conventional accounting and straight-line depreciation will be (assuming the actual benefits are equal to the expected):

| Period | Revenues | Depreciation | Income | Book Value | ROI   |
|--------|----------|--------------|--------|------------|-------|
| 1      | $1,100   | $1,000       | $100   | $3,000     | 0.03  |
| 2      | 1,210    | 1,000        | 210    | 2,000      | 0.105 |
| 3      | 1,331    | 1,000        | 331    | 1,000      | 0.331 |

The first year's operations are not acceptable given the 0.10 cost of money.

Defining depreciation expense to be the decrease in value of the asset, the results would be:

| Period | Cash Flow | Depreciation | Income | Book Value | ROI  |
|--------|-----------|--------------|--------|------------|------|
| 1      | $1,100    | $ 800        | $300   | $3,000     | 0.10 |
| 2      | 1,210     | 990          | 220    | 2,200      | 0.10 |
| 3      | 1,331     | 1,210        | 121    | 1,210      | 0.10 |

The depreciation calculations are:

$V_0 = \$3,000$ value at time 0  $d_1 = 3,000 - 2,200 = \$800$ depreciation of period 1

$V_1 = \$2,200$ value at time 1  $d_2 = 2,200 - 1,210 = \$990$ depreciation of period 2

$V_2 = \$1,210$ value at time 2  $d_3 = 1,210 - 0 = \$1,210$ depreciation of period 3.

The distortion caused by conventional depreciation accounting can be increased by assuming no (or very low) benefits until period 3. The operating results of the early years would appear to be even worse than in the example.

The second depreciation method illustrated can be called economic depreciation or present value depreciation. It is not generally accepted accounting practice.

## Cash Flow Return on Investment

Recognizing the inadequacies of conventional depreciation accounting, some managers have attempted to solve the problems by using cash flow return on investment. Since cash flows are used to evaluate the investment, why not use them to evaluate the investment's performance?

Define the cash flow return on investment to be:

$$\frac{\text{Cash flow}}{\text{Investment}}.$$

The computation seems to be appealing because depreciation is not computed, but unfortunately, the computation merely makes a bad analysis worse. Using the following example where the investment has a 0.10 internal rate of return, we obtain:

| Period | Cash Flow | Book Value | Cash Flow (ROI) |
|--------|-----------|------------|-----------------|
| 1 | $1,300 | $3,000 | 0.433 |
| 2 | 1,200 | 2,000 | 0.600 |
| 3 | 1,100 | 1,000 | 1.100 |

Some firms have actually tried to use the historical measures as required returns for additional investments. You should note that for an investment yielding 0.10 over its life, the cash flow ROIs for the three years are 0.43, 0.60, and 1.10. The measure greatly overstates the ROI the asset is actually earning.

Another difficulty of the measure is that it will tend to bias management in favor of capital-intensive methods of production, because capital cost is omitted from the numerator of the performance measure.

It is better to use the conventional ROI with income (after depreciation) in the numerator than to use the cash flow ROI, which is extremely difficult to interpret and has no theoretical foundation. The use of the measure illustrated above will get management into one or more interpretive difficulties.

## A Solution

One solution would be for the accounting profession to encourage a wide range of depreciation methods, if these methods are justified by the economic characteristics of the investment. Currently, too rapid write-off (R&D, training, plant and equipment) leads to (1) bad measures of performance and (2) non-optimal decisions.

## Summary

This chapter has been concerned with the initial recording and allocation of the costs of long-lived assets — depreciation, depletion, and amortization — over the assets' useful lives. There are many different methods for assigning the cost of a long-lived asset to each time period. The most commonly used accounting method is straight-line depreciation. It is easy to compute and well-defined. The selection of the depreciation procedure can greatly influence the reported income and financial position of a company. A distinction must be made between the accounting depreciation expense, which has no effect on a company's cash flow, and tax depreciation expense or cost recovery, which does affect cash flow.

The necessity of making assumptions in accounting practice is dramatized in the area of recording long-lived assets. The cost of these assets is sometimes difficult to measure and, even if measured in a reasonable manner, after several years the cost is likely to be a poor estimator of the value of the asset. Although part of the difficulties arise because of arbitrary accounting practices, the major problem is the attempt by the accountant to record events when the full impact of these events will not be known until some future time. For example, the value of research is uncertain until many years after the accountant's report is published. The same is true of the life of a tangible long-lived asset. Perfect accuracy relative to value should not be expected in accounting for long-lived assets.

## Review Problems

### Review Problem 7.1

The Hubbard Company owns a machine that was purchased on January 1, 2xx1, at a cost of $10,000. The machine has been depreciated on a straight-line basis with a useful life of six years and expected salvage value of $1,000. On January 1, 2xx5, the machine is traded in for a new machine with a list price of $20,000.

The company receives a trade-in allowance for the old machine of $1,200, which is estimated to be its fair market value at that time. The new machine has an expected useful life of ten years with no salvage value and will be depreciated by using the straight-line method.

Assuming the use of federal income tax procedures, prepare journal entries to record the exchange of machines on January 1, 2xx5. Prepare a journal entry to record depreciation of the new machine on December 31, 2xx5.

**Solution to Review Problem 7.1**

With federal income tax procedure, no gain or loss is recognized on the exchange. However, this affects the cost basis of the new machine.

The January 1, 2xx5 entry would be:

Machine ........................................ 21,300
Old Machine — Accumulated Depreciation ......... 7,500
    Old Machine ................................          10,000
    Cash ......................................          18,800
To record trade-in of machine for new machine.

Since the cost recognized is $21,300, the annual depreciation charges would be:

$$\frac{\$21,300}{10} = \$2,130.$$

The December 31, 2xx5 entry would be:

Depreciation Expense ............................... 2,130
    New Machine — Accumulated Depreciation .........          2,130

## Questions and Problems

1. In the course of obtaining a new machine for its factory, a company incurred the following costs. Which costs would properly be includable in the cost of the machine?

   a. The net invoice cost of the machine.

   b. A discount lost when the invoice for the machine was not paid on time.

   c. Cost of removing an old machine to make room for the new machine (the old machine had been retired a year ago and would have been removed in any event).

   d. Transportation costs of the new machine.

   e. Installation costs of the new machine.

   f. Costs of repairing the new machine: a workman dropped the machine during installation and extensive repairs were necessary before the machine could be used.

2. Depreciation accounting involves the use of estimates. At the time an asset is retired or sold, however, many of the factors affecting the annual cost of using the asset become known. For each of the following errors in estimation, indicate whether the accounting entries at the time of retirement would show a gain or loss:

   a. Estimated useful life shorter than actual.

   b. Estimated salvage value higher than actual.

   c. Estimated removal costs lower than actual.

    d. Estimated useful life longer than actual.

    e. Estimated salvage value lower than actual.

3. What is the "book value" of a depreciable asset? Is this a reasonable estimate of market value?

4. Financial analysts frequently add depreciation charges to reported income to obtain a figure that they refer to as *cash flow*. This figure is sometimes used as a substitute for reported income in evaluating securities. Is this a reasonable indicator of the flow of cash through a firm? Is it an improvement over reported income for measuring performance?

5. The president of the Federal Company was somewhat confused by accounting terminology. He recently read in a financial journal that companies were financing their capital expenditures by using depreciation allowances and retained earnings. An inspection of the most recent balance sheet revealed that depreciation allowances were $20,000,000 and retained earnings were $40,000,000. This information added to his confusion, for his treasurer had recently informed him of the desirability of postponing capital expenditures because of a lack of cash.

    Prepare a brief report that will clarify the terminology. Explain why financial analysts often speak of capital expenditures being financed from depreciation allowances. Are they correct?

6. Accountants usually insist on using objective verifiable evidence to support figures reported in the financial statements. What elements of subjectivity enter into the determination of depreciation for accounting reports?

7. The ABC Coal Company has two accounting problems:

    a. The company is about to develop a strip mining field. It is estimated that at the completion of the mining operation in ten years, it will cost the firm $10,000,000 to place the land back into an acceptable condition to conform with state legislation. How should the company treat the cost of replacing the land?

    b. The company has installed an electronic computer that has an estimated useful life of six years. It is estimated that it would cost $200,000 to remove the computer when it is to be replaced. How should the company treat the cost of removing the computer?

8. The Barnes Company purchased equipment costing $200,000 on January 1, 19x1. The equipment has an expected useful life of five years and a forecast net salvage value at retirement of $20,000. Prepare a schedule of depreciation for the years 19x1–19x5, showing for each year (1) the book value of the equipment at the beginning of the year, (2) the depreciation charge for the

year, (3) the accumulated depreciation at the end of the year, and (4) the book value of the equipment at the end of the year. Prepare a separate schedule for each of the following methods:

a. Straight-line.
b. Declining balance at twice the straight-line rate.
c. Sum-of-the-years' digits.

9. The Carlson Coal Company purchased mining property for $10,600,000 in cash. It was estimated that the property contained 400,000 tons of recoverable coal and that the land would have a value of $400,000 after the coal had been extracted. During the first year of operations, 65,000 tons of coal were recovered, of which 50,000 tons were sold. Prepare journal entries to record the purchase of the property and to recognize the cost of coal extracted and sold during the year.

10. The Collier Coal Company purchased mining property for $6,400,000 in cash. It was estimated that the property contained 300,000 tons of recoverable coal and that the land would have a value of $400,000 after the coal had been extracted. During the first year of operations, 35,000 tons of coal were recovered, of which 25,000 tons were sold. Prepare entries to record the purchase of the property and to recognize the cost of coal extracted and sold during the year.

11. The Haber Company purchased land in Arizona on which uranium had been discovered. The cost of the land was $1,000,000. Additional costs necessary to prepare the land for mining operations were $200,000. It is estimated that 5,000,000 tons of ore containing uranium will be extracted before the mine is fully mined out. During the first period of mining operations, 500,000 tons of uranium-bearing ore were dug and shipped to the refinery. The cost of getting the ore out of the ground and into railroad cars was $930,000.

    Record the transactions.

12. The Hayes Corporation acquired at a cost of $25,000,000 the assets and name of another corporation which it intends to operate as a division. The balance sheet of the acquired corporation showed the following assets:

| | |
|---|---|
| Cash and Other Liquid Assets | $ 3,000,000 |
| Inventories | 5,000,000 |
| Plant and Equipment | 16,000,000 |
| Land | 1,000,000 |

An appraisal made by an independent appraisal company listed the current values of the assets as follows:

| | |
|---|---:|
| Cash and Other Liquid Assets | $ 3,500,000 |
| Inventories | 4,700,000 |
| Plant and Equipment | 12,000,000 |
| Land | 2,500,000 |

a. At what values should the newly acquired assets be recorded?
b. If the appraisal value of the plant and equipment had been $20,000,000 instead of $12,000,000, at what values would you record the assets?

13. Equipment was purchased for $60,000 with an expected useful life of four years. The company uses the sum-of-the-years' digits method of depreciation and expects salvage value to equal the removal cost at the end of the fourth year. At the end of the third year, new equipment is purchased to replace the present equipment. The old equipment is sold for $15,000, and removal costs are $3,000.

Prepare the entries to record the retirement of the old equipment.

14. The Harkness Company traded in a car for a new model. The old car cost $3,500 and was 90 percent depreciated. The list price of the new car was $4,500, but the Keen Car Agency offered to allow $1,200 on the old car. The Harkness Company had tried to sell the old car, and the best cash price they had been offered was $475. The Keen Car Agency offered to pay $475 cash for the old car if the Harkness Company did not want to trade it in.

a. Make the journal entries to record the trade-in from the point of view of the Harkness Company.
b. Make the journal entries to record the trade-in from the point of view of the Keen Car Agency.

15. The Hardy Company ceased operations in its Illinois plant on July 1. On August 1, it was decided to dismantle the equipment and sell the plant. The cost of dismantling the equipment was $7,000. The equipment was sold as scrap, and second-hand equipment was sold for $20,000. The plant was sold for $120,000, and there were expenses of $6,000 connected with the sale. Depreciation was last accrued on the plant and equipment on the previous December 31. The January 1 balances in the plant and equipment accounts of the Illinois plant

were as follows:

| | |
|---|---|
| Plant | $2,000,000 |
| Plant, Accumulated Depreciation | 1,550,000 |
| Equipment | 400,000 |
| Equipment, Accumulated Depreciation | 320,000 |

The building depreciation was $4,000 per month, and the equipment depreciation was $3,000 per month.

Prepare journal entries to record the depreciation for the period and also the retirement of the plant and equipment of the Illinois plant.

16. Assume an investment of $4,000 has the following projected income statements. There are zero taxes. The cost of equity is 0.10.

| | 1 | 2 | 3 | 4 |
|---|---|---|---|---|
| Revenue | $1,800 | $1,600 | $1,400 | $1,200 |
| Depreciation | 1,000 | 1,000 | 1,000 | 1,000 |
| Income | $ 800 | $ 600 | $ 400 | $ 200 |

a. Compute the NPV using the cash flows.

b. Compute the economic incomes of each year (subtract an interest cost on the capital used).

Compute the NPV using economic income.

Compute the investment's internal rate of return.

c. Now assume the depreciation schedule is:

| Year | Depreciation |
|---|---|
| 1 | $1,600 |
| 2 | 1,200 |
| 3 | 800 |
| 4 | 400 |

Compute the economic incomes of each year and the NPV using economic income.

d. What is the present value depreciation of each year if 0.10 is used as the discount rate and $4,830 is used as the depreciation base?

e. Using the answer to (d), compute the incomes and ROE of each year.

f. What is the present value depreciation of each year if 0.20 is used as the discount rate and $4,000 is used as the depreciation base?

g. Using the answer to (f), compute the income and ROE of each year.

h. (continue a) Instead of an investment of $4,000, assume the book value is $9,000 and the terminal value at time 4 is $1,756.92.

Compute the NPV using the cash flows.

Compute the economic incomes of each year.

Compute the NPV using economic incomes and other relevant information.

*Chapter 8*

# Long-Term Liabilities

A **conventional bond** is a promise to pay a fixed amount (the principal) at the end of a certain number of periods and another additional amount each period as interest. The amount to be paid at the end of the last period is also referred to as the **maturity amount** or **face value**. The amount of each equal periodic interest payment may be stated as a dollar amount. In the latter case, the stated percentage is referred to as the **contractual rate**. This type of conventional bond security is sometimes called a balloon payment debt.

In terms of compound interest structure, a bond may be viewed as a combination of two components: (1) the stream of interest payments, which may be regarded as an annuity; and (2) the amount, which is a lump sum to be received after a number of periods at the maturity of the bond. The present value of a balloon payment is the present values of the two components added together to obtain the present value of the bond.

## *Example*

Compute the present value of a bond whose face value is $1,000.00, due in four years, with annual interest payments of $120 each. Money is worth 12 percent annually.

Answer:
First, the present value of the maturity amount is determined. The present value of $1 due in four periods at 12 percent interest is 0.6355. Therefore, the present value of $1,000.000 is

$$\$1,000.000 \times 0.6355 = \$635.50.$$

The present value of the interest payments is equal to the present value of an annuity of $1 per period for four periods (at 12 percent, this is 3.037). Therefore, the present value of $120.00 per period is

$$\$120 \times 3.037 = \$364.$$

Adding the two present values, we obtain the present value of the bond:

| | |
|---|---|
| Present value of maturity amount | $ 636 |
| Present value of interest payments | 364 |
| Present value of bond | $1,000 |

Several factors in the example given should be observed. Note that the contractual rate (interest payments as a percentage of maturity amount) is equal to 12 percent. The *effective* or *market rate* of interest is also 12 percent. If the two rates are equal, the present value of the bond is identical with the maturity amount. The equality will always hold whenever the effective interest rate is equal to the contractual rate.

It is likely that the effective interest rate of a bond will not be exactly equal to the contractual rate. The market rate fluctuates from day to day, depending on various economic forces.

The price of the bond can be set at a level that will allow the purchaser to earn the effective rate on the investment. That is, the price of the bond will be equal to the present value, not to the maturity amount.

If the contractual rate is less than the market rate, the bond will sell in the market for less than its face value (i.e., it will sell at a **discount**). If the contractual rate is above the market rate, the bond will sell for more than its face value (i.e., it will sell at a **premium**). The exact price is determined by present value calculations.

## *Example*

Assume that the $1,000 bond with a life of four years paying $120 interest per year was issued at an effective rate of 10 percent. Determine the price at which it would be issued.

The present value of $1 for four periods at 10 percent is 0.6830. Therefore, the present value of the maturity amount of $1,000 is

$$\$1,000.000 \times 0.6830 = \$683.00.$$

The present value of $1 per period for four periods is 3.1699. Therefore, the present value of the stream of interest payments of $120 is

$$\$120 \times 3.1699 = \$380.39.$$

The price at which the bond would be priced is calculated as follows:

| | |
|---|---|
| Present value of maturity amount | $ 683.00 |
| Present value of interest payments | 380.39 |
| Present value of bond | $1,063.39 |

Because the contractual rate of 12 percent is higher than the effective rate of 10 percent, the bond will sell at a premium. The amount of the premium is the difference between the present value and the face value of the bond.

| | |
|---|---|
| Present value of bond | $1,063.39 |
| Face value of bond | 1,000.00 |
| Premium | $ 63.39 |

## Example

Assume that the 12-percent $1,000 bond described in the previous example was issued at an effective rate of 15 percent. Determine the price at which it would be issued.

The present value of $1 for four periods at 15 percent is 0.5718. Therefore, the present value of the maturity amount of $1,000 is

$$\$1,000.000 \times 0.5718 = \$571.80.$$

The present value of $1 per period for four periods at 15 percent is 2.8550. Therefore, the present value of the stream of four interest payments of $120 is

$$\$120 \times 2.8550 = \$342.60.$$

The price of the bond is:

| | |
|---|---|
| Present value of maturity amount | $571.80 |
| Present value of interest payments | 342.60 |
| Present value of bond | $914.40 |

Because the contractual rate of 12 percent is lower than the effective rate of 15 percent, the bond would sell at a discount. The amount of the discount is the difference between the face value and the present value of the bond.

| | |
|---|---|
| Face value of bond | $1,000.00 |
| Present value of bond | 914.40 |
| Discount | $ 85.60 |

In the calculations just given, the effective rate was consistently used to compute present values. The contractual rate is not used to discount for time, although it is used to determine the amount of interest payments. The bond considered in the calculations cited above is described as a "$1,000.00, 12-percent bond with four-year maturity." In such cases, it is important to remember that the contractual rate is useful only for determining the amount of the interest payments (e.g., $1,000.00 × 12 percent = $120.00). It is not used as a rate in the present value calculations. The rate used to compute the present values is the effective interest rate.

## The Semiannual Interest Complexity

Long-term bonds frequently will pay interest semiannually. This gives rise to confusion as to what annual return is earned or what the cost is to the issuing corporation.

The return from long-term bonds is usually expressed in nominal rates of one year, even though interest is paid semiannually. For example, a $1,000 par (face value) bond paying $45 interest every six months with a contractual interest rate of 0.09 would have an effective interest rate of

$$r = \left(1 + \frac{0.09}{2}\right)^2 - 1 = 0.092025$$

or just over 0.0920 if it is sold at face value.

Assume that you can earn 0.092025 on reinvested funds and that you are given the choice between a 0.09 $1,000 bond (interest paid semiannually) or a $1,000 bond paying 0.092025. With this latter bond, you will have $1,092.025 at time 1. With the 0.09 bond, you will again have $1,092.025:

$$
\begin{aligned}
\tfrac{1}{2}(\$90)(1.092025)^{1/2} &= \$ & 47.025 \\
\text{at time 1} &= & \underline{1,045.000} \\
\text{Present value} &= & \$1,092.025
\end{aligned}
$$

The bond with a 0.09 contractual interest rate actually earns more than 0.09 if the interest is received every six months.

Assume a third bond that pays interest annually at the rate of 0.09 so that at the end of the year the investor would have $1,090. This is inferior to the conventional 0.09 bond that pays interest every six months.

If a 0.09 30-year bond with semiannual interest payments is issued at par, it is conventional practice to describe the yield to maturity as being 0.09. With semiannual interest payments, it would be more accurate to say that the yield to maturity is 0.092025. Bond yield tables that are used to value bonds would indicate that the yield to maturity is 0.09. You have to remember that this contractual rate is a nominal rate and that the effective rate is 0.092025 per year or 0.045 compounded every six months.

With a 30-year bond, we could use 60 time periods and a 0.045 interest rate to compute the present value:

$$
\begin{aligned}
\$1,000(1.045)^{-60} &= \$1,000(0.07129) &= \$\ \ \ 71.29 \\
\$45B(60, 0.045) &= \$45(20.638022) &= \ \ \ \ 928.71 \\
&\text{Present value} &= \$1,000.00
\end{aligned}
$$

If we use 0.092025, we have to use 30 time periods and annual interest costs of $\$45(1.092025)^{1/2} + \$45.00 = \$92.025$.

$$
\begin{aligned}
\$1,000(1.092025)^{-30} &= \$1,000(0.07129) &= \$\ \ \ 71.29 \\
\$92.025B(30, 0.092025) &= \$92.025(10.091942) &= \ \ \ \ 928.71 \\
&\text{Present value} &= \$1,000.00
\end{aligned}
$$

Note that the market interest rate, the number of time periods, and the annual interest payments all have to be consistent measures that apply to the same unit of time.

## A Zero-Coupon Bond

Some bonds only pay interest at the maturity of the bond. These are called zero-coupon bonds or money multiplier notes. They are also called original issue discount (OID) notes.

The valuation of a zero-coupon bond is less complex than is that of a conventional bond. If the maturity amount of the bond is $1,000 due in 30 years and if the bond is to yield 0.10 annually, the present value of the bond is

$$ PV = \$1,000(1.10)^{-30} = \$57.31. $$

A $1,000 bond (zero coupon) maturing in 30 years and yielding 0.10 will only cost $57.31 at time 0. You can see why the name "money multiplier" is an apt description.

If the company goes bankrupt in year 29, the investor will not earn 0.10.

## *Example*

Assume a ten-year bond and the effective market interest rate is 0.14.

$$ \$1,000.00 \times 0.26974 = \$269.74. $$

The issuance of a $1,000 bond would be recorded with the following entry:

| | | |
|---|---|---|
| Cash . . . . . . . . . . . . . . . . . . . . . . . . . . . . . . . . | 269.74 | |
| Bonds Payable . . . . . . . . . . . . . . . . . . . | | 269.74 |

An equivalent entry would be

| | | |
|---|---|---|
| Cash . . . . . . . . . . . . . . . . . . . . . . . . . . . . . . . . | 269.74 | |
| Bond Discount . . . . . . . . . . . . . . . . . . . . . . . | 630.26 | |
| Bonds Payable . . . . . . . . . . . . . . . . . . . | | 1,000.00 |

The interest for the first year is 14 percent of $269.74, or $37.76. The entry if the bond discount had not been separately recorded would be

| | | |
|---|---|---|
| Interest Expense . . . . . . . . . . . . . . . . . . . . . . . | 37.76 | |
| Bonds Payable . . . . . . . . . . . . . . . . . . . | | 37.76 |

The entry if the discount had been separately recorded would be

| | | |
|---|---|---|
| Interest Expense . . . . . . . . . . . . . . . . . . . . . . . | 37.76 | |
| Bond Discount . . . . . . . . . . . . . . . . . . . | | 37.76 |

Both entries increase the liability by $37.76. The interest for the second year will be 14 percent of $307.50, or $43.05. This process is repeated each year until maturity. At maturity, the recognized liability should be equal to the maturity amount.

## Reducing the Bond Liability

When a bond is paid at maturity, the liability is debited for the face amount. With a systematic amortization of premium or accumulation of discount, the bond liability will be shown at its face amount at maturity. The entry to record the retirement at maturity of a $1,000-face-value bond by a payment of cash would be as follows:

| | | |
|---|---|---|
| Bonds Payable . . . . . . . . . . . . . . . . . . . . . . . . . . . | 1,000 | |
| Cash . . . . . . . . . . . . . . . . . . . . . . . . . . . . . . . . | | 1,000 |
| To record retirement of $1,000 bond at maturity. | | |

Corporations sometimes find it desirable to pay debt prior to maturity. If interest rates have fallen since the original issue, for example, it may be advantageous to "call" the outstanding bonds at a set price and issue new bonds at the lower rate. This is facilitated if the bond agreement allows the corporation to call the bonds — that is, requires the investors to turn them in to the corporation at a fixed price — and many bond agreements do have this feature. Corporations can also purchase their bonds on the open market when interest rates fall, but since the bond price will have risen, the same potential for gain does not exist as when the bonds are callable.

If a bond is retired prior to maturity, it is unlikely that the amount paid out by the corporation will equal the current "book value" of the bond. The amortization of premium or discount is calculated on the assumption that the bond will be outstanding until maturity. But fluctuations in interest rates will cause the market price of the bonds to change over the years, although these price changes are not normally recognized in the accounts.

When a bond retires prior to maturity at a price that is *higher* than the recorded book value, a *loss* would be recognized by the corporation. If the price is *lower* than the recorded book value, a *gain* would be recognized. In accordance with current practice, these gains or losses would be shown on the income statement but classified as an extraordinary item. Thus, the gain or loss will affect net income, although it will be separately identified.

The classification of gains or losses from early extinguishment of debt as extraordinary items seems to be a departure from the rule that items must be unusual in nature and not likely to recur to qualify as extraordinary. The classification of the gains as extraordinary is required to reduce the possible confusion caused by reporting gains from debt retirement as ordinary income. In times of rising interest rates, some corporations would find it possible to refinance their debt at *higher* interest rates and yet report the gain as ordinary income in their financial statements.

## The Bond Refunding Decision

Assume there are $10,000,000 (face value) of 0.12 bonds outstanding with 20 years of life remaining. The bonds are callable at $1,050 per bond or $10,500,000 in total. The incremental costs of refunding are $2,000,000.

Now, 20-year bonds can be issued to yield 0.08. Assume zero corporate taxes.

### *An Easy Incorrect Solution*

The corporation could issue $10,000,000 of 0.08 bonds and save $400,000 of interest each year.

$$NPV = 400,000(20, j) - 2,000,000.$$

This seems to be a type of investment decision. The firm uses 0.20 to evaluate investments. Assume $j$ equals 0.20 in the above equation.

$$\text{NPV} = 400,000(4.86958) - 2,000,000$$
$$= 1,948,000 - 2,000,000 = -\$52,000.$$

Refunding is not desirable based on this calculation.

The issue that needs to be resolved is whether the 0.20 should be used as the discount rate or whether the new borrowing rate of 0.08 should be used.

### An Easy Correct Solution

We shall now compute the NPV using the new 0.08 borrowing rate.

$$\text{NPV} = 400,000(20,0.08) - 2,000,000$$
$$= 400,000(9.81815) - 2,000,000$$
$$= 3,927,000 - 2,000,000 = \$1,927,000.$$

Now refunding of the bonds has a positive NPV.

The net cash flow is positive and equal to the amount obtained using "An Easy Correct Solution".

The analysis should be on an after-tax basis, but the tax considerations introduce no special analytical complexities.

### A More Complex Calculation

The present value of the 0.12 outstanding debt using a 0.08 discount rate is:

$$1,200,000 \, B(20, 0.08) = \$11,782,000$$
$$10,000,000(1.08)^{-20} = \underline{2,145,000}$$
$$\text{PV} \qquad \$13,927,000$$

Assume \$13,927,000 of new 0.08 debt is issued (the same present value as the outstanding debt). After calling the debt and paying all the refunding expenses, we have:

| | | |
|---|---|---|
| Cash Flows In | | \$13,927,000 |
| Pay Old Debt | \$10,000,000 | |
| Refunding Expenses | 2,000,000 | 12,000,000 |
| NPV | | \$ 1,927,000 |

The NPV is again equal to the NPV using "An Easy Correct Solution".

# Conclusion

The time value of money is relevant to the understanding and the recording of financial transactions. The timing of the collection or payment is important as well as the dollar amount involved in a transaction. There are few financial transactions that do not depend in some manner on an application of the fundamentals of compound interest.

The value of a bond is equal to the sum of (1) the present value of the principal at maturity and (2) the present value of the series of interest payments. With a normal balloon payment bond (e.g., interest payments each year and the principal at maturity), the bond will sell at face value (par) if the market interest rate is equal to the contractual rate of the bond. The bond will sell at a discount if the market interest rate is more than the contractual rate. The interest expense each period is equal to the present value of the bond at the beginning of the period times the market rate of interest used to compute the present value. Semiannual interest payments introduce a computational complexity.

Leases that are essentially purchases of property are called capital leases. The accounting treatment for capital leases is to record the acquisition of a long-lived asset and the issuance of a long-term liability at the present value of the lease payments. The long-lived asset is depreciated or amortized over time, and interest expense is recognized on the long-term liability. All other leases are called operating leases. The accounting treatment for operating leases is to record the lease payments as periodic rent expense.

# Review Problems

## *Review Problem 8.1*

a. What is the present value of $1,000 due in ten years, discounted at 14 percent?
b. What is the present value of $140 per year for a period of ten years if the rate of interest used to discount the payments back to the present is 14 percent?
c. What is the sum of the two amounts obtained in parts (a) and (b)?
d. At what price would a 14-percent, $1,000, ten-year bond sell if it is to yield 14 percent? Assume annual interest payments.

### Solution to Review Problem 8.1

a. $(1.14)^{-10} = 0.26974$; therefore, $\$1,000 \times 0.269174 = \$269.74$.
b. Since $\frac{1-(1.14)^{-10}}{0.14} = \frac{1-0.26974}{0.14} = 5.21614$, $\quad \$140 \times 5.21614 = \$730.26$.

c. $269.74 + $730.26 = $1,000.
d. $1,000 (see part (c)).

## *Review Problem 8.2*

If the bond of the previous problem paid 10 percent interest per year ($100), at what price would it sell?

a. Record its issuance (use a Discount account).
b. Record the first year's interest.

**Solution to Review Problem 8.2**

$$\$1,000 \times 0.26974 = \$269.74$$
$$\$100 \times 5.21614 = \underline{\quad 521.61}$$
$$\text{Price (value) of bond} \quad \$791.35$$

| | | |
|---|---|---|
| Cash..................................... | 791.35 | |
| Bond Discount........................... | 208.65 | |
| Bonds Payable ..................... | | 1,000.00 |

The interest expense for the first year is:

$$\$791.35$$
$$\times \ 0.14$$
$$\text{Interest Expense} \quad \$110.79$$

| | | |
|---|---|---|
| Interest Expense ......................... | 110.79 | |
| Interest Payable .................... | | 100.00 |
| Bond Discount ..................... | | 10.79 |

The new liability after interest is accrued is:

$$\$791.35$$
$$+ \ 10.79$$
$$\$802.14$$

or

$$\$1,000(1.14)^{-9} = \$307.50$$
$$\$100(4.9464) \quad = \underline{\quad 494.64}$$
$$\$802.14$$

where 4.9464 is the present value of an annuity for nine years discounted at 0.14.

## Questions and Problems

1. In each of the following situations, indicate whether the bonds would be sold at the face amount, at a premium, or at a discount:

   a. A $1,000 bond with 20-year maturity. Interest coupons attached, each in the amount of $120, are payable annually. The market rate of interest is 14 percent, compounded annually.

   b. A $1,000 bond with ten-year maturity. Interest coupons attached, each in the amount of $140, are payable at 12-month intervals. The market rate of interest is 14 percent, compounded annually.

   c. A $1,000 bond due in five years. Interest coupons attached, each in the amount of $150, are payable annually. The market rate of interest is 14 percent, compounded annually.

2. Consider the formula

$$PV = \frac{1 - (1 + r)^{-n}}{r},$$

   which gives the present value of an annuity of $1 per period for $n$ periods.

   a. What is the value of $(1 + r)^{-n}$ for very large values of $n$?

   b. What is the value of PV for very large values of $n$?

   c. If $n$ is infinitely large, we have a "perpetuity". What is the present value of a perpetuity of $1 per period if $r$ is 10 percent?

3. a. What is the present value of $1,000 due in ten years? Use a 6 percent rate of interest.

   b. What is the present value of $70 per year for a period of ten years? Use a 6 percent rate of interest.

   c. What is the sum of the amounts obtained in parts (a) and (b)?

   d. At what price will a 7-percent, $1,000, ten-year bond sell if it is to yield 6 percent?

   e. Record the issuance of such a bond on January 1 and the payment of the first year's interest on December 31.

4. Determine the amount you would be willing to pay for a $1,000, 6-percent, 20-year bond. You desire a yield of 8.16 percent per year (4 percent compounded every six months). Interest is to be paid twice a year.

5. Assume that you can borrow and lend money at 10 percent interest per year and that securities yielding this return can be obtained with any maturity. You

are given the following choice:

a. $1,000 to be received annually, first payment to be received one period from now. The payments will continue forever.

b. $11,000 to be received immediately.

Assuming you can obtain either alternative (a) or (b), which would you choose?

6. Determine the present value of a five-year, $1,000, 6-percent bond that sold for a yield of 7 percent (the effective interest rate). Interest is paid annually. Prepare a bond amortization schedule. Prepare the entries to record the liability of the bond issued, the interest charges each year, and the payment of the principal.

| Period | Value of Bond Beginning of Period | Interest Expense for Period | Interest Payable | Amount Subtracted from Discount or Premium | Value of Bond End of Period |
|--------|--------|--------|--------|--------|--------|
| 1 | | | | | |
| 2 | | | | | |
| 3 | | | | | |
| 4 | | | | | |
| 5 | | | | | |

7. Determine the present value of a five-year, $1,000, 7-percent bond that sold for a yield of 6 percent (the effective interest rate). Interest is paid annually. Prepare a bond amortization schedule. Prepare the entries to record the liability of the bond issued, the interest charges each year, and the payment of the principal.

| Period | Value of Bond Beginning of Period | Interest Expense for Period | Interest Payable | Amount Subtracted from Discount or Premium | Value of Bond End of Period |
|--------|--------|--------|--------|--------|--------|
| 1 | | | | | |
| 2 | | | | | |
| 3 | | | | | |
| 4 | | | | | |
| 5 | | | | | |

8. Determine the present value of a five-year, $1,000, 5-percent bond that sold for a yield of 6 percent (the effective interest rate). Interest is paid annually. Prepare a bond amortization schedule. Prepare the entries to record the liability of the bond issued, the interest charges each year, and the payment of the principal.

| Period | Value of Bond Beginning of Period | Interest Expense for Period | Interest Payable | Amount Subtracted from Discount or Premium | Value of Bond End of Period |
|--------|--------|--------|--------|--------|--------|
| 1 | | | | | |
| 2 | | | | | |
| 3 | | | | | |
| 4 | | | | | |
| 5 | | | | | |

9. If $1 is deposited on January 1, how much money will have accumulated at the end of one year if:

   a. The bank computes interest annually, using an interest rate of 6 percent?
   b. The bank computes interest every six months, using an interest rate of 3 percent every six months?
   c. What is the compound effective annual rate of interest for the situation described in part (b)?

10. The Marshall Company authorized a bond issue of ten $1,000, 7-percent, 20-year bonds.

    a. Record the issuance of the bonds on January 1, 2xx3, so as to yield 6.09 percent annually (3 percent compounded twice a year).
    b. Record the accrual of interest on June 30, 2xx3, and the payment of interest on July 1.
    c. Record the accrual of interest on December 31.
    d. What will be the bond liability after ten years?

11. The Fenwick Company authorized a bond issue of ten $1,000, 6-percent, 20-year bonds. These low-interest bonds will sell at a discount.

    a. Record the issuance of the bonds on January 1, 2xx3, so as to yield 8.16 percent annually (4 percent compounded every six months).
    b. Record the accrual of interest on June 30, 2xx3, and the payment of interest on July 1.

    c. Record the accrual of interest on December 31.

    d. What will be the total bond liability after ten years?

12. Determine the amount you would be willing to pay for a $1,000, 8-percent, 20-year bond. You desire a yield of 10.25 percent per year (5 percent compounded every 6 months). Interest is to be paid twice a year.

# Chapter 9
# Stockholders' Equity

The divergence between accounting and finance is well illustrated by the stockholders' equity accounts of a publicly traded corporation. The accountant relies on the history of stock equity transactions and finance relies on market transactions for stock value estimates. For most managerial decisions, only the market value measures are relevant. The traditional accounting measures are relatively irrelevant aside from legal aspects.

Would it be useful if the accountant were to use the market values to adjust the reported amounts of stockholders' equity? Remember, we are dealing with a double-entry accounting system. If the market value of the stock equity is used as the basis of the accounting, another account (probably an asset account) would also have to be adjusted. But the market is using the accounting measures to value the common stock. If the accounting measures are based on the market measures of the stock, then the market has lost a useful tool for estimating value. So we have to live with the fact that the accounting measures of stockholders' equity will differ from the market value, and this difference is essential to the determination of market value. This means that a decision maker must determine whether the accounting measures or the market value of the stock is more useful. For most purposes, the market value will be most useful. In some situations, the decision maker will want to ignore the market value and use the underlying accounting measures to estimate the value of the stock without initial reference to the market value (a later reference is likely to be appropriate).

Common stock purchasers may be interested in the split between permanent legal capital and retained earnings, since the dividends may be restricted by the amount of retained earnings. However, for a common stock purchaser looking to the long run, the allocation among the different stock equity accounts may be of less importance. Long-term restrictions on the payment of dividends may be of interest, but these restrictions are not always recorded in the accounts.

## Classification of Stockholders' Equity

The accountant may classify the stockholders' equity section in various ways. The selection of the classification that is most useful will depend on the interests of the users of the financial statements. Classifications are designed to accomplish the following purposes:

1. Distinguish among equities of various classes of stockholders;
2. Distinguish between par value of stock and amounts paid in excess of, or below, par (a legal requirement);
3. Distinguish shares issued and outstanding from those that have been reacquired by the corporation;
4. Distinguish between capital arising from original contributions of stockholders and that generated through the retention of earnings; and
5. Distinguish between retained earnings available for distribution to stockholders and retained earnings restricted for various reasons.

## Par Value

Common stock may be issued with par or with stated values. These amounts may have certain limited legal significance, but are not usually of importance to buyers of common stock. When a common stock has a par value, it is generally defined by the legal requirements of the various states. The par value is often the basis of taxing the issuance and exchange of stock. The accounting entries to record the issuance of common stock are more likely to be dictated by the legal requirements than by accounting theory. Thus, instead of using one account to record the contribution of stockholders, we might use two accounts: one to record the par or stated value, and the other to record the difference between issue price and par or stated value of the stock.

The designation of par value usually has little economic significance, but merely reflects the legal requirements.

In the past, the issuance of stock for less than its par value resulted in an obligation for the stockholder to pay to the corporation the amount of the "discount" in the event of corporate insolvency. The use of "no par" stock and "low par" (such as $1.00 per share) has minimized the importance of this aspect, and stock is now not issued at a discount.

If par value is to be shown separately in the balance sheet, the positive difference between par and the amount actually paid is shown through the use of adjunct accounts. The additional amount is shown in an adjunct account referred to either as Additional Paid-in Capital, Amount Paid in Excess of Par, or simply Premium.

## Issuance of Common Stock

The issuance of common stock is usually preceded by the subscription of the stock by the prospective stockholders. This transaction may be recorded, but the corporation generally waits until the cash is actually received before recording entries relative to the issuance of the stock.

When par values are involved, the entries to record the issuance would be adapted to reflect the par value and the amount of premium or discount. The issuance of no par stock does not require this distinction.

## *Example*

Record the journal entries for the following situation.

One thousand shares of common stock, par $10, are issued for $11 per share.

| | | |
|---|---|---|
| Cash . . . . . . . . . . . . . . . . . . . . . . . . . . . . . . . . . . . . . . . . . . . . . . | 11,000 | |
| Common Stock, Par . . . . . . . . . . . . . . . . . . . . . . . . . . . . | | 10,000 |
| Common Stock, Amount Paid in Excess of Par . . | | 1,000 |

If the issue price is $9 per share, the entry is:

| | | |
|---|---|---|
| Cash . . . . . . . . . . . . . . . . . . . . . . . . . . . . . . . . . . . . . . . . . . . . . . | 9,000 | |
| Common Stock, Discount . . . . . . . . . . . . . . . . . . . . . . . . | 1,000 | |
| Common Stock, Par . . . . . . . . . . . . . . . . . . . . . . . . . . . . | | 10,000 |

## Issue of Stock for Assets

Stock may be issued for assets other than cash, such as land, buildings, and patents. The entry recording the stockholders' contribution to the corporation is based on a realistic valuation of the assets contributed. If the stock issued has an active market, recent prices of the stock might be used to estimate the value of the entire transaction. If no market exists for the stock, then the assets received should be appraised. The amount received for the stock should be assumed to equal the current value of the assets received at the time of the transaction.

For example, assume that the R Corporation issues 10,000 shares of its common stock, $1 par value, in exchange for a building and land. There is no active market for the stock, but independent appraisers hired by the company place a value of $50,000 on the building and $20,000 on the land. The transaction would be recorded as follows:

| | | |
|---|---|---|
| Building........................................ | 50,000 | |
| Land........................................... | 20,000 | |
|     Common Stock — Par ..................... | | 10,000 |
|     Common Stock — Amount Paid in Excess of Par | | 60,000 |

To record the issuance of stock in exchange for building and land.

## Treasury Stock

When a corporation repurchases its own previously issued stock, the acquired shares are referred to as **treasury stock**. The transaction may be recorded in the following manner:

| | | |
|---|---|---|
| Treasury Stock................................. | 10,000 | |
|     Cash ....................................... | | 10,000 |

To record the purchase of 500 shares of common stock for $10,000.

The Treasury Stock account is then presented in the balance sheet as a subtraction from the total of the other stock equity accounts. Although the Treasury Stock account will have a debit balance, a corporation's own shares cannot logically be regarded as an asset. When a company purchases its own stock, it is, from an economic point of view, retiring that stock. From a legal point of view, a share of stock once issued may have different characteristics from a share of stock not previously issued. For example, treasury stock may be issued at a price less than par without the purchaser being assessable for the difference between par and the purchase price. Assume that the stock in the example is reissued for $15,000.

| | | |
|---|---|---|
| Cash .......................................... | 15,000 | |
|     Treasury Stock ............................ | | 10,000 |
|     Common Stock, Amount Paid in Excess of Par.. | | 5,000 |

No gain or loss should be recognized by a corporation because of transactions in its own stock.

It can be incorrectly argued that a company that pays $10,000 for shares of stock and then reissues the shares for $15,000 has made a profit of $5,000. If it were stock of another company that was being bought and sold, a gain would be recognized. However, when the company has acquired its own stock from its stockholders and reissues the stock to other stockholders, no gain or loss is recorded.

This is consistent with the entity concept. We distinguish revenue transactions from capital transactions. **Revenue transactions** are those carried on within the scope of the purpose for which the business unit was organized — producing, selling, servicing, and so forth. Gains and losses are recognized on such transactions. **Capital transactions** are transactions involving the raising of capital — issuance and retirement of ownership equity. No gains or losses are recognized on such transactions.

## *Retained Earnings*

Historically, accountants have attempted to distinguish between the capital explicitly contributed by stockholders (where there has been an issue of stock) and capital generated from retained earnings (capital that does not require an explicit decision by the individual stockholders). This distinction serves several purposes. It indicates to some extent the past profitability of the corporation, although this indication may be distorted by cash dividends, stock dividends, reorganizations, secret reserves, disclosed reserves, and mergers. The second purpose behind the distinction is somewhat easier to accomplish. It is the fulfillment of legal requirements for the separation of contributed capital and retained earnings. The main functions of this latter requirement are to safeguard the rights of the creditors and to prevent the declaration of dividends when the payment would endanger the ability of the creditors to collection amounts due them. We want to know the amount of retained earnings in order to determine if a dividend can be declared legally.

## *Retained Earnings — Restrictions*

When retained earnings are legally restricted, this fact can be indicated in footnotes or through the use of separate accounts identifying the restrictions. Restrictions may occur through the provisions of bond indentures, cumulative preferred stock in arrears with respect to dividends, legal requirements regarding the acquisition of treasury stock, and so forth. In such cases, stockholders might wish to know the extent to which retained earnings are available for dividends.

Suppose, for example, that a company has retained earnings totaling $100,000, but provisions of a bond indenture require that dividends may be paid only to the extent that retained earnings exceed $90,000. This information may be indicated in the balance sheet through the use of separately designated accounts to show the components of retained earnings:

| | |
|---|---:|
| Retained Earnings — Restricted Due to Bond Indenture | $ 90,000 |
| Retained Earnings — Unrestricted | 10,000 |
| Total Retained Earnings | $100,000 |

## The Use of Reserves

Occasionally, corporations show balances on the equity side of the balance sheet that have the term "reserve" in their title. Usually these are components of retained earnings that have been separately identified. Among titles that have been used for such items are:

**Reserve for Contingencies**
**Reserve for Self-Insurance**
**Reserve for Foreign Operations**
**Reserve for Possible Price Decline of Inventory**
**Reserve for Uncollectibles**

The designation of such "reserves" has sometimes been used to conceal information from stockholders. Assume a company adds to such a reserve during a profitable year by including an expense in the income statement, and then avoids showing an expense in some subsequent year by debiting the reserve account rather than the expense. This would enable the corporation to smooth its reported income over the years. The accounting profession has tried to eliminate this practice and has been successful in greatly reducing the extent of its use.

For many years, accountants were relatively lax in the use of the "Reserve for Contingencies" account established by charging expense accounts for possible adverse events. In 1975, the FASB published Statement of Accounting Standards No. 5, "Accounting for Contingencies", which limits the use of provisions for contingencies.

An estimated loss from a loss contingency shall be established by a charge to income only if *both* the following conditions are satisfied:

a. It has to be probable that the loss contingency will occur (the word "probable" is used in a manner that implies a very high probability).
b. The amount of the loss can be reasonably estimated.

For a hundred years, academic accountants have warned against the use of reserve accounting to manipulate earnings. Suppose this year's earnings are "too high". The accountant can debit an expense account and credit a reserve account. This year's earnings are reduced. Assume the next year's earnings are too low. The accountant can then debit the reserve account and credit a cash or liability account (thus, the expense is not increased). The above entries may be justified or they may be attempts to stabilize earnings. In the 2006 Enron trial, Jeff Skilling was accused of using reserves to achieve the targeted earnings measures. But the establishment of a reserve for estimated uncollectable accounts can be either a reasonable attempt to recognize that not all the receivables will be collected or an effort to stabilize the earnings stream through manipulative accounting. The first explanation is legitimate. The attempt to stabilize earnings is bad accounting and likely to be a crime.

## Retained Earnings and Cash

The presence of retained earnings does not mean that there is an equal amount of cash on the asset side of the balance sheet. Retained earnings represent a portion of the stockholders' share in the total assets. There may or may not be cash. The retained earnings cannot be identified with a specific asset or group of assets.

## *Example*

**ABZ Company**
**Balance Sheet as of December 31, 20xx**

| Cash | $10,000 | Common Stock | $ 6,000 |
|------|---------|--------------|---------|
|      |         | Retained Earnings | 4,000 |
|      | $10,000 |              | $10,000 |

In the foregoing balance sheet, the cash is actually greater than the retained earnings. If the company then buys $10,000 of fixed assets, the balance sheet becomes:

**ABZ Company**
**Balance Sheet as of December 31, 20xx**

| Cash | — | Common Stock | $ 6,000 |
|------|---------|--------------|---------|
| Fixed Assets | $10,000 | Retained Earnings | 4,000 |
|      | $10,000 |              | $10,000 |

The retained earnings are unchanged, but they are $4,000 greater than the cash balance, which is now zero.

It is sometimes erroneously stated that dividends are "paid out of retained earnings". The declaration of a dividend serves to reduce the balance of retained earnings, and in many cases the amount of dividends that may legally be declared is limited by the balance of retained earnings. In the final analysis, however, a cash dividend must be paid out of cash, regardless of the balance in the Retained Earnings account. Inasmuch as the presence of retained earnings does not necessarily coincide with the holding of cash by the corporation, the amount of retained earnings is not necessarily an indication of the corporation's ability to pay cash dividends.

## Stockholders' Equity Section of the Balance Sheet

The stockholders' equity section of the balance sheet generally consists of three parts: the capital contributed by the preferred stockholders, the explicit contributions of the common stockholders, and, finally, the retained earnings. Any contra or adjunct accounts should be placed immediately under the primary account that they adjust. For example, treasury stock should be shown as a subtraction immediately below a subtotal of the common stockholders' equity.

The following illustrates a number of typical items as they might be found in the stockholders' equity section of a balance sheet.

**Stockholders' Equity**

| | | | |
|---|---|---|---|
| Preferred Stock, 1,000 Shares of Par $50 Stock Outstanding | | | $ 50,000 |
| Common Stock, 10,000 Shares of Par $10 Stock Issued | $100,000 | | |
| Common Stock, Amount Paid in Excess of Par | 7,000 | $107,000 | |
| Retained Earnings | | 45,000 | |
| | | $152,000 | |
| Less: Treasury Stock, 1,000 Shares (at cost) | | 12,000 | 140,000 |
| Total Stockholders' Equity | | | $190,000 |

From a common shareholders' perspective, the $190,000 is a relevant measure of the stockholders' equity as measured by the accountants. The observed stock price multiplied by the number of outstanding shares gives an alternative measure.

## Cost of Common Stock

The cost of common stock equity cannot be explicitly and accurately measured, since the actual return to stockholders depends not only on the forecast of the earnings of the firm, the investment, and dividend decisions that are made by the firm, but also on the interpretation by the stock market of these events and decisions.

In discussing the cost of equity capital, you should realize that this topic is the mirror image of the decision to invest in common stock. The theory of stock valuation is a crucial element of the determination of the cost of equity capital.

### A Stock Valuation Model

There are several definitions of the cost of equity capital. The standard academic definition is that the cost of equity capital is the rate of discount that equates the present value of all future expected dividends per share to the present price of the common stock. It is the return on investment required by investors so that they are willing to invest in the common stock.

Let us first define the cost of equity capital, $k_e$, as the rate of interest or return that investors require to buy the common stock. Mathematically, the cost of equity is the interest rate that equates the next dividend, $D_1$, and the expected price of the stock at the time, $P_1$, back to the price of a share today, $P$, if the next dividend is paid one period in the future. We then have

$$P = \frac{D_1 + P_1}{1 + k_e} = \frac{D_1}{1 + k_e} + \frac{P_1}{1 + k_e}. \tag{9.1}$$

The price today is equal to the present value of the next period's dividend plus the next period's price. By the same definition, the stock price at time 1 is

$$P_1 = \frac{D_2 + P_2}{1 + k_e} \tag{9.2}$$

so that, substituting equation (9.2) into equation (9.1), we find

$$P = \frac{D_1}{1 + k_e} + \frac{D_2}{(1 + k_e)^2} + \frac{P_2}{(1 + k_e)^2}. \tag{9.3}$$

Continuing this substitution process, we obtain

$$P = \sum_{t=1}^{\infty} D_t (1 + k_e)^{-t}. \tag{9.4}$$

Equation (9.4) is a basic dividend valuation model for common stock. It states that the current market value of a share of common stock is equal to the present value of all future dividends, discounted at the cost of equity capital. The cost of equity capital is that rate of return the stock market expects to receive in order to compensate it for the use of funds and the risk associated with the future dividend stream. Equation (9.4) is the simplest general formulation for the valuation of common stock. It assumes that $k_e$ can be used as the cost of equity capital for all years.

Although equation (9.4) could be solved by trial and error for any set of $D_t$'s, there are "standard" growth patterns of the dividend stream. We present a model in the next section to illustrate this methodology.

Note that the future stock prices (capital gains) are not directly in equation (9.4), but rather the future dividends are substituted for these stock prices.

## A Closed-Form Stock Price Model

One of the simplest assumptions that can be made about expected dividend behavior is that dividends are expected to grow at a constant rate through time so that $D_t = D_1 (1 + g)^{t-1}$. If dividends grow at a rate $g$ in perpetuity and $g < k_e$, then (as shown in Appendix 9.1) we can obtain

$$P = \frac{D_1}{k_e - g}, \tag{9.5}$$

where $D_1$ is the next period's dividend amount. This is a perpetual growth model where dividend growth is constant each period.

Solving equation (9.5) for the cost of equity capital, we find

$$k_e = \frac{D_1}{P} + g \tag{9.6}$$

and this is a widely accepted theoretical measure of $k_e$, the cost of stock equity capital.

### Example

A common stock is expected to pay a $1-per-share dividend at the end of the year. The stockholders want a return of 15 percent and expect dividends to grow at a rate of 14 percent per period.

$D_1 = $1$ per year (the next dividend)

$g = 0.14$, growth rate in dividends

$k_e = 0.15$, cost of stock equity capital (the return required by stockholders)

Using equation (9.5), we find that the value per share is

$$P = \frac{D_1}{k_e - g} = \frac{\$1}{0.15 - 0.14} = \$100.$$

If $g$ were to change from 14 to 10 percent, the value of a share would change to

$$P = \frac{D_1}{k_e - g} = \frac{\$1}{0.15 - 0.10} = \frac{\$1}{0.05} = \$20.$$

Note that a change in stock price, $P$, might be caused by a change in $D_1$, $g$, or $k_e$. A decrease in $P$ does not necessarily mean that $k_e$ has increased.

By observing the current annual dividend ($1) and the current price (say, $25) and using an estimate of $g$ (say, 10 percent), we could then estimate $k_e$ using equation (9.6):

$$k_e = \frac{D_1}{P} + g$$

$$= \frac{\$1}{25} + 0.10 = 0.04 + 0.10 = 14\%. \tag{9.7}$$

One might argue that investors buy price appreciation, not future dividends. For many stocks, investors may expect the first $n$ periods to have very small (or zero) dividends and, nevertheless, the current market price may be very large. The current high price, however, is only justified in a rational market by the expectation of high future dividends (or other forms of cash flow from the firm to investors). The summation of the present value of future dividends does not require that the near-term dividends be large. However, if there are several years of zero dividends and/or changing growth rates through time, then the mathematical formulation of $P$ does not reduce to an expression as simple as $P = D_1/(k_e - g)$.

What would be the value of a stock that promised never to pay cash to its investors (including a liquidation dividend payoff arising from selling the firm)? The value of these shares would be zero. There has to be the prospect of dividends (defined to be any cash distribution from the firm to its investors) for stock to have a positive value.

The constant growth rate dividend valuation model assumes that the dividend ($D_1$) is expected to grow at a constant rate $g$ forever. It may be more realistic to assume that special investment opportunities allowing a high growth rate are available not in perpetuity, but only over some finite interval of time, $T$, and after time the growth rate will be smaller.

## Conclusion

This chapter has focused on ways in which the stockholders' equity section of a firm's balance sheet may be classified to provide additional information. The information supplied by this classification includes (1) the separation of equities of various classes of stockholders; (2) the separate recognition of amounts contributed that are more or less than par value; (3) the distinction between capital initially contributed to stockholders and capital generated through retention of earnings; and (4) the division of retained earnings when dividend restrictions are involved.

The separation of various common stock equity accounts may be of limited value to users of financial statements. Except for the satisfaction of legal requirements, the classification of accounts in the common stockholders' equity section is of little benefit to long-term investors. Future dividends are likely to depend on the results of future operations and the asset-debt structure, not on past retained earnings. Yet, these classifications are commonly reflected in financial statements, and understanding their meaning should facilitate the analysis of financial data.

## Questions and Problems

1. What is the significance of the "par value" of common stock? Is it a bargain to purchase "$100 par value" stock for only $80?
2. Distinguish between "stock dividends" and "dividends on stock". Distinguish between a "stock dividend" and a "stock split".
3. Explain why it is possible for a corporation to have retained earnings of several million dollars while not being able to expand plant facilities by one million dollars without raising additional capital.
4. The balance sheet of the Dupy Corporation shows a Retained Earnings balance of $3,500,000. An analysis of the account revealed the following:

**Analysis of Retained Earnings**

| | |
|---|---:|
| Arising from past earnings | $2,500,000 |
| Donation of land by the city | 600,000 |
| Amount paid in excess of par value of preferred stock | 100,000 |
| Gain on sale of treasury stock | 180,000 |
| Amount paid in excess of par value of common stock | 120,000 |
| | $3,500,000 |

Comment on the amount shown as Retained Earnings.

5. If you found a "Reserve for Retirement Allowances" (for employees) on the equity side of a balance sheet, what would you think was the nature of the account?
6. The balance sheet of the Aeronautical Corporation at December 31, 20x1, showed the following stockholders' equity:

| | |
|---|---:|
| 6 percent Preferred Stock (par value $100 per share; authorized 30,000 shares; issued and outstanding 15,000 shares) | $1,500,000 |
| Common Stock (par value $10 per share; authorized 500,000 shares; issued and outstanding 200,000 shares) | 2,000,000 |

| Additional Paid-in Capital: | | |
|---|---|---|
| On Preferred Stock | $ 60,000 | |
| On Common Stock | 2,000,000 | 2,060,000 |
| Total Paid-in Capital | | $5,560,000 |
| Retained Earnings | | 2,800,000 |
| Total Stockholders' Equity | | $8,360,000 |

Make general journal entries for the following transactions occurring during 20x2:

a. Ten thousand shares of common stock were issued for cash at $35 per share.
b. The quarterly dividend on the preferred stock was declared but not paid.
c. Aeronautical acquired 8,000 shares of its own common stock at $32 per share.
d. A dividend of $1 per share on the common stock was declared but not paid.
e. Three thousand shares of the common stock held in the treasury were reissued at $35 per share.

7. Moran Energy Inc. is a rapidly growing domestic energy company, with operations in oil and gas exploration and production as well as onshore and offshore contract drilling. Moran's stockholders' equity section appeared as follows on December 31, 20x0:

**Stockholders' Equity**

| Common Stock, $0.25 par value, 30,000,000 shares authorized, 2,500,000 shares outstanding at December 31, 20x0 | $ 625,000 |
|---|---|
| Capital in Excess of Par Value | 20,239,000 |
| Retained Earnings | 15,549,000 |
| | $36,413,000 |

Give the journal entries to record the following events. Assume that the events took place in the order presented. Please show all calculations.

a. The company declared and issued a 10-percent common stock dividend. The market price was $34.30 per share of common stock.
b. The company issued 17,000 shares of common stock at $8.06 per share for the exercise of common stock options.
c. $19,443,000 principal amount of convertible debentures were converted into 955,000 shares of common stock.

d. The company sold 880,000 shares of common stock to the public for $24,883,000.

e. The company issued a common stock split in the form of a 100-percent stock dividend. The market value was $38.50 per share. The $0.25 par value was retained.

f. The board of directors approved a restricted stock plan whereby shares were reserved for issuance to certain officers and key employees. Restricted plan expense of $121,980 was charged to Income and credited to Unissued Restricted Stock.

g. The company earned an income of $12,187,000 in 20x1 and declared dividends of $580,000 in 20x1.

8. Assume that growth is expected to continue for perpetuity and that $P = D_1/(k_e - g)$ can be used for valuation purposes. The initial dividend is $1 and the cost of equity is 0.20.

a. What is $P$ if $g = 0.19$?
b. What is $P$ if $g = 0.10$?
c. What is $P$ if $g = 0$?
d. What is $P$ if $g = -0.05$?

9. A company's stock is selling at $50 and its dividend is $4.

a. What is $k_e$ if $g = 0.10$?
b. What is $k_e$ if $g = 0$?
c. What is $k_e$ if $g = -0.05$?

10. A company's stock is selling at $80 and its dividend for the next year is expected to be $4. The expected perpetual growth rate is 0.10 and the cost of equity is 0.15.

a. What will be the expected dividend after one year has passed?
b. What will be the price after one year?
c. What is the percentage increase in stock price?

11. Company A has a dividend of $2.10 and earnings of $3.00. The stock is selling at $210. Investors want a 0.15 return. Dividends and earnings are expected to grow at 0.14 per year.

a. Prepare a table showing the expected dividends and stock prices for the next five years.
b. Evaluate the facts of this problem and the resulting table if earnings are expected to remain constant.

## Appendix 9.1: Derivation of Stock Price Model with Constant Growth Rate

We want to show that

$$P = \frac{D_1}{k_e - g}.$$

At time $t$, $D_t = D_1(1 + g)^{t-1}$. If the current market price is defined as the present value of the future expected dividends,

$$P = \sum_{t=1}^{\infty} D_t(1 + k_e)^{-t}$$

$$= \frac{D_1}{1 + k_e}\left(1 + \frac{1 + g}{1 + k_e} + \left(\frac{1 + g}{1 + k_e}\right)^2 + \cdots\right).$$

If $k_e > g$,

$$P = \frac{D_1}{1 + k_e}\left(\frac{1}{1 - \frac{1+g}{1+k_e}}\right)$$

$$= \frac{D_1}{k_e - g}.$$

*Chapter 10*

# Distributions to Shareholders

The two major forms of cash distributions to shareholders are:

a. cash dividends
b. repurchase of its shares by a corporation.

The accounting entry for a $1,000 cash dividend declaration and payment is:

| | | |
|---|---|---|
| Stockholders' Equity .................... | 1,000 | |
| Cash .................................. | | 1,000 |

The accounting entry for a $1,000 stock purchase (the firm's own shares) by a corporation is:

| | | |
|---|---|---|
| Stockholders' Equity .................... | 1,000 | |
| Cash .................................. | | 1,000 |

The two basic entries are the same. While the detailed entries will differ, in fact, dividends and a stock repurchase of an equal amount have the same basic financial consequences to the corporation. Both transactions reduce stock equity and both reduce the cash account. Many of the different interpretations of these transactions one encounters in news and magazine articles are merely imaginative fiction.

Since the Stockholders' Equity account is subdivided in practice, there will be differences in the details of the accounting recordings, but the basic nature of the accounting entries is the same for both transactions.

## Accounting for Dividends: The Details

When a dividend is declared, a temporary account, Dividends, is debited and a liability account, Dividends Payable, is credited to reflect the amount due to the stockholders. The debit to the Dividends account ultimately reduces Retained Earnings.

When dividends on stock are declared but not yet paid, the amount of the declaration becomes a liability of the corporation. By the entity assumption, the corporation is considered to be a distinct economic unit, separate from its owners. The earnings of the corporation accrue for the benefit of stockholders and thus serve to increase the stockholders' equity. However, when the corporation's directors decide to distribute a portion or all of the earnings as a dividend, the amount of the dividend becomes a liability of the corporation. The stockholders are creditors of the corporation until the actual payment is made.

The entry to be made at the time of declaration can be:

```
Dividends......................................    1,000
        Dividends Payable............................          1,000
```
To record the declaration of a dividend; the debit reduces retained earnings.

When the cash disbursement takes place, the following entry is made:

```
Dividends Payable ...............................    1,000
        Cash.........................................          1,000
```
To record the payment of the dividend.

The Dividends account is then closed at the end of the accounting period to Retained Earnings:

```
Retained Earnings.................................    1,000
        Dividends ...................................          1,000
```
To close the dividends account.

The above entries can be simplified to:

```
Retained Earnings.................................    1,000
        Cash.........................................          1,000
```
or

```
Stockholders' Equity ..............................    1,000
        Cash.........................................          1,000
```

## Stock Dividends

Stock dividends are not dividends in a real sense. With a stock dividend, the corporation distributes additional shares of its common stock on a pro rata basis to existing shareholders. A stock dividend increases the number of shares outstanding, but leaves the assets of the corporation unchanged (except for transaction costs). The amount of a cash dividend is usually expressed (in the United States) in terms of dollars and cents per share. The amount of a stock dividend is usually expressed as a percentage or a ratio. With a 4-percent stock dividend, the holder of 100 shares of stock receives an additional 4 shares of stock.

The stock dividend, from an economic standpoint, is actually a stock split. Thus, a 100-percent stock dividend and a 2-for-1 stock split are equivalent as far as shareholders are concerned. When a stock dividend is declared and becomes effective, the new price of the shares reflects the additional shares outstanding. The actual percentage decline depends on the amount of the stock dividend.

When a 10-percent stock dividend is paid, all things being equal, the new price per share will be 1/1.1 of the old price. For example, if shares were selling for $100 before the dividend, each share would tend to sell for about $90.91 after the 10-percent stock dividend. If there were $N$ shares outstanding before the stock dividend, there would be $1.1N$ shares after the 10-percent stock dividend. The total value of the stock equity would be $100N$ before and $90.91(1.1N) = $100N$ after. The total value is unchanged.

As an additional explanation as to why a stock dividend is not comparable to a cash dividend, imagine the following situation. You are sitting in a restaurant and have just ordered a piece of cherry pie. When it arrives, it looks so good that you tell the waitress that you want two pieces. She picks up the plate with the piece of cherry pie on it, cuts the piece of pie into two, and hands both pieces back to you. The original piece of pie on the plate corresponds to your interest in the company (your share of the total pie) before the stock dividend. The two pieces on your plate after the waitress has cut the original piece in half indicates how your ownership interest would change after a 100-percent stock dividend.

An investor holding 10 shares worth $100 each would have a total investment of $1,000 before the stock dividend. After the stock dividend, the investor would own 11 shares and the stock would have a value of $90.91 per share. Again, the value of the total investment is $1,000. Logically, stock dividends should not be taxed as income, and they are not.

There are two apparent reasons why corporations use stock dividends. If, in the opinion of the board of directors, the price of the stock is too high and it is thought that the high price is limiting the extent of distribution of the stock (a lower-priced stock would have a broader market), a stock dividend may be used to reduce the price of the stock. The larger number of shares outstanding will reduce the price per share. It may increase the number of persons likely to buy the stock.

Stock dividends are also used to substitute for cash dividends. When a corporation is short of cash because of either expansion of operations or unsatisfactory results of operations, a stock dividend may act as a pacifier to uninformed stockholders until cash dividends may be increased or resumed. Retaining earnings and conserving cash may be reasonable objectives.

A stock dividend can be recorded to conform to legal requirements by debiting Retained Earnings and crediting Common Stock accounts. There is a problem in deciding the amount of retained earnings that should be transferred to the Common Stock accounts. The general practice is to use the market value of the stock issued on the date of declaration. Thus, a stock dividend of 1,000 shares of $100-par-value common stock that has a market price of $150 per share might be recorded as follows:

| | | |
|---|---|---|
| Retained Earnings . . . . . . . . . . . . . . . . . . . . . . . . . . . . . . . . . . . | 150,000 | |
|     Common Stock — Par. . . . . . . . . . . . . . . . . . . . . . . . . . . | | 100,000 |
|     Common Stock — Amount Paid in Excess of Par . . . | | 50,000 |
| To record stock dividend of 1,000 shares. | | |

## Stock Split

A stock split is also used to reduce the price of common stock. With a **stock split**, the shareholders are given a multiple of the number of shares they presently hold. There is no economic difference between a stock split and a stock dividend, although there is an accounting difference. As described above, a stock dividend is accompanied by a transfer of a portion of retained earnings to the Common Stock accounts.

Sometimes, companies issue a stock split but retain the old par value. An entry is required for a stock split if the par value of the common stock is not changed. For example, assume a company issued a two-for-one stock split but assume that it retained the $100 par value. The following entry would be made to record this stock split:

| | | |
|---|---|---|
| Capital Stock — Amount Paid in Excess of Par . . . . . . | 1,000,000 | |
|     Common Stock — Par . . . . . . . . . . . . . . . . . . . . . | | 1,000,000 |
| To record issuance of 10,000 shares of $100-par-value | | |
|     common stock for a two-for-one stock split. | | |

This entry would not affect the total invested equity capital, but it would change the amounts reported as common stock at par and as common stock at amounts paid in excess of par.

In some cases, a large increase in the number of shares may be accomplished by a stock dividend. A large stock dividend has the same effect on market price as a stock split, and a stock dividend is very similar to a stock split in which the old par value is retained.

How stock dividends and stock splits are structured and described can affect whether par values or market values are used and whether amounts are transferred from Retained Earnings or Common Stock accounts. Since amounts transferred from Retained Earnings could effectively limit the amount of retained earnings that may be distributed as cash dividends, these issues may be of some importance from a legal viewpoint. From a financial analysis viewpoint, these accounting entries are irrelevant.

## Dividends and Stock Value

With no income taxes and with other well-defined assumptions (such as perfect knowledge and certainty), a dollar retained is equal in value to a dollar distributed; thus, dividend policy is not a relevant factor in determining the value of a corporation. However, when taxes are allowed in the analysis, dividend policy affects the value of the stockholders' equity. In practice, corporations appear to be influenced in setting dividend policy by a desire to have a relatively stable dividend.

A common stock dividend is a distribution of a portion of the assets of a corporation to its common stock shareholders. The amount received by each investor is proportional to the number of shares held by the investor. In most cases, cash is distributed. When a corporation pays a dividend, its assets are reduced by the amount of the dividend. In publicly traded stock, the price per share declines by a fraction of the amount of the dividend on the day that the stock goes "ex-dividend". A person who buys the stock on or after the ex-dividend date will not receive the dividend. Because of other factors affecting the stock price, as well as tax considerations, the decline in the share price will not be exactly equal to the amount of dividend paid. The change will be a percentage of that amount.

## Dividend Policy

A corporation is not legally obligated to declare a dividend of any specific amount. A firm's board of directors makes a specific decision every time a dividend is declared. Once the board declares a dividend, the corporation is legally obligated to make the payments. Therefore, a dividend should not be declared unless a corporation is in a financial position to make the payment.

The expectation of receiving dividends (broadly defined as any distribution of value) ultimately determines the market value of the common stock. By declaring a dividend, the board of directors is not only turning over some of the assets of the corporation to its stockholders, but also influencing the expectations that stockholders have about the future dividends they can expect from the corporation.

If expectations are affected, the dividend decision and the underlying dividend policy will have an impact on the value that the market places on the common stock of the corporation.

Many financial experts believe that a highly stable dividend is advantageous to a company. The most common reason stated for this belief is that many stockholders prefer a steady income from their investments. There is at least one other important reason for thinking that a highly variable dividend rate may not be in the best interest of a company. In the long run, the value of a share of stock tends to be determined by the discounted value of the expected dividends. Insofar as this is the case, a widely fluctuating dividend rate will tend to make it difficult for current or prospective stockholders to determine the value of the stock to them; as a result, the stock is likely to sell at a lower price compared to stocks paying the same or an increasing average dividend through time, although the payments are made at a steady rate.

## Factors Affecting Investor Reaction to Dividends

Traditional concepts about the distinction between income and capital, some of which have been embodied into laws that control the behavior of certain financial institutions, are important considerations in understanding how these investors react to corporate dividend decisions and policies.

The more sophisticated thinking about financial matters tends to emphasize the total return received from an asset, and to ignore distinctions between capital gains and other forms of income except for their effect on taxes.

The total return approach treats the market value of the securities held and dividends received as one pool that can be divided up at each decision point into consumption and further investment. The fact that some of the liquid assets available have come from dividends and others from a change in the value of the investment is of secondary importance.

There are many investors who approach these same events with a different point of view. For some investors, there is an important distinction between income and capital gains. Income may be typically defined as dividends and interest. Investors who think in these terms are often quite comfortable in consuming part or all of their dividend or interest "income", but are uncomfortable about having to dispose of some of their securities in order to pay for living expenses.

The distinction between dividends and capital gains is also reinforced by tax laws that define the receipt of dividends or interest as a taxable event. By contrast, changes in the value of common stock are not taxable events unless, and until, the securities are actually sold.

One further institutional factor that should be mentioned in connection with dividends is the so-called trust legal list. Banks, insurance companies, other financial institutions, and individual trustees often manage substantial sums for the benefit of others. Over the years, many states have passed laws designed to ensure that the beneficiaries of these assets do not incur losses because trustees have purchased excessively risky investments for the trust. Various controls have been designed to accomplish this end. One is to restrict the kinds of assets that are eligible for consideration as investments by a particular kind of trustee or financial institution. Such a list of eligible assets is called a trust legal list. The laws do not specify the particular securities that are eligible for inclusion on the legal list, but rather the characteristics that a security must possess in order to be eligible. A state official is responsible for determining which securities have the necessary characteristics. To be eligible for inclusion on a legal list, a common stock may need to have paid dividends without interruption for a given length of time. A consequence of this procedure is that if a company fails to pay dividends in one quarter, it may substantially reduce the population of investors who are eligible to buy or hold its common stock.

## Corporate Dividend Practice

One consideration is the desire to have a relatively stable dividend; the second is the desire to pay out, in the long run, a given fraction of earnings. This fraction is usually referred to as the payout target. These objectives may be conflicting. Earnings tend to fluctuate substantially from year to year. If a corporation routinely paid out a given fraction of those earnings as dividends, then the dividend itself would tend to fluctuate drastically from year to year or quarter to quarter. These fluctuations would conflict with the objective of maintaining a stable dividend policy. On the other hand, if the dividend is a constant amount, then it will be a fluctuating proportion of earnings.

Assume that a corporation starts with a dividend target. If earnings are stable, then the dividend is unlikely to be changed. However, if earnings are increasing, then, with a constant dividend, the payout ratio will gradually decrease. If the increase in earnings is expected to be temporary, for example, as a result of some extraordinary event or unusually good business conditions, then it is unlikely that the company will change its dividend. However, if management believes that earnings are likely to be maintained at their new level or to increase even farther, then it is likely that the dividend will be increased. The increase will be in the direction of approaching the amount that the board of directors has set as a target payout ratio. Companies vary the payout ratio they select, and the speed with which they adjust the dividend of a period to changes in earnings; however, they tend to adhere to a target payout ratio. Over long periods of time, this policy tends to result in a dividend payout that is approximately equal to the payout target, but dividends tend to be more stable from year to year than earnings. Another important consequence of this process is that dividend decisions tend to provide information to stockholders about management's forecasts of future earnings. This will be considered in a later section.

Assume that a firm has a large amount of desirable investments and that these investments require more funds than are available internally after dividend commitments have been met. In such circumstances, one or two major alternatives must be chosen if the alternative of changing the dividend policy is thought to be unavailable. The company must either forgo some profitable investments or seek additional funds. On the other hand, if the payout ratio is set too low, relative to the level of earnings and the quantity of profitable investments available to it, the company may either find itself accumulating an unwarranted amount of liquid assets or be tempted to accept investments that are not truly consistent with the objective of maximizing the economic well-being of the stockholders. A company that consistently follows either of these policies is likely to become a target for a takeover bid, since its stock will be depressed compared to its potential value. The disadvantages of too low a dividend payout, relative to the profitable investments available to the company, are more serious from the point of view of the shareholders if the funds are being reinvested at less than competitive rates.

## The Setting of Dividend Policy

Dividend policy is likely to be set in the form of a goal rather than a rigid rule, even though a definite policy has the advantage of providing the investor, or potential investor, a clear basis for choice. Investors knowing the dividend policy of the alternative companies can choose the type of company that best fits their individual investment goals. This is desirable, because stockholders differ in the extent to which they prefer dividends rather than opportunities for capital appreciation. One must remember that, while one group might well prefer capital gains, a second group of zero-tax investors may primarily be interested in dividends. This second group of investors includes universities, foundations, and private pension funds, all of which accrue no special tax advantages from capital gains as distinct from dividends.

Sometimes a company will distinguish between a "regular" dividend and an "extra" dividend. Although this distinction does not have any cash flow significance, it is an important means by which the directors can signal their intentions to stockholders. By labeling part of a dividend payment as an "extra", the directors are indicating that they do not necessarily expect to continue those payments in future years. By declaring the remainder of the dividend payment as a regular payment, the directors indicate an intention to maintain this dividend for the foreseeable future. Extras tend to occur in the fourth quarter of a good earnings year.

## Dividend Changes and Earnings Forecasts

When a dividend increase is logical for a company, given its earnings and its traditional payout target, then the mere fact that an increase has not been declared may sometimes be interpreted as evidence that management does not expect the current level of earnings to be maintained. On the other hand, if a dividend increase takes place at a time when it is not expected on the basis of the company's historical behavior, the financial community may interpret this as evidence that management is more bullish about future prospects for the company than had previously been expected.

## Dividend Policy, Investment Policy, and Financing Policy

The dividend policy of a firm cannot be considered in isolation from its other financial policies. In particular, dividend policy is intimately connected with investment policy and financing policy. When a firm changes its dividend amount, it may, at the same time, have to change one or more of these other policies.

In any particular year, it would be surprising if the amount of cash generated internally and the schedule of available investment opportunities were exactly as anticipated. Thus, some temporary adjustments are needed. The firm can adjust either its dividend policy, its financing policy, or its investment policy. It will try to make the adjustments that are least costly to its long-term objectives.

Except as a last resort, a firm will not reduce a well-established dividend amount as a means of coping with a temporary shortage of cash. On the other hand, a one-time special dividend might be used to cope with a temporary surplus of funds if a dividend increase could be labeled as an "extra".

For industrial firms, changes in the amount of investments are the most common method of adjustment. In some cases, this can be done at relatively low cost by delaying the start of new long-term investment projects. Another alternative is to temporarily increase or decrease working capital.

## Irrelevance of Dividend Policy

Dividend policy is not relevant in determining the value of a firm if some well-defined conditions are met. The conditions are:

1. Perfect capital markets (including rational investors, perfect information available to all, certainty).
2. No transaction costs.
3. No personal taxes.
4. The investment policy of the firm is set. The amount invested is not determined by the dividend policy, but rather by the cost of equity capital.

Later we shall consider the consequences of relaxing some of these assumptions. First, we examine the impact of dividend policy on valuation assuming that these conditions hold. Let $S_t$ denote the market value of the common stock (after the investment) at time $t$, $k_e$ denote the cost of equity capital, $C$ denote actual cash generated internally over the next period, and $Q$ denote the amount of financing required to meet cash needs for the investment program. If $Q$ is larger than $C$ and no dividends are paid, $Q - C$ will have to be raised by a new equity issue. The current market value of the common stock will be

$$S_0 = \frac{S_1}{(1 + k_e)} - \frac{(Q - C)}{(1 + k_e)} = \frac{S_1 - Q + C}{(1 + k_e)},$$

where the term $S_1/(1 + k_e)$ is the present value of next period's market value and $(Q-C)/(1+k_e)$ is the amount of new equity funds. We interpret $(Q-C)/(1+k_e)$ to be the present value of the new capital that will have to be supplied by the common stockholders as a group. It is inconsequential whether existing or new equityholders provide $(Q - C)$ of financing.

Now consider the impact of a cash dividend of $D$ paid one period from now to the existing stockholders; if $D$ is paid, $Q - C + D$ will have to be raised by a new issue of common stock in order to undertake the desired investments.

## Income Taxes and Dividend Policy

The income taxes of stockholders should affect the dividend policy of a firm. To help you understand these tax implications, we shall first examine the importance of tax deferral and then show the impact of having two different tax rates, one for ordinary income and one for capital gains.

Rational stockholders should value a stock based on the after-tax returns they expect to receive from owning it. The tax status of the return depends on the form in which it is received. For a high-tax stockholder, the marginal tax rate on such income can be high when both state and federal income taxes are considered. High-tax individuals are the beneficial owners of a large fraction of all stock outstanding, but the stock may be owned indirectly through mutual funds or trusts.

The returns received by pension funds and by other nontaxable entities are not subject to either ordinary income or capital gains taxes. Payments made by the pension funds to pensioners may be taxable to the pensioner, but the amount of the tax on the distribution will not depend on whether the pension fund received its return in the form of dividends or capital gains. Thus, managers of pension funds can and should value stocks based on the before-tax returns they expect to receive from them.

The provisions of the U.S. tax code tend to lead to high-tax individuals preferring stocks whose returns are in the form of capital gains, among other securities with similar risks and characteristics. Also, by comparative advantage, pension fund holders should find that they can do better by holding stocks whose returns are in the form of dividends. There is some evidence that this occurs in practice.

## *Tax Deferral Advantage*

Consider the effect on the stockholders' wealth at the end of one period if a company, instead of paying $D$ dollars of dividends, retains and reinvests $D$ to earn a return of $r$ after corporate taxes and then pays a cash dividend of $D(1 + r)$ at time 1. This policy will be compared to a policy of paying a dividend of $D$ to the stockholders, having it taxed at a rate of $t_p$, and then having the stockholders invest $D(1 - t_p)$ to earn a taxable return of $r$ for one period or an after-tax return of $r_p$ in a second company. After one period of reinvesting $D$ and earning $r$ as well as a cash dividend, the stockholders will have $D(1 + r)(1 - t_p)$. With a cash dividend of $D$ and then investing to earn $r_p$ on $(1 - t)D$, the stockholders will have after one period

$$(1 - t)D(1 + r_p).$$

The advantage of retention and tax deferral for one period then a dividend compared to an immediate dividend is:

$$\text{Retention advantage} = (1 - t)D(r - r_p).$$

Since $r$ is larger than $r_p$ ($r_p$ is after investor tax), the advantage is in favor of the retention and deferral of tax. As long as $r$ is greater than $r_p$, the advantage will be in favor of retention.

A typical corporation is faced with the fact that it has stockholders with vastly different tax rates. Both pension funds (with zero tax rates) and high-tax investors will own the common stock of the same corporation. This makes it impossible to determine the one tax rate value for the common stockholders for a specific firm. Nevertheless, we can determine the gain or loss to an investor of different dividend policies using the models of this chapter.

## Capital Gains and Tax Deferral Advantages

We shall now assume not only the possibility of tax deferral, but also a capital gains tax rate of $t_g$, where $t_g < t_p$. If $D$ dollars are retained per share instead of being paid as a dividend and are reinvested to earn $r$ after one period, the value of a share will increase by $D(1 + r)$. Also, it is assumed that this gain is taxed at a rate of $t_g$ (implying a sale of the stock) at the end of the one period. After one period with reinvestment by the corporation earning $r$, the stockholder has $D(1 + r)(1 - t_g)$ after the capital gains tax. After one period with an immediate cash dividend and then reinvestment to earn $r_p$, the stockholder will have

$$D(1 - t_p)(1 + r_p).$$

The advantage of retention taxed at a capital gains rate compared to dividends taxed at ordinary income rates is now:

Deferral and capital gains advantage $= D(1 + r)(1 - t_g) - D(1 + r_p)(1 - t_p).$

## Example

Let us compute the deferral advantage of a corporation reinvesting $100 for one year to earn 0.10 compared to paying a dividend of $10. The stockholders can earn 0.08 on external investments and do not need current funds. Assume that the personal marginal tax rate on ordinary income is 0.30. The advantage of retaining for one period, compared to an immediate dividend, is:

Retention advantage $= (1 - t)D(r - r_p) = (1 - 0.30)100(0.10 - 0.08) = \$1.40.$

The retention alternative yields $7.00 to the stockholders at the end of the year compared to $5.60 if the dividend is paid.

If capital gains are taxed at 0.20 and if the retention of $D$ leads to a capital gain of $D(1 + r)$, we would have an advantage of retaining for one period as:

$$\begin{aligned}
\text{Retention advantage} &= D(1 + r)(1 - t_g) - D(1 + r_p)(1 - t_p)\\
&= 100(1.10)(1 - 0.20) - 100(1.08)(1 - 0.30)\\
&= 88 - 75.60 = \$12.40,
\end{aligned}$$

with the retention alternative yielding $88 to the stockholders at the end of the year compared to $75.60 if the dividend is paid.

## Cost of Retained Earnings and New Capital

Because of taxes, the cost of retained earnings is less than the cost of new equity capital. The cost of retained earnings is the return that retained earnings would have to earn on reinvestment in order for stockholders to be indifferent between the immediate receipt of the funds as a dividend and their retention. We assume zero transaction costs.

To calculate the cost of retained earnings, we examine the change in stockholders' wealth under the assumption that if reinvestment takes place at an after-corporate-tax return of $r$ leading to a value of $(1 + r)$, the entire proceeds to the investor are then taxed as ordinary income. The after-tax change in stockholders' wealth after one time period will be

$$(1 + r)(1 - t_p)$$

per dollar of reinvested funds.

If the dividend payment were to take place immediately and, after payment of ordinary income taxes on it at rate $t_p$, the residual funds were reinvested in another security of equivalent risk earning $r_p$ after personal tax, the net change in stockholders' wealth per dollar of dividend paid is

$$(1 - t_p)(1 + r_p),$$

where $r_p$ is the after-investor-tax return on the invested funds.

Define the cost of retained earnings, $r$, to be the rate of return that the firm must earn on reinvested funds for stockholder indifference between a dividend and retention. Let us equate the after-tax change in stockholder wealth per dollar of funds under the two alternatives:

$$(1 + r)(1 - t_p) = (1 - t_p)(1 + r_p).$$

Solving for $r$, we find that $r = r_p$. It can be shown that this result is independent of the number of time periods. If the firm can earn the same return as stockholders can earn after tax with the same risk, stockholders would be indifferent between having the firm pay a dividend and reinvest the funds — this is the definition of the cost of retained earnings.

If new capital is being obtained, the investor has a choice between having $1 in hand or investing in a firm that will earn $r$ and pay $r$ dividends with an after-tax present value of $\frac{r(1-t_p)}{r_p}$. Equating the two alternatives and solving for $r$, we now have

$$1 = \frac{r(1 - t_p)}{r_p}$$

$$r = \frac{r_p}{1 - t_p}.$$

With retained earnings, the cost of stockholders' equity capital was $r_p$. With new capital being obtained, the cost of stockholders' equity has now increased to $\frac{r_p}{1-t_p}$.

Having established the fact that the cost of stockholders' equity depends on whether the firm is retaining earnings, $r = r_p$, or obtaining new capital, $r = \frac{r_p}{(1-t_p)}$, we could next introduce capital gains taxes and the decision by the investor to hold or sell. These factors will also affect the cost of equity capital. Thus, the cost of equity capital, rather than being one easily determinable number, is a function of the tax law and the decisions of investors.

The solution offered above is an approximate solution since corporations will typically pay dividends and retain earnings simultaneously. More complex models would have to be used to obtain measures applicable to specific situations. However, the above equation does illustrate the fact that the cost of stockholders' equity funds depends on the source of the capital as well as on the dividend policy of the firm.

## Dividends: The Clientele Effect

Theory says that zero-tax investors will prefer high-dividend-yield stocks, whereas the high-tax investors will prefer high-growth stocks. This implies that dividend policy will affect the types of investors (the clientele) who will own a company's stock.

## Reasons for Dividends

There are several good reasons for a firm to pay dividends. Some of these have been illustrated in the models of the preceding sections. These reasons include:

1. The firm generates more cash internally than can be profitably reinvested.
2. Dividends provide stable "income" to investors (they can plan assuming the dividends will be paid).
3. The Internal Revenue Service penalizes unnecessarily retained earnings.
4. Transaction costs associated with an investor selling stock make dividends less costly if the investor needs cash income.
5. Changes in dividends have information for investors.
6. Legal lists (eligible securities for trusts) require a record of dividend payments.

7. Some investors pay zero taxes, and there is no tax advantage in deferred income taxes to this group.
8. If a firm is currently paying a dividend, it is difficult to stop without hurting some stockholders.
9. Nonpayment of dividends may encourage "raiders".
10. A market that heavily discounts the risky future (reflecting a high degree of uncertainty) will value current dividend payments more than future dividend payments.

The primary arguments against dividends are that retained earnings save flotation costs compared to a new issue, and that the payment of a dividend causes the stockholder to be taxed at ordinary rates on the amount of cash received. Since some investors prefer to defer taxes, one way to do so is to have the firm retain and reinvest earnings. Furthermore, there may be a tax advantage in taking capital gains rather than dividend income.

In addition to cash dividends, there are also:

1. Stock dividends (more shares are issued to each shareholder in proportion to holdings).
2. Repurchases of stock (a cash distribution to a self-selected group of stock-holders).
3. Liquidating dividends (this may include a return of capital).

Stock dividends are not actually dividends; rather, they represent a change in the description of the ownership (a change in the number of shares). The repurchase of stock by a corporation differs from a cash dividend in terms of the tax consequences and in that the cash is not distributed equally to all stockholders (it only goes to those stockholders who sell their stock).

## Repurchase of Shares

In the past two decades, major U.S. corporations have increasingly repurchased significant amounts of their own common shares. The reasons for this development and its implications for the theory of share valuation and public policy, however, have been subject to numerous, and often conflicting, interpretations. This chapter presents an analysis of the economics of share repurchasing, which leads to some fairly definite conclusions concerning the questions of share valuation.

The repurchase of shares is not legal under all codes of law; but in the countries where it is legal, it opens up a variety of opportunities for gains for the stockholders. In many situations, the motivation will be perfectly legitimate (a desire to shrink the size of the firm, with desirable consequences as to who receives the cash distribution), but it is also possible for one group to use this device to take advantage of information that is not available to the remainder of the investing public. The repurchase of shares is not uncommon and, barring changes in legislation, is likely to accelerate in the future.

During the past 20 years, corporations have acquired significant amounts of their own shares of common stock. The repurchase of common stock has been said to have been motivated by many factors. Among these are:

1. Repurchased stock is used by the corporation for such reasons as mergers and acquisitions of firms, stock options and stock purchase plans, and so on.
2. Stock repurchase is a form of investment.
3. Repurchasing stock increases the amount of financial leverage employed by the firm.
4. Stock repurchase is a form of dividend, and, as a form of dividend payment, stock repurchase has favorable tax consequences compared with ordinary dividends.
5. Stock repurchase can lead to a change in ownership proportions (maintenance of control being the objective).
6. By taking advantage of special information, stock repurchase can improve the wealth position of certain stockholders.
7. Stock repurchase is a method of shrinking the size of the firm (a form of liquidating dividend).
8. Repurchasing stock compared to a cash dividend may improve financial measures such as earnings per share and, consequently, the price of the stock.
9. Different expectations held by the firm and the market can lead, through repurchase, to improving the wealth position of certain stockholders.
10. Stock repurchase will increase stock price through time.

We shall consider each of these reasons separately, even though several of them are interrelated.

## Repurchase of Stock for Use by the Corporation

Corporations use shares of their own stock for several purposes, including the acquisition of other corporations. However, this is not a complete explanation as to why a corporation reacquires its own shares, since a corporation is generally able to issue new shares for the types of purposes for which the shares are acquired.

There may be valid reasons why a corporation does not want to issue additional shares, hence reacquiring shares for reissue. But it is these other reasons that are relevant, not the fact that the shares are going to be used by the corporation.

## Stock Repurchase as an Investment

A corporation cannot "invest" in its own shares. With normal investments, cash is converted into working assets. Profitable investments increase the size of the firm, and while they may be accompanied by increases in the debt or equity accounts, they are never accompanied by decreases in these accounts. However, if a firm repurchases its own shares, there is disinvestment by the corporation. With the firm's acquisition of its own shares, the assets decrease as cash is used, and the stockholders' equity also decreases. The corporate entity does not make an investment when shares are acquired.

It is possible for one group of stockholders to benefit and one group to be harmed by the repurchase of shares. The group not selling may increase the size of its investment in the firm compared to the investment of the selling group, but this is not the same as saying that the firm is investing. The term *invest* must be reserved for situations where the firm is actually committing resources to productive activities rather than a situation where the firm is becoming smaller as the result of an action.

The fact that the process of stock repurchase is not "investing" does not mean that the utilization of funds to purchase (retire) outstanding stock may not be the best use of the funds from the viewpoint of some or all of the stockholders.

## Increases in Financial Leverage

The repurchase of shares will lead to an increase in the ratio of debt to total stockholders' equity employed and will thus increase the amount of financial leverage. However, this cannot be the sole explanation of the stock repurchase process, since a cash dividend of the same amount would have an identical leverage effect. The explanation must be found elsewhere.

## A Form of Dividend

Stock repurchase is a special type of dividend. If there were no separate tax treatments between ordinary income and capital gains, and if a proportionate number of the shares were acquired from all stockholders, the economic effects would be almost identical for stock repurchase as for a cash dividend (the number of shares outstanding would change, but this would be the only difference).

If the stock is not acquired proportionately from all investors, stock repurchase is a special type of dividend, since it goes only to the stockholders who prefer cash compared to increased ownership. Those stockholders preferring to increase their investment compared to receiving cash do not sell. The self-selectivity of the process is an advantage for the stockholders as a group.

The foregoing conclusion assumes zero taxes. Once taxes are considered, stock repurchase is advantageous. The tax savings to stockholders of a stock repurchase compared to a cash dividend may be sizable. Suppose an investor owns and sells stock for $1,200 with a tax base of $1,000. The marginal tax rate for ordinary income is 35 percent and for capital gains, 15 percent. With a $1,200 cash dividend, the stockholder would net out $780 (the tax would be $420). With the $1,200 disbursed in the form of a stock repurchase, the stockholder would net out $1,170 (the tax would be $30 on a capital gain of $200).

The advantage of repurchase over ordinary dividend distribution is present for two reasons. First is the difference between the two tax rates. The second reason: with the repurchase plan, part of the payment is considered a repayment of principal tax purposes and so is not taxed at all. Although systematic repurchase over time would eventually drive the cost base close to zero, the present value methodology weighs the early tax savings high, and so the difference between systematic repurchase and ordinary dividend is still consequential when both capital gains and ordinary income are taxed at the same rate. If both personal and corporate tax rates were zero, either method of income distribution would lead to the same intrinsic value. The introduction of tax considerations, however, can affect the value of different "packages".

Tax laws can provide powerful incentives for firms with liquid assets available for distribution to purchase shares rather than pay larger dividends. Many persons will prefer capital gains to ordinary income if the marginal rate of taxation on ordinary income is large while the rate on long-term capital gains is small.

Given these incentives for returning cash to stockholders by repurchasing shares, a relevant question would seem to be: Why do firms ever pay dividends? An important reason is that there are significant investors who pay zero taxes. The second explanation is related to the attitude of the Internal Revenue Service toward share repurchasing. The current Internal Revenue Code clearly seeks to prohibit firms from disguising dividends in the form of share repurchases. Proportional repurchases from all shareholders, for example, are treated the same as dividends for tax purposes.

## Control

It is not clear that repurchasing will facilitate the retention of control. For instance, if two competing groups each owned 40 percent of the stock before the repurchase, they might well own 40 percent after the company acquires 10 percent of the shares. However, if one of the competing groups were to sell its stock to the corporation, this would alter the situation. But, in general, stock repurchase is not an effective means of beating off a raider unless the stock is actually purchased from the raider, from those stockholders most likely to sell to the raider, or from those stockholders most likely to support the raider rather than the incumbent group. In fact, the decrease in the number of the shares outstanding might make it easier for the raider to negotiate with the remaining stockholders. Thus, the control factor is not likely to be significant with a large corporation, unless the firm can identify those parties likely to sell. However, debt issuance combined with stock repurchase can discourage a raider. For example, a company, by borrowing up to its debt capacity and acquiring its own shares with the proceeds, could discourage a raider who was relying on the firm's debt capacity to increase value.

## Special Information

If one group of stockholders has special optimistic information (say, they are closely associated with management), then this group could have the corporation buy stock at the expense of the group that did not have the information and would, consequently, be willing to sell at a low price. Using special information in this manner would seem to be, at best, unethical, and is likely to be illegal. If stock is to be acquired, this information should be made known to the stockholders as well as the reasons why the stock is to be acquired. One group of stockholders should not be free to take advantage of another less well-informed group.

## Shrinking the Size of the Firm

If the objective is to shrink the size of the firm, the tax-effect rationale for using stock repurchase compared to cash dividends holds. Although shrinkage can be accomplished by a cash dividend, stock repurchase leads to part of the return being treated as a tax-free return of capital and the residual gain is taxed at a capital gain rate rather than ordinary income tax rates.

## Improving Financial Measures

The effect of stock repurchase on financial measures and the stock price is evidently of interest to the stockholders. We shall attempt to determine the conditions under which changes in the measures take place and how the stock price is affected.

1. *Book value*: If the market price paid for the common stock is less than the current book value, the book value per share will increase for the remaining shares. However, if the market price is more than the book value, the book value will decrease. It would be surprising if such changes in book value are sufficient justification for acquiring shares.

2. *Earnings per share and market price of stock*: Earnings per share will change if the firm reacquires shares rather than pays a cash dividend. Since $D$ is going to be distributed with either a dividend or share repurchase, the firm's future earning stream is unaffected but earnings per share will be higher if the repurchase strategy is followed. Although the earnings per share will be higher under repurchase, fewer shares will be outstanding, and one would expect the total value of the common stock to be the same under either strategy. If the value of the firm and the earnings are both unaffected, then the firm's price/earnings multiple is unaffected. Applying the same price/earnings multiple to the higher earnings per share, however, leads to a higher market price per share.

It is worthwhile to comment on the tax-related rationale for repurchase. Although the Internal Revenue Service does not allow the distribution to be treated as a capital gain if the firm repurchases stock pro rata (so that ownership proportions do not change), it does evidently allow less structured forms of repurchase (e.g., open market purchases or tendering) to be treated as a capital gain.

There is also another factor that may influence the method of distributing cash. Suppose you are the manager of a firm, and you have a stock option to buy the stock at $15 with the current market price being $12 (this is the expected price before the cash distribution). If a $2 cash dividend is paid, it can be expected that the price of the stock will fall to about $10 (the EPS is $1 and the price/earnings multiple is 10). If shares of the stock are acquired, the number of shares will decrease and the stock price will be larger than $10. A series of stock repurchases will tend to drive the price of the common stock upward compared to the price with a cash dividend and make it easier for the stock option to be exercised under favorable circumstances. Thus, stock repurchase is a logical strategy for firms whose policies are administered by managers holding stock options. Retaining earnings rather than paying cash dividends is still another desirable strategy tending to increase the price of a share of stock higher than it would be if the cash were distributed as a cash dividend.

## *Different Expectations*

A situation may arise in which the market assesses the value of the stock differently from management's assessment because of different expectations. If management thinks that the stock is underpriced, repurchasing of the stock will benefit those who continue to hold the stock if management's assessment is proved correct.

If management is correct, the firm can repurchase stock at any price less than what it believes to be the intrinsic value without harming the financial position of those who do not sell. If management is incorrect (overly optimistic), the extent to which the stockholders who do not sell are harmed is determined by the spread between the repurchase price and the market price.

## A Flexible Dividend

One advantage of stock repurchase in lieu of cash dividends is that investors who do not want to convert their investments into cash do not sell their stock back to the corporation. By not selling, they avoid realization of the capital gain and they do not have any taxation on the increment to the value of their wealth (they also avoid possible transaction costs).

The investors who want to receive cash sell a portion of their holdings, and even though they pay tax on their gains, this tax is apt to be less than if the cash distribution were taxed as ordinary income. By using stock repurchase as the means of the cash distribution, the company tends to direct the cash to those investors who want the cash and bypass the investors who do not need cash at the present time.

## The Stock Price Effect of Share Repurchase

Assume a corporation with $N$ shares outstanding buys $p$ of its stock each year. The immediate stock price effect is zero, but after one year there will be $(1-p)N$ shares outstanding rather than $N$ and the stock price will be higher with share repurchase than without it.

## Example

Assume a firm has 100,000 shares outstanding with a market capitalization of $2,000,000. The market price of a share is $20. The company buys 5,000 shares ($p = 0.05$) at a cost of $100,000.

The new stock price is:

$$\text{Price} = \frac{2,000,000 - 100,000}{95,000} = \$20.$$

The stock price is not changed. Assume the firm value after one year is again $2,000,000. The new value per share is:

$$\text{Price} = \frac{2,000,000}{95,000} = \$21.05.$$

The growth rate in stock price is:

$$G = \frac{p}{1-p} = \frac{0.05}{0.95} = 0.0526.$$

After ten years the stock price would be (with no other changes):

$$P_{10} = 20(1.0526)^{10} = \$33.39.$$

To this point, it was assumed that the firm had zero real growth. Now assume the real growth is $g$ per share. The growth rate of the stock price with $p$ shares purchased each year is:

$$G = \frac{g+p}{1-p}.$$

These relationships are important to managers possessing stock options with given exercise prices.

## Conclusion

Two public policy questions concerning corporate share repurchasing are apparent. First, should firms be allowed to buy back their own shares, and, if so, should they be required to give stockholders advance notice of their intentions?

Repurchasing shares can have a significant impact on the after-tax returns of stockholders. Should the form of the firm's distribution, rather than its substance, influence the amount of taxes paid by stockholders? It seems clear that as more and more firms become aware of the advantages of repurchasing shares compared with paying dividends, this issue is increasingly relevant.

Should corporations that decide to repurchase shares be required to notify stockholders of their intention? The value of the firm's stock is a function of the form of its cash distributions. Thus, it seems reasonable that shareholders should be advised of a company's distribution policy and of changes in that policy. A corporation that has repurchased shares without giving its stockholders advance notice would be implicitly placing those investors who sell their shares without this information at a disadvantage.

Corporations have offered many reasons for acquiring their own common stock. In this chapter, we listed a number of reasons and then proceeded to examine each of those reasons in turn. Two factors are of prime importance: tax effects and expectational differences between the market and management. The other explanations offered for repurchase are relatively weak.

It is very easy for a situation to develop where one group of stockholders benefits at the expense of another group; thus, a stock repurchase program must be administered with care if the attainment of a position where all stockholders are treated fairly is desired.

Under very special conditions, which are not likely to hold in the real world, the market value of a firm's stock is independent of its dividend policy. With more realistic assumptions, different firms might wish to adopt different dividend policies depending on the economic and behavioral characteristics of their stockholders.

## Questions and Problems

1. Assume that the ABC Company is earning $2 currently, is paying an $0.80 dividend, and will continue to have a 40-percent dividend payout policy in the future. All reinvested funds will earn 0.08. The stockholders require a 0.10 return on their investment and are not taxed.

   a. What is the value of a share of common stock?
   b. What would the value be if the optimal dividend strategy was followed and a $2 dividend could be maintained?
   c. If reinvested funds could earn 0.15, what would be the value of a share of common stock with the 40-percent payout policy?
   d. What would you expect to happen to $r$ if more funds were reinvested?

2. On a "per dollar of potential dividend per period" basis, calculate the advantage of (a) deferring one period and (b) deferring one period and taxing at capital gain rather than ordinary rate if the yield on reinvested funds is 20 percent, the personal tax rate on ordinary income is 60 percent, and the capital gains tax rate is 25 percent.

3. Suppose that you did not know the tax situation of the holders of your common stock, but were able to ascertain that the average personal tax rate was about 40 percent. Assume that the cost of equity for comparable common stocks is 0.12 ($k_e = 0.12$).

   What could you conclude to be the cost of retained earnings?

4. In discussing a policy of issuing annual stock dividends, a corporate public utility manager stated:

   "The stock dividend plan has done a good job for us, helping to finance our expansion, eliminating public offerings of our common stock, and enabling us to retire our preferred stock. It also made debt financing unnecessary."

   Evaluate the manager's statements.

5. The ABC Company could pay out all of its earnings as dividends; however, it wants to choose between a policy of paying out dividends as the income is earned (now and for the next three years) or alternatively reinvesting all of its earnings and paying one dividend three years from now. With no additional retained earnings, the firm can maintain a dividend of $100 per share.

   Stockholders can earn 0.10 by investing any dividends received. These earnings are subject to tax.

   Assume that capital gains and ordinary income are both taxed at a rate of 0.6.

   a. ABC has many one-period investments that yield 0.08. Should the firm invest or pay a current dividend? Find the future value of stockholders' wealth three years from now.
   b. How low a yield can an investment have and still be acceptable to the firm?
   c. Assume the firm has investments yielding 0.10. What is the improvement in value arising from retaining for one year compared with a $100 dividend?

6. It has been argued that it makes no difference whether a firm pays dividends or retains the earnings, since the value to the stockholders is the same for both.

   For example, assuming a 0.4 tax rate and an ability to find a stock that is growing at a before-tax rate of 0.10, if $100 is paid as a dividend, the investor will have after one period

$$\$100(0.6)(1.10) = \$66.$$

   If the funds are retained and invested internally to earn 0.10, and then paid as a dividend after one period, the investor will again have

$$\$100(1.10)(0.6) = \$66.$$

   Comment on the illustration.

7. The Tax Court decided several years ago that increases in the value of endowment policies under certain circumstances are income. The court drew a distinction between endowment policies and other assets such as stock whose appreciation reflects price changes over time. The gain in value of an endowment policy results from the annual addition to the investment fund of the earnings on the investments, and the gain is not directly related to price changes.

   Comment on the distinction.

8. The Big Oil Company's treasurer explained his company's dividend policy (a low dividend compared to earnings) by stating that "the stockholders did nothing to earn the money" and that "if the stockholders did not like the present policy, they could sell the stock."

   Discuss the statements.

9. A public utility announced a new plan whereby the full amount of earnings would be paid to the stockholders, the current cash dividend per share would be kept constant, and the remainder of the dividend would be in the form of a stock dividend. This policy would enable the firm to "retain and reinvest in the business a higher percentage of our earnings than we would retain under our past dividend policy and help us to finance our expansion program and cut down, if not eliminate, the need for periodic offerings of additional common stock."

   Evaluate the policy.

10. Jane Doe (zero tax) expects ABC Company to begin paying dividends on an annual basis at the end of two years. She expects the first annual dividend to be one dollar and further expects dividends to grow continuously at a rate of 4 percent thereafter. What is the maximum price she would be willing to pay for the stock today if she wants to earn at least 12 percent on her investment?

11. a. If an investor can earn 0.08 by investing in tax-exempt bonds, a corporation investing in comparable risk investments would have to earn what minimum return(s) after corporate tax to justify retention? Assume that the investor is in a 0.55 tax bracket for ordinary income and that all income from the corporation will be received in the form of cash dividends.

    b. If new capital is raised and if the investment banker takes 0.10 of the price paid by the investors, the investment made by the corporation must earn _____ after corporate tax.

12. Company XYZ has found itself with $5 million of unneeded cash, and the firm's president has indicated that he will suggest the board of directors declare an "extra" dividend of $5 per share on the million shares outstanding. The current stock price is $45 per share and current annual earnings are about $8 per share (excluding interest income on the $5 million held currently in the form of a certificate of deposit).

    The market price of $45 appears to be comprised of a basic P/E ratio of 5 on the current earnings plus the anticipated extra $5 million to repurchase stock. The firm's investment banker indicates that a purchase price of $50 per share on a tender offer would be sufficient to attract 100,000 shares for repurchase.

Assume that the P/E ratio that would be adopted by the market after the reacquisition is again 5. *Assume a zero-tax, zero-transaction-cost world.*

a. Which of the two plans (stock acquisition or dividends) should the stockholders prefer? Why?

b. If you, the corporate president, held stock options, which of the two plans would you prefer? Why?

13. The ABC Company has earned $10. It is thinking of paying a cash dividend of $10 per share. Its stockholders would be taxed at a 0.55 rate on ordinary income and 0.20 on capital gains. The stockholders can earn a 0.05 return after tax per year.

    The alternative to the cash dividend is to retain for 10 years, and then pay a cash dividend. The firm can reinvest for 10 years and earn 0.12 per year after corporate taxes.

    a. How much will an investor have after 10 years with a cash dividend now?

    b. How much will an investor have after 10 years if the first dividend is at time 10?

    c. How much will an investor have after 10 years if the first dividend is at time 10 and if the investor sells before the stock goes ex-dividend (i.e., the dividend goes to the buyer of the stock)? Assume that a dollar of retained earnings results in a dollar of stock price increase.

    d. Assume that the corporate tax rate is 0.46. If the capital had been classified as debt and if the $18.52 of before-tax income were paid as interest, how much would the investor have after 10 years?

14. Investors can earn 0.12 after personal tax (e.g., investing in tax-exempt bonds). Their marginal tax rate on ordinary income is 0.55.

    a. What return (after corporate tax) does a corporation have to earn so that the investors are indifferent to receiving a cash dividend now and a cash dividend at time 1?

    b. Answer (a) if the deferred dividend will be deferred and will be paid 10 years hence.

    c. If the corporation wants to invest new capital obtained from the investors, it has to earn at least _____. Assume that a dividend will be paid at time 1.

*Chapter 11*

# Capital Structure: Weighted Average Cost of Capital (WACC)

Capital structure is not an important consideration for management unless taxes and bankruptcy costs are considered. The value of the firm would not be affected by debt leverage if there were no taxes and no transaction costs.

When capital budgeting with time discounting was first introduced in business finance literature in the early 1950s, the common recommendation was that an investment was acceptable if the proposal's net present value was positive using the firm's weighted average cost of capital (WACC) as the discount rate (or equivalently, if the investment's internal rate of return was greater than the firm's weighted average cost of capital). Even today, more business firms are using the firm's weighted average cost of capital as the hurdle rate than any other capital budgeting decision required return. This utilization makes the firm's cost of capital calculation of great importance. Although I do not endorse the general use of the firm's cost of capital in the capital budgeting process as a single hurdle rate, it nevertheless is used; and we should compute it in a reasonable manner.

There is also the question of how the firm's value is affected by the financial mix decision. Four alternative theories deserve consideration:

1. The value of a firm, and the consequent wealth position of the stockholders, is not affected by the type of financing.
2. There is an optimum capital structure, and the utilization of this structure will maximize the value of the firm.
3. Given the present corporate tax laws, a firm should use as much debt as possible to maximize its value and the wealth position of its stockholders.
4. Given the presence of personal taxes as well as corporate taxes, common stock may have tax advantages compared to debt by means of tax deferral as well as preferential treatment of capital gains.

193

In this chapter, we examine and evaluate each of these theories and the role the firm's weighted average cost of capital plays. The key symbols to be used are:

$k_0$ = the weighted average after-tax cost of capital
$k_i$ = the before-tax average cost of debt [$k_i(1 - t)$ is the after-tax cost of debt]
$k_e$ = the after-tax average cost of equity capital
$B$ = the market value of the debt in the capital structure
$S$ = the market value of the stock equity in the capital structure
$V$ = the total market value of the firm [$V_U$ is the value of an unlevered firm; $V_L$ is the value of a levered firm (with $B$ of new debt)]
$t$ = the corporate tax rate.

## Definition

The weighted average cost of capital ($k_0$ or WACC) is defined as the sum of the weighted costs of debt ($k_i$) and equity capital ($k_e$), where the weights are the relative importance of each capital type in the firm's capital structure and the $k_i$ and $k_e$ costs are the expected average returns required by investors as an inducement to commit funds. For simplicity, we consider only one class of debt and common stock. Multiple classes of debt and preferred stock could be included without altering the logic, but the notation becomes difficult to handle.

The market value of the firm is the sum of the market values of the outstanding debt and equity.

$$V = B + S. \tag{11.1}$$

The measures of relative importance of debt and equity in the capital structure are the ratios $\frac{B}{V}$ and $\frac{S}{V}$, respectively. If we use these measures as weights, the after-tax WACC is defined to be

$$k_0 = k_i(1 - t)\frac{B}{V} + k_e\frac{S}{V}. \tag{11.2}$$

In equation (11.2), we have $k_i(1 - t)$, the after-tax cost of borrowing, and $k_e$, the cost of common stock capital, weighted, respectively, by the percentages of debt and common stock capital being used to obtain a weighted average cost of capital.

The WACC of a firm can be interpreted as being the cost of both current capital and an additional dollar of new capital if the existing capital structure is maintained.

## Example 11.1

Suppose that the market value of a company's common stock is estimated at $42 million. The market value of its interest-bearing debt is estimated at $28 million, and the average before-tax yield on the debt is 10 percent per year, which is equivalent on an after-tax basis to 6 percent per year (equal to 10 percent times 0.60, assuming a 40-percent tax rate).

Assume that the company just described is currently paying a dividend of $8 per year and that the stock is selling at a price of $100. The rate of growth of the dividend is projected to be 12 percent per year. One estimate of the cost of the common stock equity is

$$
\begin{aligned}
k_e &= \frac{D}{P} + g \\
&= \frac{\$8}{\$100} + 0.12 \\
&= 0.08 + 0.12 \\
&= 0.20, \text{ or } 20\%.
\end{aligned}
\tag{11.3}
$$

The weighted average cost of capital for the company as a whole is estimated in Table 11.1.

The 0.20 (on stock) and 0.10 (on debt) are the returns that would be required if a mixture of additional debt and common stock were to be issued. The word *average* that is used in the term *weighted average cost of capital* refers to the average of the different types of capital being used. For decisions, we want a weighted average of marginal costs for debt and stock. In situations where the issuance of the debt and common stock will not change the firm's capital structure, the marginal costs may equal the average costs.

Shareholders are exposed to the risk of bankruptcy as soon as debt in some form is introduced. Equityholders may lose their ownership interest in a company that

**Table 11.1.** Estimate of the Cost of Capital.

| Capital Source | Proportion of Total Capital | After-Tax Cost | After-Tax Weighted Cost |
|---|---|---|---|
| Common stock | 0.60 | 0.20 | 0.120 |
| Debt, interest bearing | 0.40 | 0.06 | 0.024 |
| | Weighted average cost of capital | | = 0.144 |

may again become a profitable operation. With a well-managed profitable company in a safe industry, the introduction of a small amount of nonequity capital will presumably increase the risks of bankruptcy by only a small amount. In practice, the legal possibility of bankruptcy is nearly always present, because a company will always have some debt outstanding. As the amount of debt rises, the risks of bankruptcy become greater. Every dollar of debt increases risk. The amount of the increase depends upon the amount of debt and the activities in which a company is engaged.

One advantage of debt capital comes from the financial leverage it provides for the remaining equity capital. However, increases in the debt/equity ratio will increase the year-to-year variability of earnings per share compared to the use of common stock capital. Taken by itself, this is likely to decrease the price per share that investors are willing to pay. However, the issuance of debt will also tend to increase the expected earnings per share, and this hopefully will counterbalance the increased risk.

Another important advantage of debt is that interest expense is deductible by the corporation for purposes of computing taxable income, whereas dividends on common stock are not deductible. With corporate tax rates at approximately 0.35, there is an incentive for firms to use debt as a major component of their capital structure.

It is impossible to give any simple rules for determining the optimum capital structure for a particular firm. Theoretically, the optimum structure is reached when any change in the debt/equity ratio will result in a decrease in the price per share of the common stock. Unfortunately, we do not know how much debt is the correct amount of debt. Optimum capital structure is a "judgment call".

## The Weights

We weight the cost of each type of capital by the percentage that the type of capital is to the total capital. There is a difference of opinion as to whether book values or market values of capital should be used. Those of an academic bent tend to prefer the use of market values. The logic is that the weights should reflect the economic importance of the capital, and not the historical amounts of debt and common stock as recorded by the accountants. Some practitioners favor the book values, since they are objective and tend to be used by other managers (e.g., bankers and bond analysts).

Since the issue is unresolved, a reasonable position for an analyst is to make calculations using both market and book values and let the user of the information decide which calculation is more useful. If only one calculation is being made, we would prefer the use of market value.

## Accumulated Depreciation Is Not Capital

The accounting process includes entries to expense accounts that result in credit entries to accumulated depreciation and tax deferral accounts. Since these entries can affect the calculation of cash flow from operations, it is easy to slip into the error that accumulated depreciation and tax deferral accounts give rise to capital.

## *Example 11.2*

Assume that a firm has the following balance sheet:

| Plant | $1,000 | Common Stock | $1,000 |
|-------|--------|--------------|--------|

During the next period, sales are $200 and depreciation expense is $200. The income is zero. The balance sheet after these transactions we recorded is:

| | | | | |
|---|---|---|---|---|
| Cash | | $ 200 | | |
| Plant | $1,000 | | | |
| Less: accumulated depreciation | 200 | 800 | Common stock | $1,000 |
| | | $1,000 | | |

Note that the capital consists of $1,000 common stock. The $200 of accumulated depreciation is not capital. We could revise the balance sheet and not change the conclusion that the capital is not affected by the accumulated depreciation.

| | | | |
|---|---|---|---|
| Cash | $ 200 | Accumulated depreciation | $ 200 |
| Plant | 1,000 | Common stock | 1,000 |
| | $1,200 | | $1,200 |

The location of the accumulated depreciation account on the balance sheet does not change the conclusion that it is properly considered to be a subtraction from the plant asset account.

## Existence of a Unique Optimal Financial Structure

What happens to the value of $k_0$ if the amount of financial leverage changes?

$$k_0 = k_i(1 - t)\frac{B}{V} + k_e\frac{S}{V}. \tag{11.2}$$

Let us consider how the two cost components of the cost of capital, $k_i$ and $k_e$, react to an increase in financial leverage. Assuming that investors demand more return if their investment is subject to greater risk, we conclude that $k_i$ will increase as more debt is substituted for equity because the payment stream to debtholders becomes more risky. The same logic leads to the conclusion that $k_e$ will also increase as debt is substituted for equity, since the dividend stream accruing to equity becomes more risky as debt obligations increase in size relative to the amount of equity. Furthermore, if investors are adverse to risk for any given degree of financial leverage, $k_i$ is less than $k_e$ since debtholders (as prior claimers) are subject to less risk than are equityholders. Finally, as $\frac{B}{V}$ approaches 1, $k_i$ approaches the cost of equity for zero leverage. This is true, since the most risky position a debtholder could be in is equivalent to that of an equityholder of an all-equity-financed firm. As $\frac{B}{V}$ approaches 1, debtholders in fact become implicit equityholders. Figure 11.1 depicts this assumed behavior of $k_i$ and $k_e$.

The shape of the $k_0$ curve will depend on the shapes of the $k_i$ and $k_e$ curves. The traditional or classical position assumes that $k_i$ and $k_e$ are shaped such that the resultant $k_0$ curve is U- or saucer-shaped, implying that there exists a unique minimum cost of capital structure, as depicted in Figure 11.2. Starting from the observation that most firms in any given industry (firms with roughly the same degree of business risk) tend to have roughly the same capital structure, the traditionalist might argue that $k_e$ rises significantly with increased leverage while $k_i$ begins to rise significantly only after a significant degree of leverage. The weighted average cost of capital initially falls as the leverage is increased, since the rise in $k_e$ is more than offset by the utilization of cheaper debt. At some point, however, the WACC begins to rise as $k_i$ rises more rapidly in response to the increased leverage. It is assumed that there is either a single value or a range of values of $\frac{B}{V}$ that

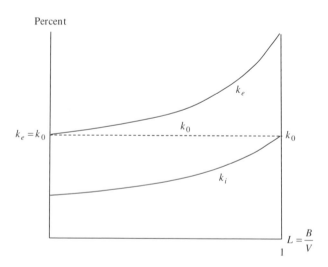

**Fig. 11.1.** A Constant Weighted Average Cost of Capital.

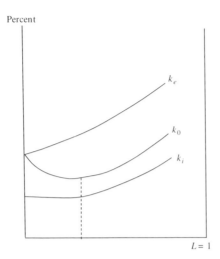

**Fig. 11.2.**    The Classical View of an Optimum Capital Structure.

minimizes $k_0$. It should be remembered that we are initially considering a zero-tax situation and one point of view.

A comprehensive theory for $k_0$ was formulated by Modigliani and Miller (hereafter M&M) in their famous 1958 *American Economic Review* article.[1] With a well-formulated set of assumptions, including no corporate taxes, $k_0$ is a constant, independent of capital structure, and it follows that any capital structure is equally desirable. A constant $k_0$ is illustrated in Figure 11.1.

The M&M position is based on the set of assumptions that (1) markets are perfect, (2) transaction costs are negligible, (3) market behavior is rational, and (4) taxes are zero. With these assumptions, all capital structures are equally desirable.

When corporate taxes (but no personal taxes and no bankruptcy costs) are considered, it can be argued that $k_0$ is a monotonically decreasing function of $\frac{B}{V}$, implying that the minimum cost of capital structure consists of nearly 100 percent tax-shielding debt financing and a minimum of equity financing.

## No Taxes

Let us consider the M&M arguments for the no-corporate-tax case. The perfect market assumption implies that with zero taxes, two nongrowth firms, which pay

---

[1] F. Modigliani and M. H. Miller, "Cost of Capital, Corporation Finance and the Theory of Investments," *American Economic Review*, June 1958, pp. 261–297.

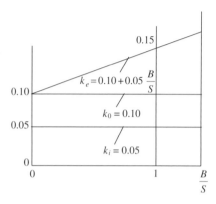

**Fig. 11.3.**　Costs of Capital.

all net income as dividends and are identical in every respect except for capital structure, should have the same market value. The market, as a whole, is purchasing the same future stream of net operating income (EBIT) from both. How that EBIT stream is divided into interest and dividend payments is inconsequential in a perfect market, and the total value of the firm will not be affected by the firm's capital structure. Two identical commodities (in this case, the future net operating income streams) cannot sell for two different prices (market values). The law of one price is assumed to hold. If a value disparity exists, the arbitrage process will remove it. Thus, with zero taxes, the value of the firm ($V$) is independent of the amount of debt, and we can write

$$V = \frac{\text{EBIT}}{k_0},\qquad(11.4)$$

where EBIT is a perpetual earnings stream (earnings before interest and taxes). Solving for $k_0$,

$$k_0 = \frac{\text{EBIT}}{V}.\qquad(11.5)$$

Given the assumptions, any amount of leverage is equally desirable.

The zero-tax M&M position is depicted in Figures 11.1 and 11.3. Given the M&M assumptions, $k_0$ is a constant.

## Example 11.3

Assume that $k_0 = 0.10$ and $k_i = 0.05$ and that these values are not a function of the amount of leverage. The value of the firm is \$10,000,000 and the firm currently has \$2,000,000 of debt and \$8,000,000 of stock. Rearranging equation (11.2) to solve for $k_e$, the cost of equity capital implied by these facts is

$$k_e = k_0 + (k_0 - k_i)\left(\frac{B}{S}\right)$$

$$= 0.10 + (0.10 - 0.05)\frac{B}{S} = 0.10 + 0.05\frac{B}{S}. \qquad (11.6)$$

Since $B = \$2,000,000$ and $S = \$8,000,000$, then

$$k_e = 0.10 + 0.05\left(\frac{2}{8}\right) = 0.10 + 0.0125 = 0.1125. \qquad (11.6)$$

The value of the WACC ($k_0$) is 0.10 (with $t = 0$):

$$k_0 = k_i\left(\frac{B}{V}\right) + k_e\left(\frac{S}{V}\right)$$

$$= 0.05(0.2) + 0.1125(0.8) = 0.01 + 0.09 = 0.10. \qquad (11.2)$$

The values of $k_i$ and $k_e$ for different degrees of leverage are plotted in Figure 11.3 from $B/S = 0$ to $B/S = 1$. In this case, $k_e$ rises linearly with respect to $B/S$.

If the firm substituted \$6,000,000 of debt for \$6,000,000 of stock with $k_i$ unchanged, we would have

$$k_e = 0.10 + (0.05)\frac{\$8,000,000}{\$2,000,000} = 0.30. \qquad (11.6)$$

While $k_e$ increases with increase in debt, the value of $k_0$ remains 0.10:

$$k_0 = \frac{2}{10}(0.30) + \frac{8}{10}(0.05) = 0.10. \qquad (11.2)$$

Other functional forms for $k_i$ lead to different functional forms for $k_e$. Normally, we expect the $k_e$ to be everywhere increasing but not linear, since we would not expect $k_i$ to be a constant with respect to changes in $B/S$.

## A Constant WACC

Let us assume that a substitution of debt for equity will increase the cost of both debt and common stock. Can the substitution be acceptable? Surprisingly, the answer is yes. Even if both costs go up, the substitution of the lower-cost debt can cause the average cost of capital to stay constant.

## *Example 11.4*

Assume that

$$k_i = 0.05 + 0.10\frac{B}{V}$$

and that

$$k_e = 0.15 + (0.15 - k_i)\frac{B}{S}.$$

Assume that the firm has $B = S$ so that $B/S = 1$, $B/V = 1/2$, $k_i = 0.10$, and $k_e = 0.20$. Then, $k_0 = 0.15$:

$$k_0 = 0.10\left(\frac{1}{2}\right) + 0.20\left(\frac{1}{2}\right) = 0.15.$$

Now assume that $B/V = \frac{2}{3}$, $S/V = \frac{1}{3}$, and $B/S = 2$:

$$k_i = 0.05 + 0.10\frac{B}{V} = 0.05 + 0.10\left(\frac{2}{3}\right) = 0.1167$$

$$k_e = 0.15 + (0.15 - k_i)\frac{B}{S}$$

$$= 0.15 + (0.15 - 0.1167)2 = 0.2167.$$

The value of $k_i$ was 0.10, and the value of $k_e$ was 0.20, so the increase in the leverage increases both costs. But the WACC is unchanged. The WACC is again 0.15:

$$k_0 = (0.1167)\frac{2}{3} + 0.2167\left(\frac{1}{3}\right)$$

$$= \frac{1}{3}(0.2333 + 0.2167) = \frac{1}{3}(0.45) = 0.15.$$

Just because debt costs less than common stock does not mean that substituting debt for common stock will reduce the average cost of capital. This is a surprising and very important observation.

## Buying a Combination of Stocks and Bonds to Delever the Firm: No Taxes

We can delever the firm to a zero-debt level. That is, an investment in the above highly levered firm can be made equivalent to an investment in the common stock of a zero-debt firm. The return on investment of $pV$ for a zero-debt firm with the same operating characteristics is $pX$ if the firm earns $X$.

With a levered firm, we have:

| Amount of Capital | Earnings |
|:---:|:---:|
| $B$ | $I$ |
| $S$ | $X - I$ |
| | $X$ |

If the investor buys $p$ of both $B$ and $S$ (a vertical slice), we have:

| Amount of Investment | Earnings |
|:---:|:---:|
| $pB$ | $pI$ |
| $pS$ | $pX - pI$ |
| $p(B + S)$ | $pX$ |

Thus, the investor always earns $pX$ with the levered firm — the same income as with the unlevered firm.

The returns from the investment in both the debt and common stock of the levered firm in the appropriate proportions will always be identically equal to the return from the investment in the common stock of the zero-debt firm, assuming that the operating results of the two firms are identical.

## Levering a Firm

The previous section showed how a firm can be delevered by the investor buying stocks and bonds of the same firm. A firm with too little leverage can also be levered by the use of personal borrowing. Investors substitute their own borrowing capacity for that of the firm to attain the amount of total leverage that is desired.

A third possible way of changing the amount of leverage of a firm is to purchase a combination of firms (one firm with too low and one firm with too high leverage) to obtain a mixture of investment that is equivalent to a medium-levered firm. Thus, if the stock of the medium-levered firm is priced high compared to the other two firms, a mixture of the underpriced securities can be purchased at a lower cost to obtain an investment equivalent to the medium-levered firm. The only limitation of this procedure is the difficulty of finding firms that differ only by capital structure. In practice, a mixture of the extreme firms (very high or very low financial leverage) will not exactly duplicate the medium firm.

## Before- and After-Tax Costs

We want to illustrate the before- and after-tax costs to the issuer of debt, preferred stock, and common stock.

## *Example 11.5*

Let us assume that the corporate tax rate is 0.35, and that investors require the following returns:

$$
\begin{array}{ll}
0.10 & \text{with debt} \\
0.078 & \text{with preferred stock} \\
0.1040 & \text{with common stock}
\end{array}
$$

Remember that preferred stock dividends offer no tax shield to the corporate issuer.

The following table shows the before-tax costs and the after-tax costs of the three different types of capital:

|  | Returns | Before-Tax Costs | Tax | Tax Savings | After-Tax Cost |
|---|---|---|---|---|---|
| Debt | 0.10 | 0.10 |  | 0.035 | 0.065 |
| Preferred stock | 0.078 | 0.12 | 0.042 |  | 0.078 |
| Common stock | 0.104 | 0.16 | 0.056 |  | 0.104 |

Assume that the firm is financed with 0.4 debt, 0.1 preferred stock, and 0.5 common stock. The before- and after-tax costs of capital are:

$$\text{Before-tax WACC} = 0.4(0.10) + 0.1(0.12) + 0.5(0.16) = 0.132$$

$$\text{After-tax WACC} = 0.4(0.065) + 0.1(0.078) + 0.5(0.104) = 0.0758.$$

To pay preferred stockholders 0.078, the firm must earn

$$(1 - 0.35)k_p = 0.078$$

$$k_p = 0.12.$$

For common stockholders to earn 0.104, the firm must earn

$$(1 - 0.35)k_e = 0.104$$

$$k_e = 0.16.$$

An investor who buys a vertical slice of the firm's securities would earn:

$$\text{Return to investor} = 0.4(0.10) + 0.1(0.078) + 0.5(0.104) = 0.142.$$

## Firm Value with Taxes

Assume a corporate tax rate of $t$. With no debt, we have:

| Amount of Capital | After-Tax Return on Capital |
|---|---|
| | $I = 0$ |
| | $X(1 - t)$ |
| $V_U$ | $X(1 - t)$ |

The firm value ($V_U$) is the present value of $X(1 - t)$ or $V_U$.

Now assume the issuance of $B$ debt paying $I$ interest and the $B$ is given to shareholders.

| Amount of Capital | Return on Capital |
|---|---|
| $B$ | $I$ |
| $S$ | $(X - I)(1 - t)$ |

But assume an investor buys all the stock and $(1 - t)$ of the debt and earns $(1 - t)I$ on the debt.

| Amount of Investment | Return on Investment |
|---|---|
| $(1 - t)B$ | $(1 - t)I$ |
| $S$ | $(X - I)(1 - t)$ |
| Sum $\overline{S + (1 - t)B}$ | $\overline{X(1 - t)}$ |

Above we found that $X(1 - t)$ of benefits with zero debt had a value of $V_U$, so

$$V_U = S + (1 - t)B$$

or

$$S + B = V_U + tB.$$

But $S + B = V_L$ where $V_L$ is the value of the leveraged firm, so

$$V_L = V_U + tB. \tag{11.7}$$

If $B$ of debt is substituted for $S$ of stock, the value of the firm increases by $tB$ and the new value of the firm is

$$V_L = V_U + tB. \tag{11.7}$$

In the absence of taxes, capital structure does not affect the value of a firm. If we are to argue that capital structure makes a difference, then we must turn to institutional reasons. One important reason is the tax law. A second reason for capital structure being important is the cost of bankruptcy.

Bankruptcy has costs arising from the court's administration of the corporation's affairs as well as the costs arising from other companies being reluctant to offer credit. Bankruptcy has costs that are not built into the basic models illustrated in this chapter.

## Valuing a Firm: Capital Structure and Corporate Taxes

Let us define $X$ to be equal to EBIT. Then we have:

$$(X - k_i B)(1 - t) = \text{the after-tax return to stockholders (assume that it is all paid as dividends to stockholders)}$$
$$k_i B = \text{the interest paid to debtholders.}$$

The total cash flows accruing to capital suppliers will be the sum of the dividends plus interest payments:

$$(X - k_i B)(1 - t) + k_i B.$$

This sum can be written as

$$X(1 - t) + (k_i B)t.$$

The return to stockholders with zero debt is

$$X(1 - t).$$

Thus, a levered firm ($B > 0$) has cash flows each period that are larger than those of the unlevered firm ($B = 0$) by $k_i Bt$. Leverage creates an annual corporate tax saving of $k_i Bt$.

Let us define the present value of the cash flows of an unlevered firm to be $V_U$ and equal to the present value of $X(1 - t)$ per period. The value of the levered firm $V_L$ has been shown above to be

$$V_L = V_U + Bt. \qquad (11.7)$$

If a theoretical maximum amount of debt is used so that $B$ equals $V_L$, then

$$\text{Maximum Debt} = \frac{V_U}{1 - t}. \qquad (11.8)$$

If with a corporate tax rate of 0.35 an unlevered firm had a value of $65,000,000, then, with maximum debt, the value of the levered firm would be

$$V_L = \frac{\$65,000,000}{1 - 0.35} = \$100,000,000. \qquad (11.8)$$

Thus, with corporate taxes included in the analysis but without considering personal taxes, the value of the zero-growth firm is maximized by utilizing as much debt as is legally permissible.

An alternative approach to equation (11.8) would be to state that the value of the firm is equal to the discounted value of the expected cash flows accruing to the capital suppliers, where the discount rate used is the borrowing rate, $k_i$, and risk is accounted for by a dollar risk adjustment factor, $R$. Then, for the unlevered firm, the value is

$$V_U = \frac{X(1-t)}{k_i} - R. \tag{11.9}$$

If debt is issued to the existing stockholders, no change in the dollar risk compensation will occur, and the expected cash flows will be

$$V_L = \frac{X(1-t) + k_i Bt}{k_i} - R = V_U + Bt - R. \tag{11.10}$$

If $R$ is not affected by the value of $B$, maximum debt should be issued to maximize the value of the firm. However, the determination of the value of $R$ would not be an easy, well-defined exercise.

## Personal Taxes

The conclusion that the optimal capital structure decision is for the corporation to issue as much debt as is permissible may be modified when we allow the firm to retain earnings and to include personal tax considerations in examining the wealth position of stockholders. This position was strongly argued by M. H. Miller in 1977.[2]

Assume that the primary objective of a corporation is to maximize the wealth position of its stockholders. Dividends received by shareholders are taxed as ordinary income. If the firm retains the earnings instead of paying them as immediate dividends and then reinvests the earnings to earn a competitive return, payment of personal taxes on the dividend is deferred (so the entire earnings rather than the after-tax dividend are reinvested). Furthermore, when the shareholders wish to obtain cash, they can sell stock and pay the capital gains tax on the present value of the reinvestment as viewed by the market rather than having dividends taxed immediately at ordinary income rates. Thus, personal tax considerations for stockholders in high tax brackets exert some pressure for a corporation to use retained earnings to finance growth.

---

[2]M. H. Miller, "Debt and Taxes," *Journal of Finance*, May 1977, pp. 261–276.

With finite investment possibilities and personal tax implications considered, stockholders with high personal tax rates might be better off having the firm use retained earnings rather than debt to finance investment opportunities.[3] While the debt financing would save corporate taxes, the personal tax savings from the use of retained earnings might be greater than the corporate tax savings resulting from the use of debt.

If the debtholders and equityholders are identical groups, tax avoidance by labeling "dividends" as "interest" can be in the owners' best interest. Although there are not exact rules, beyond some ill-defined degree of leverage, interest payments may be treated as dividends by the Internal Revenue Service and their deductibility for tax purposes disallowed.

The optimal financial structure depends in part on the tax circumstances of the shareholders and the dividend policy of the firm, and in part on the corporate tax saving associated with debt financing. No single strategy is optimal for all firms. A "zero-tax-investor"-oriented firm might pay out a large fraction of its income as dividends and employ a high degree of financial leverage (any public utility?) to meet its capital needs, whereas a "growth" firm might plow most of its earnings back and maintain a low degree of financial leverage.

## The Capital Cost of Risk

As risk is increased, the cost of capital can be expected to increase. An extensively used method of adjusting the cost of capital for risk is to use the capital asset pricing model (CAPM). The CAPM makes use of the prices that the market is setting for return-risk trade-offs rather than using subjective measures of attitudes toward risk (such as the risk preferences of specific investors). The capital asset pricing model is a major contribution to modern business finance theory and practice. To understand the CAPM and its limitations, it is necessary to understand the assumptions on which the model is based. It is a single-period model with no assumptions being made about the interaction of return and risk through time. It is assumed that the investor is only interested in the expected return and standard

---

[3]The "accumulated earnings tax" is intended to keep firms from retaining earnings expressly to avoid dividend payments. To be exempt from this onerous tax, the retained earnings must be used to finance active (plant and equipment, working capital) investments rather than passive (marketable securities, real estate) investments. This provision of the tax code has been administered in an inconsistent manner, so it is not always possible to compute the effects of corporate investment decisions on the accumulated earnings tax.

deviation (or variance) of the investment portfolio's outcomes. This is a theoretical deficiency. For some probability distributions, this ignores other information that an investor might consider to be relevant.

It is assumed that all investors must be persuaded to take more risk by the prospect of a higher expected return (they are risk-averse). The actions of an investor do not affect price. The investors are "price takers". The investors can invest at the default-free rate ($r_f$), and generally we assume that they can borrow at the same rate but this assumption is easily dropped. Investors can sell securities they do not own; that is, they can borrow securities to sell them (this is called a short sale). All investors think the same about the expected return and variance of all securities (they have homogeneous expectations), and they are all perfectly diversified.

The quantity of securities to be purchased is fixed and divisible (securities of any dollar amount can be purchased). There are no transaction costs and taxes.

Many of these assumptions could be dropped, and a model very much like the conventional CAPM would be derived. One important function served by this set of assumptions is a simplification of the model so that we are not distracted by unnecessary complexity.

## The Expected Return

Assume that an investor owns the market portfolio. In equilibrium, if we add a very small amount of a new security $i$, the expected return-risk trade-off that results from the inclusion of $i$ must equal the market's current trade-off rate. For this to happen, it can be shown that it is necessary that security $i$'s expected return be equal to

$$\bar{r}_i = r_f + (\bar{r}_m - r_f)\beta_i,$$

where

$\bar{r}_i$ = the equilibrium expected return of security $i$
$r_f$ = the return from the risk-free asset
$\bar{r}_m$ = the expected return from investing in the market
$\beta_i$ = the beta of security $i$, where $\beta_i = \text{cov}(r_i, r_m)/\sigma_m^2$ and is the measure of market risk.

The term $(\bar{r}_m - r_f)\beta_i$ is the adjustment to the risk-free $r_f$ for the risk of security $i$.

The beta measures the amount of systematic risk, that is, the risk arising because of fluctuations in the market return. There is no adjustment for risk specific to the firm (unsystematic risk) in the CAPM, since it is assumed that the unsystematic risk goes to zero given the very large number of investments (the unsystematic components are independent).

The beta of a security measures how the security's return is correlated with the market's return; thus, it is a measure of the security's systematic risk.

## Systematic and Unsystematic Returns

It is conventional theory to separate risk into two components. One component is systematic risk, or market risk that represents the change in value resulting from market value changes. Systematic risk can be somewhat reduced by the choice of securities (low-beta securities). But reducing systematic risk in this way may increase total risk, since the investor's portfolio will not be perfectly diversified. This gives rise to the second type of risk. This is residual or unsystematic risk. This risk is specific to the company (or asset) and is independent of what happens to the other securities. If the investor's portfolio consists of a very large number of securities with no security being a large percentage of the portfolio, then this unsystematic risk can be made to approach zero by a strategy of perfect diversification.

With a portfolio of 10 securities, 90 percent of the unsystematic risk is eliminated. With a portfolio of 100 securities, 99 percent of the unsystematic risk is eliminated. The systematic risk remains.

The CAPM neglects relevant factors that are actually considered by investors. For example, the common stock of electric utilities building nuclear-generating plants could have a negative impact because the CAPM does not take into consideration the specific risk of building nuclear-generating plants, but the market is likely to consider this risk even if it is non-systematic risk.

To the extent that security prices are determined by the activities of the investors who can diversify their portfolios at low cost, the prices of securities will be set in such a way that differentials in expected rates of return will reflect primarily differences in the amount of systematic risk to which the securities are exposed.

While a middle manager might find the risk of a specific asset to be of interest, the top management of a firm will want to know the effect of the asset on the overall risk of the firm. At the investor level, investors should be more interested in the effect of the specific asset on the riskiness of their portfolios than the risk of a specific asset. Managers are likely to be interested in the effect of the specific asset on the risk of their careers.

We find it useful to break down risk into two components: (1) risk that can be eliminated by diversification, which is termed unsystematic risk; and (2) risk that is still present when all unsystematic risk has been eliminated, which is termed systematic risk. The latter reflects how the investments in the portfolio are correlated with the market. Only systematic risk is relevant for a perfectly diversified investor.

The beta of a security measures its systematic risk. This is the risk associated with changes in the market's excess return.

Unsystematic risk can be diversified away. If the portfolio consists of a very large number of securities and no security being a large proportion of the portfolio, the unsystematic risk of the portfolio will approach zero. It does not take many securities for the unsystematic risk of the portfolio to approach zero.

A beta coefficient of unity indicates that a security has the same amount of systematic risk as the market portfolio. A beta coefficient greater (less) than unity indicates that the security is riskier (safer) than the market portfolio. Betas based on actual data are prepared by Merrill Lynch, Wells Fargo Bank, and the Value Line investor service as well as others. These are called historical betas. Fundamental betas would be *ex-ante* estimates based on the capital structure and operating characteristics of the firm.

One important factor should be kept in mind. We are interested in what return the market expects to earn for a given amount of risk. To determine this, we need to know the return that is expected to be earned in the market ($\bar{r}_m$) as well as how the risk of a specific security compares to the risk of the market. The model needs expectations in order to be used correctly. All we shall have are data based on past events that we shall use to estimate the variables that we need. For example, one problem is that the beta will change through time. Also, the value of $r_f$ will depend on the maturity of the government security that is used. It is not easy to use the CAPM in an exact manner.

## Use of the CAPM

Even though the assumptions on which the CAPM is based limit the generality of the model, it is still widely used. Among the uses are:

1. To estimate the cost of equity capital using

$$\bar{r}_i = r_f + (\bar{r}_m - r_f)\beta_i.$$

These estimates may be used as the basis to determine the required return to be earned by a firm's asset.
2. To evaluate securities — if the expected return is larger than

$$\bar{r}_i = r_f + (\bar{r}_m - r_f)\beta_i,$$

the security is a "bargain".

If a security has a larger expected return than the return indicated by the CAPM, all investors (with homogeneous expectations) will buy it until its expected return is lowered to be equal to

$$\bar{r}_i = r_f + (\bar{r}_m - r_f)\beta_i.$$

In like manner, if a security $i$ is expected to earn less than

$$r_f + (\bar{r}_m - r_f)\beta_i,$$

no one will buy (some will sell it short), its price will decrease, and its expected return will increase.

All securities are contained in the market portfolio in proportion to their market value. The beta of the market portfolio is 1.

Industry tends to use a "cost of capital" or a "hurdle rate" to implement the discounted cash flow capital budgeting techniques. Both of these measures are "averages" reflecting average risks and average time value conditions, and cannot be sensibly applied to unique "marginal" situations. There is no reason to think that the weighted average cost of capital can be inserted in a compound interest formula and then be applied to any series of future cash flows to obtain a useful measure of net present value that takes both the time value and risk of the investment into consideration.

The capital asset pricing model offers hope for accomplishing a systematic calculation of risk-adjusted present value. The measure reflects the investor's alternative investment return-risk trade-off opportunities in the same way as the rate of interest on a government bond reflects investment opportunities when there is no default risk. Even where there is a reluctance to accept immediately the specific calculations of the type illustrated in this chapter, there will be a change in the way that management will look at alternatives.

One important limitation of the capital asset pricing model for corporate decision making should be kept in mind. The model assumes that the investors are widely diversified, and, equally important, it assumes that the managers of the firm are willing to make investment decisions with the objective of maximizing the well-being of this type of investor. This means that unsystematic risk (for which the investor is well diversified) may be ignored in the evaluation of investments. It is well known that objectives of firms and managers are multidimensional and that there will be a reluctance to ignore risk because it does not affect the well-diversified investor. The so-called "unsystematic" risk is not something that is likely to be ignored by a management that includes among its objectives the continuity of existence of the firm.

The models we have used here are somewhat simplified. Investors are much more complex in their behavior and markets are less than perfect. Nevertheless, the conclusions reached are relevant and will be the foundation for a great deal of the financial investment models of the future. Investment decision making under uncertainty is not an easy task, but uncertainty is a characteristic of the world and the problem must be faced.

## Conclusion

One amount of debt leverage is preferred to another if moving to that leverage will improve the stockholders' wealth position. But to determine the degree of financial leverage that leads to a weighted average cost of capital that maximizes stockholders' wealth is no easy task.

Although the traditional (or classical) position states that a judicious amount of debt is to be employed, the Modigliani and Miller 1958 paper states that, with well-defined assumptions, any degree of financial leverage is equally desirable (with no corporate taxes).[4] When corporate taxes are considered, it can be argued that the theoretical minimum cost of capital structure is virtually all debt.

Care must be used in taking sides on this controversy. The traditionalists argue their position by noting that firms adopt capital structures substantially less than 100 percent debt and substantially more than 0 percent debt. The Modigliani and Miller zero-tax argument for a value that is independent of capital structure, on the other hand, is clearly spelled out in terms of their assumptions and models. While the latter are correct given their assumptions, their assumptions are worth reconsidering. The extent to which (1) markets are imperfect and (2) equity suppliers discriminate between dividends and capital gains (treated differently for tax purposes), and (3) the fact that there are both corporate and personal taxes, makes it difficult to make the definitive exact statements as to the exact optimum capital structure. Most important, there is general agreement that the different tax treatments awarded to interest and stockholder's earnings affect the relative desirability of debt and stock.

If there were no personal taxes, the use of debt in the capital structure of a corporation would enable a firm to reduce its cost of raising capital since the interest payments are deductible for corporate tax purposes. The desirability of debt compared to common stock is dramatized when the debt is purchased by the common stockholders, since in this situation there is no increase in the risk

---

[4]F. Modigliani and M. H. Miller, "Cost of Capital, Corporation Finance and the Theory of Investments," *American Economic Review*, June 1958, pp. 261–297.

to the investors. One could be led to the conclusion that a firm should issue as much debt as possible, with zero-tax stockholders purchasing the debt if they fear an excessive increase in risk arising from the highly levered capital structure. However, the Internal Revenue Service might limit the amount of this type of debt that a corporation may issue since too much debt may result in the cash distribution being relabeled as dividends.

The addition of debt, even where the debt is a relatively cheap source of capital because of the tax structure, does add risk to the stockholders if the debt is sold to nonstockholders. If there is no taxable income, the full cost of the interest falls on the corporation and ultimately on the stockholders. Thus, we can conclude that the present tax structure offers strong incentives to issue debt, but that there are frequently forces (the risk of bankruptcy and the conventions of the investment banking community) that restrain the corporation considering the issuance of unusually large amounts of debt compared to common stock.

Business managers quite properly want to know how different capital structures affect the cost of obtaining capital. They want to reduce the cost of using the firm's present capital or to reduce the cost to the firm of obtaining new capital.

Although managers may also want to use the weighted average cost of capital as the discount rate (the hurdle rate) in evaluating all investments, we are not enthusiastic about this usage. If the risk of the asset is different from the risk of the firm's other assets, or if the timing of the cash flows is different, using the one risk-adjusted discount rate (the firm's weighted average cost of capital) to evaluate all the investments is not likely to lead to correct decisions.

## Review Problems

### *Review Problem 11.1*

(a) The corporate tax rate is 0.35. Complete the following table.

| | Required Returns | Before-Tax Costs | Tax | Tax Savings | After-Tax Cost |
|---|---|---|---|---|---|
| Debt | | 0.12 | | | |
| Preferred stock | 0.11 | | | | |
| Common stock | 0.14 | | | | |

(b) The after-tax weighted average cost of capital (0.45 debt, 0.15 preferred stock, 0.40 common stock) is

$$\text{WACC} =$$

(c) An investor buying a vertical slice of the firm will earn how large a return if the required returns are earned?

**Solution to Review Problem 11.1**

(a) The corporate tax rate is 0.35.

| | Required Returns | Before-Tax Costs | Tax | Tax Savings | After-Tax Cost |
|---|---|---|---|---|---|
| Debt | 0.12 | 0.12 | | 0.042 | 0.078 |
| Preferred stock | 0.11 | 0.1692 | 0.0592 | | 0.1100 |
| Common stock | 0.14 | 0.2154 | 0.0754 | | 0.1400 |

(b) The after-tax weighted average cost of capital (0.45 debt, 0.15 preferred stock, 0.40 common stock) is

$$\text{WACC} = 0.45(0.078) + 0.15(0.11) + 0.40(0.14) = 0.1075.$$

(c) An investor buying a vertical slice of the firm will earn a return of 0.1265 if the required returns are earned.

$$r = 0.45(0.12) + 0.15(0.11) + 0.40(0.14) = 0.1265.$$

## Questions and Problems

1. Assume a 0.35 tax rate. To pay 0.10 to investors, a company must earn what return (before tax) if the security is:

   a. Debt?
   b. Preferred stock?
   c. Common stock?

   What after-tax internal rate of return must an investment earn for a corporation to supply sufficient cash flows to pay a before-tax (personal) 0.10 to:

   d. Debtholders?
   e. Preferred stockholders?
   f. Common stockholders?

2. (continue 1)

   a. Assuming 0.5 common stock, 0.4 debt, and 0.1 preferred stock, the after-tax WACC of the firm is _____.

b. A zero-tax investor holding the proportion of securities given in (a) would earn _____.

3. Assume that a firm has earned $100 of before-tax income. The corporate tax rate is 35 percent.

   a. If the security used to finance the investment is $1,000 of 10 percent debt, the firm holding the debt (supplying the debt capital) will have _____ after tax.

   b. If the security used to finance the investment is $1,000 of common stock and if the entire after-tax amount of income is paid as a dividend, the zero-tax investor holding the common stock will have _____ after tax.

4. Assume that a company borrows at a cost of 0.14. Its tax rate is 0.35. What is the minimum after-tax cost of capital for a certain cash flow if:

   a. 100 percent debt is used?

   b. 100 percent common stock is used (assume that the stockholders will accept a 0.14 return)?

5. Assume that the return on tax-exempt securities is 0.09 and that $t_p = 0.3$, $t_g = 0.20$, and $t_c = 0.35$, where $t_g$ is the rate on capital gains, $t_c$ is the corporate tax rate, and $t_p$ is the personal tax rate on dividends and interest. Equilibrium conditions exist.

   a. The return to investors on taxable bonds (with equal risk) raised as new capital can be expected to be _____.

   b. The return to investors on common stock (all capital gains) raised as new capital can be expected to be _____.

6. The tax rate for the Gas Corporation is 0.35. The following table has been prepared for the president of the firm.

| | Before-Tax Cost | After-Tax Cost | Capital Structure |
|---|---|---|---|
| Bonds | 0.10 | 0.065 | 0.4 |
| Preferred stock | 0.20 | 0.1300 | 0.1 |
| Common stock | 0.2308 | 0.15 | 0.5 |

   a. Compute the weighted average after-tax cost of capital of the firm, with the given capital structure.

   b. Compute the return before tax for an investor who splits the investment in the company in the same proportion as the sources of capital.

c. If $1,000 of each type of capital were raised, the capital would have to earn before tax:

> Bonds            $_____
>
> Preferred stock  _____
>
> Common stock     _____

7. For a company with zero debt, the cost of the first dollar of debt is 0.10, and the cost of common stock is 0.18 (these are returns required by investors). We have determined that the cost of debt is

$$k_i = 0.10 + 0.08\frac{B}{V}$$

and that there are no taxes and no bankruptcy costs. The capital market is rational and well informed.

a. What is the weighted average cost of capital?

b. Should the next issue of the company be common stock or debt if the objective is to minimize the cost of the capital?

c. What will be the cost of equity if the capital structure has equal amounts of debt and equity?

8. The following facts apply to the XYZ Company:

> Bonds can be issued to yield 0.10.
>
> Preferred stock can be issued to yield 0.08.
>
> Common stock can be issued with an expected yield to stockholders of 0.18.
>
> The tax rates are 0.4 for all sections of this problem.

a. Compute the before-tax cash flows that have to be earned to compensate investors for $1,000 of capital:

(1) Debt.    (2) Preferred stock.    (3) Common stock.

b. Compute the WACC (after-tax) if the capital structure is 0.5 debt, 0.1 preferred stock, and 0.4 common stock.

c. Compute the weighted average return for an investor who invests in the same proportion (for different securities) as the capital structure.

9. Assume the M&M zero-tax model, where $k_0 = 0.14$ and $k_i = 0.10$ for all capital structures (both $k_0$ and $k_i$ are constants).

a. Give the equation for $k_e$.

b. What is the value of $k_e$ if $B = $4$ million and $S = $8$ million?

10. Assume that tax-exempt bonds are being issued at a cost of 0.12 and risk-equivalent taxables at 0.18.

    a. Consistent with the above returns, what is the personal tax rate of the marginal investor?

    b. An investor in tax exempts in the 58-percent tax bracket would earn the equivalent of what before-tax return?

    c. If $10 billion of tax-exempt securities are issued, the annual interest savings to the issuing authorities are _____.

11.

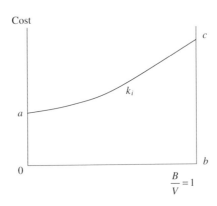

Assume that the $k_i$ curve is correctly drawn. Comment on the following statements or complete them. (There are zero taxes.)

    a. The $k_e$ curve may be below the $k_i$ curve at some point.

    b. The weighted average cost of capital is approximately equal to

    _____.

    c. If the shape of the $k_0$ curve is a horizontal straight line, then logically the $k_e$ curve will have a _____ slope.

    d. If the $k_e$ curve has a positive slope, then the $k_0$ curve must also slope upward.

12. A firm has $10 million of assets to be financed with $6 million debt and $4 million of equity. You have $2 million to invest in the firm. There are zero taxes.

    How would you invest so that your investment is equivalent to investing in an identical firm with 100 percent common stock?

13. A firm is being organized that requires an initial investment of $20 million. You have $200,000 and will buy 0.01 of the common stock if the firm is 100 percent financed with common stock. The use of $8 million of 10-percent preferred stock and $12 million of common stock is being considered.

a. If this capital structure is chosen, what investment strategy should you choose to have the same identical outcomes as investing in the common stock at the 100-percent common stock-financed firm?

b. If the firm earns $900,000, what will you earn if the common stock financing is chosen? What will you earn if the preferred stock financing is chosen and you invest as described in (a)?

14. Encircle one numeral for the correct statement.

a. If with a substitution of debt for common stock the costs of both common stock and debt increase, then the WACC will

    (1) Increase.
    (2) Decrease.
    (3) Stay the same.
    (4) Increase, decrease, or stay the same.

b. If debt is substituted for common stock, one would logically expect the cost of stock equity to

    (1) Increase.
    (2) Decrease.
    (3) Stay the same.
    (4) Increase, decrease, or stay the same.

c. In the absence of bankruptcy costs and corporate taxes, a firm with more debt than the market thinks is rational will sell

    (1) At the same value as an identical firm properly financed (as viewed by the market).
    (2) At less than a firm properly financed.
    (3) At more than a firm properly financed.
    (4) At the same value, or less than, or more than, depending on risk preferences.

15. Assume that for a public utility the following facts and estimates apply and are accepted:

$$k_i = 0.10$$
$$k_e = 0.15$$
$$\frac{B}{V} = 0.2$$
$$t = 0.46.$$

The rate commission thinks that the capital structure should be $\frac{B}{V} = 0.6$ and has made the following calculation for WACC:

$$k_0 = (1 - 0.46)0.10(0.6) + 0.15(0.4)$$
$$= (0.054)(0.6) + 0.06$$
$$= 0.0324 + 0.06 = 0.0924.$$

Briefly evaluate the calculation.

16. The earnings of firms X and Y are identically distributed (they are the same firm except for capital structure). Other facts are:

|  | Market Values | |
| --- | --- | --- |
|  | **Firm X** | **Firm Y** |
| Debt | $0 | $75,000,000 |
| Common stock | 110,000,000 | 25,000,000 |

The cost of the debt is 0.10.

   a. Assume that you are going to invest $1,000,000 in one of the firms. What would be your investment plan if you want your strategy to dominate the alternative of investing in the equity of the other firm?

   b. Explain why your plan is desirable.

17. The planning team of the ABC Insurance Company is trying to organize the capital structure of an acquisition. Both firms are paying income taxes. You are given the choice of two capital structures:

|  | Structure | Structure |
| --- | --- | --- |
| 10% Debt | 60% |  |
| 10% Preferred stock |  | 60% |
| Common stock | 40% | 40% |

ABC will own 0.40 of all securities.

   Which capital structure should the firm prefer? Explain.

18. The ABC Insurance Co. follows a policy of buying the same percentage of common stock as debt. That is, if it buys 0.20 of a company's debt, it will buy 0.20 of the company's common stock.

The Metro Insurance Co. will only buy common stock in companies that have zero long-term debt. All the companies being invested in have the same operating risk.

Assume that there are zero taxes.

Which insurance company has a more risky investment strategy? Explain.

19. Assume that a company borrows at a cost of 0.09. Its tax rate is 0.35. What is the minimum cost of capital for a certain cash flow if:

a. 100-percent debt is used?

b. 100-percent common stock is used (assume the investors accept a 0.09 return)?

20. a. The ABC Company has a simple capital structure. Management wants to substitute $100 million of 0.12 debt for common stock. What effect will the change have on the value of the firm to a zero-tax investor? The corporate tax rate is 0.35.

b. The XYZ Company is thinking of acquiring a firm that is earning before-tax $100,000 a year. XYZ's borrowing rate is 0.10, and its tax rate is 0.46. Thus, its after-tax borrowing rate is 0.65. The investment in the firm will be financed with sufficient debt to cause the amount of income taxes paid to be zero on this investment. What is the maximum amount that XYZ could afford to pay for the firm?

21. The tax rate for The Ithaca Corporation is 0.4. The following table has been prepared for the president of the firm.

| | Before-Tax Cost | After-Tax Cost |
|---|---|---|
| Bonds | 0.10 | 0.06 |
| Preferred stock | 0.12 | 0.072 |
| Common stock | 0.20 | 0.12 |

Only bond interest is deductible for income taxes. The firm has a capital structure of 0.4 debt, 0.1 preferred stock, and 0.5 common stock. Assume that the U.S. Internal Revenue Code applies.

a. Compute the weighted average cost of capital of the firm, with the given capital structure.

b. Compute the before-tax return for an investor who splits her investment in the company in the same proportion as the sources of capital.

*Chapter 12*

# Buy versus Lease

Leasing is one of the most popular means by which corporations finance assets. You name it, you can lease it — atomic fuel for nuclear power plants, hospital equipment, truck fleets, helicopters and 747s — the list is long. The total value of leased assets has been growing at a rate of more than 10 percent per year.

There have been fundamental misunderstandings about the relative merits of buying versus leasing. For example, consider the following issue. If one were indifferent to buying and leasing without considering taxes, would the addition of tax considerations drive the decision in the direction of leasing? If you said "yes" without qualifications, you have something to learn. The above improper leasing versus buying analysis with tax considerations included has probably been somewhat responsible for the tremendous popularity of leasing.

The confusion regarding the lease decision is not helped by the fact that the tax laws keep changing dramatically. Not only is it necessary to be familiar with the specifics of the current tax acts, but it is also necessary to be familiar with the Treasury Department regulations that interpret the tax laws passed by Congress.

There are two very important characteristics of leases that should be carefully distinguished and understood. The more important is the way in which a lease will affect the firm's tax situation. The second is the way in which a lease will affect the accounting reports. There are few financial decisions affected by the accounting rules as much as the leasing decision.

## FAS13: Accounting for Leases

Companies often rent property under long-term lease agreements that require fixed rental payments to be made by the *lessee* (user of the property) to the *lessor* (owner of the property) for the duration of the lease. Leasing is frequently viewed as an alternative to purchasing the property and may be an attractive means of financing needed facilities. Because the obligation for rental payments could be substantial, their effect should be disclosed in the financial statements. One way of accomplishing this is to record the present value of required lease payments as a liability. A corresponding asset would then be recognized to indicate the value of the leased property to be utilized in the company's operations. A second method would be to disclose the terms of the lease (cash outlays that will be required), but not to capitalize the asset or the liability.

The problem of the disclosure of leases in the financial statement is complicated by the varying terms and objectives of the lease agreements. At one extreme, the lessee may be viewed as simply using a service for a short period of time and paying rent for the period of use. Renting an automobile for a weekend would fit this description. At the other extreme, the lessee may be viewed as actually acquiring an ownership interest in a long-term asset, despite the fact that legal title may remain with the lessor. Leasing an automobile for four years with monthly payments that are comparable to financing terms for a purchase might fit this description.

In current practice, two types of leases are distinguished from the lessee's point of view. Leases that essentially may be regarded as purchases are called **capital leases** and are accounted for as an acquisition of a long-term asset with corresponding recognition of the payment obligation as a liability. All other leases are called **operating leases** and are treated as the utilization of services, with rental payments recognized as current expenses as they come due. The accounting for leases has been defined by Financial Accounting Standards Board Statement No. 13 and the supplementary statements issued to explain FASB (Financial Accounting Standards Board) No. 13.

There are several criteria that may be used to determine whether a lease qualifies for classification as a capital lease. Among these are provisions for the transfer of ownership of the property to the lessee during the lease term, provisions for purchase of the property by the lessee at a bargain price, a lease term that is equal to or greater than 75 percent of the useful life of the property, or the present value of minimum lease payments being equal to or greater than 90 percent of the fair value of the property at the beginning of the lease term.[1] If a lease meets *any one of these criteria*, it is classified as a capital lease. Otherwise, it is regarded as an operating lease.

---

[1]This is a simplified explanation. For more details concerning the specific requirements, see Financial Accounting Standards Board, Statement of Financial Accounting Standards No. 13, *Accounting for Leases* (Stamford, CT: FASB, 1976).

With a capital lease, the lessee must show:

a. The initial present value of the lease payments as an asset (the asset is to be depreciated through time in the same manner as any other depreciable asset).
b. The initial present value of the lease payments as a liability, to be reduced through time using present value principles.
c. The future minimum lease payments for each of the next five years and in total for the life of the lease. This total amount is reduced by the imputed interest payments, to obtain the present value of the lease.

With operating leases (leases not qualifying as capital leases), the lessee must show the future minimum lease payments for five years and the total minimum lease payments for the lives of all the operating leases. Operating leases are not shown on the balance sheet except in footnotes. The lessee's borrowing rate will be used in calculating present values.

## Example of Accounting for Leases

Assume that on January 1, 20x1, Elco Corporation rents equipment from Orco Corporation under a ten-year lease calling for rental payments of $10,000 at the end of each of the ten years. At the end of the lease period, Elco may purchase the equipment for $1. The equipment has an expected useful life of ten years and has a fair value now of $61,500. Elco pays interest of 10 percent per year to borrow money.

This may be viewed as a capital lease because the term of the lease extends beyond 75 percent of the useful life of the equipment. (It would also qualify on other grounds.) Using Appendix Table B, we find that the present value of $1 per period for ten periods at 10 percent is 6.1446. Therefore, the present value of the ten payments is

$$\$10,000 \times 6.1446 = \$61,446.$$

The asset and the lease obligation may be recorded as follows:

| | | |
|---|---|---|
| Leased Equipment . . . . . . . . . . . . . . . . . . . . . . . . . . . . . . . . | 61,446 | |
|     Liability for Leased Equipment . . . . . . . . . . . . . . . . . | | 61,446 |

The liability should be shown at its present value, and a financing charge should be recorded each year, based on the assumed rate of interest and the balance of the obligation for the year. A balance sheet on January 1, 20x1, would show an asset,

Leased Equipment          $61,446

and a liability,

Capital Lease Obligation          $61,446.

A footnote would show the following information:

Minimum lease payments for year ending December 31

| | |
|---|---:|
| 20x1 | $ 10,000 |
| 20x2 | 10,000 |
| 20x3 | 10,000 |
| 20x4 | 10,000 |
| 20x5 | 10,000 |
| Later Years | 50,000 |
| Total Minimum Lease Payments | $100,000 |
| *Less*: Amount Representing Interest | 38,554 |
| Present Value of Net Minimum Lease Payments | $ 61,446 |

The asset, Leased Equipment, must be depreciated in the usual manner. Let us assume the firm uses straight-line depreciation and that the equipment has an estimated life of ten years. The following entry would be made on December 31, 20x1:

Depreciation Cost...................................... 6,145

      Leased Equipment: Accumulated Depreciation......          6,145

It is also necessary to record the interest cost of the liability and the payment of the $10,000 lease outlay. For example, the present value of the obligation at the beginning of year 20x1 was $61,446. At the 10-percent rate, the amount of interest to be recognized for the year would be

$$\$61,446 \times 0.10 = \$6,145.$$

To record the interest, the principal payment, and the cash outlay, we have:

Interest Expense .................................... 6,145

Liability for Leased Equipment ....................... 3,855

      Cash........................................        10,000

At the end of year 1, the liability account would have a balance of $57,591. It should be noted that this is equal to the present value of the nine remaining

**Exhibit 12.1.** Amortization Table for Lease Liability.

| Period | Lease Payment | Interest Expense | Liability Reduction | Net Value of Lease Obligation |
|---|---|---|---|---|
| | | | | $61,446.00 |
| 1 | $10,000 | $6,144.60 | $3,855.40 | 57,590.60 |
| 2 | 10,000 | 5,759.06 | 4,240.94 | 53,349.66 |
| 3 | 10,000 | 5,334.97 | 4,665.03 | 48,684.63 |
| 4 | 10,000 | 4,868.46 | 5,131.54 | 43,553.09 |
| 5 | 10,000 | 4,355.31 | 5,644.69 | 37,908.40 |
| 6 | 10,000 | 3,790.84 | 6,209.16 | 31,699.24 |
| 7 | 10,000 | 3,169.92 | 6,830.08 | 24,869.16 |
| 8 | 10,000 | 2,486.92 | 7,513.08 | 17,356.08 |
| 9 | 10,000 | 1,735.61 | 8,264.39 | 9,091.68 |
| 10 | 10,000 | 909.17 | 9,090.83 | 0.85 |

lease payments discounted at 10 percent per year. At the end of year 10, when the final payment is made, the liability account would be reduced to a zero balance. Exhibit 12.1 presents an amortization table for the lease liability. Also, the asset account for Leased Equipment would have a zero net balance, as it is being depreciated over a ten-year period. The leasing arrangement is treated as an implicit purchase of equipment.

If the lease described in the above example did *not* qualify as a capital lease, it would be regarded as an operating lease. In this case, no asset or liability would be recognized. Instead, each year the company would recognize a $10,000 expense, the amount of the lease payment.

It should be noted that if the lease is treated as a capital lease, the expense of the first time-period is not equal to the $10,000 cash outlay. The total expense is:

| | |
|---|---|
| Depreciation Cost | $ 6,145 |
| Interest | 6,145 |
| Total Expense | $12,290 |

While the $6,145 of depreciation will stay constant, the interest will be reduced through time, as the liability is being reduced. The use of different depreciation methods would produce different results.

The recognition of capital leases as a liability in the financial statements is a relatively recent development in accounting practice. At one time, it was widely believed that lease obligations were different from other forms of debt and did not need to be reported on the balance sheet. This led to some companies preferring to lease rather than purchase their plant and equipment in order to reduce the amount of debt appearing on their balance sheets. This practice, which came to be known as "off-balance-sheet financing," has been restricted by FAS13.

## Lessors and Lessees

Any business entity can be a lessee. A big leasing category is transportation equipment — oil tankers, railroad rolling stock, airplanes, trucks, and autos. Other major groups of assets that are leased are computers and other data processing devices, copiers, and specialized machinery.

Lessors are frequently financial institutions with large cash flows (i.e., the insurance companies, banks, and finance and investment companies with large taxable incomes "requiring" tax sheltering). These institutions have a strong incentive to buy equipment and then lease it to equipment users who cannot take advantage of such tax benefits as accelerated depreciation because they do not have taxable income. In some cases, the plant or equipment purchased by the lessor is financed by loans made to the lessor, thereby creating a situation known as leveraged leasing.

A second type of lessor is the manufacturer-lessor. These companies use leases and rental agreements as key tools in the marketing of their products, enabling them to attract customers who might not be able to finance an outright purchase.

## The Pros and Cons of Leasing

Table 12.1 shows in summary form many of the arguments offered in favor of and against leasing. It can be seen that frequently a "pro" argument is canceled by a "con" argument, leaving the decision maker to evaluate subjectively how the factor is to be brought into the decision.

We will consider the cash flows associated with the two alternatives (buy and lease) under well-defined conditions. We will compare leasing with conventional debt accompanying the buy alternative.

Figure 12.1 shows the basic buy versus lease analysis. First, it must be decided whether or not the investment is acceptable. Second, the annual cost of buying the asset with borrowed funds must be compared with the annual cost of leasing. If the cost of buy and borrow is less than the cost of leasing, then the third and final step is to consider whether it is desirable to finance the investment with debt or with a mixture of debt and stock equity.

**Table 12.2.** Ten Pros and Cons of Leasing.

| Pro | Con |
|---|---|
| 1. It is 100 percent debt financing. | 1. A lease may preclude other debt financing if it is a firm obligation to pay. |
| 2. With a short-term lease, there is less risk of being "stuck" with a bad asset if the useful life is less than expected; there is no argument about life with IRS. | 2. No residual value if life is longer than expected. |
| 3. The short-term lease gives flexibility. | 3. Lease terms may be adjusted upward at the end of the lease. |
| 4. Maintenance may be cheaper than if you did it yourself. | 4. The same maintenance contract can probably be purchased if you buy. |
| 5. An operating lease is off-balance-sheet financing. | 5. Many experts reconstruct financial statements to include operating leases. |
| 6. With a lease, it is easier to justify investments (higher return on investment since there is zero or a small investment). | 6. It does not fool as many as it used to. The lease should be capitalized. |
| 7. A lease is easy and quick to obtain. | 7. Not always. Some lease arrangements are very complex. |
| 8. Higher book income is generated in early years. | 8. This is a result of accounting convention; also, later incomes will be less. |
| 9. Lower property taxes are paid. | 9. Property taxes are likely to be built into lease payments. |
| 10. There are tax savings. | 10. There are tax dissavings. |

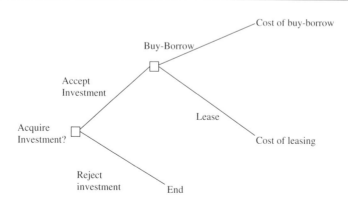

**Fig. 12.1.** Buy-Borrow versus Lease: Lessee.

## Three Basic Problems

There are three basic problems in analyzing buy versus lease decisions. One is the definition of the cash flows to be used. The second is the choice of the rate of discount. The third problem is to match the appropriate rate of discount with the choice of cash flow.

For simplicity's sake, we shall recommend the use of after-tax cash flows. For purposes of simplification, a zero tax rate will initially be used so that the before-tax and after-tax cash flows are identical for the first example.

A major problem with the cash flow calculation is the inclusion or exclusion of the debt component of the lease flows. The objective is to make the lease analysis comparable in terms of debt characteristics with the buy analysis. Generally, this means extracting debt-equivalent tax deduction elements of the lease cash flows.

There are three basic options from which the rate of discount can be chosen:

1. The after-tax borrowing rate,
2. The before-tax borrowing rate, or
3. Some type of risk-adjusted rate such as the weighted average cost of capital.

If we assume that there are four possible sets of cash flows (there are, in reality, more) and three possible discount rates (again, there are, in reality, more), then there are twelve different ways of combining the two elements. If we then recognize the possibility of using different rates of discount to discount different types of cash flows for either the buy or the lease component, we can readily see why there has not been agreement on the method of analyzing buy versus lease decisions.

It is necessary to compare the cash flows and the present value of one alternative (buy) with the other alternative (lease). Rather than reviewing the basic theory and practice of capital budgeting, we shall jump into the middle of that discussion and conclude that one should use the net present value method since it is at least as good as any other method and, for many purposes, better.

## Separating Financing and Investment

It is necessary to evaluate the financial aspect of leasing and to separate the financing and investment elements. We shall assume that we are discussing a lease that is highly similar to a purchase with the borrowing of the purchase price. The lease contract being considered has all the characteristics of a long-term legal debt obligation. The lessee must pay the specified sum to the lessor at the specified times of payment or suffer legal consequences. A lease that can be broken by the lessee without substantial penalty is not the type of lease being discussed in this section.

In the situation being analyzed, committing one's company to a set of lease payments is equivalent to committing the company to a set of comparable debt service payments. Any knowledgeable financial analyst would immediately capitalize financial leases even if they were technically operating leases. For example, if it is disclosed that a given company is obliged to pay, say, $36,829 per year for three years to a leasing firm, the present value of those lease obligations at the existing opportunity cost of debt, say, 10 percent, would be

$$\$36,829 \times B(3, 0.10) = \$36,829 \times 2.4869 = \$91,590.$$

The analyst would modify the existing balance sheet data by adding $91,590 worth of lease-equivalent assets to the firm and $91,590 worth of debt-equivalent liabilities. The relevant comparison for decision purposes is buy and borrow versus lease.

## The Problem Even with a Zero-Tax Situation

We shall try to isolate the basic components of the buy versus lease decision. Consider the following set of situations:

### Example 12.1: Buy-Borrow versus Lease

*The Assumptions*

1. No tax considerations.
2. No uncertainty regarding cash flows.
3. The investment has no salvage value.

*The Problem*

The economic life of the equipment is three years. You have already decided to proceed with the project, but the problem is whether to buy the machine at a cost of $90,000 or lease it from the manufacturer at an annual lease fee of $36,829 for three years. The lease is "net, net", meaning that you provide all the maintenance and insurance.

*The Analysis*

A call to the local banker reveals that the bank is willing to lend your firm the $90,000 at an interest rate of 10 percent. This, the bank lending officer informs you, will require annual payments of \$36,190. The bank credit officer did the following calculations to obtain the annual payments. Let $R$ be the annual payment; then,

$$R \times B(3, 0.10) = \$90,000 \quad \text{or} \quad R = \frac{\$90,000}{2.4869} = \$36,190.$$

## The Decision

Since buy-borrow is cheaper than lease by \$639 per year for the three years, you arrange for the loan and purchase the equipment. The firm would rather pay \$36,190 to the bank than \$36,829 to the lessor. It can be shown that the lease has an implicit cost of 11 percent.

Given these facts, we see that buy-borrow is preferred to lease if it is already decided that we need the equipment. Thus, our decision at the second node of the decision tree depicted in Figure 12.2 is to buy-borrow. Now consider the first decision — the acquisition decision.

## Example 12.2: Acquire the New Equipment?

### The Problem

The incremental cash flows associated with an equipment acquisition would be \$38,000 per year (estimated annual revenue from sale of product less cost of production excluding equipment cost). The equipment costs \$90,000.

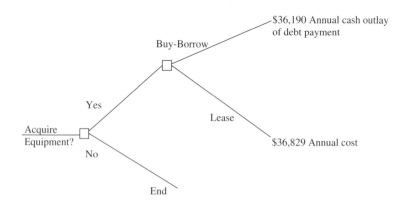

**Fig. 12.2.**  Buy-Borrow versus Lease: Lessee.

## The Analysis

The firm normally uses the weighted average cost of capital (WACC) as its "hurdle rate" in investment analysis. The WACC is estimated to be 14 percent.

| Method of Financing | Cost | Weighted in Capital Structure | Weighted Cost |
|---|---|---|---|
| Debt | 0.10 | 0.5 | 0.05 |
| Equity | 0.18 | 0.5 | 0.09 |
| | | | 0.14 = WACC |

If we use 14 percent as the discount rate, the net present value analysis for acquiring the equipment is:

| Time | Cash Flow | Present Value Factor @ 14% | Present Value @ 14% |
|---|---|---|---|
| 0 | −$90,000 | 1.0000 | −$90,000 |
| 1–3 | $38,000 | 2.3216 | $88,221 |
| | | Net present value @ 14% | = −$ 1,779 |

The net present value of acquiring the equipment is negative using the WACC as a discount rate. But, if we lease the equipment, the net present value is clearly positive at any discount rate since leasing provides an expected net benefit of $38,000 − $36,829 = $1,171 per year.

Using 14 percent, these benefits have a net present value of $2,719.

## The Decision

This analysis would seem to indicate that the firm should reject the buy alternative, but that leasing is acceptable (leasing has a positive net present value with any positive rate of discount). But Example 12.1 already showed that if the equipment is acceptable, the firm should buy-borrow, not lease!

## The Proper Comparison

The analysis in Example 12.2 leading to the acceptance of leasing and the rejection of the buy alternative is faulty. We cannot logically compare "buy" and "lease"; rather, we compare "buy-borrow" and "lease" or compare "buy" with a lease alternative that is placed on a basis that is comparable to "buy". The lease alternative implicitly includes debt financing flows, while the "buy" alternative has no such flows. A comparison of the net present values as structured above is likely to be faulty.

## A Lease Is a Debt

Assume an investment analysis that uses cash flows with debt flows subtracted from the basic investment flows (stock equity flows are being used). Any conventional investment with an internal rate of return greater than the cost of debt can be made to appear better (a greater net present value) by including the debt flows in the analysis or by increasing the debt used to finance the investment and focusing on the net present value of the residual cash flows. Since lease payments are effectively debt service, it is important that comparability be established between the lease and buy alternatives in acquisition analysis. There are essentially three methods of neutralizing the financial differences between the two alternatives.

The first method would be to recognize the lease payments as debt service and discount these payments at the cost of debt, thereby comparing the cost of buying with debt against acquiring with lease. In the illustration, the debt equivalent of leasing (the present value of the lease payments at 10 percent) is

$$\$36,829 \times B(3, 0.10) = \$36,829 \times 2.4869 = \$91,590.$$

If funds are borrowed and the equipment is purchased, the present value of the debt service and flows is $90,000, and so buy-borrow is preferred to leasing that costs $91,590.

The second method of comparing buy-borrow and lease is to include the debt flows in the buy analysis. The net debt flows of buying are $38,000 - \$36,190 = \$1,810$ per year. The net benefits from leasing are $1,171 per year, which is less than the buy-borrow net benefits of $1,810.

The third method is comparable to the second. We contend that the decision tree approach of Figure 12.1 is an appropriate approach. If acquisition is desirable and leasing is an alternative, we can compare the annual equivalent costs of financing the acquisition by debt and by leasing. Since the benefit stream of cash flows from acquisition is the same under either acquisition strategy, the differential cash flows between buy-borrow and lease arise solely from the differences in the contractual obligation of the two alternatives. Debt financing costs $36,190, and the lease costs $36,829; therefore, buy-borrow is more desirable than leasing.

These three procedures tell us what to do if we have decided to accept the equipment. They do not tell us whether or not the equipment is desirable. With no uncertainty, the investment is desirable. With uncertainty, both buying and leasing may not be acceptable. The decision depends on the analysis of the project's risk.

## The Effect of Taxes

Let us assume that the equipment acquisition is deemed desirable and that the method of acquisition is the only question. Taxes exert substantial influence and must be considered. With respect to income taxes, the total lease payments are tax-deductible, whereas depreciation and interest payments on debt are deductible under the buy-borrow alternative.

How do these tax factors affect the decision? Let us proceed with our previous illustration. Now assume that the lessor offers to lease at $36,190 per year, the same as the debt service payments to the bank if the $90,000 were borrowed. This would result in indifference if there were zero taxes. Do taxes force the analysis toward lease or buy-borrow in this case?

Suppose that the tax rate is 40 percent. If the $90,000 is borrowed, the debt repayment schedule would be:

| Period | Amount Owed Beginning of Period | Interest at 10% | Principal Payment | Total Payment |
|--------|--------|--------|--------|--------|
| 1 | $90,000 | $ 9,000 | $27,190 | $ 36,190 |
| 2 | 62,810 | 6,280 | 29,910 | 36,190 |
| 3 | 32,900 | 3,290 | 32,900 | 36,190 |
|  |  | $18,570 | $90,000 | $108,570 |

If straight-line depreciation is used by the firm for taxes, the total tax deductions resulting from buy-borrow and leasing would be:

| Period | Interest | Straight-Line Depreciation | Buy-Borrow Total Tax Deductions | Lease Tax Deductions |
|--------|--------|--------|--------|--------|
| 1 | $ 9,000 | $30,000 | $ 39,000 | $ 36,190 |
| 2 | 6,280 | 30,000 | 36,280 | 36,190 |
| 3 | 3,290 | 30,000 | 33,290 | 36,190 |
|  | $18,570 | $90,000 | $108,570 | $108,570 |

The tax deduction each year with leasing is $36,190 or $108,570 for three years. The sums of the deductions arising from both buy-borrow and leasing are

$108,570, but the timing of the cash flows clearly favor the buy-borrow alternative, even if straight-line depreciation expense is used for taxes rather than accelerated depreciation.

Note that if the firm used accelerated depreciation, as it normally would for tax purposes, the buy-borrow alternative would be even more preferable. Total tax deductions would again be the same, but the timing would be even more favorable in the early years to buy-borrow. In this situation where there was initially indifference and zero taxes, the inclusion of taxes moved the decision toward buy-borrow.

## *A Method of Solution*

If we use straight-line tax depreciation and the after-tax borrowing rate of 0.06, the net cost of buy-borrow is

$$\$90,000 - 0.4(\$30,000)2.673 = \$90,000 - \$32,076 = \$57,924.$$

The $32,076 is the present value of the tax savings resulting from the use of straight-line tax depreciation.

Let

$r =$ the after-tax borrowing rate

$t_c =$ the corporate tax rate

$L =$ the annual lease payment

$B(n, r) =$ the present value of an annuity for $n$ periods discounted at $r$ interest rate.

The after-tax present value cost of leasing is

$$(1 - t_c)LB(n, r) = \$36,190(1 - 0.4)B(3, 0.06) = \$58,042.$$

Buy has a smaller after-tax present value cost than does leasing. We can use $(1 - t_c)LB(n, r)$ to compute the present value of leasing, since the after-tax borrowing rate is being used as the discount rate.

This calculation is a reasonable solution to the problem of determining whether leasing or buying with borrowing is more desirable. This very easy method of solution is possible, since the firm is willing to use the after-tax borrowing rate to discount all the cash flows. If any other discount rate is used, we must use a more complex method of solution. The use of the after-tax borrowing rate has the advantage of causing the after-tax present value of the debt flows associated with borrowing to be equal to zero. This makes the buy-borrow and the lease calculations equivalent.

You should not be lulled into the belief that if there is no difference between buy-borrow and lease on a before-tax basis, the after-tax analysis will always demonstrate that buy-borrow is less costly. Suppose that the lessor offered the equipment at $32,901 per year, with payment due at the beginning of the year rather than at the end. The present value of the lease payments at the before-tax cost of debt is again $90,000,

$$\$32,901 + \$32,901 \times B(2, 0.10) = \$90,000,$$

which is the same as the present value of the debt service cash flows, and there is before-tax indifference. But the present value of the after-tax cash flows of leasing discounted at the after-tax cost of debt,

$$(1 - 0.4)(\$32,901)[1 + B(2, 0.06)] = \$55,933,$$

is in this case less than the present value of the after-tax cash flows from buy-borrow with straight-line depreciation ($57,924). Leasing is now less costly than buy-borrowing. Changing the timing of the lease payments and the tax deductions affects the relative desirability of buy-borrow and lease, even though the before-tax present values are not changed.

There are no easily applied consistently correct rules of thumb in buy versus lease analysis — a complete after-tax discounted cash flow analysis is the safest way of making the decision.

## Risk-Adjusted Discount Rate

We shall now assume that management is willing to discount debt flows using the borrowing rate, but wants to use a "risk-adjusted rate" for other cash flows. These "other" cash flows include (1) depreciation tax savings (or the equivalent) and (2) residual value.

## *Example 12.3*

Assume that both the lease payments and debt payments with buy-borrow are $36,190. The firm evaluates investments using a risk-adjusted rate ($j$) of 0.20.

The total annual tax deduction with leasing is $36,190, but we have to break that down into "interest" and "depreciation". For leasing, the "depreciation" equivalent is equal to the "principal" portion of the lease payment.

Using the before-tax borrowing rate of 0.10, we obtain a present value (debt equivalent) of lease payments of

$$\$36,190B(3, 0.10) = \$36,190(2.4869) = \$90,000.$$

The implicit debt amortization schedule for the lease is:

| Period | Beginning Liability | Interest (0.10) | Principal Payment |
|--------|--------------------|-----------------|--------------------|
| 1 | $90,000 | $9,000 | $27,190 |
| 2 | 62,810 | 6,280 | 29,910 |
| 3 | 32,900 | 3,290 | 32,900 |
|  |  |  | $90,000 |

The tax savings associated with the investment-like aspects of the lease are:

| Period | Lease Outlay | Interest | "Depreciation" or Principal | Tax Rate 0.4 | Cash Flow (tax savings) | Preset Value of Tax Savings ($j = 0.20$) |
|--------|-------------|----------|----------------------------|--------------|-------------------------|----------------------------------------|
| 1 | $36,190 | $9,000 | $27,190 | 0.4 | $10,876 | $ 9,063 |
| 2 | 36,190 | 6,280 | 29,910 | 0.4 | 11,964 | 8,308 |
| 3 | 36,190 | 3,290 | 32,900 | 0.4 | 13,160 | 7,616 |
|  |  |  | $90,000 |  | $36,000 | $24,987 |

For the buy alternative using straight-line depreciation, we have:

| Period | Buy | Cash Flow (tax savings) | Present Value of Tax Savings ($j = 0.20$) |
|--------|-----|-------------------------|-------------------------------------------|
| 1 | $30,000 × 0.4 = | $12,000 | $10,000 |
| 2 | 30,000 × 0.4 = | 12,000 | 8,333 |
| 3 | 30,000 × 0.4 = | 12,000 | 6,944 |
|  |  | $36,000 | $25,277 |

The depreciation tax savings of buy are larger than the depreciation-equivalent tax savings of leasing. Since all other things are equal, buy is better than leasing.

These depreciation tax savings are the only cash flows for both alternatives that are not debt types of flows, and it can be argued that only these flows and not the financing-type flows should be discounted at a risk-adjusted rate.

Inspection of the tax saving numbers reveals that at any positive rate of interest, the buy stream (even with zero residual value) is to be preferred to the leasing stream. A decrease in the lease payments from $36,190 is necessary to increase the relative desirability of lease compared to buy-borrow. Using $j = 0.20$, the after-tax present value cost of buying is $90,000 - $25,277 = $64,723.

If we had incorrectly used $j = 0.20$ to discount all the after-tax cash flows of leasing, we would have

$$(1 - t_c)LB(3, 0.20) = (1 - 0.4)\$36,190(2.1065) = \$45,741.$$

This calculation indicates that leasing has a smaller net cost than does buying. It is an incorrect calculation because it implicitly includes the debt component in the lease cash flows that are being discounted at 0.20. If we included the debt flows in the buy analysis and discounted at 0.20, the net cost would be \$45,451. The cost is reduced, since 0.10 debt is being discounted at 0.20.

## *Debt Calculations Using 0.20*

| Period | Interest | $(1 - 0.4)$ Interest | Principal Payment | After-Tax Cash Flows | Present Value Using 0.20 |
|--------|----------|----------------------|-------------------|----------------------|--------------------------|
| 1 | \$9,000 | \$5,400 | \$27,190 | \$32,590 | \$27,158 |
| 2 | 6,280 | 3,768 | 29,910 | 33,678 | 23,388 |
| 3 | 3,290 | 1,974 | 32,900 | 34,874 | 20,182 |
| | | | | Present value of outlays = | \$70,728 |

$$\text{Net present value of debt} = \$90,000 - \$70,728 = \$19,272.$$
$$\text{Net cost of buying} = \$64,723 - \$19,272 = \$45,451$$

or

$$\text{Net cost of buying} = \$70,728 - \$25,277 = \$45,451,$$

where \$70,728 is the present value of the debt outlays, and the \$25,277 is the present value of the tax savings from depreciation.

## Residual Value

Assume that 0.06 is the correct interest rate and that the same facts apply as earlier when the lease payments are \$35,555 per year, except that the expected residual value is \$1,070 if the firm buys. The present value of depreciation tax savings \$32,076 plus the present value of residual value (\$898) is \$32,974 for buy-borrow using 0.06. This is equal to the present value of the tax shield of the noninterest portion of the lease payments (\$31,396) plus the \$1,578 of savings because the present value of before-tax lease payments (\$88,422) is less than the present value of debt flows of buying ($90,000). Figure 12.3 shows that if the appropriate discount rate is greater than 0.06, leasing is more desirable than buy-borrow.

Instead of plotting the present value of the nondebt flows as in Figure 12.3, we could plot the net cost of the two alternatives as in Figure 12.4.

With a zero rate of discount, the net cost of buying is

$$\$90,000 - 0.4(\$90,000) - \$1,070 = \$52,930$$

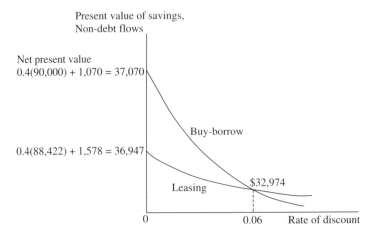

**Fig. 12.3.**   Buy versus Lease with $1,070 of Residual Value (Present Value of Savings).

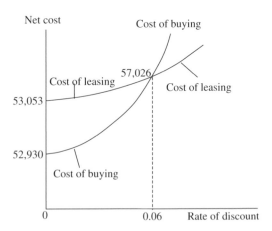

**Fig. 12.4.**   Net Costs (Residual value = $1,070).

and the net cost of leasing is

$$\$88,422 - 0.4(\$88,422) = \$53,053.$$

If we use 0.06 to discount the tax savings, the net cost of leasing is:

$$
\begin{aligned}
\text{PV of lease (before tax)} &= \quad \$88,422 \\
\text{PV of tax savings} &= \quad \underline{\phantom{0}31,396} \\
\text{Net cost of leasing} &= \quad \$57,026
\end{aligned}
$$

The net cost of buying with residual value of $1,070 is also $57,026 using 0.06:

$$\$90,000 - \$32,076 - \$898 = \$57,026.$$

With a lower interest rate than 0.06, buy-borrow is more desirable than leasing; and with a higher interest rate, leasing wins (has a lower cost). At 0.06, there is no difference.

## The Issues

We have illustrated a procedure that allows the use of any rate of discount for computing the present value of the tax savings from depreciation (or the depreciation equivalent of leasing) and the present value of the residual value.

Some analysts will want to discount depreciation tax savings using a risk-free rate since these cash flows are nearly certain. Others will prefer the after-tax borrowing rate since it avoids certain types of error and is consistent with the opportunity cost of new debt capital. Finally, some will prefer to include an adjustment for risk in computing the present value of depreciation tax savings and residual value (or for one of them).

If an interest rate larger than the after-tax borrowing rate is used, care must be taken to place the buy-borrow analysis on a comparable basis to the lease analysis. The lease analysis tends to include debt flows; and if a high interest rate is used, this creates a bias for leasing. The solution recommended is to compute a debt equivalent of leasing and analyze separately the investment characteristics of leasing so that leasing and buying are comparable.

## Three Decisions

Firms have three decisions to make before an asset can be leased. First, the firm has to decide whether or not the project is worthwhile. Second, a decision has to be made whether the financing should be done with straight debt or with leasing. Third, the firm must consider using equity rather than leasing or debt. We are not concerned with the sequence in which the decisions are made as long as it is recognized that there are three decisions. For example, it might be decided that, if the project were to be accepted, buying would be more desirable than leasing, but it still would not be desirable to acquire the project.

The financing can influence whether or not the project is desirable. For example, a buy analysis might lead to a reject analysis, but since the lease terms are so favorable, leasing might cause the project to be acceptable. Acceptability implies that the asset passes some type of risk and present value analysis.

If it is decided that straight debt rather than leasing is desirable, it is still possible that the firm will decide to use common stock or some other type of financing. The buy versus lease decision should be made comparing the lease contract with straight debt financing so that the two alternatives are as comparable as we can make them. But after that decision is made, it may still be correct for the firm to reject debt in favor of some other type of financing.

## Conclusion

Leasing is an important financing method. For firms without access to debt money, it may be the only way of acquiring assets. But for many potential lessees, the option to buy is available, and, with ready access to the debt-capital market, the most relevant decision is to compare buy-borrow and lease since lease commitments may be, in effect, debt-type obligations. Furthermore, in focusing on the incremental cash flows of buy-borrow and lease, the use of the after-tax borrowing rate enables us to choose the form of the debt. The use of a conventional investment hurdle rate ($j$) or WACC to discount total lease flows with the formula $(1 - t_c)LB(n, j)$ is in error.

Many firms have made the wrong financing decision by not following these principles. Comparing buy (without including debt flows) with lease flows using a high discount rate and cash flows of $(1 - t_c)L$ creates an inherent bias toward the leasing alternative, and we suspect that the phenomenal growth rate in leasing is, in part, the result of faulty analysis.

There are no easy rules of thumb to help decide which alternative is preferable even when the intangibles are ignored. Calculating and comparing the after-tax cash flows of the two alternatives and computing the present values will provide a guideline with respect to these factors if the correct discount rate and correct cash flows are employed.

# Review Problems

## *Review Problem 12.1*

Assume that the A Corporation can obtain a 10-year noncancellable lease of $12,500 per year for an asset that it wants. The lease payment is due at the end of each year. The asset will have zero value at the end of 10 years.

The asset would cost $70,000 if purchased. It will earn gross cash flows of $13,500 per year.

Corporate taxes are 0.35. The asset fits in the 5-year Accelerated Cost Recovery System (ACRS) class life.

The corporation can borrow money repayable in equal installments at an after-tax cost of 0.07. It has a weighted average cost of capital of 0.15.

Assume that the firm has decided to acquire the asset. Assume that the firm is willing to use the after-tax borrowing rate.

The net tax cost of buying is _____.

The net tax cost of leasing is _____.

**Present Value of Depreciation of $1,000,000 of Assets Under ACRS**

(all the table values have a decimal in front of the first digit)

| Discount Rate | Class Life | | | |
| | 3 Years | 5 Years | 10 Years | 15 Years |
| --- | --- | --- | --- | --- |
| 01 | 979156 | 969618 | 949194 | 928486 |
| 02 | 959001 | 940615 | 902132 | 864282 |
| 03 | 939507 | 912912 | 858479 | 806496 |
| 04 | 920645 | 886436 | 817933 | 754358 |
| 05 | 902386 | 861118 | 780223 | 707203 |
| 06 | 884707 | 836893 | 745105 | 664453 |
| 07 | 867582 | 813701 | 712360 | 625607 |
| 08 | 850988 | 791487 | 681788 | 590226 |
| 09 | 834904 | 770198 | 653211 | 557930 |
| 10 | 819309 | 749784 | 626466 | 528385 |
| 11 | 804183 | 730201 | 601407 | 501299 |
| 12 | 789507 | 711404 | 577900 | 476415 |
| 13 | 775263 | 693353 | 555825 | 453508 |
| 14 | 761435 | 676010 | 535071 | 432377 |
| 15 | 748007 | 659340 | 515539 | 412848 |
| 16 | 734962 | 643309 | 497136 | 394764 |
| 18 | 709968 | 613040 | 463395 | 362398 |
| 20 | 686343 | 584973 | 433263 | 334347 |

**Solution to Review Problem 12.1**

$$\text{Net cost of buying} = \$70,000 - 0.35(\$70,000)(0.813701)$$
$$= 70,000 - 19,936$$
$$= \$50,064$$
$$\text{Net cost of leasing} = \$12,500(1 - 0.35)B(10, 0.07)$$
$$= \$57,067.$$

## Questions and Problems

1. Assume zero taxes. Equipment can be leased at $10,000 per year (first payment one year hence) for ten years or purchased at a cost of $64,177. The company has a weighted average cost of capital of 15 percent. A bank has indicated that it would be willing to make the loan of $64,177 at a cost of 10 percent.

   Should the company buy or lease? There are no uncertainties. The equipment will be used for ten years. There is zero salvage value.

2. (continue 1) If the bank was willing to lend funds at 9 percent, should the company buy or lease?

3. (continue 2) If the company pays $64,177 for the equipment, it will save $10,000 a year on lease payments for ten years.

   What internal rate of return will it earn on its "investment"?

4. (continue 1) Now assume a marginal tax rate of 0.4. Assume that the funds can be obtained for 0.10 at a bank. The company uses sum-of-the-years' digits depreciation for taxes.

   Should the firm buy or lease? (Assume that the present value of the depreciation deductions is 0.79997 per dollar of depreciable assets using 0.06 as the discount rate.)

5. (continue 1) Now assume a marginal tax rate of 0.4 and that a loan can be obtained from the bank at a cost of 9 percent.

   Should the firm buy or lease? Using 0.054, the present value of depreciation is 0.811. Use 0.054 as the discount rate.

6. (continue 5) Assume that the lease payments of $10,000 start immediately and that they are paid at the end of each year. There are 10 payments.

   Compute the present value of leasing; compare the present value with that obtained for problem 5.

7. Assume that there is a 0.4 marginal tax rate. An asset with a life of three years can be bought for $25,313 or leased for $10,000 per year. Funds can be borrowed at a cost of 0.09 (payments of $10,000 per year).

a. What is the present value of the debt (the liability) if the funds are borrowed at a cost of 9 percent? Assume that the payments to the bank are $10,000 per year.

b. What is the present value of the lease payments of $10,000 (the liability)?

8. (continue 5)

a. Include the borrowing cash flows in the buy analysis. Assume equal payments of debt. How does this change the net cost?

b. Assume that the net cost of buying was computed using the cost of capital of 15 percent. Now include the borrowing cash flows. How will this change the net cost of buying (you do not have to compute the present value)?

9. What factors might make a lessor's expected cost of acquiring and disposing of equipment less than the lessee's expected cost?

10. Why are leasing companies (lessors) so highly levered?

11. Consider the following investment:

| Cash Flows at Time | | | |
|---|---|---|---|
| 0 | 1 | 2 | Internal Rate of Return |
| −$1,000 | $576 | $576 | 10% |

If debt can be obtained at a cost of 5 percent, determine the net present value of the equity cash flows discounted at 15 percent if:

a. No debt is used to finance the investment.

b. $500 of debt is used to finance the investment.

c. $900 of debt is used to finance the investment.

d. Repeat the calculations using 5 percent as the discount rate.

12. Suppose that $100,000 is borrowed at 8 percent and is to be repaid in three equal annual installments. Prepare a debt amortization table and show that the net present value of the after-tax cash flows of the debt is zero using the after-tax cost of debt as the discount rate. The tax rate is 40 percent.

13. MBI has offered to sell or lease computing equipment to Cornell University that has an expected life of three years. If purchased, the initial cost would be $2 million. If leased, the annual lease payments would be $800,000 per year. Cornell can borrow money at about 7 percent on its endowment and pays no taxes. Ignoring salvage value, what should Cornell do?

## Chapter 13

# Preferred Stock

## Preferred Stock: A Hybrid

Preferred stock is a security that, similar to debt, promises a well-defined (specified) but not necessarily constant contractual cash flow (dividend) to the holders of the security. Unlike debt, it does not cause the firm to be subject to bankruptcy if the dividends are not paid. The term *preferred stock* implies that this security is in a more favorable position than the common stock. This conclusion is not likely to be valid for an individual investor paying taxes at a high rate on dividends. A corporate investor might like preferred stock because of a 70% "dividend-received deduction" (in the United States, normally only 0.30 of the dividend income received by a corporation is subject to tax).

The corporate tax savings associated with interest on debt make it difficult for preferred stock to compete with debt in the nonregulated sector of corporate activity. Also, the capital gains and tax deferred possibilities for individual investors of common stock give common stock tax advantages over preferred stock with a contractual dividend and little chance of capital gains.

Preferred stock has historically been important to regulated public utilities, and it is likely to be approximately 10 percent of a typical public utility's capital structure.

Preferred stock is a hybrid form of capital, possessing a mixture of debt and common stock characteristics. Like the interest on debt, its dividends may be fixed over time. However, "participating" preferred stock shares income with common stock according to some prearranged formula, and other preferred stock may pay a dividend that is linked to some independent measure such as the yield on government bonds. Like common stock, preferred stock is generally treated as equity capital for corporate tax purposes, so its dividends are paid from corporate earnings that have been taxed. Preferred stock generally has a perpetual life, although it may have a finite life, and it may have a call price specified and even a sinking fund where stock is to be repurchased by the firm in the open market. It is important to the issuing firm and to the investor that nonpayment of the preferred stock dividend does not trigger bankruptcy. Normally, common stock dividends cannot be paid until all past due preferred dividends have been paid or the preferred stockholders have been compensated by some other means. Preferred stock dividends have to be approved by the board of directors before they become a legal liability of the corporation. Preferred stock generally does not have voting rights, but if a preferred stock dividend is passed over, the preferred stockholders sometimes have the right to select one or more members of the board of directors.

Although the dividends on some preferred stock are allowed as a tax deduction, currently in the United States dividends of preferred stock are not normally deductible for taxes by a corporation (unlike the interest payment of debt). This tends to limit the use of preferred stock by corporations. However, in some parts of the world, preferred stock dividends are treated in the same manner for taxes as interest; thus, in those parts of the world, this drawback would not apply. It is logical to have securities that bridge the gap between debt, where failure to pay interest results in bankruptcy, and common stock, where there is no stated commitment to pay dividends. From the investors' viewpoint, compared to common stock, preferred stock reduces somewhat the amount of uncertainty associated with future dividend payments.

## Accounting for Preferred Stock

The preferred stock is classified in the stockholders' equity section of the balance sheet, although it should be separated from the common stock equity. The preferred stock will generally have a par value that will determine the credit to the preferred stock account. If the amount contributed by the preferred stockholders is greater or less than par, the difference should be recorded in a contra account or adjunct account.

## *Example*

Record the journal entries for the following situations:

a. One thousand shares of 5 percent, cumulative preferred stock, par $100, are issued for $100 per share.

| | | |
|---|---|---|
| Cash . . . . . . . . . . . . . . . . . . . . . . . . . . . . . . . . . . . . . | 100,000 | |
| Preferred Stock . . . . . . . . . . . . . . . . . . . . . . . . . | | 100,000 |

b. Assume the above stock is issued at $110 a share.

| | | |
|---|---|---|
| Cash.......................................... | 110,000 | |
| Preferred Stock.............................. | | 100,000 |
| Preferred Stock: Amount Paid in Excess of Par... | | 10,000 |

The Preferred Stock, Amount Paid in Excess of Par account is an adjunct account to Preferred Stock; in the balance sheet, it should be added to Preferred Stock.

Some accountants have argued that such amounts should be added to the common stockholders' equity because, in the event of liquidation, the preferred stockholders would receive only the par amount of their shares. This argument is contrary to the basic assumptions of a going concern. The accounts should show the amounts initially paid by the various classes of shareholders rather than liquidation values.

c. Assume the above stock is issued for $92 per share.

| | | |
|---|---|---|
| Cash ......................................... | 92,000 | |
| Preferred Stock, Discount ........................ | 8,000 | |
| Preferred Stock .............................. | | 100,000 |

The discount account is a contra account (a subtraction) to Preferred Stock; in the balance sheet, it should be subtracted from Preferred Stock.

d. A dividend of $5 per share is declared on the preferred stock.

| | | |
|---|---|---|
| Preferred Stock Dividends........................ | 5,000 | |
| Dividends Payable ........................... | | 5,000 |

If the interest on bonds is not paid, the bondholders have legal recourse and can cause the corporation to be declared insolvent. When dividends on preferred stock are not paid, however, the preferred stockholders have no such recourse because the corporation is not legally required to pay dividends on preferred stock.

A history of failure to pay dividends will affect the corporation's ability to raise capital through issuing preferred stock in the future. It could even result in the preferred shareholders receiving rights to elect members of the board of directors. Since there is no legal liability, the accountant makes no entry at the time a preferred stock dividend is passed over. This is consistent with the assumption that the accounting is being done for the corporate entity rather than for a particular group of shareholders. However, the preferred stock arrearage is of interest to all stockholders, and the amount of arrearage should be disclosed on the balance sheet either in a footnote or by the separation and identification of part of the retained earnings.

## Measuring the Cost of Preferred Stock

The cost of preferred stock is defined as the discount rate that equates the future expected preferred dividends (and call price if callable) to the present market price. Let $P$ denote the current price of a share of preferred stock, $D$ the annual constant dividend payment, and $k_p$ the return required by investors or cost of the preferred stock. The current price of a share, if noncallable, may be defined in terms of $D$ and $k_p$. The dividend is assumed to be a perpetuity with first payment one year from now:

$$P = \frac{D}{k_p}. \tag{13.1}$$

Solving for $k_p$, we obtain

$$k_p = \frac{D}{P} \tag{13.2}$$

under the assumption that the issuing firm expects to pay the dividend for perpetuity. So, the current cost of noncallable preferred stock to the issuing corporation is the stock's dividend yield.

If interest rates and stock yields should fall after selling a new issue and the issue is not callable, the issuing firm is stuck with perpetual financing at a high cost. For example, if the interest rate on a $100 preferred stock were 10 percent at time of issue (a $10 per year cash dividend) and if the market now requires a 0.08 return, the stock would have to be repurchased in the open market for

$$P = \frac{10}{0.08} = \$125$$

if the firm wished to retire the obligation. If, on the other hand, a call provision were specified at, say, $110, the firm could call the $10 obligation per annum for $110 and replace it with a $110 par value, 8-percent issue paying only $8.80 per annum and issued at par. The company replaces a security promising to pay $10.00 a year with a security paying $8.80 a year. This is a saving of $1.20 per year. The $110 issue price of the 8-percent preferred stock is enough to retire the currently outstanding preferred stock.

If there were no call provision and the company paid $125 to retire a share, the new security issued at $125 with a par value of $125 and paying 0.08 would have an annual dividend of $10 and the company's financial position would not improve.

Investors prefer the preferred stock to be noncallable so that if interest rates fall, the stock's value goes up. Thus, investors will require a higher yield on the callable preferred stock issue than on the noncallable issue. For example, if a noncallable issue is selling for 10 percent, an otherwise comparable callable issue would have to promise to pay somewhat more than 10 percent if the investor is to pay the same price for both issues.

In the example, if the 10-percent preferred stock were noncallable and if the fall in interest rates to 0.08 occurred in the first year, the investor who sells would receive $10 of dividends and $25 of capital gains for a total return on investment of 35 percent. With the preferred stock callable at $110, there would be only $10 of capital gains and the return on investment would be 20 percent.

## *Example 13.1*

XYZ Corporation has decided to issue preferred stock. The preferred stock will carry a $10 dividend and will be sold for $105 with a call price of $110. The firm expects lower interest rates (say, 8 percent) in approximately two years and therefore expects to call the issue at time 2. We can solve by trial and error for the cost of this preferred stock issue or equivalently the return earned by the investor:

$$\$105 = \sum_{t=1}^{2} \frac{\$10}{(1+k_p)^t} + \frac{\$110}{(1+k_p)^2}.$$

In this case, $k_p$ is approximately 12 percent while the one-period dividend yield of $\frac{10}{105}$ is approximately 9.5 percent. The call provision seems to make the cost of the preferred stock greater than the dividend yield, but this is misleading. Assume that without a call provision after two years the stock price goes up to $125. The two-period economic cost is

$$\$105 = \sum_{t=1}^{2} \frac{\$10}{(1+k_p)^t} + \frac{\$125}{(1+k_p)^2}.$$

Solving for $k_p$ (by trial and error), we find that without a call provision $k_p$ is now 18.25 percent. In this example, the call provision reduces the cost of the preferred stock if the issue price of $105 is assumed to be independent of the call provision.

## Factors Affecting the Cost of Preferred Stock

Preferred stock is similar to debt, and the factors affecting the cost of debt are also important here. There is, however, one additional factor that has to be discussed: the dividend-received deduction. If a corporation purchases equity capital (preferred or common stock) of another corporation, and if it owns less than 20 percent of the voting stock, 70 percent of the dividends it receives on that stock is nontaxable income for the receiving corporation. On the other hand, all interest the corporation receives on taxable debt securities held is taxable. Insurance companies in particular find that the dividend-received deduction, plus the relative predictability of the dividend flow, makes preferred stock a desirable form of investment.

Not as risky as common stock and offering a high after-tax yield on the investment, a substantial amount of preferred stock is held by insurance companies. In fact, the demand for preferred stock by these companies is so great that the before-tax yield on preferred stock is sometimes less than the before-tax yield on the debt of the same issuing firm, despite the fact that the preferred stock is obviously more risky insofar as the debt has first claim to earnings and prior claim on assets in case of liquidation.

To explain why preferred stock may yield less than debt, let us examine the after-tax yield of debt. The effective after-tax yield on debt of a corporation being taxed at a rate of $t_c$ is $(1 - t_c)k_i$. The after-tax cost of preferred stock is

$$(k_p - 0.30k_p t_c) = k_p(1 - 0.30t_c) \qquad (13.3)$$

if the preferred stock yields $k_p$ before tax to the holder. If both debt and preferred stock securities yielded the same before-tax return, the after-tax yield on the preferred stock would be greater than that on the debt since $(1 - t_c)$ is less than $(1 - 0.30t_c)$. For example, if $t_c = 0.35$ and $100 of interest is received, the investing corporation nets $65 after tax. If $100 of dividends are received, the tax is $10.50 and the corporation nets $89.50.

If the preferred stock is only slightly more risky than the debt, then it could yield less than debt before tax and still return enough in excess of the yield on debt after tax to compensate a corporate investor for the additional risk.

## Mergers and Acquisitions

Preferred stock has frequently been issued in connection with mergers and acquisitions. Often the preferred stock is issued with a conversion feature, so in the long run there is a probability it will become common stock capital. Preferred stock allows the acquired firm's owners a prior claim relative to common stock and reasonably definite dividends while simultaneously giving the acquiring firm a form of leverage without strapping it with the rigid obligations of debt.

This provides a justification for the fact that some firms do issue preferred stock. However, on a pure explicit cost comparison with debt, preferred stock tends to be inferior (have a higher after-tax cost). A firm not making sufficient taxable income to use the tax shield of the debt may have incentive to use preferred stock, as will a firm close to its debt capacity.

## Variable-Rate Preferred Stock

Some treasurers of corporations would like to invest in preferred stock having before-tax yields about the same as (or somewhat less than) short-term debt if some of the risk of preferred stock can be removed.

One risk that investors would like to see removed is the risk that the price of preferred stock will fall because the market's required return has gone up.

Variable-rate preferred stocks is one method of insuring that the stock price will not fall. Rather than paying a fixed dividend, this type of security pays a dividend that is a fixed fraction of the highest of as many as three government bond yields (e.g., the T-bill rate, the U.S. Treasury 10-year constant maturity rate, and the U.S. Treasury 20-year constant maturity rate). The advantage of a variable-rate preferred stock is that its market price should always be close to its face value. If the payment risk does not change, it will differ only because the linkage to the U.S. Treasury securities does not perfectly reflect the market's required return on preferred stock.

To protect the issuing firm against very large cash outlay commitments, a maximum dividend rate is established. To protect the investor against very low dividends, a minimum dividend rate is established. While not necessary to the basic concept of the security, these provisions are generally present, but the levels of maximum and minimum vary greatly. Also, the differential between the maximum of the three U.S. Treasury returns and the preferred stock dividend also differs from issue to issue. These factors are set by market conditions (supply and demand) for this particular type of security.

## Preferred Stock versus Common Stock

The primary advantage to an investor of holding preferred stock compared with common stock is that the preferred stock return is somewhat more predictable (more certain). The issuing company will generally make a real effort to try to avoid defaulting on the preferred stock dividend. Since the return to preferred stock is reasonably well defined and since the preferred stockholders precede the common stockholders (the preferred dividends are paid before the common dividends), preferred stock is a popular type of security for executing mergers and acquisitions.

From the point of view of an issuing corporation's common stockholders, preferred stock offers the opportunity to introduce a form of leverage (the preferred stockholders generally have a maximum dividend return) that could benefit the common stockholders if the corporation does very well in the future. The preferred stockholders do not normally participate in any bonanza that might occur since their dividend rate is either fixed or, if variable, generally has a set maximum.

It is wrong to assume that preferred stock fills a unique demand for an investment security in the market that other securities cannot fill. Dividends from common stock are as eligible for the dividend-received deduction available to corporate investors as preferred stock. Second, a portfolio of a firm's debt and common stock can be constructed to have a return that behaves closely to the return on preferred stock. Although preferred stock may appear to a corporate issuer to be more desirable than common stock because of its financial leverage characteristics, this advantage is likely to be illusory. With the present tax law, preferred stock has no special attributes for which an efficient market would be willing to pay a premium; thus, its cost is not likely to be cheaper than other forms of financing.

If the types of risks associated with an investment in common stock and preferred stock purchased individually (not a mixture) are what the market desires and if the risks and returns could not be exactly duplicated in any other way, then it would be possible for a firm with preferred stock outstanding to sell at a premium. As a theoretical as well as a practical matter, it is unlikely that the investors need the preferred stock to accomplish their investment objectives. If an explanation is to be found for the issuance of preferred stock, it is likely to be found in institutional considerations.

The issuing corporation does not have a tax shield with either preferred stock or common stock, so there is no advantage for the corporation issuing preferred stock to be found in the tax laws. The common stock can give rise to retained earnings (deferring taxes to the investor) and the prospect of capital gains from these retained earnings. The preferred stock does not offer these possibilities; thus, it is at a disadvantage. For zero-tax investors, neither preferred stock nor common stock has any specific advantage for the investor. Debt is likely to be more desirable than either security because of the tax shield provided to the issuer by the interest expense.

With a regulated public utility, preferred stock offers the investor some protection against arbitrary actions by the regulatory commission in regard to the return to be allowed on common stock equity. The preferred stock dividend is contractual, whereas the common stock dividend is a combined result of the judgments and actions of the regulatory commission and the corporation's board of directors.

In the case of zero-tax investors, it would be difficult to argue that preferred stock is inferior to common stock. We could still argue that preferred stock is inferior to debt.

## Convertible Exchangeable Preferred Stock

Let us assume that a corporation is operating at a level that leads to zero taxes. There are no current tax benefits associated with the issuance of debt. If exchangeable (into debt at the option of the issuing firm) preferred stock can be issued at a lower before-tax yield than debt, it will have a lower cost than debt.

But what if the corporation starts earning sufficient income to start paying taxes? The corporation would then prefer to have outstanding debt rather than preferred stock. The "exchangeable" feature of the security allows the corporation to force the investors to accept debt for the preferred stock. If both the preferred stock and debt cost 0.15 before tax, with a 0.35 tax rate, the after-tax cost of debt becomes 0.0975. This is a significant saving compared with the 0.15 cost of preferred stock.

The corporate investor that purchased the preferred stock with its 70 percent dividend-received deduction will not be pleased with the forced exchange into a debenture. The corporate investor can sell, convert into common stock, or merely accept the exchange. The interest rate on the bond is likely to be at least as large as the preferred stock dividend, and will be somewhat safer. Zero-taxed investors, such as pension funds, are likely to find the debentures of more value than will a corporation taxed at a marginal rate of 0.35.

The fact that the security is exchangeable at the option of the issuing corporation reduces the expected overall cost to that corporation, but it does decrease the attractiveness of the security to the normally taxed corporate investor.

The individual investor or the zero-taxed institutional investor would welcome the exchange, since the bond interest is safer than the preferred stock dividend. The investor cannot initiate the exchange and thus has to wait until the corporate issuer finds it advantageous to force the exchange.

The conversion feature is valuable to the investor since the investor can convert into common stock at any time. If the preferred stock's conversion value is $1,900 at the time of maturity, and the cash value if redeemed is $1,000, the value of the conversion right at that time will have a value of approximately $900. If the issuing corporation can call the bond prior to maturity, the value of the conversion feature may be cut off before it reaches $900, but it is likely to have some positive value.

The investor is not likely to opt for conversion prior to call or maturity unless the common stock dividend exceeds the preferred stock dividend or the debenture interest (the relative safety to the debenture interest and principal should also be considered), and even then there are strong reasons (risk avoidance) for not converting. The corporation is likely to call the convertible security if it can call and if the conversion value exceeds the call price.

The corporation can move the security from being preferred stock to being a debenture (desirable if the corporation changes from having zero taxable income to needing tax deductions). It can also call the security if the conversion value is larger than the call price and change the security into common stock.

The convertible exchangeable preferred stock is a sensible security, and we would expect the corporate and personal tax laws as written to encourage a variety of securities. As long as the tax law distinguishes between securities that are essentially the same, we can expect corporate financial officers to try to exploit this fact.

## Private Equity

Private equity firms find it convenient to use preferred stock to increase the return earned on the common stock of an investment.

Assume that with an investment of $1,000,000 (common stock) a private equity firm will earn $1,200,000 at time 1. A 20% return is not adequate and it has reached its debt capacity. However, it can issue $500,000 of preferred stock paying 0.10. The projected cash flows are:

|  | 0 | 1 | IRR |
|---|---|---|---|
| Basic Investment | −$1,000,000 | +$1,200,000 | 0.20 |
| Preferred Stock | +$ 500,000 | −$ 550,000 | 0.10 |
| Common Stock | −$ 500,000 | +$ 650,000 | 0.30 |

With the use of the preferred stock, the expected return on common stock is increased from 0.20 to 0.30.

If 0.30 is not a sufficiently high return, a larger amount of preferred stock could be considered.

## Preferred Stock as an Investment

Corporations have the dividend-received deduction as an incentive for them to invest in preferred stock. Individuals and zero-taxed investors do not have that incentive, and normally tend to not hold straight preferred stock in their portfolios. Straight debt with its tax deductibility for interest at the corporate issuer level is apt to be lower cost to the issuing corporation and should have a better risk-return relationship for the noncorporate investor than preferred stock.

Unless the tax laws are changed, preferred stock tends to be dominated for the noncorporate investor by straight debt and by common stock. A change in the tax laws could change this conclusion.

## Conclusion

It is not at all obvious that a firm's common stockholders benefit from the issuance of preferred stock over other financial instruments, if the issuing firm is paying income taxes. Like debt, preferred stock provides leverage that is likely to increase the rate of return on common stock investment as well as increase the riskiness of that return. But because debt also provides leverage at a lower after-tax cost, unless the firm does not wish to run the risk associated with debt, has reached its institutionally acceptable debt ceiling, or does not have taxable income, the stockholders would be better off with the issuance of debt to achieve financial leverage, assuming the firm does have debt capacity.

Tax considerations play an important role in the financing decision. Since all earnings before interest and taxes are available to pay interest on debt, and taxes must be paid prior to paying any income out as preferred dividends, the tax savings from debt can be used to retire the debt, while a lower-yielding preferred stock's dividend can continue as a claim perpetually. Thus, in a sense from a long-run perspective, preferred stock is more risky.

If debt capacity is available, debt has tax advantages compared to preferred stock. If the firm does not wish to issue debt (or cannot issue debt because of institutional barriers or restrictive covenants in its existing debt instruments), then the choice of whether to issue preferred stock or common stock is relevant and the risks and returns of each alternative must be weighed.

## Questions and Problems

For all problems, assume there is a 70 percent dividend-received deduction for a corporate investor (30 percent of the dividend is taxed). The corporate tax rate is 40 percent.

1. Assume that there is a corporate investor wanting to invest $10 million in your firm. Debt or preferred stock can be issued at a cost of 0.10. The firm needs $10 million of capital. Assume a 0.4 corporate tax rate.

   a. On a straight cash flow basis, should a firm issue debt or preferred stock?

b. If $1 million of earnings before interest and taxes (EBIT) is available, on a cash flow basis, are the investing firms better off with debt or preferred stock?

c. What amount does the firm have to earn to pay $1 million of interest? To pay $1 million of preferred stock dividends?

d. What is the before-tax percentage cost of 0.10 debt? Of 0.10 preferred stock?

e. What is the after-tax cost of each?

f. What does an investment have to earn *after tax* to be financed by debt? By preferred stock? Assume a break-even objective for the firm.

2. How much does a corporate investor net out (after tax) from $100 of interest? From $100 of preferred stock dividends?

3. What are the risks to a corporate investor buying preferred stock?

4. If callable preferred stock is issued at a price of $100 and promises to pay $9 per annum, what is the cost (as a percentage) of the issue after tax to the issuing firm if the call provision is expected to be exercised two years from now at a price of $105?

5. A corporation has earned $100 (before tax) and is paying the after-tax residual to its stockholders. Assume

$$k_i = k_p = 0.10.$$

The tax rate on all securities is 0.4, but there is a 0.70 dividend-received deduction for corporations investing in stock.

To a corporate stockholder, what is the after-tax dollar return if the security is a debt? A preferred stock? A common stock?

6. Assume a 0.4 tax rate. To pay 0.10, a company must earn what percentage return (before tax) if the security is:

a. Debt?

b. Preferred stock?

c. Common stock?

7. Describe the economic consequences of a corporation issuing 0.08 debt to finance an investment of $1 million in 0.08 preferred stock. The corporate tax rate is 0.4.

# Chapter 14

# Managerial Performance

This chapter will evaluate different quantitative financial measures of performance including return on investment and economic income. The arguments of this chapter are applicable to entire firms, self-contained operating components of a firm, or components that are not self-contained but in which there is a reasonable transfer pricing procedure. To compute any quantitative performance measurement of an operating unit, it is necessary to arrive at reasonable income and investment measures for the unit. There are a few shortcuts in undertaking an intelligent analysis of financial statements. A knowledge of accounting theory and practice is desirable to ensure a sound interpretation. Equally important is the fact that the analysis should be detailed and varied.

There are various tools of analysis that are helpful when used intelligently. But no tool of analysis is better than the information on which it is based. This is not an area in which one will find exact answers; often, the analysis will raise additional questions. Also, it should be noted that financial analysis based on published accounting data tends to be a short-run analysis. The long-run well-being of the firm is related to future conditions, competitive environment, technology, and other items that the accountant does not measure (such as the caliber of the younger executives of the firm). The financial analysis discussed in this chapter is a historical approach based on past events, not forecasts of the future. Accountants follow well-defined rules of the game (which we have called "Generally Accepted Accounting Principles") in preparing published financial statements. These rules and the contexts in which they are set must first be understood if accounting reports are to be properly used.

One of the most important and most difficult tasks of an administrator is to measure the performance of subordinates. Sometimes a measure is useful for one purpose, but not for another. The fact that a golf drive went 250 yards is useful in judging the force with which the ball was hit, but knowledge of the total distance covered is not useful in judging whether the drive was good or bad. We need information relating to the location and distance of the hole before we can make that type of decision.

How do we measure the performance of a member of management? The first step is to establish objectives. The second step is to see how well these objectives are met. We shall assume that a prime objective of the firm is to maximize profits; from the accountant's point of view, this is an important consideration. Other objectives such as maintaining continuity of existence will not be considered.

The extent of success in attaining objectives may be assessed quantitatively or qualitatively. The qualitative criterion will include things such as relations with superiors and subordinates, training of subordinates, professional attainments, civic activities, and ability to get things done. The qualitative factors are relevant in judging performance, but are more the province of the industrial psychologist than of the accountant or the financial manager.

## Performance Measurement and Managerial Compensation

Measuring managerial performance for praise or compensation determination is a difficult task. Any measure used is subject to valid objections. It is desirable that there be congruence between the firm's goals and the measures that are used. One cannot expect managers to consciously take actions that are desirable for the firm if those actions will adversely affect their career path or compensation.

My recommendation is to use several measures. Since all measures will be subject to some sort of gaming by management, the use of several good measures reduces the likelihood that managers will consciously make undesirable decisions.

We will review four basic measures that can be used:

1. Accounting measures (e.g., income return on investment, economic income, etc.).
2. Market measures (the return earned on an investment in the company's common stock).
3. Non-accounting but quantitative measures (e.g., customer and employee satisfaction).
4. Qualitative measures (subjective evaluations).

## Accounting Measures

The accounting measures we will consider are:

1. Sales revenue.
2. Operating margins: percentages or dollar amounts.

3. Income.
4. Return on investment or return on equity or return on assets.
5. Economic income (residual income or economic value added).
6. Earnings per share (for a period of years).

Sales revenue is an attractive accounting measure since there are relatively few arguments as to the magnitude. Add measures of the share of market and growth in sales, and one can become enthusiastic about the usefulness of the sales measures. But we should also consider profitability.

The operating margin is a popular profitability measure: subtract from sales revenue the direct costs of generating the revenue. For example, the operating margin of a retail store is sales minus the cost of the merchandise sold. With a manufacturer, the definition of the expenses to be subtracted to compute the margin is not as exact as for a retailer.

If sales are $100 and the cost of goods sold is $60, the operating margin can be expressed as a dollar amount, $40, or as a percentage, 40%. Operating margins as a control mechanism are very useful. If operating margins are maintained, it is likely that a positive bottom line (income) will result. On the other hand, many expenses (including capital costs) are omitted from the calculation. Thus, the operating margin can only be one of several measures that are used.

Income is revenue minus expenses as defined by Generally Accepted Accounting Principles. Unlike the operating margin, it includes the fixed expenses as well as the variable expenses.

The primary area where the income measure is deficient is the expense of the equity capital used. The implicit cost of the equity capital used is normally not deducted in computing the income.

It is essential that the costs of the capital used affect the performance measures. The two common measures are return on investment in some form and economic income. Economic income deserves to be used more extensively (its use is growing rapidly).

## Return on Investment (ROI)

Advocating the use of *return on investment* (ROI) implies that it is a better measure of performance than is obtained from using just the income of the operating unit. While this is normally the situation, not all subsidiary operating units should be judged using ROI, and ROI should always be only one of several measures. For many operating units, marketing efforts are not autonomous, and it is more appropriate to use cost minimization rather than profit maximization (or its near-equivalent, maximization of ROI, subject to constraints).

It should be realized that ROI is not necessarily the best measure of performance, but that ROI can be a useful measure. Consider what a good ROI measure can accomplish. We have first a measure of income; but before concluding that the income level is satisfactory, we relate the income to the amount of assets used to earn the income. While $1 million of earnings may be termed to be very good, if you are told that the operating unit used $100 million of capital to earn the $1 million, your conclusion might well shift from good to bad. To evaluate performance, it is necessary to consider the amount of assets used in earning the income. Thus, the use of ROI has advantages over the use of income only.

Instead of ROI, some firms use the *return on equity* (ROE). While the two measures have comparable uses, the ROE measure has several limitations:

a. It is affected by capital structure (which may not be controllable by the management being measured).
b. It adversely affects certain types of decisions (investment and divestment) because it is a percentage.
c. Equity investment creates biases unless the analyst distinguishes between investments in the equity of a subsidiary and investments in real assets.

The second limitation (b) applies equally to ROI as it does to ROE. Other terms commonly used instead of ROI are *return on net assets employed* (RONAE), *return on funds employed* (ROFE), *return on capital applied* (ROCA), and *return on assets* (ROA).

## Components of ROI

For some purposes, it is useful to break ROI into two components (this is sometimes referred to as the Du Pont formulation):

$$\text{ROI} = \frac{\text{Income}}{\text{Assets}}$$
$$= \frac{\text{Income}}{\text{Sales}} \times \frac{\text{Sales}}{\text{Assets}},$$

where income is measured after interest and taxes.

The term sales/assets measures the degree of asset utilization. The term income/sales measures profitability. The product of the two terms gives the return on investment.

The primary contribution of ROI (or ROE) is that management is held responsible for the capital used. However, return on investment may be used in a somewhat flawed manner (may adversely affect certain types of investment or asset retention decisions).

## Valuation of Assets

Important valuation problems arise in the areas of intangibles, inventories, investments, and fixed assets. These problems must be recognized by the analyst in using accounting data.

The problem of valuing intangibles may be avoided if the analyst subtracts them from the asset total (intangibles may be considered a residual, valued by earning power in excess of what would normally be expected from the tangible assets). This procedure substitutes the problem of valuation of the corporate entity for the problem of specific asset valuation. It is difficult to measure either the cost of the intangibles or their value.

The analyst has several choices in the valuation of fixed assets, including finding the current market values of these assets or determining their original or replacement costs and the extent to which their useful lives have expired. The measures may differ greatly. Usually the analyst will accept the reported (book) amounts, although the information given on the balance sheet may have no relationship to the current market values or to the original cost or to the current replacement costs of these assets.

These comments about the asset measures on the balance sheet may seem to be indirect criticisms of current financial reporting practices. The accounting profession, the FASB, and the SEC have improved accounting and reporting practices, but financial statements prepared to serve the uses of many varied groups cannot always provide the information required for particular decisions of a specialized nature. The recommended use of fair value has reduced the past criticisms of the use of historical cost measures.

## The Income Statement

It may be reassuring to read that a share of stock earned exactly $3.12 for the year. This is a positive and clear-cut statement, although it may be misleading. The measurement of the income of an enterprise for a short period of time is a difficult process. The shorter the time period, the more difficult the measurement.

One of the main difficulties is the inclusion or exclusion of items that are essentially adjustments of prior years' incomes and not revenues of this period or expenses of gaining the revenues of this period. The inclusion of an item of this nature, when large, can distort the measurement of the period's operating income or an estimate of the next period's income.

## ROI and Investment Decision Making

The use of ROI to evaluate performance can affect investment decisions because the manager knows that after accepting an investment its operations will affect the performance measurement. This leads to an incentive for the divisional (or other subcomponent) manager to reject investments that yield a lower return on investment than is being earned on the currently owned assets, even though the incremental investments are attractive for the firm.

Top management should be concerned not only with the return on investment of the assets being used, but also with the growth in assets and income. *Growth* as well as return on investment is important. A static division earning a 30-percent ROI may well be evaluated as being badly managed, whereas it may be concluded that a division that is growing and earning 15 percent is well managed.

The investment decision problem resulting from a desire to maintain a high ROI highlights the necessity of not relying on one performance measure (ROI or something else), but rather bringing in sufficient measures to restrain the impulse of persons trying to circumvent the control-evaluation system. Any defense of ROI should be based on a desire to use it as one method of evaluating the performance of investments, not so that it may be used to evaluate the desirability of under-taking investments. ROI is not an acceptable method of evaluating prospective investments.

## The Case of the Resource Benefiting the Future

Measures of performance used in an incorrect manner will tend to lead to incorrect conclusions. There is a necessity to improve the measures and to use them intelli-gently. Consider the case of a division manager of a timber company who has the opportunity to invest in 500,000 acres of prime timber land. The catch is that the trees on the land are all seedlings and they will not mature for 30 years. It is agreed by the planning group that the land is a good investment. However, the manager's performance is measured using return on investment. The manager knows that the land will increase the denominator (investment) now, but it will be 30 years before the numerator (income) is also increased. Since the division manager only has five years to go before retirement, the investment in land is rejected.

This case has a reasonable solution. The land should be excluded from the investment base in measuring performance unless the value increment is allowed to affect the income. Unless something like this is done, there will be a distortion in the investment performance analysis, and thus distortion in the investment decision-making criteria applied.

Now consider a plant being built with excess capacity to service the expected demand of year 2030. Is the normal performance measurement scheme capable of taking this situation into consideration? Probably it is not. Generally Accepted Accounting Principles do not do a good job of assigning expenses through time.

## The Computation of Income and ROI

It is widely known that straight-line depreciation or accelerated depreciation, except in very well-defined and specific situations, will distort measures of ROI. Also, the ROI that results for each year will differ from the internal rate of return computed at the time of acquisition, even when the expected results are realized.

Define theoretical depreciation (this is not the accounting depreciation) to be *the decrease in value of the investment during the time period.* Although the definition becomes more complex if there are additional investments made during the period, the theory can be used to compute the income that is used in the ROI calculations. The following example is used as a vehicle to show that return on investment, when properly calculated, gives useful performance measurement information.

Assume the net cash flows (and net revenues) associated with an investment costing $3,000 at time zero are:

| Time | Cash Flow |
|------|-----------|
| 1 | $1,300 |
| 2 | 1,200 |
| 3 | 1,100 |

The firm uses straight-line depreciation and has a time value of money of 10 percent. This investment has a yield (internal rate of return) of 10 percent. There are zero taxes.

Exhibit 14.1 shows the income and investments for each of the three years of use. The fact that each year has identical returns on investment equal to the internal rate of return of the investment seems to be a coincidence. However, if we inspect Exhibit 14.2, which shows the present value of the investment at three moments in time ($V_i$ is the value at time $i$), we see that in each period the decrease in value is $1,000 (the value of $V_3$ is zero), and that in this very special situation the use of straight-line depreciation is correct (if the cash flows are different, the depreciation schedule would be different). The present value at time 0 is $3,000; at time 1, $2,000; and at time 2, $1,000.

**Exhibit 14.1.**  Equal ROIs.

| Year | Cash Flows or Net Revenues | Depreciation | Income | Investment at the Beginning of the Period | ROI Income Divided by Investment |
|------|------|------|------|------|------|
| 1 | $1,300 | $1,000 | $300 | $3,000 | 0.10 |
| 2 | 1,200 | 1,000 | 200 | 2,000 | 0.10 |
| 3 | 1,100 | 1,000 | 100 | 1,000 | 0.10 |

**Exhibit 14.2.**  The Present Values.

| Time | Flows | Period 1 Present Value Factors | Time 0 Present Values | Period 2 Present Value Factors | Time 1 Present Values | Period 3 Present Value Factors | Time 2 Present Value |
|------|------|------|------|------|------|------|------|
| 1 | $1,300 | 0.9091 | $1,182 | | | | |
| 2 | 1,200 | 0.8264 | 992 | 0.9091 | $1,091 | | |
| 3 | 1,100 | 0.7513 | 826 | 0.8264 | 909 | 0.9091 | $1,000 |
| | | | $V_0 = \$3,000$ | | $V_1 = \$2,000$ | | $V_2 = \$1,000$ |

Define depreciation expense to be the change in economic value. The procedure works with any set of cash flows. There need not be distortion in ROI because of the method of depreciation. In this simplified example, the internal rate of return on the investment is equal to the firm's time value of money, and the cash flows of each period equal the net revenues. Different assumptions would add to the complexity of the calculations, but these complications can be solved.

## *The Economic Income Method*

Some managers call this method the *residual income method* and others call it *economic value added* or EVA. The main characteristic of the method is that interest on equity is deducted from income to obtain the net income. This procedure is very useful if we properly define income and investment, if the correct interest rate is used, and if interest is appropriately assigned to time periods. Unfortunately, the above requirements may not be fulfilled in a manner that will give theoretically sound (and useful) results if one uses conventional accounting in a situation where the benefits are increasing through time. Using the previous example, we illustrate an application of the economic income method.

Define economic income as net revenue less a capital consumption expense (depreciation) and the interest cost of the investment. Continuing the ROI example, the expected economic incomes for the three years are:

|  | Year 1 | Year 2 | Year 3 |
|---|---|---|---|
| Revenues | $1,300 | $1,200 | $1,100 |
| Depreciation | $1,000 | $1,000 | $1,000 |
| Interest Cost | 300 | 200 | 100 |
| Economic Income | $ 0 | $ 0 | $ 0 |

Note that if the internal rate of return is used as the interest rate (the basis of computing the interest cost), the economic incomes are equal to zero. Zero economic income is not a bad result, since investors earn the asset's internal rate of return which is above the firm's required return.

When the actual revenue of year 1 is $1,500 (beating the $1,300 expected revenue), there will be $200 of economic income.

Now assume the internal rate of return is 0.20 but the firm uses a 0.10 capital cost to compute the economic incomes. The revenues are now $1,600, $1,400, and $1,200 for years 1, 2, and 3, respectively. The asset again costs $3,000. The expected economic incomes are now:

|  | Year 1 | Year 2 | Year 3 |
|---|---|---|---|
| Revenues | $1,600 | $1,400 | $1,200 |
| Depreciation | $1,000 | $1,000 | $1,000 |
| Interest Cost | 300 | 200 | 100 |
| Economic Income | $ 300 | $ 200 | $ 100 |

The net present value (NPV) of the economic incomes is

$$NPV = \frac{300}{1.1^1} + \frac{200}{1.1^2} + \frac{100}{1.1^3} = \$513.15.$$

This $513.15 is also equal to the NPV of the cash flows:

$$NPV = \frac{1,600}{1.1^1} + \frac{1,400}{1.1^2} + \frac{1,200}{1.1^3} - 3,000 = \$513.15.$$

The present value of the economic income measures is tied to (and consistent with) the NPV measures used to evaluate the investment.

Some consultants call this economic income calculation "economic value added." This is unfortunate since the economic value added by the investment is $513.15 at time zero. The operations in the first year (with revenues of $1,600) result in the following value at time 1:

$$\text{Value at time } 1 = \frac{1,400}{1.1^1} + \frac{1,200}{1.1^2} + 1,600 = \$3,864.46.$$

Since the time zero value of the investment is $3,513.15, the economic value added at time 1 is $351.31, not the $300 of economic income computed above. The measure that is being computed is an income measure, not a value or a value change measure.

## Comparing ROI and Economic Income

Economic income offers several significant advantages over ROI as a performance measure. First, and most importantly, the use of ROI might discourage division managers from accepting investments that offer returns that are larger than the firm's required risk-adjusted returns, but that are less than the ROI the division is currently earning. If the new investment is accepted, the division's ROI will be decreased.

For example, suppose a division is now earning $30 million (a perpetuity) on an investment of $100 million. Then,

$$\text{ROI} = \frac{\$30,000,000}{\$100,000,000} = 0.30.$$

The division can invest an additional $50 million and earn 0.15 ROI or $7.5 million per year (a perpetuity) on this new investment. The firm's required return for this investment is 0.10; thus, the investment is economically desirable. Should the division accept the new investment? If it is accepted, the division's ROI is reduced from 0.30 to

$$\text{ROI} = \frac{\$37,500,000}{\$150,000,000} = 0.25.$$

Based on the adverse effect on the division's ROI, a manager might reject this economically desirable investment. This problem does not arise if economic income is used. The economic income before the new investment is

Initial Economic Income $= \$30,000,000 - \$10,000,000 = \$20,000,000.$

Note that the $15,000,000 interest cost is computed on the $50 million of new investment plus the $100 million initial investment, not just the portion financed by debt. After the investment, the economic income increases from $20,000,000 to

$$\text{New Economic Income} = \$37,500,000 - \$15,000,000 = \$22,500,000.$$

Based on economic income, there is an incentive for the division manager to accept the desirable investment and increase the economic income by $2,500,000.

The second problem with ROI is related to the first. ROI gives faulty evaluations of relative division performance. Consider two divisions, one with a ROI of 0.30 and the second with a ROI of 0.25. Which of the two division managers is doing the better job? Above, we showed that accepting the economically desirable investment reduces the division's ROI from 0.30 to 0.25. The division earning 0.25 is being managed better than the division that earns 0.30 and that rejects good investments. Using economic income to measure performance solves this problem that exists with ROI.

The third advantage of economic income is that it allows more flexibility. For example, if short-term interest rates are 0.20 and long-term rates are 0.12 (the pattern of 1980), the 0.20 interest rate could be used for working capital items in computing economic income. The ability to use different interest rates for different assets introduces a flexibility that ROI lacks.

## Summary of Complexities

The complexities of applying economic income to performance measures or compensation are:

1. The method of calculating depreciation expense.
2. The choice of the capital cost (interest rate).
3. The changing value of assets (e.g., inflation or technological change).
4. Risk.
5. Non-controllable factors affecting the measure.

## Summary of Economic Income Advantages

Economic income offers three primary advantages:

1. Any investment with a positive net present value or an internal rate of return larger than the firm's required return will have positive economic incomes.
2. The use of economic income will tend to not adversely affect investment or divestment decisions.

3. With the use of economic income, management is charged for the capital it uses; thus, management has a direct incentive to use capital economically.

Economic income is a very sensible measure.

## Market Measures

The stockholders are the firm's residual owners and they are interested in the stock's total return. How well did the CEO perform? What was the stockholders' total return?

The stock's return does not always track the CEO's performance, especially in the short run. A company may do well but the stock might go down (e.g., with an interest rate increase). Nevertheless, tying a CEO's compensation to the stock's market performance is sensible (as long as it is not the only basis of compensation calculation).

There are several comparisons that can be made. The firm's performance can be compared to a defined target return, the return earned by the market, or the returns earned by a set of comparable firms.

In addition to relating compensation to the current year's performance, it is reasonable to reward today's managers in the future for performance for the next ten years. It is desirable to give today's managers an incentive to make decisions with a concern for the future.

### *Earnings Per Share*

The earnings per share of common stock is widely used in investment analysis. It may be helpful in evaluating the investment worth of a share of stock, and it may also provide an indication of managerial performance.

Basically, earnings per share is the ratio of the earnings available to common stockholders divided by the average number of common shares outstanding.

$$\text{Earnings per Share} = \frac{\text{Earnings Available to Common Shareholders}}{\text{Average Shares Outstanding}}.$$

Many companies have relatively complex capital structures, and it is not unusual for these companies to present several earnings per share in their income statements. There are many complexities that can arise in the computation of earnings per share, most of which are beyond the scope of this book. However, we will consider some basic features of the earnings per share calculation that apply to most cases.

Earnings available to common stockholders generally consist of the net income for the period less any dividends or accumulations attributable to preferred stockholders. When there are extraordinary items, earnings per share should be calculated on the basis of income before extraordinary items, as well as net income. Thus, two earnings per share figures would be shown.

The number of shares outstanding may vary during a period because of business combinations, acquisitions of treasury stock, public issuances of stock, and so forth. In such cases, the calculation of earnings per share is based on a weighted average of shares outstanding during the period. Thus, if a company had 1,000,000 shares outstanding for four months during the year, and 2,000,000 shares outstanding during eight months, the weighted average would be 1,666,667 shares.

Companies with complex capital structures generally report two sets of earnings per share figures: primary earnings per share, and fully diluted earnings per share. Both of these sets of figures measure the earnings per share that would have been determined if certain securities had been converted and options had been exercised during the period. The distinction between the two sets of figures lies in the assumptions about which securities should be treated as though they had been converted into common stock.

## *Book Value Per Share*

The book value per share is the amount each share would receive if the company were liquidated on the basis of the historical accounting amounts reported on the balance sheet.

$$\text{Book Value per Share} = \frac{\text{Shareholders' Equity}}{\text{Shares Outstanding}}$$
$$= \frac{\$5,080}{166.4}$$
$$= \$30.53.$$

We have used the average numbers of shares outstanding. The end-of-period number of shares could just as logically be used.

The book value per share calculation is straightforward if the company does not have different classes of stock. The calculation becomes more complex when different classes of stock exist, because stockholders' equity items have to be allocated among the different classes of stock and the amount allocated to each class is then divided by the number of shares outstanding. With regard to the fact that the balance sheet valuations do not reflect or approximate fair market values, the book value per share figure is not likely to be very useful or meaningful for decision making.

## *Times Interest Earned*

The holders of debt are concerned about the security of their investment. The times interest earned ratio focuses on the safety or coverage of periodic interest payments.

$$\text{Times Interest Earned} = \frac{\text{Operating Income}}{\text{Interest Expense}}.$$

Looking at one year's figures can be misleading. Long-term creditors wish to have interest expense covered throughout the debt period. A company's operating income may differ quite dramatically from its cash flows from operations. Revenues and expenses may differ from cash receipts and disbursements.

## *Debt-Equity Ratio*

The debt-equity ratio gives an indication of an enterprise's ability to sustain losses without jeopardizing the interests of creditors. This ratio is based only on information provided in the balance sheet. Although stockholders' equity serves as a buffer to protect the creditors' interests, it should be kept in mind that the earning prospects of the enterprise are also relevant in judging a firm's ability to survive the long run. The debt-equity ratio is only one of several factors to be taken into consideration.

There are numerous ways in which the debt-equity ratio may be expressed. Four widely used and cited definitions will be presented here. These definitions can be used to express the balance between debt and equity, which together constitute the resources of an enterprise. These definitions can also be used to express the relative risk from relying on debt or equity.

One definition of the debt-equity ratio is the ratio of total debt to stockholders' equity.

$$\text{Debt-Equity Ratio} = \frac{\text{Total Debt}}{\text{Stockholders' Equity}}.$$

A second definition of this ratio focuses on a narrower definition of debt that includes only long-term debt. This definition excludes short-term debt as well as other debt that will not be paid according to a fixed payment schedule.

$$\text{Debt-Equity Ratio} = \frac{\text{Long-Term Debt}}{\text{Stockholders' Equity}}.$$

A third definition of the debt-equity ratio focuses on the relationship between total debt and total investment (e.g., total debt plus stockholders' equity). This ratio essentially provides the percentage of total investment composed of total debt.

$$\text{Debt-Equity Ratio} = \frac{\text{Total Debt}}{\text{Total Debt and Stockholders' Equity}}.$$

A fourth and final definition of the debt-equity ratio focuses on the relationship of long-term debt to total investment.

$$\text{Debt-Equity Ratio} = \frac{\text{Long-Term Debt}}{\text{Total Debt and Stockholders' Equity}}.$$

These four definitions of the debt-equity ratio focus on how well the creditors are protected.

## *Limitations of Ratio Analysis*

Although the use of ratios can prove helpful in analyzing financial data, there are some pitfalls. The first thing to keep in mind is that ratios based on accounting records will inherit many of the deficiencies of the accounting data. For example, ratios that incorporate long-lived assets in their calculations will be affected by the convention of recording assets at cost rather than current value and by the alternatives available for recording depreciation. Thus, two companies may be virtually identical, but the use of straight-line depreciation by one and accelerated depreciation by the other will result in differences when such things as the return on assets or the book value per share are computed. This could be overcome by making suitable adjustments in the data to place all firms on a comparable basis, but the analyst usually lacks sufficient data for doing this.

Another danger to be alert for is the arithmetic effect of certain types of transactions on the ratios. For example, the quick ratio is supposed to provide an indication of the company's ability to meet its current obligations when due. Suppose a company has cash of $40 million, accounts payable of $30 million, and no other current assets or liabilities. The current ratio and quick ratio would both be 1.33 to 1. Now suppose that the company used $20 million to pay a like amount of accounts payable. This transaction should have no special significance, as both the very liquid assets and the current liabilities would be reduced by the same amount — to $20 million and $10 million, respectively. The impact on the quick ratio is significant. This ratio would now be 2 to 1.

Ratios are most meaningful when viewed in comparison with those of other firms of a similar nature and when the trend of a period of years is established. Business services such as Dun & Bradstreet and Robert Morris Associates compile lists of important ratios for many industries, and these may be used in comparing the ratios of a particular company to those of its industry. One would expect, for example, that a firm in the meat-packing industry would have a smaller income as a percentage of sales than firms in the pharmaceutical industry. Comparing the operating ratios of a meat-packing firm with those of other meat-packing firms would give more meaningful results than comparisons with averages for all manufacturing industries.

## *Efficient Markets and Accounting*

In the past, accounting theory (and the choice among accounting alternatives) has been done on an *a priori* basis. This book was written in that spirit. For example, we first assume it is desirable to match revenues and the expenses associated with those revenues. The accounting entries that are appropriate for recording depreciable assets stem from that assumption. In recent years, another school of thought has arisen which suggests that we should consider the existing evidence as to how the financial markets actually use the accounting information presented. One of the major theories that forms the basis of this new school is the efficient market hypothesis.

The extreme position of those who advocate the efficient market hypothesis claims that all the market requires is basic financial information. We can expect the market to digest that information with the result that the market price will fully reflect the basic information, even if the accounting practice is not consistent with the best accounting theory. Thus, variations in accounting practice will not affect the market price of a firm's common stock, as long as the basic data are disclosed.

The efficient market hypothesis comes in several forms. We shall consider only three: the weak, the semi-strong, and the strong forms.

### *The Weak Form*

The efficient market theories had their origin in research that tended to prove that stock market prices were a random walk. According to the weak form of the efficient market hypothesis, to predict tomorrow's price of a share of common stock we need only today's price. Yesterday's price (the past history of the stock) or the volume of shares traded tell one nothing about tomorrow's price. The expected value of tomorrow's price is today's price (assuming a short time horizon). If valid, this state of the world eliminates a wide range of security analyses that look at patterns of stock price changes.

The implications for accounting practice of the "weak form" center on the accounting for securities that have a wide market. If stock prices follow a random walk, and if the expected value of tomorrow's price is today's price, then the accountant has a justification for showing such securities at market value.

## The Semi-Strong Form

The semi-strong form of the efficient market hypothesis states that the market incorporates all the known information about a stock, the current price reflects this information, and this information is incorporated in the price very rapidly. Thus, an investor cannot use the known public information to make a more-than-normal return.

Let us assume that two otherwise identical firms are presenting income statements, but that one firm uses the straight-line method in depreciating its equipment while the other firm uses the double declining balance method. The differences in accounting are fully explained with supporting schedules in their respective reports. The efficient market hypothesis, given the assumptions, suggests that both common stocks would sell for exactly the same price. The market would adjust for the accounting practices, so only the real differences would remain. In this case, there are no real differences; thus, the stock prices of the two firms would be identical.

A person who believes in the semi-strong form of the efficient market would argue that more attention should be directed toward obtaining completeness of disclosure and improving the timing of the announcements containing information rather than toward the form of the presentation. A person who doubted that the market was perfectly efficient in the semi-strong form might agree with the importance of completeness of information disclosure and the importance of timing, but he or she would still argue that the form of presentation made a difference to enough investors so that the accounting problems were still a relevant area and the improvement of accounting practices was a valid endeavor. In addition, since the processing of information has a cost, the accountant has an obligation to refine the information and present it in as good form as is feasible so that information processing costs can be reduced.

While one might not agree completely with the semi-strong form of the efficient market hypothesis, it would be incorrect to argue that the market is perfectly fooled by differences in accounting practices and makes no adjustment for such differences. If one firm is using FIFO (first-in, first-out) and a second firm is using LIFO (last-in, first-out), the market is likely to be making some type of adjustment for the fact that two different accounting assumptions are being used.

We would expect the market to make reasonably good adjustments where the supplemental information is clearly presented, but in some cases, where the information is not clear or is not publicly available, the adjustments may not be as effective. This brings us to the strong form of the efficient market hypothesis.

## The Strong Form

The strong form says that one cannot make abnormal profits with either publicly held information or nonpublic information. Thus, insiders cannot make abnormal profit if they trade using that information. It is difficult to test the strong form (it is against the law for insiders to trade using privileged information; therefore, obtaining information about the trading of insiders is extremely difficult). The author would guess that if one had good inside information, one could make abnormal profits. However, there is a tendency for a person who is too close to a situation to not appraise it objectively; thus, the strong form might have some validity. It is possible that insiders do not do as well as an envious outsider might think.

If we believe that the strong form does not hold and that insiders do have an edge in trading, then this conclusion affects the manner in which confidential accounting information is handled. For example, we would not want the employees of an independent certified public accounting firm to own or trade in the stock of a company the firm is auditing. The same conclusion holds for the executives of an industrial firm. If common stock is to be held by the executives, the stock should be held with other investments in a blind trust so that the timing of buy and sell decisions cannot be the result of information that is available only to a few. Thus, the strong form is important to accounting in a negative sense. Since we tend to reject the strong form, we think the information possessed by insiders is important, and rules should be established that prevent individuals from exploiting that information.

## Implications

The development of the efficient market hypothesis has implications for the development of accounting theory and practice. It is important for accountants to realize that there are many intelligent analysts interpreting the data and, as long as sufficiently accurate information is presented, the analyst is likely to work around differences in the exact form of a balance sheet or income statement. For example, accounting practice might insist on the use of fair value for presenting marketable securities, but this should not preclude the presentation of other market values such as bid and offer prices in a footnote. There are several possible ways in which securities may be presented in a balance sheet. It is possible that *a priori* reasoning may be able to suggest that one method is better than another method, and a more reasonable presentation might result in a decrease in information processing costs for the analysts.

## Non-Accounting Quantitative Measures

Given the generally accepted criticisms of accounting (e.g., it is cost-based), most analysts of business affairs search for other quantitative measures to complement (or replace) the accounting measures. These measures include:

1. Market penetration.
2. Customer satisfaction.
3. Employee satisfaction and turnover.
4. Units sold.
5. Diversity measures.
6. Quality control measures (percentage of defectives).

If reliable useful measures can be obtained, then the non-accounting quantitative measures can take their place with the accounting measures. In many situations, they will be more important than the accounting measures since they give a hint of the level of future incomes.

## Qualitative Measures

There are many qualitative aspects that enter into an evaluation. For example, a manager might be reliable and easy to work with. A manager might have laid the foundation for future growth by hiring outstanding managers and researchers. Does the manager generate enthusiasm and creativity? Has the manager enhanced the firm's reputation among customers and suppliers? There are many ways in which the manager can enhance the firm's future profitability and value by actions that do not lead to current profitability. To evaluate a manager's performance, it is necessary to consider these factors.

In addition, firms can have goals other than a measurable effect on profitability. This might involve the local society or society in a broader sense (e.g., protecting the environment beyond the legal requirements).

Intangibles are factors not easily measured, but they can be important to the long-run success of a corporation.

## Managerial Compensation

The basis of compensation should be both the operating results of the manager's specific unit and the results of the firm. The manager should have joint loyalties.

The basis of compensation should include quantitative objective measures, but not to the exclusion of qualitative measures. The existence of the qualitative considerations reduces the tendency of managers to game the system.

To some extent, some of the compensation should be deferred and be tied to the firm's future performance. We want managers to make decisions from a long-run perspective. The basis of compensation should be both accounting measures and market measures. The return earned by the shareholders should affect the compensation of the managers.

## Agency Theory Applied to Corporate Management and Performance Measurement

Problems of agency arise when a principal employs an agent to perform a task, and the interests of the principal and the agent are not identical. The corporate form is fertile soil for agency problems to take root. Consider the relationships between shareholders (the principal) and management (the agent). For many reasons including the increase in power, management might want the firm to grow while the shareholders would be better off with a small firm and a large cash distribution. It is necessary for the compensation method to be efficient in terms of eliminating the possibility of a management to undertake knowingly undesirable investments from the viewpoint of shareholders.

There can also be agency problems with different levels of employees. Consider the CEO and traders of a bank. They are all employees. They all want to increase the bank's profits. But the traders might have bonus arrangements that encourage them to take excessive risks from the CEO's perspective in order to earn a large bonus. This strategy might be good for the traders, but bad for the expected profits of the bank. A trader who wins becomes rich. A trader who loses gets an identical job with the bank across the street.

Another type of agency problem arises when one group is in a position to take advantage of a second group. Let us consider a firm financed by $9 million of 0.08 debt and $500,000 of common stock. There are zero taxes. Without any new investments, there is certainty of the firm earning $800,000 (before interest) and being able to pay the $720,000 interest on the debt. The stockholders would earn $80,000 per year. The firm is considering a $1 million investment financed by 0.08 debt. With this investment, there is 0.5 probability that no debt interest will be paid. The initial debtholders do not want the $1 million of new debt to be issued.

Obviously, the initial debtholders will attempt to structure their indentures so that they limit the ability of the stockholders to change the nature of the business in a manner that adversely affects the position of the debtholders. This is a variation of an agency problem.

Agency costs consist of several types. One is the transaction cost. Buyers of debt have to hire a lawyer that protects the debt buyers' interests. Corporations hire consultants to establish systems so that the traders of derivatives cannot bankrupt the firm. These are transaction costs or agency costs. Another type of agency cost arises because of the necessity to reward the agent in a manner that makes the agent's interests congruent with the principal's interests.

## Non-Controllable Factors

An oil company executive's firm is losing $500 million per year. The CEO is in danger of being fired. Then oil prices double and the firm makes $800 million. It is the same manager managing in the same way, but the economic environment has changed. Obviously, some attempt could be made to separate out the factors that are and are not controllable by the manager. But this is difficult, and is apt to introduce subjective measures into the evaluation.

This problem is an example of the qualitative aspects of performance evaluation.

## A Non-Zero Net Present Value

The basic example used in this chapter sets the net present value of the investment equal to zero, that is, the internal rate of return of the investment is equal to the time value factor for the firm. Obviously, this will only rarely be the case. We expect most investments to have expected returns in excess of their required return. For example, let us assume that the three-year investment costs $2,760 instead of $3,000. The net present value of the investment at the time of acquisition is $240, and its internal rate of return is 0.15. There are several possible paths we can take. Two methods will be described. The most straightforward would be to use 0.15 as the rate of discount to compute the depreciation expenses and returns on investment.

Using 0.15 as the rate of discount, we obtain:

| Period | Revenues | Depreciation | Income | Investment | ROI |
|--------|----------|--------------|--------|------------|------|
| 1 | $1,300 | $844 | $416 | $2,760 | 0.15 |
| 2 | 1,200 | 919 | 281 | 1,876 | 0.15 |
| 3 | 1,100 | 957 | 143 | 957 | 0.15 |

The primary difficulty with this solution is that the time value of money is defined to be 0.10, not 0.15. Thus, the values of the investment at each time period are greater than those shown above. A second solution is to immediately adjust the value of the investment to $3,000, the present value of the benefits, despite the fact that the investment cost is only $2,760. This procedure would not be acceptable for conventional financial accounting purposes because of the implicit threat of manipulation, but it would be acceptable for internal managerial purposes. It is a very appealing procedure because it is relatively simple and yet is correct from the standpoint of accounts reflecting values.

## Incentive Consideration

The use of book value based on cost to measure the investment (the denominator in the ROI calculation and the basis of the interest cost in the economic income calculation) or even the use of estimates of price-level-adjusted cost is subject to severe criticism. There is no reason why a system based on values estimated by management cannot be used for internal purposes instead of cost-based conventional accounting. Here we have an opportunity to apply ingenuity to bypass a valid objection by managers to cost-based accounting.

Rather than asking an accountant or another staff person to supply the number on which the managers are to be judged, let us ask the managers to supply the value estimate. The procedure would be simple. Take a set of eligible managers and ask them to "bid" periodically for the assets they want to manage and for which a change in management is appropriate. The manager whose bid is accepted takes the asset, and the bid becomes the accounting base for performance evaluation. If the manager bids too high, that manager gets the asset but will find it hard to meet the return on investment and economic income requirements. If the manager bids too low, a competing manager will win, or alternatively the "board" may reject the bid and ask for revised bids. There is one major difficulty with this procedure. Managers can rig the time shape of projected earnings so that early targets can be easily attainable. This tendency would have to be controlled by the top managers awarding the bid. Large deferred benefits would have to be discounted.

The proposed procedure would have many advantages. It would establish an investment base whose measure is acceptable to both the operating manager and the top level of management (the former sets the value, the latter must accept it). The accountant serves the very important and proper function of supplying relevant information that is used by the managers in making their respective judgments and bids. The ROI and economic income measures are improved because the investment base is appropriate to the specific investment and manager being evaluated rather than being the result of a series of historical accidents (such as the year of purchase and the method of depreciation). Most important, it requires managers to set, describe, and quantify their plans for the utilization of the assets. It would tie together planning, decision making, and control.

## Deferred Benefits

Conventional depreciation accounting combined with the uses of ROI is at its worst when the benefits produced by the asset are expected to increase through time or when the benefits are deferred. The early years are greatly penalized by conventional accounting, with the managers having an incentive to avoid such investments so that their performance evaluations do not suffer.

For example, assume an investment costing $3,000 is expected to have the following benefit stream:

| Period | Benefits |
|--------|----------|
| 1 | $1,100 |
| 2 | 1,210 |
| 3 | 1,331 |

The firm's cost of money is 0.10 and is equal to the investment's discounted cash flow internal rate of return. The results using conventional accounting and straight-line depreciation will be (assuming the actual benefits are equal to the expected):

| Period | Revenues | Depreciation | Income | Investment | ROI |
|--------|----------|--------------|--------|------------|-----|
| 1 | $1,100 | $1,000 | $100 | $3,000 | 0.03 |
| 2 | 1,210 | 1,000 | 210 | 2,000 | 0.105 |
| 3 | 1,331 | 1,000 | 331 | 1,000 | 0.331 |

The first year's operations are not acceptable.

Defining depreciation expense to be the decrease in value of the asset, the results would be:

| Period | Revenue | Depreciation | Income | Book and Value Investment | ROI |
|--------|---------|--------------|--------|---------------------------|-----|
| 1 | $1,100 | $ 800 | $300 | $3,000 | 0.10 |
| 2 | 1,210 | 990 | 220 | 2,200 | 0.10 |
| 3 | 1,331 | 1,210 | 121 | 1,210 | 0.10 |

The value ($V_i$) and depreciation ($d_i$) calculations are:

$$V_0 = \$3,000 \text{ at time } 0 \quad d_1 = \$3,000 - \$2,200 = \$800 \text{ in period } 1$$
$$V_1 = \$2,200 \text{ at time } 1 \quad d_2 = \$2,200 - \$1,210 = \$990 \text{ in period } 2$$
$$V_2 = \$1,210 \text{ at time } 2 \quad d_3 = \$1,210 - \$0 = \$1,210 \text{ in period } 3.$$

The distortion caused by conventional accounting can be increased by assuming no (or very low) benefits until period 3. The operating results of the early years would appear to be even worse than in the example.

## Cash Flow Return on Investment

Recognizing the inadequacies of conventional depreciation accounting, some managers have attempted to solve the problems by using cash flow return on investment. Since cash flows are used to evaluate the investment, why not use them to evaluate the investment's performance?

Define the cash flow return on investment to be:

$$\text{Cash Flow Return on Investment} = \frac{\text{Cash flow}}{\text{Investment}}.$$

The computation seems to be appealing because depreciation is not computed, but unfortunately, the computation merely makes a bad analysis worse. Using the previous example where the investment has a 0.10 internal rate of return, we would obtain:

| Period | Cash Flow | Investment | Cash Flow ROI (Cash Flow/Investment) |
|--------|-----------|------------|--------------------------------------|
| 1 | $1,300 | $3,000 | 0.433 |
| 2 | 1,200 | 2,000 | 0.600 |
| 3 | 1,100 | 1,000 | 1.100 |

Some firms have actually tried to use the historical measures as required returns for additional investments. You should note that for an investment yielding 0.10 over its life, the cash flow ROIs for the three years are 0.43, 0.60, and 1.10. The measure greatly overstates the ROI the asset is actually earning.

Another difficulty of the measure is that it will tend to bias management in favor of capital-intensive methods of production, because capital cost is omitted from the numerator of the performance measure.

It is better to use the conventional ROI with income (after depreciation) in the numerator than to use the cash flow ROI, which is extremely difficult to interpret and has no theoretical foundation. The use of the measure illustrated above will get management into one or more interpretive difficulties. There are alternative methods of using cash flow return on investment that are improvements over the method illustrated.

## Planning Implications

The fact that there may be a conflict between the investment criteria used and the performance measures means that corporate planning must take into consideration the fact that all desirable investments (from the corporate standpoint) may not be submitted upward. It would be naive to expect a division manager to recommend a plant with 60 percent excess capacity where the analysis of mutually exclusive investments indicates that this is the best alternative, if the performance measures for a period of five years will be adversely affected by the choice. Rather, the division manager is likely to bury this type of alternative so that the board of directors is not confused by the number of alternatives and this "undesirable" alternative specifically.

The managers have a similar type of conflict when they evaluate major investments that satisfy normal investment criteria, but have adverse effects on the ROIs and earnings per share of the next few years because of conventional accounting.

The planner rejecting investments with positive net present values may gain short-run benefits (nondepressed earnings), but will have a long-run cost in that future earnings will be depressed compared to what they could have been.

One alternative is to use the recommended investment criteria and hope to modify the accounting conventions that cause the distortions. Failing that, management can alternatively attempt to explain the characteristics of the investment (and the deferred benefits) to the investing community.

The best solution would be for the accounting profession to encourage a wide range of depreciation methods, if these methods are justified by the economic characteristics of the investment. Currently, too rapid write-off (R&D, training, plant and equipment) leads to (1) bad measures of performance and (2) non-optimal decisions.

## Conclusion

Annual or quarterly accounting profits can be a poor measure of what has been accomplished during any relatively short period of time. Also, it is often difficult to assign responsibility for a deviation from the profit objective. Many economic events with long-run implications are not recorded by the accountant. One should not use any performance measure without considering those factors not normally appearing in the management information system.

In some cases, the ROI or economic income should not be used for operating units because it is too difficult to measure either the income or the investment. Normally, the measure of ROI can be used to gain an impression of managerial performance, but the use of ROI should always be supplemented by economic income measures. This is necessary if the top management of a firm is attempting to measure the effectiveness of the utilization of assets controlled by persons at different levels of the firm. The economic income is a very useful means of accomplishing this, if efforts are made to measure income and investment in a useful way. Economic income combined with economic depreciation is very good. Performance measures can be made as complex or simplified as you wish.

In conclusion, to measure performance you *can* use ROI (never by itself), but economic income is strongly recommended. To make investment decisions, you *cannot* use ROI effectively.

Although performance measurement is a difficult task when exact reliable measures of income and investment are not feasible, it is necessary that all managers evaluate persons for whom they are responsible. As guides and indicators, ROI and economic income have their uses.

## Questions and Problems

1. As of the end of December, the current liabilities of the Large Steel Company are $800 million and its liquid assets are $600 million. The funds generated by operations in the past year were $1 billion, and it is expected that this rate will continue in the future.

   How many days of funds generation would be needed to pay the amount of current liabilities in excess of liquid assets?

2. (continue 1) The Large Steel Company also has $1 billion of long-term debt in addition to the $800 million of current liabilities.

   How many days of funds generation would be needed to pay the amount of total liabilities in excess of liquid assets?

3. The Large Steel Company has $1.5 billion of current assets, $0.8 billion of current liabilities, and $1 billion of long-term debt. It generates $1 billion of funds per year.

   Compute some meaningful measures relating assets, debt, and funds generation.

4. The following information applies to the ABC Company for the coming year:

| | |
|---|---:|
| Earnings before interest and taxes | $3,000,000 |
| Interest | 300,000 |
| Principal repayment | 1,200,000 |
| Depreciation (for taxes and accounting) | 800,000 |
| Tax rate | 0.40 |

What before-tax cash flow has to be earned to meet the debt requirements in the coming year?

5. Does the use of inventory necessarily affect the amount of cash that is held by a corporation?

6. Why is EBIT generally used in the interest coverage ratio rather than income after taxes?

7. A bank loan officer is considering lending $2 million on a 60-day note to a corporation.

What quantitative measures should the loan officer compute? If the loan is for 20 years, how should the analysis differ?

8. The following facts apply to two companies for the year ending December 31 of the same year:

| | Company A | Company B |
|---|---|---|
| Income | $10,000,000 | $10,000,000 |
| Funds flow | 16,000,000 | 16,000,000 |
| Interest payments | 4,000,000 | 3,000,000 |

No long-term debt (principal) payments are due for either firm for 10 years.

Before evaluating the liquidity of the two firms, what additional information would you desire?

9. The basic defensive interval (BDI) is defined as:

$$BDI = \frac{\text{total defensive assets}}{\text{forecasted daily operating expenditures}}.$$

The defensive assets include those assets that can readily be turned into cash (liquid assets) such as cash, marketable securities, and accounts receivable.

Evaluate the usefulness of the BDI.

10. An analyst wants a cash flow coverage ratio prepared from the point of view of the common stockholders of a firm. The firm has a long-term debt and preferred stock outstanding.

Prepare a useful ratio for the analyst.

11. To earn $78 after tax, how much has to be earned before tax? The tax rate is 0.4.

12. The depreciation expense for taxes is $80 and the debt principal payment is $110.

    With a tax rate of 0.4, what do the before-tax earnings have to be in order to have sufficient cash to pay the debt principal?

13. Does a high current ratio indicate a well-managed company?

14. What would be the effect on the all-asset earning rate in the year in which equipment is acquired of using sum-of-the-years' digits rather than a straight-line depreciation procedure?

15. A leading company in the paper industry included the following information in an annual report:

    "Timberlands are carried at $1 per cord of estimated standing softwood on November 30, 1904, plus subsequent purchase acquisitions at cost, less deple-tion based on timber cut. The carrying values of timberlands do not reflect regrowth in areas which have been cut or current market values for stumpage which are believed to be substantially higher than carrying values."

    Comment on the procedure followed.

16. Assume you were thinking of investing $1,000,000 in a common stock. If you were given today's stock price, would you pay anything to find out yesterday's price? Explain.

17. (continue 16) Would you pay anything for the entire past history of stock prices of that stock?

18. Assume you believe 100 percent in the semi-strong form of the efficient market hypothesis. In June, you are considering investing $1,000,000 in the common stock of a firm whose fiscal year ends December 31 and whose annual report came out in March. Would you look at the last year's annual report? Explain.

19. Assume you believe 100 percent in the strong form of the efficient market hypothesis. A friend is working in the accounting department of a large publicly traded firm. He inadvertently discloses the quarter's income, which is very different from the forecasted income. Ignoring legal and moral issues, would you trade? Explain.

20. Should a public accounting firm allow its employees to hold stock in publicly owned firms that are being audited by the firm?

21. "The company's stock has reached a new high, therefore you should sell." Evaluate this advice.

22. "The company's stock has reached a new low, therefore you should buy." Evaluate this advice.

23. "We cannot record the investment in stock at its market value, since we know that value of the stock will change in the future." Evaluate this statement.

24. There have been many cases where the market has seemed to be fooled by bad accounting. Some companies whose stocks had sold at high prices are now in bankruptcy. Do these examples "prove" that the market is not efficient?

25. A business case states that the stock of the company being studied dropped from a 20x1 peak of $31 a share to $10 by mid-20x2. It then states, "In the light of this development the management had ruled out a new issue of common stock as a source of financing capital expenditures so long as the price of the company's common stock remained depressed."

    Do you agree with the position?

*Chapter 15*

# Mergers and Acquisitions: Consolidations

Two firms may join together (a merger) to form a new joint firm, or one firm may acquire all the common stock of another firm (an acquisition). The consequences of both restructurings are the same. Almost all firms are either actively engaged in merger activity or worried about being acquired. Thus, the topic is important to management.

Mergers and acquisitions occur for many different reasons, ranging from the desire for risk reduction to the necessity of doing something with extra cash currently held for which the firm has no other special plans. Consider the following four acquisitions of oil companies:

1. Socal (now Chevron) acquired Gulf Oil for US$13.2 billion in 1984.
2. Texaco acquired Getty Oil for US$10.2 billion in 1984.
3. DuPont acquired Conoco for US$7.4 billion in 1981.
4. U.S. Steel acquired Marathon Oil for US$6.5 billion in 1981.

All four acquisitions occurred because the management of the acquiring firm thought that the oil reserves were undervalued by the market. Socal and Texaco were seeking additional oil reserves. DuPont and U.S. Steel were diversifying out of their basic industries because they saw relatively low profits and high risks in those industries (chemicals and steel). The diversification efforts were not effective.

## Reasons for Mergers

### *Obtaining Resources*

Many specific reasons are given for mergers and acquisitions. For example, if a firm wants to start a new type of activity, an acquisition of a firm may be quicker than doing it from scratch. Another reason for mergers is that retention of earnings saves investor taxes; thus, it is a sensible strategy compared to a cash dividend and may be the best internal use of resources from the viewpoint of stockholders.

There are many reasons for mergers and acquisitions. Among them are:

1. Synergy (real and imaginary), the process whereby it is hoped that 2 plus 2 equals 5, but sometimes it equals 3.
2. Financial considerations (including tax effects).
3. Bargain prices and availability of capital.
4. Psychological reasons (empire building by managers and raiders).
5. The P/E effect.
6. The reduction of risk (diversification).

One of the more important reasons for a merger is that it will lead to the acquisition of resources such as:

1. Management talent.
2. Markets.
3. Products.
4. Cash or debt capacity.
5. Plant and equipment (replacement cost is less than the price).
6. Raw material.
7. Patents.
8. Know-how (processes or the management team).

## *Diversification*

Another reason for mergers and acquisitions is diversification (risk reduction). Risk diversification is a difficult objective to evaluate. Individual investors can diversify for themselves. A corporation does not have to diversify for its investors.

Mergers and acquisitions are generally assumed to reduce risk for the acquiring firm, but this is not necessarily so. If the risk of the acquired firm is sufficiently large, it tends to contaminate the financial position of the firm acquiring it. Paying too much for an acquisition can also adversely affect the acquirer's risk.

Despite this, certain types of mergers tend to reduce risk. Assume two firms have operations that are perfectly independent of each other, both in an economic and statistical sense. In this situation, investors who keep their investment size the same in a merger will reduce their risk. We are assuming that the failure of one firm will not cause a failure of the second firm, and that operations are not affected by the merger. For example, say one group of investors owns a firm where there is a 0.5 probability of success and 0.5 probability of failure. If that firm is merged with a second firm with the same probabilities of success and failure but whose operations are independent, and if the original investors now own 50 percent of the merged firms, there would only be a 0.25 probability of both portions of the merged firm failing. Hence, in this case, risk has been reduced (the expected return may be unchanged).

For simplicity's sake, we generally assume the goal of a firm is profit maximization (in present value terms) in order to maximize the well-being of the common stockholders. We should periodically question this assumption, since corporations are also in existence to serve other groups, for example, management.

When a firm diversifies by merging with or acquiring a firm in another industry, who benefits? Let us consider the position of the shareholder and, for purposes of focusing on diversification, let us assume zero investor tax rates. The objective of diversification is risk reduction. The advice not to put all one's eggs in one basket is good advice if the objective is to avoid a feast-or-famine situation.

The individual shareholder can diversify easily by buying stocks in different firms in different industries or by investing in mutual funds. The stockholder of a company does not need the company to incur costs to achieve diversification.

If diversification can generally be efficiently achieved by investors, then why do firms diversify? Naturally, there are many investors who are not well diversified and would like the corporation to diversify on their behalf. More importantly, management has its major asset invested in the firm, and this asset is difficult to diversify. The major assets of managers are their careers. If a company goes bankrupt or enters a period of financial difficulty, the middle-aged manager pays a heavy price. Hence, it is reasonable for such a manager to seek a higher level of security by trying to stabilize the income of the corporation.

## *Synergy*

A popular reason offered for mergers is that the two firms joined together will be more valuable than the sum of the values of the two independent firms. There will be synergy. Synergy is a process whereby when 1 and 1 are added, more than 2 is obtained. Two firms joined together may be worth more than they are worth individually. There are several reasons why a merger of the two firms may result in total profits larger than the sum of the two individual profits. Two firms may be more valuable after a merger than as separate entities because:

1. One firm may be badly managed and the other firm may have managerial talent.
2. One firm may have assets (e.g., plant or liquid assets) that can be effectively used by the other firm, or intangible assets such as technological, marketing, or production know-how.

3. Horizontal integration — increases markets (and possibly reduces competition).
4. Vertical integration — increases operating efficiencies by integration of production.
5. Joint utilization of service facilities, or organization and elimination of duplication.

All of the former might lead to operating efficiencies (lower costs). Horizontal integration might also lead to decreased competition, which, although not socially desirable, might well be welcomed by management (this type of merger would tend to be discouraged by government bodies).

A form of synergy can be derived since the market adds value for size. A firm of large size tends to be able to obtain capital at a lower cost. Consistent with this is management's hope that the market will pay a higher P/E ratio for the stock of a larger, less risky firm.

Profits may also increase when a resource-poor company acquires a resource-rich company because the marginal value of that resource is greater for the resource-poor company. Thus, there are oil companies with wide distribution networks acquiring firms with large amounts of oil reserves but inadequate distribution systems.

## Tax Implications

A tax-loss company might acquire a profitable company in order to use its tax loss, or a profitable firm might acquire a tax-loss company. (To take advantage of the loss, the loss company must be operated; it cannot be acquired just for the tax loss.)

The tax motivation for a merger is sometimes not apparent to the public since both firms involved are reporting incomes. It must be remembered that a firm with accounting income might still have a tax loss.

Frequently, acquisitions of privately owned firms occur because the owners of the acquired firm want to prepare their estates for the inevitable moment of death. There are advantages to an estate in having marketable stock whose value is relatively easily determined, rather than having partial ownership in a privately owned corporation. In the latter case, it is necessary to estimate the value of the firm, and this valuation process is far from being as objective as a stock market price.

## Growth

The question might be asked as to why a firm would acquire another firm when the acquiring firm could enter the industry by developing its own product and productive facilities. Acquisition is much faster and sometimes safer than "doing it yourself." Management has its own reasons for wanting rapid growth. Growth through merger and acquisition means more power and prestige as well as the potential for higher salaries and bonuses.

## Size

Size itself may be one of the reasons for a merger (not the only reason, it is hoped). Size is thought to reduce financing costs and may offer bargaining power in negotiating with suppliers.

It is also possible that some managers value size as reflecting a type of personal achievement, but this is not likely to be a significant factor as a general explanation of mergers.

## Anti-Raiding Maneuver

Some mergers take place in order to fight off other raiders. A reluctant bride might well prefer a friendly marriage to a white knight rather than succumb to a raid by a black knight. Managers are people, and it is reasonable to expect that they will fear not being able to continue as they did in the past. They would like to choose their next boss. This desire may give rise to a merger with a friendly firm (a white knight), even though the number one choice (if feasible) would be to continue with unchanged operations.

## Different Expectations

If the managers and owners of two firms have different expectations, they will compute different values, and this might create a situation where an exchange can take place.

Other factors that create such a situation are different perceptions of the time value of money (or different actual time values) and different risk attitudes. Different opinions help to create mergers.

## Antitrust Considerations

The U.S. Justice Department, the Federal Trade Commission, and the European Union act as watchdogs to prevent mergers that tend to lessen competition or tend to create a monopoly. There are some who would also like them to prevent the largest firms in the economy from acquiring any smaller firms in any industry.

Since it tends to lessen competition or create a monopoly, the prevention of any merger or acquisition will obviously be a judgment call if the two firms involved are in the same industry. Well-defined distinctions between legal and illegal mergers are very difficult to define. The application of laws depends to a large extent on the political and philosophical leanings of the persons administering the law.

It is reasonable to expect that a conglomerate acquisition (unrelated businesses) will be more likely to be approved by the Government than will a horizontal acquisition (say, a department store chain acquires another department store chain). A vertical integration (either integrating backward by acquiring a material or parts supplier or forward by acquiring a sales outlet) will tend to be less acceptable than a conglomerate acquisition, but more acceptable than a horizontal acquisition.

## Acquisition for Cash

A firm finding itself with extra cash above that required for normal operations essentially has four choices:

1. Expand *present* activities.
2. Add *new* activities.

   a. "Do-it-yourself" with basic building blocks.

   b. Acquire an ongoing activity by the merger and acquisition process.

3. Give the excess cash to stockholders via the following methods:

   a. Dividends.

   b. Other cash distributions (such as the repurchase of shares by the firm).

4. Retire debt.

If the cash is not available, any of the above can also be financed by raising new capital.

We will concentrate in the following sections on the merger alternative using either accumulated cash or new capital. The objective is assumed to be to increase value. The first step will be to determine the premium that the acquiring firm can afford to pay.

## *Determining the Premium*

We want to determine how much cash a firm can offer for an acquisition when as an alternative it can pay a cash dividend and its investors can buy shares of the same firm in the capital market. We will assume that the investor's objective is to acquire the shares of common stock in the firm being acquired.

Let $P_0$ be the current market price of the firm to be acquired and $x$ equal the stock price multiplier. The investor's tax rate is $t_p$. The bid price is defined to be:

$$\text{Bid price} = xP_0.$$

Assume that a firm has $D$ available either for reinvestment or for a cash dividend. To make the investor indifferent to retention or a dividend, we want the same number of shares purchased with retention as with dividend (we initially assume that capital gains and dividends earned by a corporation are not taxed).

The shares to be purchased by the investor with the after-tax proceeds of a cash dividend of $D$ are

$$\Delta N = \frac{D(1 - t_p)}{P_0},$$

where $P_0$ is the current common stock price and $t_p$ is the tax on the investor's ordinary income.

With retention and a bid price of $x P_0$, the shares purchased by the firm with the $D$ dollars are

$$\Delta N = \frac{D}{x P_0}.$$

Equating the above two equations yields

$$\frac{D(1 - t_p)}{P_0} = \frac{D}{x P_0}.$$

Solving for $x$, we obtain

$$(1 - t_p) = \frac{1}{x}$$

or

$$x = \frac{1}{1 - t_p}.$$

## Example 15.1

Assume that the stock being acquired is actually selling for $40 and that this is its value. Let $t_p = 0.6$. To compare a dividend and firm acquisition, we first compute the stock price multiplier that results in indifference.

$$x = \frac{1}{1 - t_p} = \frac{1}{0.4} = 2.5.$$

$$\text{Bid price} = x P_0;$$

$$2.5 \times \$40 = \$100 \text{ per share.}$$

With a dividend of $100, the investors net $40 after tax. The cash buys one share with a tax basis of $40. With retained earnings of $100, the firm can pay $100 per share for one share. The tax basis is $0 for the investors and $100 for the corporation.

If the $100 is retained and $100 is paid by the corporation for a share, then one share can be purchased. If the $100 is paid as a cash dividend, the $60 of tax is paid and a share can be purchased for $40. The company can pay 2.5 times the current market price and leave the taxable investor with the same number of shares of stock of the acquired firm as if the investor had purchased the stock directly.

This analysis ignores the capital gains tax that would take place on sale and assumes that the alternative to retention by the firm is a cash dividend.

## A Holding Company

Although holding companies are not a widely used form of business organization, it is not unusual to see a chain of firms owning each other.

### *Example 15.2*

Assume A owns B which owns C which owns D which owns E. The common stock of A is $10,000. Mr. Jones owns 51 percent of A's common stock financed with borrowed funds.

|  | A | B | C | D | E |
|---|---|---|---|---|---|
| Assets | $50,000 | $500,000 | $5,000,000 | $50,000,000 | $500,000,000 |
| Debt | 40,000 | 400,000 | 4,000,000 | 40,000,000 | 400,000,000 |
| Common stock | 10,000 | 100,000 | 1,000,000 | 10,000,000 | 100,000,000 |

Now assume that:

1. A owns 50 percent of B's common stock.
2. B owns 50 percent of C's common stock.
3. C owns 50 percent of D's common stock.
4. D owns 50 percent of E's common stock.

E has $100,000,000 of common stock and $500,000,000 of assets, and Jones controls it all with an investment of $5,100 financed with the bank's money.

The consolidated balance sheet shows the immense amount of debt.

**Consolidated Balance Sheet**

| | |
|---|---:|
| Debt | $444,440,000 |
| Common stock, minority interest | 55,550,000 |
| Common stock | 10,000 |
| | $500,000,000 |

This is an extreme case, since all of A's assets consist of stock in B, all of B's assets consist of stock in C, etc.

# EBIT and EBITDA

Two profitability measures not normally presented by the accountants but widely used by finance people and managers are EBIT (earnings before interest and taxes) and EBITDA (earnings before interest, taxes, depreciation and amortization). Private equity firms, in particular, use these measures in determining the value of a prospective acquisition.

EBIT is particularly useful when the capital structure of the acquisition candidate is financed with debt, since the amount of taxes is reduced to close to zero and EBIT is more relevant than after-tax earnings.

EBITDA is a cash flow measure of operations. If the capital expenditures have already been made, eliminating the depreciation and amortization deductions in computing the positive flows from operations is sensible. If additional capital expenditures will be needed in the future, then the final valuation should reflect these as additional outlays.

## Valuation for Acquisition

The four basic methods of valuating a firm for acquisition are:

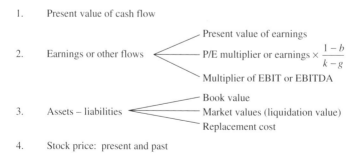

1.  Present value of cash flow

2.  Earnings or other flows
    - Present value of earnings
    - P/E multiplier or earnings $\times \dfrac{1-b}{k-g}$
    - Multiplier of EBIT or EBITDA

3.  Assets – liabilities
    - Book value
    - Market values (liquidation value)
    - Replacement cost

4.  Stock price: present and past

The cash flow approach to valuation treats a firm being considered for acquisition the same as any real asset. The cash flows are the relevant input.

Since a firm has an earnings history, there is a temptation to use the earnings as the input. One can compute the present value of the earnings. If interest on all capital is subtracted in computing the earnings of each year, the present value of the earnings will be the same as the net present value of the cash flows.

An alternative valuation approach using earnings is to multiply the earnings by a price/earnings multiplier. The basic valuation model is

$$P = \frac{D}{k-g} = \frac{(1-b)E}{k-g}.$$

If we multiply $E$ (the earnings per share) by $\frac{(1-b)}{(k-g)}$, where

$$1 - b = \text{the retention rate}$$
$$k = \text{the required return}$$
$$g = \text{the growth rate},$$

we obtain the value of a share. This can be made to be equivalent to computing the net present value of the cash flows and the present value of the earnings, if all the inputs are consistent, but the equivalency should not be assumed. If we divide both sides by $E$, we have for the $P/E$ multiplier

$$\frac{P}{E} = \frac{1-b}{k-g}.$$

Instead of using the income flows, some analysts prefer to use other flow measures (e.g., EBIT or EBITDA). Instead of using flows, one can also use the assets and the liabilities for valuation. The easy measures to use are the book values (the data are readily available), but either market values (including liquidation values) or replacement costs are likely to be more useful. Not considering the flows is not recommended.

With the acquisition of a firm whose stock is traded on a market, the present and past stock prices are relevant. Investors will consider any offer in relation to the current stock price and are likely to compare any offer to the recent past prices (even though past prices are not relevant in a theoretical economic sense).

### *Other Factors to be Considered*

The existence of assets that can be sold, or debt capacity that is available, will affect the value of an acquisition. Some assets will not be recorded (e.g., recent knowledge acquired through research) or will be stated on the financial statements at understated costs (e.g., land).

An important consideration for management is an analysis of the effect of the acquisition on the riskiness of the firm. This will be high on management's list of relevant considerations.

## The P/E Ratio

We want to investigate the financial effects of a high-P/E ratio firm (P) acquiring a low-P/E firm (S). Table 15.1 shows the financial information for the two firms and for their combination.

## *Example 15.3*

If P gives 25,000 shares having a market price of $80 per share (having a total value of $2,000,000) for S, there will be 125,000 shares outstanding. What is their value if the earnings per share is $11.20?

It is incorrect to argue that the P/E of P + S will be the same as the P/E of P, leading to a price of $11.20 × 8 or $89.60. The new price/earnings ratio can be expected to be a weighted average of the old P/E ratios, where the weights are the total earnings of each of the companies divided by the total earnings of both companies.

$$\text{New P/E} = \frac{E_P}{E_P + E_S}(\text{P/E of P}) + \frac{E_S}{E_P + E_S}(\text{P/E of S})$$
$$= \frac{\$1,000,000}{\$1,400,000}(8) + \frac{\$400,000}{\$1,400,000}(5)$$
$$= 5.714 + 1.429 = 7.143.$$

**Table 15.1.** Financial Information for Firms P and S.

| | The Merger of P and S | | |
| | P | S | Pro Forma (P + S) |
|---|---|---|---|
| Total market value | $8,000,000 | $2,000,000 | $10,000,000 |
| Total earnings | $1,000,000 | $400,000 | $1,400,000 |
| Number of shares | 100,000 | 100,000 | 125,000 |
| Earnings per share | $10 | $4 | $11.20 |
| Market price | $80 | $20 | $80 |
| P/E ratio | 8× | 5× | 7.143× |

This leads to a market value of a share of P + S equal to 7.143($11.20) = $80. The total market value is

$$\$80(125{,}000) = \$10{,}000{,}000,$$

which is equal to the sum of the values of firms P plus S. Value is being neither created nor destroyed by the acquisition.

With no change in operations, expectations, or payouts, the post-acquisition P/E ratio should be a weighted average of the pre-acquisition P/Es, where the weights are the relative amounts of earnings of each component.

To understand better the logic of why the P/E of firm P + S is less than that of firm P, we will determine the implied growth rates for P and for S. Table 15.2 shows the current dividend, the cost of equity, and the retention rate. For example, P earned $10 and paid a $6 dividend; therefore, the retention rate is 0.4.

Using the one-stage growth model,

$$P = \frac{D}{k_e - g}$$

and, if $D = (1 - b)E$, then

$$P = \frac{(1 - b)E}{k_e - g}.$$

Solving this relationship for $g$, we obtain the implicit growth rate:

$$g = k_e - (1 - b)\frac{E}{P}.$$

For firm P, we have

$$g = 0.15 - \frac{1}{8}(1 - 0.4) = 0.15 - 0.075 = 0.075.$$

**Table 15.2.** Additional Information.

|  | P | S |
| --- | --- | --- |
| Current dividend | $6.00 | $2.00 |
| Cost of common stock equity ($k_e$) | 0.15 | 0.15 |
| Retention rate ($b$) | 0.4 | 0.5 |

With zero debt, and a return on investment of $r$ for new investments, then

$$g = rb$$

$$0.075 = 0.4r$$

$$r = 0.1875.$$

For firm S, we have a lower implied growth rate:

$$g = k_e - \frac{E}{P}(1 - b)$$

$$= 0.15 - \frac{1}{5}(1 - 0.5) = 0.05.$$

The implicit return on new investments is

$$g = rb$$

$$0.05 = 0.5r$$

$$r = 0.10.$$

Firm S has a lower growth rate than does P; we also see that S is expected to earn only 0.10 on new investments, whereas P is expected to earn 0.1875. P's higher P/E ratio implies that the market is more optimistic about its future growth and earnings opportunities.

Each $P/E$ ratio and dividend retention percentage implies a different growth rate (and thus a different return on new investment). Table 15.3 gives a few illustrative values for a retention rate of 0.6 and a 0.15 cost of equity capital.

The relationship $g = rb$ assumes that there is zero debt. If we changed that assumption, the growth rate formulation would be somewhat more complex.

**Table 15.3.** Implied Growth Rates and Returns.

| $P/E$ | $\frac{E}{P}$ | $0.60\frac{E}{P}$ | $g = 0.15 - 0.60\frac{E}{P}$ | $r = \frac{g}{0.4}$ |
|---|---|---|---|---|
| 20 | 0.05 | 0.03 | 0.12 | 0.30 |
| 10 | 0.10 | 0.06 | 0.09 | 0.225 |
| 5 | 0.20 | 0.12 | 0.03 | 0.075 |
| 4 | 0.25 | 0.15 | 0 | 0 |

Note: $b = 0.4$; $k_e = 0.15$; $g = k_e - (1 - b)\frac{E}{P}$; $g = rb$.

Thus, assuming that a firm can be acquired for its current market value, it is not important if the current P/E of the candidate for acquisition is above or below the acquirer's P/E. It is important whether the acquisition can be expected to result in an increase in the acquirer's P/E as a result of a change in operations (changing retention rates or debt utilization), a decrease in financing costs ($k_i$ and $k_e$), or real synergistic effects such as better rates of return on reinvestment or direct reduction of cost (higher current earnings). If the weighted average post-acquisition P/E ratio exceeds the weighted average pre-acquisition P/E ratio, or if earnings improve, the acquisition will tend to be beneficial to stockholders of both the acquired and acquiring firms.

## *Dilution of Earnings*

Assume that earnings per share are now $1.20 and that they are growing at 5 percent per year. If the acquisition takes place, the earnings per share will only be $0.80, but the expected growth rate will now be 10 percent per year. The earnings per share are diluted.

How long will it take for the earnings with the acquisition to equal the earnings without the acquisition? Let both sets of earnings grow for $n$ years so that the two earnings are equal:

$$(1.05)^n 1.20 = (1.10)^n 0.80$$

$$\left(\frac{1.10}{1.05}\right)^n = 1.5$$

$$n \ln(1.0476) = \ln 1.5$$

$$n = \frac{0.405465}{0.04652} = 8.716 \text{ years.}$$

After 8.716 years without the acquisition, the earnings will be

$$(1.05)^{8.716}(\$1.20) = 1.53(\$1.20) = \$1.84.$$

After 8.716 years with the acquisition, the earnings will be

$$(1.10)^{8.716}(\$0.80) = 2.295(\$0.80) = \$1.84.$$

Many managers would state that 8.716 years is too long to wait for an uncertain improvement in earnings per share and would reject the acquisition.

# The Cost of an Acquisition

If an acquisition requires the issuance of 1,000,000 shares, where the shares of the acquiring firm before the acquisition announcement were selling at $80 per share, the cost of the acquisition can be defined to be

$$\$80(1,000,000) = \$80,000,000.$$

If there are 3,000,000 shares outstanding before the acquisition, and 4,000,000 shares after, and if the total value of the post-acquisition firm's stock is $400,000,000, we could define the cost to be

$$\$400,000,000 \times \frac{1,000,000}{4,000,000} = \$100,000,000,$$

since one-fourth of the shares are being given away to achieve the acquisition. However, this is stretching the definition of cost, since the firm would not be worth $400,000,000 without the acquisition.

If the 3,000,000 shares are worth $80(3,000,000) = $240,000,000 before the acquisition and $300,000,000 after the acquisition, the original stockholders will have a $60,000,000 improvement in their wealth position (before tax). The total value of the firm after the acquisition is assumed to be $400,000,000.

Although common stock is frequently issued for an acquisition, since the transaction can be nontaxable to the investors, cash, debt, and preferred stock are also used.

If instead of issuing new common stock shares, in the example, a purchase price of $80,000,000 cash is paid and if the firm's value after acquisition is $320,000,000 (equal to $400,000,000 minus the $80,000,000 purchase price), then the stockholder's position will now improve from $240,000,000 to $320,000,000, for a gain of $80,000,000.

# Leveraged Buyouts

In a leveraged buyout (LBO), a firm is acquired by a group of investors. The financing for the purchase is characterized by the use of a large amount of debt. There are two basic types of leveraged buyouts. One type is engineered by the current management whose members become significant stockholders in the new firm. The second type is structured by outsiders, but almost invariably they will attempt to retain the more important members of management.

A very large LBO of the first type was the acquisition of Metromedia Broadcasting Corporation by a group called J. W. K. Acquisition Corporation. The acquisition price was over US$1 billion. In fact, Metromedia itself issued US$1.3 billion worth of high-yield bonds to help finance the acquisition (the funds were used to buy back the company's common stock). To place this amount of debt in perspective, the total recorded assets of Metromedia was US$1.3 billion. J. W. K. Acquisition Corporation was controlled by the management of Metromedia.

As long as banks and other investors are willing to finance very highly leveraged acquisitions, LBOs will prosper. They are a very important financial development of the end of the 20th and the beginning of the 21st centuries.

## Greenmail

Historically, a corporation (or a corporate management) finding that it was being pursued by an undesirable suitor (a black knight) would arrange to buy the shares held by the black knight at a premium price. The intentions of the raider may be perfectly honorable, but the perceptions of the management might be different. The greenmail process is not fair to all shareholders. One select group of investors is given the opportunity to sell at a premium price. Congress passed a law that imposes a tax penalty on any firm engaged in greenmail and this effectively stopped the process. Now, the same offer to buy has to go to all shareholders.

## Golden Parachutes

If the defensive tactics of a target firm have not worked, then management's final option is to have a safety net. A contractual agreement is prepared that guarantees a manager a given sum if his or her employment is terminated because of an acquisition or merger (a change of control).

## Accounting Issues

It is not unusual for a corporation to own shares of common stock in one or more other corporations. The percentage of ownership may vary from a few shares, representing a small percentage of ownership, to 100 percent of the shares outstanding. In the absence of an actual merger, when the percentage of ownership is large, it is usually desirable to treat the separate corporations as if they were a single entity, resulting in consolidated financial statements. Regardless of the extent of the holdings involved, we must determine the manner of treating intercorporate investments on the balance sheet and of recognizing the income attributable to these holdings.

## Accounting for Long-Term Investments

Assume that one corporation is purchasing shares of common stock in a second corporation but that the percentage of ownership is relatively small. In this situation, it would not be appropriate to consider the financial affairs of the two corporations as if they were one corporation.

Let us assume that Corporation A has purchased a small percentage of the outstanding shares of Corporation B. If Corporation A views these shares as a *temporary investment*, it would classify the investment as a marketable security (a current asset). If the shares are a *long-term investment*, however, the accounting treatment is somewhat different. Corporation A owning common stock in B may:

a. Maintain the investment account at cost.
b. Adjust the investment account as market value changes.
c. Record the investment at the lower of cost or market value.
d. Record the investment at cost and adjust for Corporation A's equity in the subsequent changes in undistributed earnings (or losses) of Corporation B.

Each of these procedures will now be discussed.

## Cost

The advantage of using cost is that the cost of the investment may be documented with well-defined objective evidence and the use of cost here is consistent with the basis used to record other long-lived assets. The disadvantage of recording the investment at cost is that, with time, cost becomes a poor estimator of value. It is not significant information for A to indicate that it paid $100,000 for shares of Corporation B stock 30 years ago. The cost is likely to have little relationship to the value of these shares today.

How is the income of A affected by the income earned by B? The use of cost to record the asset implies that income is recognized as the dividends are received on the shares. But dividends received may be a poor measure of the economic gain arising from possessing an investment in securities. The problem becomes even more acute when the stock holdings are so large that the investing corporation can influence the dividend policy of the company whose stock it holds. In such a case, it would be possible to manipulate the reported earnings of Corporation A by altering the dividend distributions of Corporation B. Therefore, this income measuring procedure should be used only when the investor corporation does not have a significant influence over the affairs of the company in which the investment is held.

## Market

Recording the investment at market value is an improvement over the use of cost. The measure of the asset reflects what the market thinks the investment is currently worth. It has the characteristic of resulting in a valuation that will fluctuate as the stock market fluctuates. However, for many investments, there is not an effective market. This is true of wholly owned subsidiaries or where several companies join forces to form a subsidiary. In these situations, market valuation cannot be used. Nevertheless, in situations where a well-defined market price does exist, and where the holdings can be readily sold at the market price (this would not be the case if holdings were very large or the market thin), the market price provides the best measure of the fair value of the investment for most purposes.

If market prices are used to record the value of the investment, then changes in market prices must be recognized as affecting the stockholders' equity. One possibility is to treat the change as income (or a loss). Any dividends received are recorded as revenue with this procedure.

## *Equity*

The fourth procedure, usually referred to as the **equity method**, retains an objective basis for recording the investment, yet does not adhere to original cost as the measure of the investment. After recording the investment at its initial acquisition cost, adjustments are made to reflect the proportionate share of the earnings (or losses) of the company whose shares have been purchased. The recognition is not contingent on the declaration of a dividend.

This procedure is particularly appropriate when the purchasing corporation has control of the other corporation and can influence the amount of dividends paid. The earnings of the period provide a more objective means of determining the economic benefits that accrue from the investment in this situation than do the dividends.

When earnings are reported by the purchased company, a proportionate share of the earnings is added to the Investment account and recognized as revenue by the acquiring company. When dividends are received, they are not considered to be revenue. The revenue has already been recognized based on the equity in the earnings of the company. The receipt of cash is recorded as an exchange of assets — the Investment account is reduced and Cash is increased — but there is no effect on income.

## Consolidated Financial Statements

When the percentage of ownership of one company in another is large, it is often desirable to provide statements showing the operating results and financial position as though the separate corporations were combined into a single operating unit.

Such **consolidated financial statements** frequently replace the single-company statements prepared in the manner described in the previous chapters of this book. The consolidated statements are regarded as so important that they overshadow the financial statements of the separate corporations, and many corporations provide only the consolidated statements in their annual reports.

When one corporation owns a substantial proportion of the shares of another corporation, the investing corporation is called the **parent corporation**. Any corporations in which it has substantial investments are known as **subsidiaries**. In preparing consolidated statements, the accountant ignores the legal fact that the companies are each separate entities. Instead, the companies are treated as though they were a single entity and the accounting treatment is adjusted accordingly. Taking the economic point of view, it is reasonable to cast aside the legal fiction of separate entities and combine the financial affairs of several corporations when the corporations do, in fact, operate as a single unit.

## *Accounting Assumptions*

The consolidated statements are based on information contained in the separate company statements. Adjustments are likely to be necessary for purposes of consolidating the affairs of the several corporations. For example, the investment in subsidiaries is shown as an asset on the statements of the parent company. This would be true of any of the basic methods described in the first part of this chapter. When the companies are consolidated, the original investment of the parent and the corresponding portion of the stock equity of the subsidiary at the time of purchase must be eliminated. These two items are redundant from the consolidated entity viewpoint, because the net assets of the subsidiaries (which the Investment account represents) will be included in the assets of the combined unit.

The parent company's share of stock equity of the subsidiary as of the date of stock purchase must be eliminated because it does not represent an outstanding capital element of the consolidated company. From the consolidated entity point of view, it is akin to treasury stock. The Investment account must be eliminated, because the consolidation procedures effectively change the purchase of common stock into the purchase of assets and the assumption of liabilities. It would be double counting to include both the parent company's investment and the subsidiary's net assets in the consolidated statement.

The need for another adjustment arises when the subsidiary sells goods to the parent (or the parent to the subsidiary). Profit is recognized at the time of a sale to outsiders. From the separate company point of view, the parent company is an outsider to the subsidiary and vice versa. In accounting for the separate legal entities, then, it is appropriate to recognize profits on sales transactions between the two companies. When the two companies are treated as a single entity, however, adjustments must be made for intercompany sales transactions. They are now considered to be mere transfers within the same organization, and no profit is recognized. The profit that has been recognized in the separate company accounts for such transactions must therefore be eliminated when consolidated statements are prepared.

## Consolidated Balance Sheets

The preparation of a consolidated balance sheet requires the combining of various account balances of the separate legal entities. Before such combinations can be accomplished, however, certain adjustments and eliminations must be made in the data.

Although we will describe these adjustments in terms of accounting entries, it should be pointed out that these entries are for worksheet purposes only and are not recorded in the journals of either company. From the legal point of view, it is the consolidated entity that is an accounting fiction, a mere creature of the accountant designed to provide economic information in a relevant context. Thus, the consolidated entity does not exist in a strict legal sense, although it is convenient to assume its existence for the purpose of providing information.

The first example will assume that the parent, Company A, has purchased 100 percent of the common stock of Company B. For simplicity's sake, the amount paid in this example will be equal to the book value of the stock.

## *Example*

Company A buys 100 percent of the common stock of Company B for $10,000. Immediately after the purchase, the separate balance sheets of the two companies appear as follows:

**Company A**
**Balance Sheet as of December 31, 20xx**

| Assets | | Liabilities and Stockholders' Equity | |
|---|---|---|---|
| Investment in Company B | $10,000 | Liabilities | $15,000 |
| Miscellaneous Assets | 30,000 | Common Stock | 20,000 |
| | | Retained Earnings | 5,000 |
| | | Total Liabilities and | |
| Total Assets | $40,000 | Stockholders' Equity | $40,000 |

## Company B
## Balance Sheet as of December 31, 20xx

| Assets | | Liabilities and Stockholders' Equity | |
|---|---|---|---|
| Miscellaneous Assets | $18,000 | Liabilities | $ 8,000 |
| | | Common Stock | 7,000 |
| | | Retained Earnings | 3,000 |
| | | Total Liabilities and | |
| Total Assets | $18,000 | Stockholders' Equity | $18,000 |

The first step in preparing the consolidated balance sheet is to organize the data from the separate statements in a worksheet. This is done in the first two columns of the following worksheet. We then proceed with the necessary eliminations and adjustments, and add the remaining items to obtain data for the consolidated balance sheet (the right-hand column of the worksheet).

| Accounts | Company A | Company B | Eliminations Dr. | Eliminations Cr. | Consolidated Balance Sheet |
|---|---|---|---|---|---|
| Miscellaneous Assets | $30,000 | $18,000 | | | $48,000 |
| Investment in Co. B | 10,000 | | | (1) $10,000 | |
| | $40,000 | $18,000 | | | $48,000 |
| Liabilities | $15,000 | $ 8,000 | | | $23,000 |
| Common Stock | 20,000 | 7,000 | (1) $ 7,000 | | 20,000 |
| Retained Earnings | 5,000 | 3,000 | (1) 3,000 | | 5,000 |
| | $40,000 | $18,000 | $10,000 | $10,000 | $48,000 |

The elimination entry is a credit to the Investment account of Company A to eliminate the investment in Company B (but leaving the assets of Company B) and debits to eliminate the stock equity of Company B as of the time of purchase.

Let us assume that the elimination entry was not made and that the consolidated balance sheet was prepared by naively adding the asset, liability, and stock equity accounts of the two corporations.

| | |
|---|---|
| Miscellaneous Assets | $48,000 |
| Investment in Co. B | 10,000 |
| | $58,000 |
| Liabilities | $23,000 |
| Common Stock | 27,000 |
| Retained Earnings | 8,000 |
| | $58,000 |

The former statement shows total assets of $58,000, but this includes a double counting of $10,000 of B's assets, because not only are the real assets of Company B included but also the investment of Company A in Company B. The value of the investment of A in B is derived from the assets that are already included; thus, to include the investment again would be double counting. In like manner, the stock equity is overstated by $10,000, because not only are the rights of the investment of A in B included but also the rights to the assets of B, and this is also counting the same thing twice.

Based on the figures shown in the last column of the worksheet, the consolidated balance sheet would appear as follows:

### Company A and Subsidiary
### Consolidated Balance Sheet as of December 31, 20x1

| Assets | | Liabilities and Stockholders' Equity | |
|---|---|---|---|
| Miscellaneous Assets | $48,000 | Liabilities | $23,000 |
| | | Common Stock | 20,000 |
| | | Retained Earnings | 5,000 |
| | | Total Liabilities and | |
| Total Assets | $48,000 | Stockholders' Equity | $48,000 |

Complications would be introduced if Company A purchased 100 percent of the common stock at a price different from the book value of the stock equity of Company B. For example, if Company A had paid $12,000 for stock with a book value of $10,000, this would indicate that Company A thought there was $2,000 of intangible values such as goodwill or that the other assets were undervalued. If the former is assumed to be true, the elimination entry would be:

| | | |
|---|---|---|
| Common Stock — B | 7,000 | |
| Retained Earnings — B | 3,000 | |
| Goodwill | 2,000 | |
| Investment in Co. B | | 12,000 |

Again, the investment and the stock equity of Company B are eliminated. In this situation, an intangible asset of $2,000 is recognized inasmuch as Company A paid $2,000 more than the book value of the assets. If we can trace the excess of the purchase price to specific asset accounts, then those asset accounts, rather than the Goodwill account, should be debited.

Instead of increasing specific asset accounts or creating a Goodwill account, the difference between the amount paid and the book value of the stockholders' equity is sometimes debited to an account called Excess of Investment Cost over Book Value. This account is then treated as a noncurrent asset. The disadvantage of this procedure is that it results in a poorly defined asset item that the average reader of financial reports will have difficulty in interpreting. It is better for the accountant to make the decision as to whether the amount paid in excess of book value is a result of undervaluation of specific assets or the presence of goodwill. If assets are understated, they should be written up to a realistic value. If there are intangibles connected with the utilization of the assets, resulting in the expectation of high future earnings, it is reasonable to record the amount as goodwill.

Assume that Company A had paid $8,000 for the common stock. This is an amount less than the book value. The book value of the assets is overstated, and there is a type of negative goodwill. Negative goodwill indicates that the earning power of the assets is actually less than we might expect from assets of this nature or, equivalently, that the assets are overstated. The elimination entry might be:

| | | |
|---|---|---|
| Common Stock — B | 7,000 | |
| Retained Earnings — B | 3,000 | |
| Investment in Co. B | | 8,000 |
| Excess of Book Value over Investment Cost | | 2,000 |

The credit item Excess of Book Value over Investment Cost would not appear on the balance sheet. It should be allocated among the identifiable assets, reducing assets to their value at the time of acquisition. As explained earlier, it is, in a sense, negative goodwill. Instead of crediting the amount Excess of Book Value over Investment Cost, we may credit the specific assets that are overvalued. This is appropriate if we are able to identify the assets that are overstated. It has the double advantage of being more straightforward, thus easier to understand, as well as presenting better information relative to the valuation of the assets owned.

## Minority Interest

Another complication arises when Company A purchases less than 100 percent of the common stock outstanding. This gives rise to a **minority interest** in the consolidated corporation. If we assume the same situation as the previous one, except that Company A purchases 80 percent of the common stock for $8,000, the elimination entries would be:

| | | |
|---|---|---|
| Common Stock — B ........................... | 7,000 | |
| Retained Earnings — B ........................ | 3,000 | |
|     Investment in Co. B ......................... | | 8,000 |
|     Minority Interest ............................. | | 2,000 |

The minority interest would appear on the consolidated balance sheet of Company A between the liabilities and the stockholders' equity, or as part of the stockholders' equity section. It represents the interest of outside stockholders of the subsidiary in the assets of the consolidated corporation.

In the example cited, A paid an amount equal to the book value of B times the percentage of ownership acquired by A (the percentage of ownership being measured by the fraction of common stock shares it acquired). Let us now assume that A paid $12,000 for 80 percent ownership in B. There are two possible methods of treating this situation.

If A paid $12,000 for 80 percent of the ownership, then the value of the entire stockholders' equity could be inferred to be $15,000. Let $X$ equal the value of B; then,

$$0.8X = \$12,000,$$

$$X = \$15,000.$$

The book value of the stockholders' equity is $10,000; thus, there is $5,000 of goodwill (or any of the other possible interpretations previously described). The following elimination entry might be made:

| | | |
|---|---|---|
| Common Stock — B ........................... | 7,000 | |
| Retained Earnings — B ........................ | 3,000 | |
| Goodwill ..................................... | 5,000 | |
|     Investment in Co. B ......................... | | 12,000 |
|     Minority Interest ............................. | | 3,000 |

The minority interest is equal to 20 percent of $15,000, the inferred value of Company B.

The foregoing treatment, which assumes it is appropriate to adjust the total assets of B, is reasonable. In current practice, however, accountants recognize goodwill only to the extent that it has been paid for. Thus, they would record only

$4,000 of goodwill. The $4,000 is computed as follows:

| | |
|---|---:|
| Investment by A | $12,000 |
| Equity in Identifiable Assets of B (80% of total value) | 8,000 |
| Goodwill | $ 4,000 |

In this case, the following elimination entry would be made:

| | | |
|---|---:|---:|
| Common Stock — B ........................... | 7,000 | |
| Retained Earnings — B ......................... | 3,000 | |
| Goodwill ...................................... | 4,000 | |
| Investment in Co. B ........................... | | 12,000 |
| Minority Interest .............................. | | 2,000 |

The minority interest is equal to 20 percent of the $10,000 book value of the stockholders' equity of Company B.

The second treatment assumes that it is reasonable to record the goodwill for the portion of the firm purchased by the parent, but it is not reasonable to record the goodwill of the minority interest. This is consistent with the usual accounting convention of recording intangible assets only when they are explicitly purchased. The value of goodwill relating to the minority interest may be imputed from the parent corporation's purchase, but inasmuch as the minority shareholders did not explicitly pay for goodwill, it is not recorded under this assumption.

In the following example, we shall assume that A paid $5,600 for 80 percent ownership. Again, there are two possible methods of recording this situation, but we shall illustrate only the procedure that assumes it is appropriate to adjust the asset valuation completely. We first find the value of the stockholders' equity. If 80 percent is worth $5,600, then the entire stockholders' equity is worth $7,000 (instead of the book value of $10,000). The elimination entry would be:

| | | |
|---|---:|---:|
| Common Stock — B ........................... | 7,000 | |
| Retained Earnings — B ......................... | 3,000 | |
| Investment in Co. B ........................... | | 5,600 |
| Excess of Book Value over Investment Cost ....... | | 3,000 |
| Minority Interest .............................. | | 1,400 |

The minority interest is equal to 20 percent of $7,000, the inferred value of the stockholders' equity of Company B. The Excess of Book Value over Investment Cost would be allocated to the various specific assets and liabilities in preparing the consolidated statement. The specific assets of B are assumed to be overstated in the aggregate by $3,000.

## Intercompany Transactions

In addition to the entries eliminating the investment of the parent in the subsidiary and the stockholders' equity of the subsidiary, there may be intercompany transactions that require elimination entries. For example, B may be in debt to A. Assume B owes A $2,000. The elimination entry would be:

| | | |
|---|---|---|
| Accounts Payable — B ......................... | 2,000 | |
|     Accounts Receivable — A ..................... | | 2,000 |

Failure to eliminate the receivable on the books of A and the payable on the books of B would be like a husband declaring himself a millionaire because his wife lost that sum to him in a gin rummy game. For intrafamily purposes, the data may be of interest; but in a consolidated statement, which treats the combined operations as a single unit, the receivable and payable offset one another.

If B declares a cash dividend, A and B might record the declaration in their accounts. The following elimination entry would be required if the dividend has been declared and recorded by both parties but not yet paid (assume the total dividend is $4,000, of which $3,200 will go to A):

| | | |
|---|---|---|
| Dividends Payable — B......................... | 3,200 | |
|     Dividends Receivable — A..................... | | 3,200 |

If A has sold a product to B, some of which is still in B's inventory, and there is an element of profit in the price charged by A, it is necessary to eliminate the profit from the inventory of B and from the retained earnings of A. Assume A has made a profit of $0.25 per dollar of sale, and that B has inventory that was purchased from A at a cost of $4,000. It is necessary to make the following eliminations:

| | | |
|---|---|---|
| Retained Earnings — A......................... | 1,000 | |
|     Inventory — B................................. | | 1,000 |

This entry eliminates the $1,000 of intercompany profits from the inventory of B and the retained earnings of A (the debit could be to the Income Summary of A).

In the presence of a 20-percent minority interest, some accountants would make the foregoing entry, but some would eliminate only 80 percent of the profit in the inventory. They would contend that profit is realized to the extent of the minority interest share. The minority interest is thus viewed as an "outsider" by the company. Other accountants argue that if the sale were made following the same procedures as if the companies were separate entities and not parent and subsidiary, then none of the profit should be eliminated (this would be consistent with a legal interpretation of the entity). In current practice, the entity concept prevails, which suggests that all of the intercompany profits would be eliminated, regardless of the minority interest.

When a debt exists between a parent and subsidiary, the entire amount of the debt is eliminated despite the presence of minority interests. This should be interpreted as a rule established for uniformity, because other possible procedures might be equally acceptable from a theoretical point of view. For example, the elimination of a fraction of the amount (equal to the fraction of ownership) could be justified, because the interests of the minority stockholders make the debt due to "outsiders". This would not be the case if the subsidiary were 100 percent owned by the parent.

A prevalent assumption, which supports the elimination of the entire amount of intercompany profits, is known as the *entity theory of consolidations*. With this assumption, the consolidated group is regarded as an entity, and the minority interests are considered not as "outsiders" but as persons who have contributed capital to the complete enterprise. Thus, their equity is treated as part of the stockholders' equity in the consolidated statement, and all transactions with subsidiaries are handled as if they were entirely within the single unit with no "outside" interests involved.

## Consolidation in a Later Period

In the periods after purchase, the basic elimination entry for consolidation is the same as the one made at the time of purchase. The significance of this treatment is that the incomes earned and retained since the purchase of stock are not eliminated. However, additional elimination entries may be necessary for debts owed by one of the corporations to another or for proper recognition of other transactions such as the earnings since acquisition. Also, there are complexities when one of the firms sells to another firm. These complexities are beyond the scope of this book.

## The Spin-off: Splitting the Corporation

Just as it is desirable for some corporations to merge, it may be desirable for other firms to divest a unit or units. There are several situations where divestment may logically be desirable. In the first place, the unit may be more valuable to another corporation because synergy of some type would result. In fact, all the reasons for mergers are, with slight adjustments, reasons for divestment.

There is another basic reason for divestment. Assume a corporation has a major unit that is not healthy. The financial difficulty of the major unit may overshadow the fact that other units of the corporation have excellent prospects. In such a situation, bond covenants might prevent the spinning off of profitable units, since these units are a major part of the debt security. However, there may be no reason why a suitable split of the debt cannot be arranged so that the debtholders are approximately as well off (or better off). Adding warrants or conversion features is one method of accomplishing the acceptance of a corporate spin-off.

A third reason for divestment exists when the central core of the corporation adds overhead costs but little or no value. In fact, it can be that the large size of the corporation reduces managerial flexibility as well as prevents identification by employees with the well-being of the corporation. Smaller organizational units standing on their own bottoms might collectively be more valuable than an entire set of units operating as one corporation.

There are several different ways of splitting a corporation. With a *spin-off*, the shareholders of the parent receive shares in the unit being separated (this transaction tends to be tax-free and inexpensive). With a *carve-out*, the shares are issued to the public (cash is raised). With a *split-off*, the shareholders choose to convert some or all of their shares into the shares of the divested corporation (the process protects the parent's stock price).

## Conclusion

The acquisition of a corporation by another corporation is an investment decision. If one is convinced that investments should be evaluated using the net present value method, it would be disconcerting if an investment decision involving the acquisition of a corporate entity could be correctly made using a simplistic device such as conjecting the change in the firm's P/E ratio. It is not clear that a management is able to acquire a firm with a low P/E (such as a firm with low growth opportunities) and fold it into a firm with a high P/E and obtain a benefit, unless the market assumes that the growth rate will change under the new management.

We can expect that the prospect of quick and easy profits arising from financial wheeling and dealing will sometimes give rise to decisions made from the point of view of short-run considerations rather than from the long-term profitability of the decision. We cannot force management to set objectives of one type or another. We can hope that a better understanding of the significance of mergers will lead to better analysis on which to base decisions. Just combining two firms does not automatically lead to an increase in value.

Mergers and acquisitions will always be with us as one way in which a firm may grow (while the investors of the acquired firm change the nature of their investment). We may see the government defining limitations on situations where firms may merge, but it would be surprising to see legislation that discouraged mergers and acquisitions of firms in different industries from taking place.

Financial planners must consider the possibilities of mergers and acquisitions from two different perspectives. One is the opportunity to acquire new firms, and the other is that their firm is a possible candidate for someone else to acquire. It is extremely difficult for managers to view a merger completely objectively. If their firm is acquiring another firm, the process is looked at as being beneficial to all parties. If their firm is being acquired, the acquiring firm is a "raider".

A firm with under-utilized assets and little debt that is undertaking less-than-profitable investments and has outstanding large amounts of preferred stock is a likely merger candidate. The foregoing reasons may not all be valid, but these situations do tend to attract merger-oriented firms. The financial planner should keep this in mind. Hopefully, the decisions that are made will be aimed at maximizing the well-being of the stockholders.

There are many motivations that lead to mergers and acquisitions. The payment of a large premium over market price does not necessarily indicate an unwise decision by the acquirer. Unfortunately, sometimes management might not be able to reveal all its reasons for offering the large premium. Thus, stockholder unrest can arise where there would not be unrest if all the facts were known. But even worse, there can also be situations where management's analysis is faulty and the purchase price is excessive. Time will reveal which is the true situation. Looking back, any one of us can be wiser than the wisest manager trying to make merger decisions under conditions of uncertainty.

## Review Problems

### *Review Problem 15.1*

If the common stockholders of ABD Corporation are taxed at 0.52 and if they buy XYZ stock at $100, how much could the corporation ABD pay for XYZ stock and have the investors indifferent? They will hold and not sell.

**Solution to Review Problem 15.1**

$$x = \frac{100}{1 - t_p} = \frac{100}{1 - 0.52} = \$208.33.$$

## Questions and Problems

1. a. The ABC Company has a simple capital structure. Management wants to substitute $100 million of 0.12 debt for common stock.

   What effect will the change have on the value of the firm to a zero-tax investor who owns all the stock? The corporate tax rate is 0.35.

   b. The XYZ Company is thinking of acquiring a firm that is earning before tax $100,000 a year. The borrowing rate of XYZ is 0.10, and its tax rate is 0.35. Thus, its after-tax borrowing rate is 0.054. The investment in the firm will be financed with sufficient debt to cause the amount of income taxes paid to be zero on this investment.

   What is the maximum amount that XYZ could afford to pay for the firm?

2. The following facts apply to two companies, A and B, whose operations are completely independent.

|  | A | B |
|---|---|---|
| P/E | 20 | 5 |
| Earnings per share | $1 | $2 |
| Shares outstanding | 10,000,000 | 1,000,000 |

   Assume that A acquires B in exchange for 500,000 shares of common stock.

   a. What will be the new earnings per share (EPS) for A?
   b. What would you expect the new P/E of A (after acquisition) to be? Assume a rational market.
   c. What will be the total market value of A's common stock after the acquisition? Assume a rational market.

3. The ABC Company is considering acquiring the Doggy Corporation. The Doggy Corporation is earning before interest and taxes $2 million per year and expects to continue to earn that (for perpetuity), and it has zero debt.

   The ABC Company can borrow at a cost of 0.10 and would have a capital structure of 100 percent debt for the Doggy Corporation if it acquired it. The corporate tax rate is 0.35.

   Consider only corporate taxes. What is the present value of the Doggy Corporation to the ABC Company? Assume that the following calculation is accepted for $V_U$:

$$V_U = \frac{X(1-t)}{0.10} = \frac{\$1,300,000}{0.10} = \$13,000,000,$$

where 0.10 is the appropriate discount factor for the zero-debt cash flows.

4. Answer the following statements as true or false.

   a. Firm A with a high P/E acquires Firm B with a low P/E. The EPS of A will increase immediately as a result of the acquisition.

   b. Continuing (a), the EPS for a period 10 years from now will certainly be larger for A as a result of the acquisition.

5. The RS Company is currently earning $10 per share and expects to grow at a rate of 0.05 per year. If RS merges with T Company, which is growing at 0.14, the earnings will be reduced to $8 per share and the growth rate will be 0.09.

   In how many years will the earnings per share of the merged firms equal the earnings per share of RS without the merger?

6. The ABC Company has the following capital structure:

| | Proportion | Cost | Weighted Cost |
|---|---|---|---|
| Debt | 0.8 | 0.10 | 0.080 |
| Common stock | 0.2 | 0.16 | 0.032 |
| | | | 0.112 |

The common stock of a company with an identical operating risk as ABC can be acquired for $1,000,000. The stockholders' equity cash flows of the acquisition are:

| 0 | 1 | 2 | |
|---|---|---|---|
| −$1,000,000 | $120,000 | $120,000 | The benefits are a perpetuity. |

This second firm has $200,000 of debt (net of any disposable assets) paying 0.06 ($12,000) per year. There are zero taxes.

Should the acquisition be accepted if the ABC returns establish the required returns?

7. Distinguish between the information supplied by consolidated financial statements and financial statements prepared for separate corporations (with financial linkages).

8. On January 15, 20xx, Company Q purchased all the common stock of Company Y for $40,000. At the time of purchase, the balance sheets of the two companies

were as follows:

|  | Company Q | Company Y |
|---|---|---|
| Other Assets | $ 65,000 | $50,000 |
| Investment in Company Y | 40,000 | |
|  | $105,000 | $50,000 |
| Liabilities | $ 30,000 | $10,000 |
| Common Stock | 50,000 | 25,000 |
| Retained Earnings | 25,000 | 15,000 |
|  | $105,000 | $50,000 |

Prepare a consolidated balance sheet as of January 15, 20xx.

9. On December 31, 20xx, the Oliver Corporation acquired 100 percent ownership of the Stanley Corporation by issuing 500,000 shares of common stock. The two companies were then legally merged. The market price of Oliver Corporation stock was $70 per share. At the time of acquisition, the balance sheets of the two corporations were as follows:

|  | Oliver Corporation | Stanley Corporation |
|---|---|---|
| Assets | $200,000,000 | $40,000,000 |
| Liabilities | $ 95,000,000 | $ 5,000,000 |
| Common Stock | 75,000,000 | 10,000,000 |
| Retained Earnings | 30,000,000 | 25,000,000 |
|  | $200,000,000 | $40,000,000 |

a. Prepare journal entries to record the acquisition, assuming the Stanley Corporation ceases to exist as a separate corporate entity.
b. Show the balance sheet of the Oliver Corporation after the merger.

10. Company A buys 100 percent of Company B for $55,000.

| Accounts | Company A | Company B | Eliminations | Consolidated Balance Sheet |
|---|---|---|---|---|
| Other Assets | $ 90,000 | $70,000 | | |
| Investment in Co. B | 55,000 | | | |
|  | $145,000 | $70,000 | | |
| Liabilities | $ 25,000 | $15,000 | | |
| Common Stock | 40,000 | 25,000 | | |
| Retained Earnings | 80,000 | 30,000 | | |
|  | $145,000 | $70,000 | | |

11. Company C buys 100 percent of Company D for $130,000.

| Accounts | Company C | Company D | Eliminations | Consolidated Balance Sheet |
|---|---|---|---|---|
| Other Assets | $ 65,000 | $130,000 | | |
| Investment in | | | | |
| Co. D | 130,000 | | | |
| | $195,000 | $130,000 | | |
| Liabilities | $ 40,000 | $ 20,000 | | |
| Common Stock | 65,000 | 30,000 | | |
| Retained Earnings | 90,000 | 80,000 | | |
| | $195,000 | $130,000 | | |

12. Company E buys 100 percent of Company F for $80,000.

| Accounts | Company E | Company F | Eliminations | Consolidated Balance Sheet |
|---|---|---|---|---|
| Other Assets | $110,000 | $140,000 | | |
| Investment in | | | | |
| Co. F | 80,000 | | | |
| Excess of Book | | | | |
| Value over | | | | |
| Investment | | | | |
| | $190,000 | $140,000 | | |
| Liabilities | $ 70,000 | $ 40,000 | | |
| Common Stock | 50,000 | 45,000 | | |
| Retained Earnings | 70,000 | 55,000 | | |
| | $190,000 | $140,000 | | |

## Chapter 16

# Convertible Bonds

We shall consider in this chapter debt securities that are convertible at the option of the owner into a given number of common stock shares. These securities do not classify neatly as being either debt or stock equity, since they are hybrids containing characteristics of several types of securities. These hybrid securities tend to be difficult to value. In fact, one of the advantages of these securities is that the company issuing them and the investors considering buying them may have different estimates of value.

Convertible securities are popular among investors who want a fixed (well-defined) interest income but also an upside potential. The convertible feature opens up the possibility of large gains for investors if the stock rapidly appreciates in value. There is only a small probability of large losses because of the security's bond characteristics. The bond feature tends to guarantee periodic interest payments and the payment of principal at the given maturity date (if the bond is not previously retired) if the stock price does not increase sufficiently to justify conversion. These conversion features are not without a cost to investors; convertible bonds carry a lower interest rate than do comparable bonds without the conversion feature. This discussion of convertible securities will be in terms of convertible bonds, even though much of the discussion also applies to convertible preferred stock.

Consider a $1,000 face value or par value $1,000 bond that is convertible into 20 shares of common stock. The conversion price is $50 per share (equal to the face value of $1,000 divided by 20). If the common stock price goes above $50, then the conversion privilege is of the value to the investor who has to sell. For example, if the common stock is currently selling at $60 per share, the conversion value of the bond is $1,200. The market price of the bond will be at least $1,200. The holder of the bond can realize at least $1,200 on the sale of the bond. Without the conversion feature and with no change in interest rates, an investor would only realize $1,000 on sale (if interest rates had fallen significantly, the investor might be able to realize $1,200 or more, even without the conversion feature).

A person buying a convertible bond is receiving the rights to future interest and principal payments plus the privilege of converting to common stock if it is desirable. If the price of the common stock increases sufficiently to justify the conversion, the bondholder benefits from the conversion feature. The issuing corporation benefits from the conversion feature by being able to issue debt with a lower interest rate than it would otherwise have to pay. In addition, at some time in the future there may be conversion of the debt into common stock, thus decreasing the amount of debt outstanding, without making a cash outlay for the principal.

Conversion terms of a bond may change through time either because of built-in conditions in the bond indenture or because of stock dividends and stock splits. Informed investors in convertible bonds will insist on protection against dilution with stock dividends and splits.

The period of time during which the conversion features apply may not be the same as the bond maturity. It is important that the bond contract be read carefully by a conservative investor considering purchase so as to reduce the number of unpleasant surprises.

## Description of Convertible Bond

The financial characteristics of a convertible bond can be described in three different ways:

1. It is a bond with a call option to convert to common stock.
2. It is the sum of its expected value as debt plus the expected value as stock.
3. It is common stock with downside insurance if the common stock does not go up sufficiently to warrant conversion.

Let us assume that a very risky company wants to issue debt, but it cannot find buyers for its bonds unless it pays more interest than it can afford. Adding a conversion feature may attract investors. For example, if the stock price is $40, the bonds can be defined to be convertible into 20 shares (there is a 25-percent conversion premium).

A convertible bond is a hybrid. It is a debt, but if the stock price goes up to $60 by maturity, the investor will have a valuable option of converting it into 20 shares of common stock. If the bond is not callable for a period of time, the investor has some probability of large gains. If the stock price does not go up, the investor has the fallback position of receiving $1,000 at maturity.

One of the important advantages of convertible bonds is that they offer interesting risk possibilities. There is only a very small probability of losing large amounts, and there is a probability of large gains (if the common stock increases in value rapidly). There is also a high probability of a small loss. There is an opportunity loss arising from accepting lower interest than with straight debt (the loss occurs if the conversion feature turns out to have little or no value). Since it is an opportunity loss, it is implicit rather than explicit (larger interest payments could have been earned on bonds without the conversion feature); therefore, it is not apparent to some investors.

An advantage of convertible bonds for a speculator is that the bonds sometimes have a smaller margin requirement than stock. Thus, the investors can lever their investment with more dollars invested in bonds than they can invest in common stock.

## Conversion Premiums

### *Basic Relationships*

We first establish basic convertible bond relationships that are useful for analysis. Let

$B = $ the face value of the debt;

$s = $ the number of shares of common stock into which a bond can be converted, i.e., the conversion ratio;

$B_0 = $ the value now of the security as straight debt;

$M_0 = $ the convertible bond's market value now;

$P_0 = $ the common stock's market value now.

Investors are frequently interested in two measures: the premium over bond value and the conversion premium. We shall compute these measures as percentages, although they are sometimes presented in dollar amounts.

The premium over straight bond value incurred by buying the convertible bond is defined as

$$\frac{M_0 - B_0}{B_0}. \qquad (16.1)$$

The conversion premium is defined as

$$\frac{B - sP_0}{sP_0}. \qquad (16.2)$$

This gives the percentage increase in common stock price required for the bond (as common stock) to be worth as much as the common stock that could be purchased.

## Example 16.1

An 8-percent $1,000 bond is convertible into 20 shares of common stock. The stock is currently selling at $45 per share and the bond is selling at $1,200. Assume that the bond as straight debt would have a value of $800. The premium over straight bond value is

$$\frac{M_0 - B_0}{B_0} = \frac{\$1,200 - \$800}{\$800} = \frac{\$400}{\$800} = 0.50.$$

The conversion premium is

$$\frac{B - sP_0}{sP_0} = \frac{\$1,000 - 20(\$45)}{20(\$45)} = \frac{\$100}{\$900} = 0.11.$$

The bond is currently selling at 50 percent over its value as straight debt and has an 11-percent conversion premium.

Other factors of interest to the investor are the call premium and the period of no call (the issuing firm cannot call during this period). The higher the call premium and the longer the period of no call, the more protection the investors have against being forced to sell or to convert their bonds before they want to. During the period that the issuing corporation cannot call, the investor's potential gains are unlimited. If the issuing corporation can call, the potential gain is limited by the likelihood of the firm calling. A called convertible bond can always be converted within a given time period into common stock if an investor so desires. One criterion used when determining whether or not to call is the drain on cash resulting from the dividends on stock compared to the cash drain of the interest payments. Equally important is whether or not the conversion value of the bond is above the call price.

If the common stock in Example 16.1 were paying $1 per share per year, conversion would mean cash dividends of $20 per year compared to $52 per year of after-tax interest (assuming a 0.35 corporate tax rate, the after-tax cost of the $80 contractual interest is $52). Let the stock price at time $t$ be $P_t$. The corporation might well decide that conversion was desirable as soon as the conversion value $(sP_t)$ went above the call price (or enough above so that the investors would convert rather than take advantage of the opportunity to liquidate their investment without transaction costs at the call price). The investors, for their part, would compare $80 of interest and $20 of common stock dividend, the taxes on these returns, and the safety given by the bond feature by the security, and would likely decide to postpone conversion until the cash dividend were increased or they were forced to convert by the bonds being called.

## Value of a Convertible Bond

If $P_t$ is the stock price at time $t$, the present value of a convertible bond, $M_0$, can be expressed in terms of the present value of the interest and principal or the present value of the conversion value. If $P_t$ never goes above the conversion price, the face value of the bond is used as the estimate of future value (there will be no conversion) and the bond is valued as straight debt. If $P_t$ goes above the conversion price, we can assume that the bond is converted at time $t$, where $t$ is chosen to maximize the net present value. If the second calculation (value with conversion) is larger than the value as straight debt, the conversion feature has some value.

## *Example 16.2*

A 30-year, 0.08 bond ($1,000 face value) is convertible into 25 shares of common stock. The price of the common stock is currently $50 per share, and the common stock price is expected to increase steadily to $391 at the end of year 30 (a 7-percent growth rate). The common stock is paying a $2-per-share dividend that is expected to continue for the entire 30 years. The yield for comparable bonds without a conversion feature is 0.09. We want to determine the present value of the convertible bond if it is converted just before maturity. Assume that the investor does not pay taxes.

The value of the convertible bond with conversion in 30 years using 0.09 as the opportunity cost and the common stock price of $391 per share (25 shares are worth $9,775) is

$$\sum_{t=1}^{30} \$80\,(1.09)^{-t} + 25\,(\$391)\,(1.09)^{-30}$$

$$= (\$80 \times 10.2737) + (\$9,775 \times 0.0754)$$
$$= \$821.90 + \$737.07$$
$$= \$1,558.94.$$

The value of the security as a straight bond is $897.30, using 0.09 and 30-year present value factors:

$$\$1,000 \times 0.0754 = \$\ \ 75.40$$
$$\$80 \times 10.2737 = \underline{\ \ 821.90}$$
$$\$897.30$$

The total value of the bond is equal to the sum of the straight bond plus the value of the conversion feature. If the price of the bond is $1,558.94, the value being placed on the conversion privilege is

$$\text{value of conversion package} = \$1{,}558.94 - \$897.30 = \$661.64$$

on the basis of converting at time 30.

## The Investment Decision

### *Comparing Convertibles and Debt*

How does one make the decision to buy a convertible bond? First, we shall compare the convertible bond to straight debt; then, we shall compare buying a convertible bond or common stock of the same firm.

Assume that straight debt is paying $k_i$ interest and that the convertible debt will pay $k$. Assume that the call premium of $C$ will be received at time $n$ only if the convertible bond is purchased. The incremental net present value (NPV) of the cash flows from investing in the convertible bond rather than the straight debt is

$$\text{NPV} = [B(k - k_i)]\, B(n, k_i) + C(1 + k_i)^{-n}. \qquad (16.3)$$

The investor in the convertible receives $(k - k_i)B$ less interest for $n$ years than the investor in straight debt, but does receive $C$ (the call premium) at time $n$ that the straight debt does not pay.

Setting the NPV equal to zero, we can solve for $n$, the number of years that can pass with the investor earning at least a return of $k_i$ if the bond is called on or before $n$ years have passed. If the bond is called after $n$ years have passed, and if the conversion value is not larger than the call price, the investor will earn less than $k_i$. Solving for $n$, we obtain

$$n = \frac{\ln\left[(k_i C / B(k_i - k)) + 1\right]}{\ln(1 + k_i)}. \qquad (16.4)$$

### *Example 16.3*

Assume that a convertible bond is callable at a price of $1,090 ($C = \$90$). The convertible yields 0.082 and comparable straight debt yields 0.10. The investor is zero tax.

Solving for $n$,

$$n = \frac{\ln\left[\left(k_i C / B\,(k_i - k)\right) + 1\right]}{\ln\,(1 + k_i)} \tag{16.4}$$

$$= \frac{\ln\left[\left(0.10 \times \$90/0.018(\$1,000)\right) + 1\right]}{\ln\,(1.10)} = \frac{\ln\,1.5}{\ln\,1.10} = \frac{0.40547}{0.09531} = 4.25.$$

Assume that the bond is callable after two years. In the first two years, the investor can earn unlimited returns (the firm cannot call). In years 2.0 to 4.25, the investor can earn more than $k_i$, but the gains are limited by the fact that the firm can call any time after 2.0 years.

Assuming that the conversion value at time 4.25 is less than the call price and that the firm will call as soon as the conversion value equals the call price, the investor will earn a return after year 4.25 that is less than $k_i$. If the bond is held to maturity, without call or a conversion taking place, the investor will earn $k = 0.082$. This is the contractual rate on the convertible bond originally issued at par.

Now assume that the firm can only call after year 6. The investor can earn unlimited gains until year 6 ($n$ is less than 6, so the exact value of $n$ does not affect the value of the bond to the investor). However, since $n$ is less than 6, we know that the stock price has to go above the conversion price prior to year 6 or the investor will earn less than $k_i$.

The primary importance of the model [equation (16.4)] is that it highlights the importance of $k$, $k_i$, $C$, and the period during which the firm cannot call. Also, because the likelihood of the stock increasing above the call price before $n$ time periods is of importance, the conversion premium that is set is of concern to the investor.

## Comparing Convertibles and Common Stock

Instead of comparing the convertible bond and straight debt, investors frequently compare investing in the convertible debt and investing in common stock. There are several approaches, but we will compare buying a bond convertible into $s$ shares of common stock or buying $s$ shares of common stock.

## Example 16.4

$k_i = 0.10$, $k = 0.09$, $s = 20$ and there are no taxes
$B = \$1,000$ (cost of convertible bond)
$P_0 = \$42$, dividend $= \$2$ per share

Since $s = 20$, assume that the investor buys 20 shares of common stock. Twenty shares of common stock will cost

$$\$42 \times 20 = \$840.$$

The stock will pay dividends of

$$\$2 \times 20 = \$40 \text{ per year.}$$

Buying the convertible bond costs an extra $160:

$$\$1,000 - \$840 = \$160,$$

and this bond will earn an extra $50 of interest per year compared to the $40 common stock dividend:

$$\$90 - \$40 = \$50.$$

The net present value from investing in the convertible bond rather than the common stock, assuming the interest advantage lasts forever, is

$$\text{NPV} = -\$160 + \frac{\$50}{0.10} = \$340.$$

We can determine how long the interest advantage has to exist for the initial $160 investment to be recovered:

$$-\$160 + \$50 \, \text{B} \, (n, 0.10) = 0$$
$$\text{B} \, (n, 0.10) = 3.2$$
$$n = 4.05 \text{ years.}$$

We can also solve for $n$ more generally. Let $C_0$ be the additional outlay resulting from buying the bond instead of the stock:

$$-C_0 + (\text{Int} - \text{Div}) \, \text{B} \, (n, k_i) = 0.$$

Solving for $n$ yields

$$n = \frac{\ln \left[ (\text{Int} - \text{Div})/(\text{Int} - \text{Div} - k_i C_0) \right]}{\ln (1 + k_i)}. \tag{16.5}$$

For the example, we have

$$n = \frac{\ln \left( \$50/(\$50 - \$16) \right)}{\ln 1.10} = \frac{0.3857}{0.0953} = 4.05 \text{ years.}$$

Some investors like to compute a payback period for the extra $160 investment:

$$\frac{\$160}{\$50} = 3.2 \text{ years.}$$

This measure is widely used on Wall Street to evaluate the investment desirability of a convertible.

The 4.05 years previously determined takes into consideration the time value of money. The 3.2 does not consider the time value of money.

So far, we have assumed a constant common stock dividend. If the dividend is increasing, then we decrease the net present value of investing in the bond compared to investing in the common stock.

The advantage of comparing an investment in the convertible bond and an investment in the common stock is that it holds the common stock price appreciation neutral (it is present with both buying alternatives) so that we can concentrate on the characteristics of the convertible debt.

## Interest Rate and Conversion Premium

The price that is set for a convertible bond is a function of the interest rate on the bond and the conversion premium. The smaller the conversion premium, the smaller the interest rate on the convertible bond has to be. Conversion premiums are usually between 20 and 30 percent.

## *Example 16.5*

Let us analyze the following two alternatives for a 20-year bond. The stock price is now $40.

| | Interest Rate | Shares | Conversion Premium | Conversion Price |
|---|---|---|---|---|
| Alternative 1 | 0.08 | 25 | $\dfrac{\$1,000 - 25\,(\$40)}{25\,(\$40)} = 0$ | $40 |
| Alternative 2 | 0.10 | 20 | $\dfrac{\$1,000 - 20\,(\$40)}{20\,(\$40)} = 0.25$ | $50 |

Which alternative is better for the issuing firm?

Alternative 2 has an extra $20-per-year interest on a $1,000 bond. But it saves five shares at the time of conversion. If the stock price is $40 or less and conversion does not take place, alternative 2 leads to an extra $20-per-year (before-tax) cost and zero benefits. The bonds are not converted with either alternative. Alternative 2 is inferior to alternative 1.

If the stock price goes to $P_n$ where $P_n$ is larger than $50, then alternative 2 saves five shares worth $P_n$ each. For the issuing firm, we have a NPV of

$$\text{NPV} = -20\,\text{B}\,(n, k_i) + 5\,(P_n)\,(1 + k_i)^{-n}.$$

If the stock price is between $40 and $50, then at time $n$ alternative 1 costs $25\,P_n$ while alternative 2 costs $1,000.

The NPV of alternative 2 compared to alternative 1 is

$$\text{NPV} = -20\,\text{B}\,(n, k_i) + \left(25\,P_n - \$1,000\right)(1 + k_i)^{-n}.$$

If $P_n = \$40$, the NPV is a negative 20 B$(n,k_i)$ and alternative 1 is preferred. If $P_n = \$50$, $n = 20$, and $k_i = 0.10$, we have

$$\text{NPV} = -20(8.5136) + (\$1,250 - \$1,000)(0.1486) = -170 + 37 = -133.$$

Alternative 1 is better than alternative 2.

With $n = 20$, $P_n$ has to be at least as large as $229 for alternative 2 to be better:

$$\text{NPV} = -20\,(8.5136) + 5\,P_n\,(0.1486) = 0$$

$$5\,P_n = \frac{\$170}{0.1486} = \$1,144$$

$$P_n = \$229.$$

The analysis can also be done for different values of $n$ and different call strategies. An earlier conversion will increase the importance of the extra five shares.

## The Investor

Why should an investor buy a convertible bond? We shall assume that the investor has already decided to invest in the common stock of the corporation. We consider only the question as to whether or not this proposed convertible debt is a better investment than the common stock.

To simplify the analysis for both the investor and the issuing firm, we will assume that:

1. There is zero conversion premium;
2. The interest payment per period will initially be larger than the cash dividend on the common stock;

3. There is antidilution protection (the number of shares the bond is convertible into is adjusted for stock dividends and stock splits).

Assume that the convertible bond is being issued at a price of $40 and that it is convertible into one share of common stock currently selling at $40 per share. The bond pays $4 interest per year and the stock pays $3 of dividends per year. Should the investor buy the bond or the stock? Both interest and dividends are taxed the same.

The convertible security just described is better than the purchase of an equivalent number of shares of common stock in the same company for a zero-tax investor or for an individual. The most significant advantage occurs because the contractual interest payment is larger as well as safer than the cash dividend. For the investor, the bond dominates the common stock because there is no possible way in which it can be inferior. If the stock price goes up and the cash dividend exceeds the interest being paid, the investor might want to convert and thus will hold the common stock (the same number of shares will be held as if the common stock had been purchased initially). If the common stock price falls below the conversion value, the call price and the maturity value supply some protection (the existence of a maturity date ensures that the investor will at least receive the maturity value). But this protection is an extra bonus given that we had already established the relative merits of the bond and the common stock.

Normally, the investor will consider this value to be a major reason for purchasing the security. If the conversion value falls below the maturity price, the investor has downside protection.

If the firm wants to avoid the interest payments and if the conversion value exceeds the call price, the firm can call and force conversion. However, if the firm wants to avoid the interest payments, and the call price exceeds the conversion value, then a call by the firm will require a cash outlay. Unfortunately, the same factors (unprofitable operations) that might cause the firm to want to avoid paying the interest will also tend to prevent it from calling the bonds prior to maturity, if calling the bonds causes a cash outlay to take place.

If the firm can pay the interest because of adequate cash flow but cannot use the interest tax shield because of low taxable profits, the firm might wish to call the debt to convert the interest payment into the smaller cash dividend. A conversion value larger than the call price combined with an expectation that the interest tax shield could not be used in the future would simplify the decision to call. But even with forced conversion, the investor is at least as well off as if the common stock had been purchased initially.

If the conversion value is currently larger than the call price, the issuing firm might call now if there is a probability of a future change in the firm's well-being and a resultant decrease in stock price, so that the firm would not be able to force conversion in the future.

## The Issuing Firm's Perspective

The negative features of the convertible security from the viewpoint of the issuing firm are that it promises to pay interest periodically and that there is an amount due at maturity. The interest payment is contractual and thus has more risk to the firm than do common stock dividends. Also, if the interest payment is larger before taxes than the common stock dividend, and if the firm's tax status were to change so that the firm could not use the tax shield, the debt could be more costly. If the stock price drops below the call price, a calling of the bond would result in a cash outlay; thus, forcing conversion might be impossible for a firm with cash problems.

Another way of describing this difficulty is to define it in terms of the downside protection being offered to the investors. Although the downside protection is an advantage to the convertible bond purchaser, it is a disadvantage to the common stockholders (it increases their risk).

The primary advantage for the issuing firm of this type of convertible security compared to common stock is the tax deductibility of the interest. If $100 million of convertible debt is paying $10 million of interest instead of $10 million of common stock dividends, the firm with a 0.35 tax rate will save $3.5 million per year. This is a significant incentive for using the convertible security rather than common stock. But this advantage exists for all securities classified as debt.

The IRS will object to debt that is too much like common stock and will attempt to block the use of the interest payment as a tax deduction. However, any convertible debt is part debt and part common stock, so the issue is already on the table. The only question is the extent to which the logical use of convertible debt can be extended by the use of securities that have desirable characteristics from the issuing firm's viewpoint. The basic fault is in a tax code that attempts to distinguish in a substantive manner between the cash distributions of common stock and debt. It is not possible to distinguish between them in an exact manner with a hybrid security.

The issuing firm will be happy with its decision to issue the convertible debt rather than common stock as long as the after-tax cost of the interest is less than the cash dividend that would have been paid, and if at the time of call or maturity the conversion value is marginally larger than the call price.

Suppose that the price of the common stock falls and the debt is called when the conversion value is less than the call price so that the firm has to make a cash outlay. In that case, it is possible that the issuance of common stock would have been better. However, if the time of call is reasonably long after the time of issue, it is likely that the cash savings from the interest tax shield will have a larger present value than will the cost of the call (the difference between the call price and the value of the equivalent shares of the common stock at time of call, when the call price is larger than the conversion value).

If the call price is set relatively low, there is likely to be a very small probability that the firm will regret the issuance of the convertible debt compared to the issuance of an equivalent number of common stock shares. The guidelines established by the Treasury or by Congress as to what acceptable debt is (thus, the interest payments will be tax-deductible) will be crucially important in determining how close a firm can move to the theoretically optimum security (a very low call price and a small conversion premium at time of issuance).

An important argument against the issuance of convertible debt is that it does result in a dilution in the stockholder's equity position. The holder of a convertible security can share in the winnings if the events turn out to be desirable. This is real dilution. If events do not go well, with the result that the stock price does not increase, then an overhang of potential dilution is created, and there is still debt outstanding.

Another important consideration is that financial analysts tend to consider convertible bonds as common stock equivalents in evaluating the common stock, and bond rating agencies tend to consider convertibles as debt in arriving at bond ratings. This is looked at by financial officers as a double penalty, and is considered as a negative factor arguing against the issuance of convertible debt.

Tax considerations work both for and against convertible bonds. The tax deduction of convertible bond interest gives the bonds an advantage compared to common stock. But the lower explicit interest costs compared to non-convertible debt result in lower tax shields; thus, there is less value added per $1,000 bond as a result of using the convertible bond (which is part equity capital).

## Bonds with Warrants

A warrant gives the investor the right to buy a share of stock (or a fraction of a share) at a given exercise price. The exercise price is paid to the issuing corporation. In addition to convertible bonds, bonds with detachable warrants are also used by corporations. The advantage of the detachable warrant is that, upon exercise, the investor still has a bond investment with its fixed return and the corporation has debt outstanding. If the number of shares of stock associated with each bond is less with detachable warrants than with a conversion feature, there would tend to be less dilution of the current stockholders' position. A possible drawback from the corporation's point of view is that, after the exercise of the warrants, there is still debt outstanding, and this reduces the debt-issuing ability of the firm (assuming that it wants to issue more debt). To solve this objection, the face value of the bond may be accepted for the exercise price.

One advantage of issuing bonds with warrants is that the issue price is split between debt and stock equity (the value of the warrant is classified as stock equity). The issue price of a convertible bond is classified as debt.

The two types of securities (convertible bonds and bonds with detachable warrants) are very similar, and it is difficult to describe substantive differences aside from differences in accounting.

## Dilution

Dilution for the present shareholders takes place when their percentage of ownership is reduced by the issuance of new shares or new securities. Convertible securities are attractive to issuers, since the conversion feature tends to reduce the explicit interest cost. But a convertible security carries with it a threat of dilution of the stockholders' equity that is not present with straight debt. However, the dilution may be less than if common stock were issued immediately. Also, there is always the chance that the bonds will not be converted, and the corporation will have raised funds at a lower ex post cost than straight debt. (This means that the stock price failed to rise above the conversion price, so stockholders may still be unhappy.)

## *Example 16.6*

Assume that a corporation is considering issuing 1 million shares of common stock at a price of $40 or 40,000 convertible $1,000 bonds with a 20-year maturity. Each bond would be convertible into 20 shares of common stock. There are currently 5 million shares of common stock outstanding.

As long as there is a positive conversion premium (it is 25 percent), the bonds will lead to less potential dilution than will the issuance of common stock. The purchaser of the bond is paying a price for the downside protection offered by the bond features.

Whether convertible bonds or bonds with warrants attached will lead to more dilution will depend on the terms of the specific securities. We might expect detachable warrants to lead to less dilution, since the investor will have a debt security no matter what happens with the warrant. On the other hand, the warrant upon being exercised will require an additional cash investment; thus, we cannot guess at the potential advantage.

## Convertible Bonds and the Black–Scholes Model

Since a convertible bond is a combination of a conventional bond and an option to convert into common stock, it follows that methods of valuing options are also of interest in the valuation of convertible bonds. An important step in convertible bond valuation is the application of the Black–Scholes model to valuation of both the option feature and bond feature of convertible debt as an investment.[1]

## Why Should an Investor Convert Voluntarily?

If the common stock's cash dividends become larger than the interest payments on the debt, the investor has a decision. The choice is between more cash flow with the larger risk associated with common stock dividends and a safer but smaller amount of cash. If the investor converts, the investor is making an assumption that the expected present value of cash dividends is larger than the present value of the interest payments. In addition, it is expected that the price of the common stock will remain sufficiently high so that one does not lose in the future by giving up the safer maturity payment of the debt. If all these conditions are satisfied, the investor has a conversion decision, but because of the risk it is not obvious that the investor should convert voluntarily. Except in rare situations where there are high, relatively safe cash dividends, the investor is better off holding the convertible bonds than converting. The put option has value.

If the bond's market price is larger than the conversion value, it is better to hold or sell than it is to convert voluntarily. The investor is reluctant to give up the call option (the right to convert to common stock) or the put option (the right to the face value of the convertible debt at maturity).

## Why Should a Firm Force Conversion?

The opportunity for a firm to force conversion arises when the conversion value of the bond is larger than the call price. Normally, a price cushion is required to reduce the likelihood of the firm paying out cash. There are several reasons why a firm might want to force its investors to convert into common stock by calling the

---

[1] The Black–Scholes model is a mathematical model for the valuation of an option. See F. Black and M. Scholes, "The Valuation of Option Contracts and a Test of Market Efficiency," *Journal of Finance*, May 1972, pp. 399–417; F. Black and M. Scholes, "The Pricing of Options and Corporate Liabilities," *Journal of Political Economy*, May–June 1973, pp. 637–654.

bond. It might be a way to strengthen the capital structure so that new debt can be issued. Another reason for the firm to force conversion is that the cash outlays of outstanding common stock are less than with debt. For example, a growth stock may be paying zero dividends; thus, the after-tax interest payments are saved if conversion is forced. Also, calling the bonds results in the elimination of the implicit put option held by the investors.

Assume a $1,000 bond paying 0.10 interest is convertible into 40 shares of common stock. The common stock pays a $1-per-year dividend and is selling at a price of $50. The call price of the bond is $1,080. Should the company call? The corporate tax rate is 0.35.

The company can call, since the conversion value, $50 \times 40 = $2,000, is larger than the call price. If the bonds are called, the rational investors must convert rather than accept the call price. The conversion value is larger than $1,080. The bonds converted into common stock will require $40 per bond of cash outlays for dividends. The bonds now require $100 of interest outlays, which are $65 after tax. The $40 is less than $65. The investors will receive $40 of dividends instead of $100 of interest; thus, they do not have their position improved by the call. The position of the present stockholders is improved by the call, since the firm's cash outflow is reduced. In addition, the downside protection offered by the bond (the put option held by investors) is eliminated.

Earnings per share will also be affected by the conversion. Interest costs will be reduced, and the number of shares outstanding will be affected (the exact effect will depend on whether we are computing earnings per share with or without dilution and on the nature of the conversion feature).

In some situations, the amount of debt not yet converted has become very small and calling the debt is a reasonable way of eliminating an unnecessary financial complexity.

There is a sound financial theory that convertible bonds should be called as soon as the market price of the bond is high enough above the call price to insure conversion. If called at lower prices, there might be cash outlays associated with the retirement of the debt. Just as an investor prefers to hold the convertible bond rather than convert because of the downside protection offered by the bond, the corporation wants to force conversion so that the legal obligation to pay interest and principal are replaced by the more flexible commitments to common stock.

## Hedge Funds

In recent years, hedge funds have bought between 70 and 80 percent of the convertible bonds issued. The funds buy the convertibles and sell the stock short.

If the stock price goes down, they win on the short sale and do not lose much (if anything) on the convertible bonds. If the stock price goes up, they win on the convertible but lose on the short sale. Obviously, the amounts of gains and losses will depend on the exact nature of the transactions. The strategy has its risks (no "free lunch").

## Conclusion

The value of warrants, options, calls, and the conversion feature of convertible securities are all governed by the same economic rationale. If they can be converted immediately, their minimum value as common stock is set by their immediate conversion value. Their actual value will depend on a host of factors, among which are the current common stock market price, the distribution of future stock prices, the time value of money, and the risk preferences of the market.

Convertible bonds may be an attractive investment in a common stock growth situation (thus, tending to ensure conversion) and as a substitute for common stock where there is a possibility of the growth not taking place (thus, investors are willing to pay for the downside protection). If there are no common stock growth possibilities, the investor would prefer straight debt. If there is certainty of growth (no risk of the conversion feature being worthless), the investor is likely to do better investing in the common stock or warrants or calls. Thus, a convertible bond is a type of security that fills the needs for an investor with a risk preference for a chance of a large gain and a very small chance of a large loss, but with a large chance of a small loss (an opportunity cost).

## Review Problems

### Review Problem 16.1

Assume a $1,000, 20-year convertible bond that has a contractual interest rate of 0.10. Straight debt pays 0.12. The corporate tax rate is 0.46.

The stock price at time of issue is $20. The bond is callable at a price of $1,100 after one year.

(a) If the conversion premium at time of issue is 0.25, the conversion price per share is _____. The bond is convertible into _____ shares.

(b) A zero-tax investor will earn more than 0.12 if the bond is called prior to _____ years.

(c) Assume that a 0.10 bond is convertible into 25 shares of common stock currently selling at $40 per share. The stock is paying a $3-per-share dividend. The bond is being issued at a price of $1,000.

Would you buy the common stock or the convertible bond, assuming you (an individual) are going to buy one or the other? Explain.

## Solution to Review Problem 16.1

(a) $20(1.25) = $25$ conversion price.

$$\frac{\$1,000}{\$25} = 40 \text{ shares.}$$

(b)

$$n = \frac{\ln\left[(Ck_i/B\,(k_i - k)) + 1\right]}{\ln\,(1 + k_i)} = \frac{\ln\left[(\$100(0.12)/\$20) + 1\right]}{\ln\,1.12}$$

$$= \frac{\ln\,1.6}{\ln\,1.12} = \frac{0.47}{0.1133} = 4.15 \text{ years.}$$

The basic formulation is

$$C\,(1 + k_i)^{-n} - B\,(k_i - k)\,B\,(n, k_i) = 0.$$

(c) Buy the bond. It is at least as good as the common stock costing the same for the same number of shares, plus:

   (1) $100 interest > $75 dividend today.
   (2) Downside protection.
   (3) Same upside potential.

## Questions and Problems

1. A $1,000 bond can be converted into 20 shares of common stock. The stock is now selling at $36.
    What is the bond's conversion premium?
2. (continue 1) If the stock price were to increase 38.9 percent, what would be the conversion value of the bond?
3. (continue 1) If the present value of the convertible bond as straight debt is $780, what is the bond's premium on straight bond value if the market price of the bond is $940?
4. a. Assume that a 20-year convertible bond is paying 0.06 interest per year. Straight debt is yielding 0.10.
        What is the value of the convertible as straight debt?
   b. If the bond is selling for $940, what value is the market placing on the conversion feature?

5. (continue 4) Assume that the bond is expected to be called after five years at a call price of $1,090.

   What is the net present value of the investment in the convertible bond at time 0, assuming a zero-tax investor who paid $1,000 for the bond?

6. (continue 4 and 5) What is the net present value at time 0 if the bond is convertible into 20 shares and the stock is selling at $70 per share when the bond is called at time 5?

7. The ABCD Company is issuing a 7-percent, 20-year convertible debt callable at a price of $1,080 at any time. The conversion price has been set at a 30-percent price premium over the current stock price. The bonds have been recommended to a pension fund manager. The argument has been made, "You will earn a high return since we can expect the stock price to easily double within the next 10 years." However, it is agreed that it is unlikely that the annual rate of growth in stock price will exceed 10 percent per year. Comparable-risk straight noncallable debt is being issued at a yield of 11 percent.

   Should the bonds be bought if they sell at par? Explain.

8. A zero-tax investor is considering purchasing either straight debt or a convertible bond issued by firms of identical risk. The straight debt has a coupon of 0.12 and the convertible debt, 0.05. The call price of the convertible bond is $1,140 and the bond can be called at or after time 2. Both bonds can be bought at par.

   The investor expects the common stock price to increase, so that the stock price is larger than the conversion price at and after time 3, but not prior to that time.

   a. Which security should be purchased? Why?

   b. How long can it be (maximum time) before the stock price forces the bond price above the call price, if the investor is to earn more than 0.12?

9. The ABC Company has been given two choices by an investment banker. One is to issue 5-percent convertible 20-year bonds ($1,000 par). The stock price is now $10 per share, and the conversion premium would be 100 percent. The other alternative would be a 4-percent interest rate and a 25-percent conversion premium.

   The bonds would be noncallable. The company does not pay a cash dividend on its stock, and it does not intend to start in the near future.

   The company has recently issued 20-year straight debt costing 0.10. The company has a 0.40 tax rate.

   Which of the two alternatives should the company prefer? Explain.

10. Company F is considering the terms of a convertible bond that it is going to issue. The following facts apply:

| Alternative | Interest | Conversion Premium |
|:---:|:---:|:---:|
| 1 | 0.08 | 0.15 |
| 2 | 0.09 | 0.20 |

The bond issue size is $10 million. The bonds will have a maturity of 10 years and will be noncallable. The tax rate is 0.46. The stock price is $50.

a. How many shares would the bonds be convertible into with the 0.15 premium?

b. How many shares would the bonds be convertibles into with the 0.20 premium?

c. With the 0.20 conversion premium, there is an extra after-tax cost of $_____ per year.

d. What does the price of the common stock have to be at time 10 for alternative 2 to be preferred? Assume the firm has an opportunity cost of money of 0.10.

11. A $1,000 convertible bond is to be issued with a call premium of $90 and a coupon of 0.12. Straight debt could be issued at a cost of 0.16. The bond is callable any time after year 4.

Is this convertible bond a good investment, compared to straight debt, if a zero-tax investor thinks that the bond will be called at year 5? Explain with numerical justification.

12. Assume that the stock price is above the conversion price.

When should an investor holding the convertible bond voluntarily convert into common stock? List three necessary conditions (not necessarily sufficient conditions).

13. Design a convertible bond that is very much like debt.

14. Design a convertible bond that is very much like common stock.

*Chapter 17*

# Inventories

At the end of each period, the accountant allocates the total costs of opening inventory and purchases between an expense of the current operating period and costs of future operating periods. The costs applicable to the current period are recognized as cost of goods sold (an expense) in the income statement, whereas the costs applicable to future periods are placed in the Ending Inventory asset account.

Accountants would like to report relevant values in the balance sheet, match revenues and expenses in the income statement, minimize current income tax obligations, and present measures with a high degree of reliability. Some of these objectives are in conflict with one another; thus, a choice as to the accounting method must be made.

## Classifications of Inventory

**Inventories** are goods that are held for sale in the ordinary course of business, or goods that will be used or consumed in the production of goods to be sold. Manufacturing concerns typically have three inventory accounts. Costs assigned to goods and materials on hand that have not yet been placed in production are reported as **raw materials inventory**; costs assigned to partially completed goods are reported as **work-in-process inventory**; and costs assigned to completed but unsold goods are reported as **finished goods inventory**.

Inventories are often the largest item among the current assets for merchandising and manufacturing concerns. Sales can be lost if inventories are inadequate, but excessive inventories can expose a company to significant financing costs and potential losses from spoilage and obsolescence.

## What Costs Are to Be Inventoried?

There is no clear-cut distinction between costs that may or may not be assigned to inventories. There is a general agreement that inbound freight costs are to be included; and some accountants argue that purchasing costs, materials handling costs, and storage costs are also properly included as costs of inventory. The costs arising from inefficiency or prolonged storage of the items in inventory are expenses.

Another example of a cost that should be excluded from inventory is a lost purchase discount. Lost discounts are not a cost of the purchased material. Costs of shipping goods to customers are considered to be expenses.

From a practical point of view, it is not unreasonable for a merchandising firm to place into the inventory account only the net invoice price, freight, and handling costs of placing the merchandise in its storage place. Other costs would normally be considered expenses of the period. This procedure excludes from inventory the purchasing department costs, accounting department costs, and costs of warehousing the inventory, and these costs are considered to be expenses of the period in which they are incurred. There can be times when it is appropriate to place costs of warehousing an inventory. This will be the situation when the warehousing was expected at the time of purchase and the warehousing enhances the value of the product or enables the firm to reduce ordering costs. For example, storing grain or other seasonal commodities from harvest time until it is sold in another season may normally be expected to add value. Where the warehousing was not planned (added value is less than cost), adding storage costs to the cost of the product is not justified.

## Costs of Manufacturing Firms

What costs may be included in inventory if the firm is engaged in a manufacturing process? A narrow definition would include in inventory only the direct variable costs (this would usually include only direct material and direct labor). A cost is *variable* if when production doubles in amount, the total variable cost will also double. A somewhat broader viewpoint would include all other variable costs connected with the manufacturing process (indirect variable materials, indirect variable labor, and other variable costs such as power would be included). The generally accepted accounting treatment of manufacturing costs is somewhat more inclusive. All costs connected with the manufacturing process may be considered costs of inventories. This differs from the two preceding alternatives by the inclusion of some or all fixed costs in the costs of inventories. Examples of costs that are not includable in inventories are selling expenses, income taxes, advertising expenses, expenses of shipping out, and sales invoice preparation. They are classified as expenses and charged to Income.

A firm engaged in a manufacturing process will usually have several accounts that are not required for a merchandising firm. The inventory cost of a manufacturing firm will usually be divided among raw materials, work in process, and finished goods. The problem of allocating the factory costs among these three categories is beyond the scope of this book. Once these allocations are made, however, the accounting treatment of manufacturing inventories is similar to that of merchandise inventories.

## Cost Flow Assumptions

With either a merchandising or a manufacturing firm, it is necessary to make some assumptions about the order in which costs flow through the accounts. It is necessary to distinguish between the *flow of the physical units* of inventory that pass through the plant and are shipped to customers and the *flow of accounting costs*. The flow of the physical units may be the result of a materials handling arrangement that ensures that the oldest goods are sold or used first. The accounting costs of inventory that are charged to expense may or may not be the costs of the oldest goods on hand. This would depend on which of several accounting conventions is adopted by the company. The following are the four alternative flow assumptions most often used in practice:

1. The oldest goods are sold or used first — FIFO (first-in, first-out).
2. The last goods purchased are sold or used first — LIFO (last-in, first-out).
3. The goods are intermingled and goods used are of average cost and age — Average Cost.
4. The specific units used are identified.

In practice, the *physical flow* of goods frequently will not correspond to the method chosen by the accountant to record the *flow of costs*.

## *Flow of Costs: FIFO*

The **FIFO (first-in, first-out) procedure** of accounting for inventory charges the costs of the first goods purchased to expense. This means that the cost of the goods appearing in inventory will be the cost of the goods most recently purchased.

## Example

Beginning inventory: 100 units @$2.00 = $200.00

**Purchases during the Month**

| | | | |
|---|---|---|---|
| Jan. 15 | 200 units @ $2.10 = | $ | 420.00 |
| Jan. 24 | 300 units @ $2.20 = | | 660.00 |
| Jan. 30 | 100 units @ $2.25 = | | 225.00 |
| | 600 units | | $1,305.00 |

During the month of January, the company sold 500 units.

Compute the cost of goods sold and ending inventory.

**Cost of Goods Sold:**

| | |
|---|---|
| 100 units @ $2.00 = $ 200.00 | (beginning inventory) |
| 200 units @ $2.10 = 420.00 | (Jan. 15 purchase) |
| 200 units @ $2.20 = 440.00 | (Jan. 24 purchase) |
| 500 units $1,060.00 | |

**Ending Inventory:**

| | |
|---|---|
| 100 units @ $2.25 = $225.00 | (Jan. 30 purchase) |
| 100 units @ $2.20 = 220.00 | (Jan. 24 purchase) |
| 200 units $445.00 | |

The results may be checked by adding the inventory and the cost of goods sold ($1,060 + $445 = $1,505). This should be equal to the opening inventory plus the cost of the goods purchased during the period ($200 + $1,305 = $1,505).

FIFO results in an inventory measure that is reasonable (the goods have recently been purchased), but the cost of goods sold consists, to some extent, of items purchased in past periods and might not reflect current costs.

## Flow of Costs: LIFO

The **LIFO (last-in, first-out) procedure** of accounting for inventory charges the cost of the goods most recently purchased to expense. This means that the cost of the goods appearing in ending inventory will be the cost of the oldest goods purchased. This will be the opening inventory plus additions (or less deductions) during the period. If there have been changes in the cost of goods purchased over a period of years, this inventory figure can become far removed from either the actual cost of the goods on hand or their current value. The cost of goods sold is a reasonable measure unless old inventory with old prices is sold (sales dip into inventory).

## Example

Assume that the Sample Company is using a LIFO procedure. Compute the cost of goods sold and the ending inventory. (See the FIFO section.)

**Cost of Goods Sold:** 100 units @ $2.25 = $ 225.00 (Jan. 30 purchase)
        300 units @ $2.20 =   660.00 (Jan. 24 purchase)
        100 units @ $2.10 =   210.00 (Jan. 15 purchase)
        500 units       $1,095.00

**Ending Inventory:** 100 units @ $2.00 = $ 200.00 (beginning inventory)
        100 units @ $2.10 =   210.00 (Jan. 15 purchase)
        200 units       $ 410.00

The results may be checked by adding the ending inventory and the cost of goods sold ($1,095 + $410 = $1,505). This should be equal to the opening inventory plus the cost of the goods purchased during the period ($200 + $1,305 = $1,505).

Although LIFO may seem to provide a solution to the problem of changing prices, it does have serious limitations. A particular disadvantage is the valuation of ending inventory. Although the costs of most recent purchases are charged as expenses for the determination of gross margin, the ending inventory figure may be based on the lower costs of purchases of past time periods. Thus, the asset figure resulting from the use of LIFO is not likely to reflect the current values of the goods remaining in inventory. By failing to adjust the inventory, LIFO fails to recognize the gains and losses that may result from price changes. These economic gains and losses should be taken into account in evaluating managerial performance. Even if these are beyond the control of management, they should nevertheless be separately reported so that the normal operating results may be more effectively appraised. If these elements are to some degree controllable by management, their determination should form part of the managerial reporting process.

The FIFO inventory assumption causes these market gains and losses to be commingled with the results of ordinary operations in the single figure of gross margin. When LIFO is used, the market gains and losses are usually eliminated from gross margin, but they still are not separately determined.

If LIFO is used to compute a firm's federal income taxes, then in the U.S. the firm is also required to use LIFO for its financial statements.

## Flow of Costs: Weighted Average Cost

The **weighted average cost procedure** of accounting for inventory charges to expense an average of the costs of the goods purchased during the period and the opening inventory. The ending inventory figure is also based on this average. This is a weighted average. The following example illustrates the application of the weighted average procedure.

## *Example*

Assume that the Sample Company is using a weighted average cost procedure. Compute the cost of goods sold and the ending inventory.

**Goods Available**

| | | |
|---|---|---|
| Opening Inventory | 100 @ $2.00 = | $ 200.00 |
| Jan. 15th purchase | 200 @ $2.10 = | 420.00 |
| Jan. 24th purchase | 300 @ $2.20 = | 660.00 |
| Jan. 30th purchase | 100 @ $2.25 = | 225.00 |
| | 700 | $1,505.00 |

$$\text{Weighted Average Cost} = \frac{\$1,505}{700} = \$2.15 \text{ per unit.}$$

$$\text{Cost of Goods Sold} = \$2.15 \times 500 = \$1,075.00$$
$$\text{Ending Inventory} = \$2.15 \times 200 = \phantom{0}430.00$$
$$\$1,505.00$$

## *Flow of Costs: Identification of Costs of Specific Units*

In some situations, accountants will identify the actual costs of specific units. In most cases, this procedure will be too expensive; and in some cases, it will be impossible. The benefits of such a system are, at best, doubtful except where high-cost items are being sold and the cost of specific items can be easily traced.

Even if the cost of each specific unit could be identified, it is not clear that specific identification would be a desirable accounting procedure. It would open the door to possible manipulation of income and thus reduce the reliability of accounting data. If the company had some reason for wanting its income to be higher or lower in a particular period, it could accomplish this goal by choosing the specific units to be delivered.

## Evaluation of Cost Flow Assumptions

The cost flow assumption used in determining inventory cost can have an impact on the income reported by a company in any given year. There is a great deal of flexibility permitted in the choice of method, and many methods are used in practice.

The cost flow assumption of FIFO closely parallels the normal physical movement of goods through the firm. Also, the balance sheet inventory balance is likely to be fairly close to current value. When LIFO is used, the balance sheet figure may be based on prices of goods acquired many years ago, which often means that the balance sheet balances are unrealistic in terms of today's prices.

It is claimed that the LIFO procedure has advantages in regard to income determination. If a company is to remain in business, it must maintain a certain level of inventory. Therefore, when an item is sold, it must be replaced, and it might be argued that the profit on sale should be based on the cost of replacing the item rather than its original cost. To the extent that the costs of the most recent purchases reflect current replacement costs, LIFO will provide a measure of operating income that embodies this viewpoint. LIFO, however, does fail to record market gains and losses.

A major drawback of LIFO is that when there is a decrease in the physical volume of inventory below that of the beginning of the accounting period, costs charged to current income will include costs of earlier purchases. These costs might be stated at prices that represent very old purchases and thus not measure current replacement costs. This dependence on physical inventory volume may permit some manipulation of income through timing of purchases.

LIFO does have real advantages in decreasing income taxes in times of rising prices. This is because the more recent, higher-priced purchases are charged as expenses so that income is lower than it otherwise would be. If prices were to decline, however, LIFO would then result in higher income (and thus higher taxes) than FIFO. Current U.S. income tax regulations require that companies using LIFO for tax purposes must also use this flow assumption in their accounting reports.

## Cost-or-Market, Whichever Is Lower

The FIFO, LIFO, and weighted average cost procedures are all concerned with determining the cost of the ending inventory. If FIFO or average cost is used to implement cost-or-market, one must compare the cost (as determined by using one of these procedures) to the market price of the item and take the *lower* amount for the valuation of the inventory. This procedure results in a conservative inventory figure, because the inventory is *written down* to market but *never up* to market. The inconsistency may be explained by the rule that recognizes losses but does not recognize gains until they are realized. Once an inventory item is written down to market, it is *not* written back up to cost if the market subsequently exceeds initial cost.

The journal entry to record the write-down to market takes various forms. The debit may be to cost of goods sold or to a loss amount. The credit may be to the Inventory account or to a contra asset account, Allowance for Market Valuation, which is subtracted from the Inventory account for statement purposes.

The cost-or-market rule has been attacked by accounting theoreticians on the grounds that it is not consistent (inventories are written down to market, but never up to market) and that it is not even consistently conservative (in the next period, the income may be higher if the inventories are written down in this period, and the inventory of this period is included in the cost of goods sold next period). It also suffers from confusion as to what is meant by *market*.

On the positive side is the fact that the write-down to market is desirable to prevent the subsequent year's earnings from being charged with excessive costs and to prevent the inventory presentation from being overstated on the balance sheet. However, write-ups to market might also be desirable to be better able to judge managerial performance in the next period and to present more realistic inventory figures on the balance sheet. Reliable market value would be preferable to the lower of cost-or-market procedure.

The Internal Revenue Code does forbid the use of LIFO combined with cost-or-market for tax purposes.

## Example

At the end of the calendar year, the Sample Company's raw material inventory sheet showed the following items. Using "cost-or-market, whichever is lower," determine the dollar amount of raw material inventory.

| Material | Units | Cost per Unit | Market Price per Unit | Cost | Market | Lower of Cost-or-Market |
|---|---|---|---|---|---|---|
| A | 100 | $1.00 | $0.80 | $ 100 | $ 80 | $ 80 |
| B | 200 | 2.00 | 2.10 | 400 | 420 | 400 |
| C | 150 | 3.00 | 3.00 | 450 | 450 | 450 |
| D | 300 | 2.20 | 2.00 | 660 | 600 | 600 |
| | | | | $1,610 | $1,550 | $1,530 |

There are two acceptable answers. Cost-or-market applied to the individual inventory items provides an inventory figure of $1,530. On the other hand, applying this rule to the inventory as a whole, the figure of $1,550 is obtained. Determining the lower of cost-or-market by individual items will always give the lower inventory figure and is therefore more conservative.

# Financial Accounting Standards No. 157

FAS 157 was issued in September 2006 and was effective for financial statements issued for fiscal years beginning after November 15, 2007. The fair value measures of FAS 157 apply to some inventory measures. For example, paragraph A5 (C) states:

> C. The in-use valuation premise might be incorporated in the fair value of the asset through the market participant assumptions used to measure the fair value of the asset. For example, if the asset is work-in-process inventory that is unique and market participants would complete the inventory into finished goods, the fair value of the inventory would assume that any specialized machinery necessary to complete the inventory into finished goods would be available to market participants.

But paragraph C24 severely limits the application of fair value concepts to inventory:

> C24. This Statement also does not apply for the market value measurement that results when measuring inventories at the lower of cost or market under ARB No. 43, Chapter 4, 'Inventory Pricing.' ARB 43, Chapter 4, places upper and lower limits on the measurement that may not result in a fair value measurement.

The lower of cost or market calculations as illustrated above still apply rather than fair value. We can expect inventories to be valued at fair value to be consistent with other asset values in the future.

# Inventory and Finance

There are two relevant financial aspects of inventory. First, the accounting measures of inventory stocks and flows affect both the income measure and balance sheet. Second, the level of inventory held affects the amount of capital needed as well as the income of the period. The availability of inventory affects the likelihood of making a sale as well as the costs of carrying inventory.

The determination of the optimum level of inventory under conditions of certainty is the result of balancing the costs of ordering with the costs of carrying inventory. With uncertainty, the firm also has to balance the costs of having too much inventory with the costs of having too little. Inadequate inventory levels lead to disruptions in production and lost sales opportunities. Excessive inventories tie up capital in assets that are not earning an adequate return. Excessive and leftover inventory can lose value through obsolescence and cause excessive storage cost.

## Inventory Models versus "Just in Time"

One managerial technique that has been exported from Japan to the United States is the "just in time" inventory model. Rather than having large safety stocks, the next shipment arrives just as the last unit is used. This reduction in inventory levels results in increased profits. Also, by reducing set-up costs (including set-up time), the order size (or production run) is further reduced, again resulting in less inventory.

Despite the great appeal of a zero-inventory decision model, we will take the position that the optimum level of inventory will depend on the facts and must be determined. A "just in time" inventory procedure may be right where the instantaneous supply is certain or when there is zero cost of being short of inventory. With other facts, a "just in time" policy may not be attractive. Imagine flying across the Atlantic Ocean in a Boeing 747 that had just enough fuel to reach the other side of the ocean if the tail wind is a constant 40 miles per hour. Most of us would prefer a margin for error arising from carrying extra fuel.

## An Inventory Model

Although inventories are held for speculation (the price is expected to increase or a strike is anticipated), we shall only consider the situation when inventories are held for transactions (either for production or for sales).

First, we assume that the rate of usage (demand) and all other factors are known with certainty.

The economic order quantity (EOQ) model is the most simple and most widely used of all the formal mathematical inventory models. It gives exact answers that are correct if the assumptions are valid.

Let

$K$ = the order cost (per order);
$r$ = the carrying cost (per unit per time period);
$D$ = the total expected demand (during the time period).

If we define $Q$ to be the optimal order size (the EOQ), then the average inventory on hand is $\frac{Q}{2}$. Total carrying costs for the period can now be defined to be $r\left(\frac{Q}{2}\right)$. The number of orders required is $\frac{D}{Q}$, and, hence, purchase order costs are $K\left(\frac{D}{Q}\right)$. Total cost, $TC$, for the period considering holding and ordering costs is given by

$$TC = r\left(\frac{Q}{2}\right) + K\left(\frac{D}{Q}\right).$$

As $Q$ increases, the carrying cost, $r\left(\frac{Q}{2}\right)$, increases. But as $Q$ increases, the cost of ordering, $K\left(\frac{D}{Q}\right)$, decreases.

To minimize this expression requires that its derivative be taken, set equal to zero, and solved for $Q$.[1]

$$Q = \left(\frac{2KD}{r}\right)^{1/2}.$$

Assumptions implicit in the EOQ model are:

1. A known, constant demand over the period and known delivery times.
2. No change in holding costs per unit or order costs.
3. No change in prices through time and no quantity discounts.

If $K$ (order costs) is equal to or close to zero, then $Q$ will be equal to or close to zero. If set-up or order costs are very small, then the amount ordered will be very small and the resulting inventory, which is $Q/2$, will be very small. The "just in time" rule would be effective with small amounts of inventory arriving each time.

## The Value of Inventory Reductions

What is it worth to a firm to reduce its average inventory by $1 million? The answer is $1 million plus any reductions in costs such as insurance, storage, taxes, and so on. The financial incentive to have a theoretically correct inventory policy is large.

## Inventory Levels and Uncertainty

If we relax the assumption of certainty, then the firm will want to have inventory to prevent stockouts.

---

[1]

$$\frac{dTC}{dQ} = \frac{r}{2} - \frac{DK}{Q^2} = 0.$$

The optimum order size is

$$\frac{r}{2} = \frac{DK}{Q^2} \quad \text{and} \quad \frac{rQ}{2} = \frac{DK}{Q}$$

or

$$Q = \left(\frac{2KD}{r}\right)^{1/2}.$$

The two components of total cost are equal if $Q$ is the optimum order size.

Let

$k_u$ = the cost per unit of not having enough inventory (cost of underage);
$k_0$ = the cost per unit of having excess inventory (cost of overage).

Define $p$ to be the probability that the next unit of inventory is demanded and $(1 - p)$ that it is not demanded. We assume that if the unit has not been ordered, it cannot be reordered when the actual demand is established.

We want the expected cost of underage to be equal to the expected cost of overage:

$pk_u$ = the expected cost of having a unit demanded and not having it;
$(1 - p)k_0$ = the expected cost of not having a unit demanded but having it in inventory.

At the margin,

$$pk_u = (1 - p)k_0.$$

Solving for $p$ yields

$$p = \frac{k_0}{k_0 + k_u}.$$

## Example

Assume that

$$k_0 = \$20$$

$$k_u = \$80$$

since each unit costing $20 can be sold for $100. A leftover unit is worthless.
The probability of demand is:

| Units Demand $D$ | Probability | Probability of Demand Being at Least as Large as $D$ |
|:---:|:---:|:---:|
| 0 | 0.10 | 1.00 |
| 1 | 0.20 | 0.90 |
| 2 | 0.30 | 0.70 |
| 3 | 0.20 | 0.40 |
| 4 | 0.10 | 0.20 |
| 5 | 0.10 | 0.10 |
| 6 | 0.00 | 0.00 |

Solving for $p$, we obtain

$$p = \frac{k_0}{k_0 + k_u} = \frac{20}{20 + 80} = 0.2.$$

The number of units that should be obtained is 3 or 4 (the fourth unit does not add to profit). The expected profit of ordering three or four units is $140:

**Order 4 Units**

| Demanded | Units Sold | Profits on Units Sold | Leftover Units | Cost of Leftover Units | Net Profit | Probability |
|---|---|---|---|---|---|---|
| 0 | 0 | $ 0 | 4 | $80 | −$ 80 | 0.10 |
| 1 | 1 | 80 | 3 | 60 | $ 20 | 0.20 |
| 2 | 2 | 160 | 2 | 40 | 120 | 0.30 |
| 3 | 3 | 240 | 1 | 20 | 220 | 0.20 |
| 4 | 4 | 320 | 0 | 0 | 320 | 0.10 |
| 5 | 4 | 320 | 0 | 0 | 320 | 0.10 |
| | | | | | Expected profit = $ 140 | |

**Order 3 Units**

| Demanded | Units Sold | Profits on Units Sold | Leftover Units | Cost of Leftover Units | Net Profit | Probability |
|---|---|---|---|---|---|---|
| 0 | 0 | $ 0 | 3 | $60 | −$ 60 | 0.10 |
| 1 | 1 | 80 | 2 | 40 | $ 40 | 0.20 |
| 2 | 2 | 160 | 1 | 20 | 140 | 0.30 |
| 3 | 3 | 240 | 0 | 0 | 240 | 0.20 |
| 4 | 3 | 240 | 0 | 0 | 240 | 0.10 |
| 5 | 3 | 240 | 0 | 0 | 240 | 0.10 |
| | | | | | Expected profit = $140 | |

The expected profit calculation for ordering two units is $120:

**Order 2 Units**

| Demanded | Units Sold | Profits on Units Sold | Leftover Units | Cost of Leftover Units | Net Profit | Probability |
|---|---|---|---|---|---|---|
| 0 | 0 | $ 0 | 2 | $40 | −$ 40 | 0.10 |
| 1 | 1 | 80 | 1 | 20 | $ 60 | 0.20 |
| 2 | 2 | 160 | 0 | 0 | 160 | 0.30 |
| 3 | 2 | 160 | 0 | 0 | 160 | 0.20 |
| 4 | 2 | 160 | 0 | 0 | 160 | 0.10 |
| 5 | 2 | 160 | 0 | 0 | 160 | 0.10 |
| | | | | | Expected profit = $120 | |

If we allow reordering but the time to replenish inventory is not known, then there will be need for safety stock.

From a finance point of view, every dollar that is released from inventory saves a dollar of capital. Unfortunately, we cannot then conclude that it is desirable to reduce inventory. Management must balance the costs and benefits of inventory reduction. Carrying inventory has a cost, but so does excessive reordering or being caught short of inventory.

In some cases, it might be feasible to reduce the ordering costs or the downtime associated with production changeovers. Uncertainty as to timing of replacement can also be reduced with good management. Thus, the inventory models and the values of the variables should not be taken as given, but rather the possibility of changing the process to improve efficiency should be investigated.

## Conclusion

There are many complex problems associated with accounting for inventories. For example, in determining the cost of the inventory, we encounter problems of determining what costs are to be included in inventory and what assumptions should be made about cost flow (FIFO, LIFO, or weighted average). A lower of cost-or-market rule may also be used.

FIFO assumes that the most recent costs should be assigned to inventory; thus, its use results in recent costs being reflected in the balance sheet and older costs being reflected in the income statement. LIFO assigns the most recent costs to cost of goods sold; thus, its use results in recent costs being reflected in the income statement and older costs being reflected in the balance sheet. Since the costs assigned to inventory may be very old, the balance sheet valuations that result from the use of LIFO may not be reliable estimates of current market value.

## Questions and Problems

1. Which of the following costs would be properly includable in the inventory of a retailing firm?

   a. Advertising costs.
   b. Gross invoice cost of merchandise purchased (discount was available but not taken).
   c. Gross invoice cost of merchandise purchased (discount was taken).
   d. Net invoice cost of merchandise purchased.

e. Transportation cost applicable to goods purchased.

f. Transportation cost applicable to goods delivered to customers.

2. Which of the following costs would be properly includable in the inventory of a manufacturing firm?

   a. Direct labor cost.

   b. Salaries of shop foremen.

   c. Sales representatives' salaries.

   d. Salary of vice president in charge of manufacturing.

   e. Depreciation of factory building.

   f. Depreciation of sales office.

3. For each of the following products, describe the *physical flow* that one might normally expect the products to follow through a firm.

   a. Bakery products.

   b. Nails in a bin.

   c. Bottled milk.

   d. Gasoline in underground tanks.

   e. Coal in a pile.

   f. Wine in a vat.

4. Discuss the procedure of "cost-or-market, whichever is lower" in light of the basic accounting assumptions of consistency, conservatism, and objectivity.

5. Assume that a company must use the same inventory flow assumption consistently from year to year. Which flow assumption would generally result in the highest reported income during an extended period of rising prices? Which during an extended period of falling prices?

6. In anticipation of increased steel prices, the Auto Company purchased a four months' supply of steel. As of December 31, the costs of carrying this steel in inventory were $10,000,000 (the steel had an invoice price of $200,000,000).

   Should the steel inventory be shown on the December 31 statements at $200,000,000 or $210,000,000?

7. The Ithaca Gas Company has a problem arising from the seasonal nature of its product. People use more gas in the winter to heat their homes and to cook. This creates the problem of peak loads. The problem is made even more difficult by the fact that there are five or six exceptionally cold days each winter, during which time the demand for gas increases tremendously. Rather than build pipelines for the peak loads, the daily fluctuations are handled by the use of gas tanks. The peak loads created by seasonal demands have

been somewhat solved by the use of underground storage. Gas is pumped underground under pressure during the summer and then used in the winter. Of the $10,000,000 worth of gas pumped underground during the first year of operating the underground storage, it is estimated that $7,000,000 will never be recovered (this amount of gas is required to build up the pressure so that gas may be taken out).

Should the $7,000,000 be treated as inventory? Does a manufacturing firm have a similar problem?

8. The Rusty Steel Company shifted to the LIFO method of accounting for inventory in 1929. At that time, the inventory of Type A-1 steel plate was 1,000 tons, with a cost of $100 per ton.

In 1932, the company decided to continue using LIFO, but it also incorporated the "cost-or-market, whichever is lower" criterion. Cost was computed by using a LIFO assumption as to flow. At that time, the inventory of Type A-1 steel plate was $2,000 tons, and the market value was $40 per ton (cost ranged from $50 to $100 per ton). The following entry was made to write the inventory down to market:

| | | |
|---|---|---|
| Loss on Inventory Price Decline................ | 80,000 | |
| Inventories ............................ | | 80,000 |

From 1932 to 2010, inventories of Type A-1 steel plate increased each year, and the market value was never lower than $40 per ton. In 2010, the finished goods inventory of A-1 steel plate decreased to 500 tons. In 2010, a ton of steel plate of this type cost $200 per ton to produce (the market value was greater than $200).

a. Comment on the write-down of inventory in 1932 and the procedure used since then (LIFO plus cost-or-market).

b. How would the income for 2010 be affected by the fact that inventory was decreased by at least 1,500 tons?

9. The D. Jones Ship Company received an order on July 1, 2010, to build a 110,000-ton tanker. The costs connected with obtaining the sale were $20,000, and these were all incurred in 2010. It is estimated that the tanker will take 24 months to build.

How should the selling costs be treated? How should the costs connected with constructing the ship be treated? When should the revenue from the sale of the ship be recognized?

10. Consider the two following situations and determine the disposition of the cost of warehousing.

a. The ABC Company purchased a truckload of mink coats. Demand was not as strong as expected and, rather than sell the leftover coats at a large loss, it was decided to store them until the next year.
b. The XYZ Lumber Company had the opportunity to purchase a large quantity of rare wood paneling. It expected to be able to sell this paneling over the next 18 months. The company actually sold it in 12 months.

11. During the month of April, the Jansen Manufacturing Company's Raw Materials account was debited for $511,000. A review of the entries to the account disclosed the composition of the debits to be as follows:

| | |
|---|---|
| Materials Purchased (gross price) | $450,000 |
| Freight-in (including demurrage charges of $3,000) | 15,000 |
| Receiving Department Costs | 25,000 |
| Materials Handling and Storage Costs | 10,000 |
| Allocation of Selling Department Costs | 5,000 |
| Shipping Department Costs | 6,000 |
| | $511,000 |

The company follows a procedure of crediting a Purchase Discount Revenue account when purchase discounts are taken. Terms of purchase are 2/10, n/30.

Analyze and adjust the Raw Materials account as necessary.

12. The Winchester Store shows the following information relating to Commodity A, which it handles.

Inventory, January 1: 100 units @ $6.50
Purchases for January: 400 units @ $7.00
Inventory, January 31: 175 units

a. What value should be assigned to the ending inventory, assuming the use of LIFO?
b. What is the cost of goods sold for January, assuming the use of FIFO?
c. What is the value of the ending inventory, assuming cost is determined on the basis of a weighted average and valuation is at cost-or-market, whichever is lower? Market on January 31 is $6.75.

13. From the following data, determine the inventory valuation by applying the rule of cost-or-market, whichever is lower.

| Commodity | Quantity | Unit Cost | Unit Market |
|-----------|----------|-----------|-------------|
| A | 100 | $1.15 | $1.05 |
| B | 400 | 2.40 | 2.75 |
| C | 500 | 4.00 | 4.35 |
| D | 700 | 3.45 | 3.10 |

14. During the month of January, the James Manufacturing Company's Raw Materials account was debited for $450,000. A review of the entries to the account disclosed the composition of the debits to be as follows:

| | |
|---|---|
| Materials Purchased (gross price) | $400,000 |
| Freight-in (including demurrage charges of $3,000) | 12,000 |
| Receiving Department Costs | 20,000 |
| Materials Handling and Storage Costs | 8,000 |
| Allocation of Selling Department Costs | 7,000 |
| Shipping Department Costs | 3,000 |
| | $450,000 |

The company follows a procedure of crediting a Purchase Discount Revenue account when purchase discounts are taken or lost. Terms of purchase are 2/10, n/30.

a. Analyze and adjust the Raw Materials account as necessary.
b. Describe briefly a general rule for determining what costs are to be considered as Cost of Material Purchases.

15. The Blue Front Store shows the following information relating to Commodity A, which it handles.

Inventory, January 1: 100 units @ $5.00
Purchases, January 300 units @ $6.00
Inventory, January 31: 200 units

a. What value should be assigned to the ending inventory, assuming the use of LIFO?
b. What is the cost of goods sold for January, assuming the use of FIFO?
c. What is the value of the ending inventory, assuming cost is determined on the basis of a weighted average and valuation is at cost-or-market, whichever is lower? Market on January 31 is $5.80.

16. During the month of June, Sample Company sold 350 units. The following information is given on purchases.

| Beginning Inventory | June 1 | 100 units | $1.00 | $100 |
|---|---|---|---|---|
| | June 10 | 150 units | 1.10 | 165 |
| | June 20 | 200 units | 1.25 | 250 |
| | June 28 | 100 units | 1.40 | 140 |

Compute the cost of goods sold and ending inventory, using:

a. FIFO.

b. LIFO.

c. Average Costs.

17. The Inflate Company has 100 units of inventory that cost $5.00 per unit. It sells the 100 units for $7.00 per unit and replaces them at a cost of $6.50 per unit.

a. Determine the income, using:

   i. FIFO.

   ii. LIFO.

b. Determine the inventory, using:

   i. FIFO.

   ii. LIFO.

c. What did the ending inventory actually cost?

18. (continue 17) Assume the market value at the end of the period (replacement cost) is $8. How might you bring this information into the reporting?

*Chapter 18*

# The Cash Flow Statement

Financial Accounting Standards Statement No. 95 (Statement of Cash Flows) dated November 1987 establishes standards for cash flow reporting. It supersedes statements dealing with changes in financial position and fund flow statements.

The bottom line of the cash flow statement is either "Net cash provided by (used in) investing activities of continuing operations" or the cash balance "Cash and cash equivalents at end of year." The second term is a more exact term since it requires that all items affecting the cash balance during the year be included in the report.

## Three Main Sections

The three main sections of the cash flow statement are:

1. Cash flows from operations.
2. Cash flows from investing activities.
3. Cash flows from financing activities (including effect of exchange rate changes on cash).

## Cash Flows from Operations

The continuous process of producing and selling the company's product or service is one of the main sources of cash of an enterprise. The cash from operations, however, will only rarely be equal to the operating income. The accrual basis of accounting involves the recognition, for income determination purposes, of several types of economic events that do not involve cash. For example, some of the expenses of a period do not use cash during the period.

Frequently, the income statement for the period is used as the starting point for deriving the cash flow statement. To compute the net cash from operations, it is necessary to add back to operating income those expenses that did not utilize cash and to subtract those revenue or other income items that did not generate cash. An alternative treatment is to start with revenues that increase cash and then deduct only those expenses that utilize cash. The disadvantage of the latter procedure is that it does not make specific reference to the income figure reported in the income statement. The two procedures may be reconciled, however. The current discussion will be limited to the process that starts with income.

The main items that may necessitate adjustments to income to obtain the cash from operations are:

> Depreciation of fixed assets;
>
> Depletion of natural resources;
>
> Amortization of patents and other intangibles;
>
> Loss or gain on sale or retirement of noncurrent assets (The cash or other current assets received from the sale is a source of funds, but this is not likely to be equal to the gain recognized. Sales of noncurrent assets are shown separately in the statement.);
>
> Accumulation of bond discount or amortization of premium; and
>
> Expenses associated with future income tax liabilities.

## *Example*

Given the following conventional statement, compute the cash from operations.

| | | | |
|---|---|---|---|
| Sales | | | $50,000 |
| *Less:* | | | |
| | Labor, etc. | $35,000 | |
| | Depreciation | 12,000 | |
| Total Expenses | | | 47,000 |
| Net Income | | | $ 3,000 |

The cash from operations may be computed by adding back to income those expenses that did not use funds.

| | |
|---|---|
| Income Reported | $ 3,000 |
| Add back expenses not using funds (depreciation) | 12,000 |
| Cash from Operations | $15,000 |

This procedure is very widely used. Depreciation must be explicitly added to obtain the total cash flow. It should be recognized that depreciation actually has no effect on working capital, but is merely added back to income to offset the result of the accounting entry that resulted in its being deducted from revenue to determine the amount of income.

The accounting entry to accrue depreciation is a debit to depreciation expense and a credit to the fixed asset account (usually a contra account, such as Accumulated Depreciation, is used). The asset that has been decreased is a long-lived asset. Thus, cash and working capital are not affected by the accrual of depreciation, and depreciation should not be deducted from revenues if we are computing funds from operations. If it has been subtracted (i.e., if we are starting from income rather than from revenue), it is necessary to add back to income the amount of depreciation deducted from revenue to obtain the cash from operations.

Leaving out the tax consequences, *cash is not generated by charging or accruing depreciation; it is created by sales.* Charging more or less depreciation will have no effect on the amount of working capital. The depreciation charge affects the income of the period, and it will affect the amount that has to be added back to income to compute the funds from operations. If we start with income, depreciation expense is added back to income, since depreciation does not use cash.

If the tax consequences of depreciation are considered, depreciation may be regarded as having an effect on cash. The amount of depreciation charged for tax purposes affects the current payment or the liability recognized for taxes. The tax itself is the current outlay affected. The amount of depreciation charged for financial accounting purposes does not affect cash.

The depletion charges taken by firms in extractive industries (mining, oil, and so forth) should be treated in a manner similar to that of depreciation. Because the depletion charge does not result in a decrease of cash, it must be added back to income to obtain cash from operations. In general, the expense arising from the amortization of any long-lived asset must be added back whenever the cash from operations figure is to be derived from income.

## Gain or Loss on Sale of Noncurrent Assets

When noncurrent assets are sold, the difference between the book basis for the asset (cost less depreciation or amortization) and the amount received is recognized as a gain or loss. Such gains and losses are included in the income calculation, but are often stated separately. Long-lived assets that may be sold include land, buildings, equipment, and investments.

From the viewpoint of cash changes, we are not concerned with the amount of gain or loss recognized, but rather with the amount of cash received in the transaction. The sale of a noncurrent asset is not considered to be a part of current operations, but the cash would be shown as a source of cash. Therefore, if the working capital received is included, the loss or gain arising from the sale of these assets must be eliminated in computing cash from operations. Any loss must be added back to income if it has been subtracted. Any gain recognized must be subtracted if it has been included in income. Including the gains and losses from the transaction in addition to the cash received would result in double counting.

## Example

A fixed asset with a book value of $10,000 is sold for $12,000 cash.

a. What is the gain or loss recognized?
b. What amount of cash is generated by the transaction?
c. What adjustment must be made to the income for the period to obtain the funds from operations?

**Solution**

a. The gain is $2,000.
b. Cash of $12,000 is generated by the transaction.
c. The $2,000 gain must be subtracted from income (assuming that it has been included in other income). Not to subtract the $2,000 would mean that cash of $14,000 would be reported to have been generated, but only $12,000 of working capital would actually have been received (the $14,000 is equal to the $2,000 gain plus the $12,000 of cash received).

## Example

A fixed asset with a book value of $10,000 is sold for $8,000 cash.

a. What is the gain or loss recognized?
b. What current assets are generated by the transaction?
c. What adjustment must be made to the income for the period to obtain the funds from operations?

**Solution**

a. The loss is $2,000.
b. Cash of $8,000 is generated by the transaction.

c. The $2,000 book loss must be added back to income (assuming that it had been subtracted to obtain the income figure). Not to add back the $2,000 would mean that a loss which did not utilize cash was subtracted in computing cash from operations.

## *Bond Discount or Premium*

The normal entry for recording interest accrued on a bond payable that had been issued at a discount is:

| | | |
|---|---|---|
| Interest Expense | 40 | |
| Bond Discount | | 2 |
| Interest Payable | | 38 |

The expense is $40, but the decrease in working capital (by an increase in current liabilities) is only $38. When the interest is paid, cash is reduced by $38. The difference between the interest expense and the cash outlay of $2 is caused by the fact that long-term liabilities have been increased by $2 (the credit to Bond Discount in effect increases the long-term debt). Thus, the interest expense for the period is not equal to the decrease in cash.

The adjustment that should be made is to add $2 back to income, if $40 of interest expense has been subtracted in obtaining income.

Bonds issued at a premium require an adjustment in the opposite direction. In this case, the amount of cash used would be greater than the expense recognized, as indicated by the normal accrual entry:

| | | |
|---|---|---|
| Interest Expense | 45 | |
| Bond Premium | 5 | |
| Interest Payable | | 50 |

The $5 is a use of cash, but only the interest expense is deducted in determining income. The additional current outlay due to the amortization of the premium reduces cash.

## Cash Flows from Investing Activities

This section includes the cash from the sale of long-lived assets or the reclassification of special cash "funds". This includes the sale of investments (but not marketable securities classified as current assets), land, buildings, and equipment.

Cash set aside for building purposes, debt retirement, and so forth is sometimes classified as a cash usage. When the fund is liquidated, any residual cash may be a source. Gains from transactions involving long-lived assets are excluded, but the cash acquired in such transactions is included. Cash is commonly utilized to purchase long-lived assets (land, buildings, equipment, investments, patents, and so forth) or to retire long-term debt.

## Cash Flows from Financing Activities

An important source of cash is the issuing of new securities, both long-term debt and stock equity. This includes common and preferred stock, bonds, long-term notes, and warrants.

Dividends paid on both common and preferred stock will appear in this section as cash outlays. Purchase of company stock is another common outlay.

If the company has capital leases, this will be a cash outlay reported in this section. Any investment inflows or investment outflows are included in this section.

## Transactions Not Affecting Funds

Most of the problems arising in the preparation of statements of changes in financial position are not connected with those transactions that are sources of cash or distributions of cash, but are the result of transactions that do not affect cash. A transaction of this nature is the accrual of depreciation and depletion. Appropriations of retained earnings are also of this nature. The establishment of an account such as Deferred Income Taxes does not involve cash; thus, it should not affect the cash from operations (the expense will have to be added back to income). A stock dividend (in contrast with a cash dividend) is another transaction that does not directly affect the working capital position of the firm.

## Managerial Uses

A cash flow statement is useful because it tells us where the cash is coming from and where it is being used. It is, by necessity, a summary, but it does indicate what is happening to the cash position of the firm and why it is happening. This is of importance to management as well as investors.

Although the statement as defined is useful, management needs additional information. Explanations of why the cash balance has changed are desirable, and forecasts of what is going to happen to cash in the future are often essential. This information is necessary to ensure that the proper amount of cash will be on hand for the operations of future periods. As productive facilities are enlarged, the treasurer of the corporation must ensure that cash is on hand to pay for the construction of the facilities. As the facilities are placed into operations, new workers must be paid, materials purchased, and so forth. All these items require that cash be available long before the product being produced is sold.

## EBIT (Earnings Before Interest and Taxes)

To compute EBIT, start with the corporate income and add back the amounts of interest and taxes.

The most common way of using EBIT is to multiply EBIT by a constant to obtain a value for the corporation.

Financial analysts use several different flow measures and multipliers. The multipliers are applied to either historical measures or forecasts for the next period. We will consider three different multipliers:

a. $M_0$ — applied to after-tax earnings (E).
b. $M_1$ — applied to earnings before interest and taxes (EBIT).
c. $M_2$ — applied to earnings before interest, taxes, depreciation, and amortization (EBITDA).

Let $P$ be the value now of a share of common stock. Then, by definition of $M_0$,

$$P = M_0 E$$

or

$$M_0 = \frac{P}{E}.$$

If $P = \frac{D}{k-g}$, then the theoretical value of the earnings multiplier is

$$M_0 = \frac{D}{E(k-g)} = \frac{(1-b)E}{E(k-g)} = \frac{1-b}{k-g}.$$

Assume we want to determine the multiplier ($M_1$) to use if EBIT (defined to be $X$) is used rather than E (after-tax earnings).

Again, let $P$ be the value now of a share of common stock. Then,

$$P = M_1(\text{EBIT}) = \frac{D}{k-g} = \frac{(1-b)E}{k-g} = \frac{(1-b)(1-t)X}{k-g}.$$

Solving for $M_1$, we get

$$M_1 = \frac{(1 - b)(1 - t)}{k - g}$$

since $X = $ EBIT.

## *Example*

Assume that

$$X = \$100, t = 0.35, b = 0.4,$$
$$E = \$65, D = \$39, k = 0.12, g = 0.02, \text{EBITDA} = \$150.$$

Then,

$$P = \frac{D}{k - g} = \frac{\$39}{0.12 - 0.02} = \$390.$$

Calculating the multipliers for $E$ and $X$,

$$M_0 = \frac{1 - b}{k - g} = \frac{0.6}{0.12 - 0.02} = 6$$

$$M_1 = \frac{(1 - b)(1 - t)}{k - g} = \frac{0.6\,(0.65)}{0.10} = 3.9.$$

The firm value using $E = \$65$ and $M_0 = 6$ is

$$P = M_0 E = 6(65) = \$390.$$

The firm value using $M_1 = 3.9$ and $X = \$100$ is

$$P = M_1 X = 3.9(100) = \$390.$$

# EBITDA (Earnings Before Interest, Taxes, Depreciation, and Amortization)

The most popular valuation method for private equity and other corporate acquisitions is to use EBITDA and a EBITDA valuation multiplier ($M_2$).

Now $P$ is

$$P = M_2(\text{EBITDA}) = \frac{(1-b)(1-t)X}{k-g}$$

and

$$M_2 = \frac{(1-b)(1-t)X}{(k-g)(\text{EBITDA})}.$$

Above we define EBITDA = $150, and $M_2$ is

$$M_2 = \frac{(1-b)(1-t)X}{(k-g)(\text{EBITDA})} = \frac{(0.6)(0.65)100}{(0.12-0.02)150} = \frac{39}{15} = 2.6.$$

$$P = \frac{39}{15}(150) = \$390 \quad \text{or} \quad 2.6(150) = \$390.$$

For all the calculations, the firm value is $390. This occurs since the values of all three multipliers are linked. In practice, the multiplier for EBITDA is likely to be determined by a group of wise men (using judgment) rather than finance theorists, and the three values are likely to be different rather than being exactly equal.

It is likely that these multipliers cannot be applied to a different firm with a different cost of equity and a different growth rate. Above, the multipliers were computed based on specific information. Other information will lead to different multipliers.

## The International Accounting Surge

Currently, the U.S. accounting standards are established by the Financial Accounting Standards Board (FASB) located in Norwalk, Connecticut. The FASB supplies very detailed rules and guidance for the accounting process of public corporations.

In the distant future, we can expect the rules and guidance offered by the International Accounting Standards Board (IASB) to be given more or less equal standing. The IASB allows more judgment than the FASB in applying principles.

The objective will likely be to provide information useful for making economic decisions not following a set of bookkeeping rules. A long-term objective is to have one set of rules throughout the world so that financial statements originating in different countries are comparable.

## Conclusion

We can expect the use of fair value for both assets and liabilities to increase. Thus, the use of historical costs can be expected to decrease except for cash and near cash.

Though easy, rules will be incorrectly discarded (if not already discarded). Thus, justifying an accounting process because it is conservative will not be (is not) accepted.

A faithful representation of assets, liabilities, and income will be more important than being able to verify the exact correctness of the measures. It will be recognized that estimation is an important and inescapable element of the accounting process.

Keeping in mind the above set of objectives will help you be a better accountant or user of accounting information.

We have attempted to show that there are a variety of measures, some objective and some highly subjective, that can be used by the decision makers in attempting to determine the value of a firm. There are exact methods of calculation, but there are not exact reliable measures of value.

Accounting information must be adjusted for purposes of determining the value of a firm. The liquidation value of the assets sets a minimum price and value, but any value in excess of this minimum must find its justification in the present value of the projected cash flow expected to be generated in the future. The going concern value of the assets, with the assets gaining their value from the cash flow, is the relevant factor. The prime advantage to be gained by using cash flow versus conventional income is that it is theoretically correct and it does not tie us to the results of accounting procedures that are not designed for this specific type of decision. If the decision makers want to use the current income as the basis for making their investment decision, care should be taken since the computation may not be equivalent to the use of cash flows. However, even if they do not use the income measure directly, the decision makers will use it indirectly as the basis for their evaluation of future dividends.

The cash flow statement of changes in financial position has become an important and widely used financial report, helping the reader to understand changes in the cash position of the firm. Although reporting what happened is desirable and necessary, management also wishes to estimate sources and uses of cash in planning for the future. One can form impressions from the historical records, but managerial decisions must be based on projections. We should place the cash flow statement in proper perspective. The statement is not a substitute for either the income statement or the balance sheet, but is a useful supplement to these two reports.

## Questions and Problems

1. "Higher depreciation accruals have reduced the need of corporations to borrow." Comment on this statement.

2. A leading business periodical stated that "the two primary sources of funds for corporate expansion are retained earnings and the allowance for depreciation." Comment on this statement.

3. There are two major categories of transactions that do not affect the funds flow, yet may have a profound impact on the operations of a company and may even affect the company's need for financing. Describe these two types of transactions and give an example of each.

4. The No-Ash Coal Company recorded the following transactions. Indicate how each would be treated on a statement of changes in financial position, assuming that funds are defined as the cash balance. If the transaction involves a source or use of cash, indicate the amount that would appear on the statement as a result of the transaction. Each transaction may be identified as one of the following:

   a. A source of cash.
   b. A use of cash.
   c. An income statement adjustment that has no effect on cash.
   d. A transaction that has no effect on cash because it involves changes only in non-cash items.
   e. A transaction that represents neither a source of cash nor an application of cash.

   The transactions were as follows. The company:

   (1) Paid a dividend on preferred stock paid in cash, $25,000.
   (2) Purchased raw materials costing $87,000 on credit.
   (3) Sold an old truck for $300 that cost $2,000 and was 80 percent depreciated. Loss recognized on the sale amounted to $100.
   (4) Received $280,000 in payments on accounts receivable.
   (5) Purchased a new machine with a list price of $27,000. Received a discount of 10 percent for paying cash.
   (6) Acquired a new building with fair market value of $200,000 by issuing $200,000 in long-term notes to the builder.

5. How does the presence of bond premium affect the computation of the cash from operations?

6. Explain how the gain or loss on the sale of fixed assets should be treated in computing the cash from operations.
7. Shown are comparative balance sheets and an income statement for the Roberts Company. Prepare a cash flow statement for the year ended December 31, 20X2.

## The Roberts Company
### Comparative Balance Sheets as of December 31

|  | 20X2 | 20X1 |
|---|---|---|
| Cash | $150,000 | $125,000 |
| Accounts Receivable | 197,000 | 160,000 |
| Inventories | 50,000 | 85,000 |
| Machinery and Equipment | 75,000 | 50,000 |
| Bonds Payable, Discount | 5,250 | 5,500 |
|  | $477,250 | $425,500 |
| Allowance for Uncollectibles | $ 2,000 | $ 1,000 |
| Accumulated Depreciation | 10,000 | 7,000 |
| Accounts Payable | 53,000 | 70,000 |
| Bonds Payable | 100,000 | 100,000 |
| Common Stock* | 150,000 | 50,000 |
| Retained Earnings† | 162,250 | 197,500 |
|  | $477,250 | $425,500 |

* Represents 10,000 shares outstanding on December 31, 20X2, and 5,000 shares on December 31, 20X1.

† A $100,000 stock dividend was issued in 20X2.

## The Roberts Company
### Income Statement for Year Ended December 31, 20X2

| Sales | $400,000 | |
|---|---|---|
| Less Allowance for Uncollectibles | 3,000 | $397,000 |
| Expenses | | |
| Cost of Goods Sold | $260,000 | |
| Operating Expenses | 60,000 | |
| Taxes | 7,000 | |
| Interest Expense | 5,250 | 332,250 |
| Net Income | | $ 64,750 |

8. Assume the following facts apply to Bernake Corporation ($t_c = 0.35$):

$$E = \$195, \quad X = \$390, \quad M_0 = 20, \quad \text{Interest} = \$90.$$

a. What is the value of the corporation using earnings to stockholders ($E$)?
b. Assume the EBIT multiplier is 10 ($M_1 = 10$). What is the firm value?
c. Assume that the depreciation expense accrual is $260 and that the EBITDA multiplier is 6. What is the firm value?

9. During the year 20X2, the Foster Company purchased buildings that cost a total of $3,400,000. The Buildings account and the related Accumulated Depreciation were shown in the comparative balance sheets of the company as of December 31, 20X1 and 20X2, as follows:

|  | **20X2** | **20X1** |
|---|---|---|
| Buildings | $5,600,000 | $3,100,000 |
| Accumulated Depreciation | 2,500,000 | 1,700,000 |
|  | $3,100,000 | $1,400,000 |

The company's income statement for the year 20X2 included the following items:

| Depreciation of Buildings | $1,200,000 |
|---|---|
| Gain on Sale of Buildings | $ 600,000 |

Determine the cost of the buildings that were sold during 20X2 and the total amount received from the sale of buildings.

# Appendices

**Table A**  Present value[a] of $1.00 $(1 + r)^{-n}$.

| n/r | 1% | 2% | 3% | 4% | 5% | 6% | 7% | 8% | 9% | 10% | 11% | 12% | 13% | 14% | 15% |
|---|---|---|---|---|---|---|---|---|---|---|---|---|---|---|---|
| 1 | 0.9901 | 0.9804 | 0.9709 | 0.9615 | 0.9524 | 0.9434 | 0.9346 | 0.9259 | 0.9174 | 0.9091 | 0.9009 | 0.8929 | 0.8850 | 0.8772 | 0.8696 |
| 2 | 0.9803 | 0.9612 | 0.9426 | 0.9246 | 0.9070 | 0.8900 | 0.8734 | 0.8573 | 0.8417 | 0.8264 | 0.8116 | 0.7972 | 0.7831 | 0.7695 | 0.7561 |
| 3 | 0.9706 | 0.9423 | 0.9151 | 0.8890 | 0.8638 | 0.8396 | 0.8163 | 0.7938 | 0.7722 | 0.7513 | 0.7312 | 0.7118 | 0.6931 | 0.6750 | 0.6575 |
| 4 | 0.9610 | 0.9238 | 0.8885 | 0.8548 | 0.8227 | 0.7921 | 0.7639 | 0.7350 | 0.7084 | 0.6830 | 0.6587 | 0.6355 | 0.6133 | 0.5921 | 0.5718 |
| 5 | 0.9515 | 0.9057 | 0.8626 | 0.8219 | 0.7835 | 0.7473 | 0.7130 | 0.6806 | 0.6499 | 0.6209 | 0.5935 | 0.5674 | 0.5428 | 0.5194 | 0.4972 |
| 6 | 0.9420 | 0.8880 | 0.8375 | 0.7903 | 0.7462 | 0.7050 | 0.6663 | 0.6302 | 0.5963 | 0.5645 | 0.5346 | 0.5066 | 0.4803 | 0.4556 | 0.4323 |
| 7 | 0.9327 | 0.8706 | 0.8131 | 0.7599 | 0.7107 | 0.6651 | 0.6227 | 0.5835 | 0.5470 | 0.5132 | 0.4817 | 0.4523 | 0.4251 | 0.3996 | 0.3759 |
| 8 | 0.9235 | 0.8535 | 0.7894 | 0.7307 | 0.6768 | 0.6274 | 0.5820 | 0.5403 | 0.5019 | 0.4665 | 0.4339 | 0.4039 | 0.3762 | 0.3506 | 0.3269 |
| 9 | 0.9143 | 0.8368 | 0.7664 | 0.7026 | 0.6446 | 0.5919 | 0.5439 | 0.5002 | 0.4604 | 0.4241 | 0.3909 | 0.3606 | 0.3329 | 0.3075 | 0.2843 |
| 10 | 0.9053 | 0.8203 | 0.7441 | 0.6756 | 0.6139 | 0.5584 | 0.5083 | 0.4632 | 0.4224 | 0.3855 | 0.3522 | 0.3220 | 0.2946 | 0.2697 | 0.2472 |
| 11 | 0.8963 | 0.8043 | 0.7224 | 0.6496 | 0.5847 | 0.5268 | 0.4751 | 0.4289 | 0.3875 | 0.3505 | 0.3173 | 0.2875 | 0.2607 | 0.2366 | 0.2149 |
| 12 | 0.8874 | 0.7885 | 0.7014 | 0.6246 | 0.5568 | 0.4970 | 0.4440 | 0.3971 | 0.3555 | 0.3186 | 0.2858 | 0.2567 | 0.2307 | 0.2076 | 0.1869 |
| 13 | 0.8787 | 0.7730 | 0.6810 | 0.6006 | 0.5303 | 0.4688 | 0.4150 | 0.3677 | 0.3262 | 0.2897 | 0.2575 | 0.2292 | 0.2042 | 0.1821 | 0.1625 |
| 14 | 0.8700 | 0.7579 | 0.6611 | 0.5775 | 0.5051 | 0.4423 | 0.3878 | 0.3405 | 0.2992 | 0.2633 | 0.2320 | 0.2046 | 0.1807 | 0.1597 | 0.1413 |
| 15 | 0.8613 | 0.7430 | 0.6419 | 0.5553 | 0.4810 | 0.4173 | 0.3624 | 0.3152 | 0.2745 | 0.2394 | 0.2090 | 0.1827 | 0.1599 | 0.1401 | 0.1229 |

(*Continued*)

**Table A**   (*Continued*)

| n/r | 1% | 2% | 3% | 4% | 5% | 6% | 7% | 8% | 9% | 10% | 11% | 12% | 13% | 14% | 15% |
|---|---|---|---|---|---|---|---|---|---|---|---|---|---|---|---|
| 16 | 0.8528 | 0.7284 | 0.6232 | 0.5339 | 0.4581 | 0.3936 | 0.3387 | 0.2919 | 0.2519 | 0.2176 | 0.1883 | 0.1631 | 0.1415 | 0.1229 | 0.1069 |
| 17 | 0.8444 | 0.7142 | 0.6050 | 0.5134 | 0.4363 | 0.3714 | 0.3166 | 0.2703 | 0.2311 | 0.1978 | 0.1696 | 0.1456 | 0.1252 | 0.1078 | 0.0929 |
| 18 | 0.8360 | 0.7002 | 0.5874 | 0.4936 | 0.4155 | 0.3503 | 0.2959 | 0.2502 | 0.2120 | 0.1799 | 0.1528 | 0.1300 | 0.1108 | 0.0946 | 0.0808 |
| 19 | 0.8277 | 0.6864 | 0.5703 | 0.4746 | 0.3957 | 0.3305 | 0.2765 | 0.2317 | 0.1945 | 0.1635 | 0.1377 | 0.1161 | 0.0981 | 0.0829 | 0.0703 |
| 20 | 0.8195 | 0.6730 | 0.5537 | 0.4564 | 0.3769 | 0.3118 | 0.2584 | 0.2145 | 0.1784 | 0.1486 | 0.1240 | 0.1037 | 0.0868 | 0.0728 | 0.0611 |
| 21 | 0.8114 | 0.6598 | 0.5375 | 0.4388 | 0.3589 | 0.2942 | 0.2415 | 0.1987 | 0.1637 | 0.1351 | 0.1117 | 0.0926 | 0.0768 | 0.0638 | 0.0531 |
| 22 | 0.8034 | 0.6468 | 0.5219 | 0.4220 | 0.3418 | 0.2775 | 0.2257 | 0.1839 | 0.1502 | 0.1228 | 0.1007 | 0.0826 | 0.0680 | 0.0560 | 0.0462 |
| 23 | 0.7954 | 0.6342 | 0.5067 | 0.4057 | 0.3256 | 0.2618 | 0.2109 | 0.1703 | 0.1378 | 0.1117 | 0.0907 | 0.0738 | 0.0601 | 0.0491 | 0.0402 |
| 24 | 0.7876 | 0.6217 | 0.4919 | 0.3901 | 0.3101 | 0.2470 | 0.1971 | 0.1577 | 0.1264 | 0.1015 | 0.0817 | 0.0659 | 0.0532 | 0.0431 | 0.0349 |
| 25 | 0.7798 | 0.6095 | 0.4776 | 0.3751 | 0.2953 | 0.2330 | 0.1842 | 0.1460 | 0.1160 | 0.0923 | 0.0736 | 0.0588 | 0.0471 | 0.0378 | 0.0304 |
| 26 | 0.7720 | 0.5976 | 0.4637 | 0.3607 | 0.2812 | 0.2198 | 0.1722 | 0.1352 | 0.1064 | 0.0839 | 0.0663 | 0.0525 | 0.0417 | 0.0331 | 0.0264 |
| 27 | 0.7644 | 0.5859 | 0.4502 | 0.3468 | 0.2678 | 0.2074 | 0.1609 | 0.1252 | 0.0976 | 0.0763 | 0.0597 | 0.0469 | 0.0369 | 0.0291 | 0.0230 |
| 28 | 0.7568 | 0.5744 | 0.4371 | 0.3335 | 0.2551 | 0.1956 | 0.1504 | 0.1159 | 0.0895 | 0.0693 | 0.0538 | 0.0419 | 0.0326 | 0.0255 | 0.0200 |
| 29 | 0.7493 | 0.5631 | 0.4243 | 0.3207 | 0.2429 | 0.1846 | 0.1406 | 0.1073 | 0.0822 | 0.0630 | 0.0485 | 0.0374 | 0.0289 | 0.0224 | 0.0174 |
| 30 | 0.7419 | 0.5521 | 0.4120 | 0.3083 | 0.2314 | 0.1741 | 0.1314 | 0.0994 | 0.0754 | 0.0573 | 0.0437 | 0.0334 | 0.0256 | 0.0196 | 0.0151 |
| 35 | 0.7059 | 0.5000 | 0.3554 | 0.2534 | 0.1813 | 0.1301 | 0.0937 | 0.0676 | 0.0490 | 0.0356 | 0.0259 | 0.0189 | 0.0139 | 0.0102 | 0.0075 |
| 40 | 0.6717 | 0.4529 | 0.3066 | 0.2083 | 0.1420 | 0.0972 | 0.0668 | 0.0460 | 0.0318 | 0.0221 | 0.0154 | 0.0107 | 0.0075 | 0.0053 | 0.0037 |
| 45 | 0.6391 | 0.4102 | 0.2644 | 0.1713 | 0.1112 | 0.0727 | 0.0476 | 0.0313 | 0.0207 | 0.0137 | 0.0091 | 0.0061 | 0.0041 | 0.0027 | 0.0019 |
| 50 | 0.6080 | 0.3715 | 0.2281 | 0.1407 | 0.0872 | 0.0543 | 0.0339 | 0.0213 | 0.0134 | 0.0085 | 0.0054 | 0.0035 | 0.0022 | 0.0014 | 0.0009 |

(*Continued*)

**Table A** (*Continued*)

| n / r | 16% | 18% | 20% | 22% | 24% | 26% | 28% | 30% | 32% | 34% | 36% | 38% | 40% | 45% | 50% |
|---|---|---|---|---|---|---|---|---|---|---|---|---|---|---|---|
| 1 | 0.8621 | 0.8475 | 0.8333 | 0.8197 | 0.8065 | 0.7937 | 0.7813 | 0.7692 | 0.7576 | 0.7463 | 0.7353 | 0.7246 | 0.7143 | 0.6897 | 0.6667 |
| 2 | 0.7432 | 0.7182 | 0.6944 | 0.6719 | 0.6504 | 0.6299 | 0.6104 | 0.5917 | 0.5739 | 0.5569 | 0.5407 | 0.5251 | 0.5102 | 0.4756 | 0.4444 |
| 3 | 0.6407 | 0.6086 | 0.5787 | 0.5507 | 0.5245 | 0.4999 | 0.4768 | 0.4552 | 0.4348 | 0.4156 | 0.3975 | 0.3805 | 0.3644 | 0.3280 | 0.2963 |
| 4 | 0.5523 | 0.5158 | 0.4823 | 0.4514 | 0.4230 | 0.3968 | 0.3725 | 0.3501 | 0.3294 | 0.3102 | 0.2923 | 0.2757 | 0.2603 | 0.2262 | 0.1975 |
| 5 | 0.4761 | 0.4371 | 0.4019 | 0.3700 | 0.3411 | 0.3149 | 0.2910 | 0.2693 | 0.2495 | 0.2315 | 0.2149 | 0.1998 | 0.1859 | 0.1560 | 0.1317 |
| 6 | 0.4104 | 0.3704 | 0.3349 | 0.3033 | 0.2751 | 0.2499 | 0.2274 | 0.2072 | 0.1890 | 0.1727 | 0.1580 | 0.1448 | 0.1328 | 0.1076 | 0.0878 |
| 7 | 0.3538 | 0.3139 | 0.2791 | 0.2486 | 0.2218 | 0.1983 | 0.1776 | 0.1594 | 0.1432 | 0.1289 | 0.1162 | 0.1049 | 0.0949 | 0.0742 | 0.0585 |
| 8 | 0.3050 | 0.2660 | 0.2326 | 0.2038 | 0.1789 | 0.1574 | 0.1388 | 0.1226 | 0.1085 | 0.0962 | 0.0854 | 0.0760 | 0.0678 | 0.0512 | 0.0390 |
| 9 | 0.2630 | 0.2255 | 0.1938 | 0.1670 | 0.1443 | 0.1249 | 0.1084 | 0.0943 | 0.0822 | 0.0718 | 0.0628 | 0.0551 | 0.0484 | 0.0353 | 0.0260 |
| 10 | 0.2267 | 0.1911 | 0.1615 | 0.1369 | 0.1164 | 0.0992 | 0.0847 | 0.0725 | 0.0623 | 0.0536 | 0.0462 | 0.0399 | 0.0346 | 0.0243 | 0.0173 |
| 11 | 0.1954 | 0.1619 | 0.1346 | 0.1122 | 0.0938 | 0.0787 | 0.0662 | 0.0558 | 0.0472 | 0.0400 | 0.0340 | 0.0289 | 0.0247 | 0.0168 | 0.0116 |
| 12 | 0.1685 | 0.1372 | 0.1122 | 0.0920 | 0.0757 | 0.0625 | 0.0517 | 0.0429 | 0.0357 | 0.0298 | 0.0250 | 0.0210 | 0.0176 | 0.0116 | 0.0077 |
| 13 | 0.1452 | 0.1163 | 0.0935 | 0.0754 | 0.0610 | 0.0496 | 0.0404 | 0.0330 | 0.0271 | 0.0223 | 0.0184 | 0.0152 | 0.0126 | 0.0080 | 0.0051 |
| 14 | 0.1252 | 0.0985 | 0.0779 | 0.0618 | 0.0492 | 0.0393 | 0.0316 | 0.0253 | 0.0205 | 0.0166 | 0.0135 | 0.0110 | 0.0090 | 0.0055 | 0.0034 |
| 15 | 0.1079 | 0.0835 | 0.0649 | 0.0507 | 0.0397 | 0.0312 | 0.0247 | 0.0195 | 0.0155 | 0.0124 | 0.0099 | 0.0080 | 0.0064 | 0.0038 | 0.0023 |
| 16 | 0.0930 | 0.0708 | 0.0541 | 0.0415 | 0.0320 | 0.0248 | 0.0193 | 0.0150 | 0.0118 | 0.0093 | 0.0073 | 0.0058 | 0.0046 | 0.0026 | 0.0015 |
| 17 | 0.0802 | 0.0600 | 0.0451 | 0.0340 | 0.0258 | 0.0197 | 0.0150 | 0.0116 | 0.0089 | 0.0069 | 0.0054 | 0.0042 | 0.0033 | 0.0018 | 0.0010 |
| 18 | 0.0691 | 0.0508 | 0.0376 | 0.0279 | 0.0208 | 0.0156 | 0.0118 | 0.0089 | 0.0068 | 0.0052 | 0.0039 | 0.0030 | 0.0023 | 0.0012 | 0.0007 |
| 19 | 0.0596 | 0.0431 | 0.0313 | 0.0229 | 0.0168 | 0.0124 | 0.0092 | 0.0068 | 0.0051 | 0.0038 | 0.0029 | 0.0022 | 0.0017 | 0.0009 | 0.0005 |
| 20 | 0.0514 | 0.0365 | 0.0261 | 0.0187 | 0.0135 | 0.0098 | 0.0072 | 0.0053 | 0.0039 | 0.0029 | 0.0021 | 0.0016 | 0.0012 | 0.0006 | 0.0003 |

(*Continued*)

**Table A**   (*Continued*)

| n/r | 16% | 18% | 20% | 22% | 24% | 26% | 28% | 30% | 32% | 34% | 36% | 38% | 40% | 45% | 50% |
|---|---|---|---|---|---|---|---|---|---|---|---|---|---|---|---|
| 21 | 0.0443 | 0.0309 | 0.0217 | 0.0154 | 0.0109 | 0.0078 | 0.0056 | 0.0040 | 0.0029 | 0.0021 | 0.0016 | 0.0012 | 0.0009 | 0.0004 | 0.0002 |
| 22 | 0.0382 | 0.0262 | 0.0181 | 0.0126 | 0.0088 | 0.0062 | 0.0044 | 0.0031 | 0.0022 | 0.0016 | 0.0012 | 0.0008 | 0.0006 | 0.0003 | 0.0001 |
| 23 | 0.0329 | 0.0222 | 0.0151 | 0.0103 | 0.0071 | 0.0049 | 0.0034 | 0.0024 | 0.0017 | 0.0012 | 0.0008 | 0.0006 | 0.0004 | 0.0002 | 0.0001 |
| 24 | 0.0284 | 0.0188 | 0.0126 | 0.0085 | 0.0057 | 0.0039 | 0.0027 | 0.0018 | 0.0013 | 0.0009 | 0.0006 | 0.0004 | 0.0003 | 0.0001 | 0.0001 |
| 25 | 0.0245 | 0.0160 | 0.0105 | 0.0069 | 0.0046 | 0.0031 | 0.0021 | 0.0014 | 0.0010 | 0.0007 | 0.0005 | 0.0003 | 0.0002 | 0.0001 | 0.0000 |
| 26 | 0.0211 | 0.0135 | 0.0087 | 0.0057 | 0.0037 | 0.0025 | 0.0016 | 0.0011 | 0.0007 | 0.0005 | 0.0003 | 0.0002 | 0.0002 | 0.0001 | |
| 27 | 0.0182 | 0.0115 | 0.0073 | 0.0047 | 0.0030 | 0.0019 | 0.0013 | 0.0008 | 0.0006 | 0.0004 | 0.0002 | 0.0002 | 0.0001 | 0.0000 | |
| 28 | 0.0157 | 0.0097 | 0.0061 | 0.0038 | 0.0024 | 0.0015 | 0.0010 | 0.0006 | 0.0004 | 0.0003 | 0.0002 | 0.0001 | 0.0001 | | |
| 29 | 0.0135 | 0.0082 | 0.0051 | 0.0031 | 0.0020 | 0.0012 | 0.0008 | 0.0005 | 0.0003 | 0.0002 | 0.0001 | 0.0001 | 0.0001 | | |
| 30 | 0.0116 | 0.0070 | 0.0042 | 0.0026 | 0.0016 | 0.0010 | 0.0006 | 0.0004 | 0.0002 | 0.0002 | 0.0001 | 0.0001 | 0.0000 | | |
| 35 | 0.0055 | 0.0030 | 0.0017 | 0.0009 | 0.0005 | 0.0003 | 0.0002 | 0.0001 | 0.0001 | 0.0000 | 0.0000 | 0.0000 | | | |
| 40 | 0.0026 | 0.0013 | 0.0007 | 0.0004 | 0.0002 | 0.0001 | 0.0001 | 0.0000 | 0.0000 | | | | | | |
| 45 | 0.0013 | 0.0006 | 0.0003 | 0.0001 | 0.0001 | 0.0000 | 0.0000 | | | | | | | | |
| 50 | 0.0006 | 0.0003 | 0.0001 | 0.0000 | 0.0000 | | | | | | | | | | |

*Note:* [a] *r* is the rate of discount and *n* is the number of time periods.

**Table B** Present value of $1.00 received[a] per period $(1 - (1 + r)^{-n})/r$.

| n/r | 1% | 2% | 3% | 4% | 5% | 6% | 7% | 8% | 9% | 10% | 11% | 12% | 13% | 14% | 15% |
|---|---|---|---|---|---|---|---|---|---|---|---|---|---|---|---|
| 1 | 0.9901 | 0.9804 | 0.9709 | 0.9615 | 0.9524 | 0.9434 | 0.9346 | 0.9259 | 0.9174 | 0.9091 | 0.9009 | 0.8929 | 0.8850 | 0.8772 | 0.8696 |
| 2 | 1.9704 | 1.9416 | 1.9135 | 1.8861 | 1.8594 | 1.8334 | 1.8080 | 1.7833 | 1.7591 | 1.7355 | 1.7125 | 1.6901 | 1.6681 | 1.6467 | 1.6257 |
| 3 | 2.9410 | 2.8839 | 2.8286 | 2.7751 | 2.7232 | 2.6730 | 2.6243 | 2.5771 | 2.5313 | 2.4869 | 2.4437 | 2.4018 | 2.3612 | 2.3216 | 2.2832 |
| 4 | 3.9020 | 3.8077 | 3.7171 | 3.6299 | 3.5459 | 3.4651 | 3.3872 | 3.3121 | 3.2397 | 3.1699 | 3.1024 | 3.0373 | 2.9745 | 2.9137 | 2.8550 |
| 5 | 4.8534 | 4.7135 | 4.5797 | 4.4518 | 4.3295 | 4.2124 | 4.1002 | 3.9927 | 3.8897 | 3.7908 | 3.6959 | 3.6048 | 3.5172 | 3.4331 | 3.3522 |
| 6 | 5.7955 | 5.6014 | 5.4172 | 5.2421 | 5.0757 | 4.9173 | 4.7665 | 4.6229 | 4.4859 | 4.3553 | 4.2305 | 4.1114 | 3.9975 | 3.8887 | 3.7845 |
| 7 | 6.7282 | 6.4720 | 6.2303 | 6.0020 | 5.7864 | 5.5824 | 5.3893 | 5.2064 | 5.0330 | 4.8684 | 4.7122 | 4.5638 | 4.4226 | 4.2883 | 4.1604 |
| 8 | 7.6517 | 7.3255 | 7.0197 | 6.7327 | 6.4632 | 6.2098 | 5.9713 | 5.7466 | 5.5348 | 5.3349 | 5.1461 | 4.9676 | 4.7988 | 4.6389 | 4.4873 |
| 9 | 8.5660 | 8.1622 | 7.7861 | 7.4353 | 7.1078 | 6.8017 | 6.5152 | 6.2469 | 5.9952 | 5.7590 | 5.5370 | 5.3282 | 5.1317 | 4.9464 | 4.7716 |
| 10 | 9.4713 | 8.9826 | 8.5302 | 8.1109 | 7.7217 | 7.3601 | 7.0236 | 6.7101 | 6.4177 | 6.1446 | 5.8892 | 5.6502 | 5.4262 | 5.2161 | 5.0188 |
| 11 | 10.3676 | 9.7868 | 9.2526 | 8.7605 | 8.3064 | 7.8869 | 7.4987 | 7.1390 | 6.8051 | 6.4951 | 6.2065 | 5.9377 | 5.6869 | 5.4527 | 5.2337 |
| 12 | 11.2551 | 10.5753 | 9.9540 | 9.3851 | 8.8632 | 8.3838 | 7.9427 | 7.5361 | 7.1607 | 6.8137 | 6.4924 | 6.1944 | 5.9176 | 5.6603 | 5.4206 |
| 13 | 12.1337 | 11.3484 | 10.6350 | 9.9856 | 9.3936 | 8.8527 | 8.3577 | 7.9038 | 7.4869 | 7.1034 | 6.7499 | 6.4235 | 6.1218 | 5.8424 | 5.5831 |
| 14 | 13.0037 | 12.1062 | 11.2961 | 10.5631 | 9.8986 | 9.2950 | 8.7455 | 8.2442 | 7.7862 | 7.3667 | 6.9819 | 6.6282 | 6.3025 | 6.0021 | 5.7245 |
| 15 | 13.8650 | 12.8493 | 11.9379 | 11.1184 | 10.3797 | 9.7122 | 9.1079 | 8.5595 | 8.0607 | 7.6061 | 7.1909 | 6.8109 | 6.4624 | 6.1422 | 5.8474 |
| 16 | 14.7179 | 13.5777 | 12.5611 | 11.6523 | 10.8378 | 10.1059 | 9.4466 | 8.8514 | 8.3126 | 7.8237 | 7.3792 | 6.9740 | 6.6039 | 6.2651 | 5.9542 |
| 17 | 15.5622 | 14.2919 | 13.1661 | 12.1657 | 11.2741 | 10.4773 | 9.7632 | 9.1216 | 8.5436 | 8.0216 | 7.5488 | 7.1196 | 6.7291 | 6.3729 | 6.0472 |
| 18 | 16.3983 | 14.9920 | 13.7535 | 12.6593 | 11.6896 | 10.8276 | 10.0591 | 9.3719 | 8.7556 | 8.2014 | 7.7016 | 7.2497 | 6.8399 | 6.4674 | 6.1280 |
| 19 | 17.2260 | 15.6785 | 14.3238 | 13.1339 | 12.0853 | 11.1581 | 10.3356 | 9.6036 | 8.9501 | 8.3649 | 7.8393 | 7.3658 | 6.9380 | 6.5504 | 6.1982 |
| 20 | 18.0455 | 16.3514 | 14.8775 | 13.5903 | 12.4622 | 11.4699 | 10.5940 | 9.8181 | 9.1285 | 8.5136 | 7.9633 | 7.4694 | 7.0248 | 6.6231 | 6.2593 |

*(Continued)*

**Table B**  *(Continued)*

| n/r | 1% | 2% | 3% | 4% | 5% | 6% | 7% | 8% | 9% | 10% | 11% | 12% | 13% | 14% | 15% |
|---|---|---|---|---|---|---|---|---|---|---|---|---|---|---|---|
| 21 | 18.8570 | 17.0112 | 15.4150 | 14.0292 | 12.8211 | 11.7641 | 10.8355 | 10.0168 | 9.2922 | 8.6487 | 8.0751 | 7.5620 | 7.1015 | 6.6870 | 6.3125 |
| 22 | 19.6604 | 17.6580 | 15.9369 | 14.4511 | 13.1630 | 12.0416 | 11.0612 | 10.2007 | 9.4424 | 8.7715 | 8.1757 | 7.6446 | 7.1695 | 6.7429 | 6.3587 |
| 23 | 20.4558 | 18.2922 | 16.4436 | 14.8568 | 13.4886 | 12.3034 | 11.2722 | 10.3711 | 9.5802 | 8.8832 | 8.2664 | 7.7184 | 7.2297 | 6.7921 | 6.3988 |
| 24 | 21.2434 | 18.0139 | 16.9355 | 15.2470 | 13.7986 | 12.5504 | 11.4693 | 10.5288 | 9.7066 | 8.9847 | 8.3481 | 7.7843 | 7.2829 | 6.8351 | 6.4338 |
| 25 | 22.0232 | 19.5235 | 17.4131 | 15.6221 | 14.0939 | 12.7834 | 11.6536 | 10.6748 | 9.8226 | 9.0770 | 8.4217 | 7.8431 | 7.3300 | 6.8729 | 4.4641 |
| 26 | 22.7952 | 20.1210 | 17.8768 | 15.9828 | 14.3752 | 13.0032 | 11.8258 | 10.8100 | 9.9290 | 9.1609 | 8.4881 | 7.8957 | 7.3717 | 6.9061 | 6.4906 |
| 27 | 23.5596 | 20.7069 | 18.3270 | 16.3296 | 14.6430 | 13.2105 | 11.9867 | 10.9352 | 10.0266 | 9.2372 | 8.5478 | 7.9426 | 7.4086 | 6.9352 | 6.5135 |
| 28 | 24.3164 | 21.2813 | 18.7641 | 16.6631 | 14.8981 | 13.4062 | 12.1371 | 11.0511 | 10.1161 | 9.3066 | 8.6016 | 7.9844 | 7.4412 | 6.9607 | 6.5335 |
| 29 | 25.0658 | 21.8444 | 19.1884 | 16.9837 | 15.1411 | 13.5907 | 12.2777 | 11.1584 | 10.1983 | 9.3696 | 8.6501 | 8.0218 | 7.4701 | 6.9830 | 6.5509 |
| 30 | 25.8077 | 22.3965 | 19.6004 | 17.2920 | 15.3724 | 13.7468 | 12.4090 | 11.2578 | 10.2737 | 9.4269 | 8.6938 | 8.0552 | 7.4957 | 7.0027 | 6.5660 |
| 31 | 26.5423 | 22.9377 | 20.0004 | 17.5885 | 15.5928 | 13.9291 | 12.5318 | 11.3948 | 10.3428 | 9.4790 | 8.7331 | 8.0850 | 7.5183 | 7.0199 | 6.5791 |
| 32 | 27.2696 | 23.4683 | 20.3888 | 17.8735 | 15.8027 | 14.0840 | 12.6466 | 11.4350 | 10.4062 | 9.5264 | 8.7686 | 8.1116 | 7.5383 | 7.0350 | 6.5805 |
| 33 | 27.9897 | 23.9886 | 20.7658 | 18.1476 | 16.0025 | 14.2302 | 12.7538 | 11.5139 | 10.4644 | 9.5694 | 8.8005 | 8.1354 | 7.5560 | 7.0482 | 6.6005 |
| 34 | 28.7027 | 24.4986 | 21.1318 | 18.4112 | 16.1929 | 14.3681 | 12.8540 | 11.5869 | 10.5178 | 9.6086 | 8.8293 | 8.1566 | 7.5717 | 7.0599 | 6.6091 |
| 35 | 29.4086 | 24.9986 | 21.4872 | 18.6646 | 16.3742 | 14.4982 | 12.9477 | 11.6546 | 10.5668 | 9.6442 | 8.8552 | 8.1755 | 7.5856 | 7.0700 | 6.6166 |
| 40 | 32.8347 | 27.3555 | 23.1148 | 19.7928 | 17.1591 | 15.0463 | 13.3317 | 11.9246 | 10.7574 | 9.7791 | 8.9511 | 8.2438 | 7.6344 | 7.1050 | 6.6418 |
| 45 | 36.0945 | 29.4902 | 24.5187 | 20.7200 | 17.7741 | 15.4558 | 13.6055 | 12.1084 | 10.8812 | 9.8628 | 9.0079 | 8.2825 | 7.6609 | 7.1232 | 6.6543 |
| 50 | 39.1961 | 31.4236 | 25.7298 | 21.4822 | 18.2559 | 15.7619 | 13.8007 | 12.2335 | 10.9617 | 9.9148 | 9.0417 | 8.3045 | 7.6752 | 7.1327 | 6.6605 |

*(Continued)*

**Table B** *(Continued)*

| n/r | 16% | 18% | 20% | 22% | 24% | 26% | 28% | 30% | 32% | 34% | 36% | 38% | 40% | 45% | 50% |
|---|---|---|---|---|---|---|---|---|---|---|---|---|---|---|---|
| 1 | 0.8621 | 0.8475 | 0.8333 | 0.8197 | 0.8065 | 0.7937 | 0.7813 | 0.7692 | 0.7576 | 0.7463 | 0.7353 | 0.7246 | 0.7143 | 0.6897 | 0.6667 |
| 2 | 1.6052 | 1.5656 | 1.5278 | 1.4915 | 1.4568 | 1.4235 | 1.3916 | 1.3609 | 1.3315 | 1.3032 | 1.2760 | 1.2497 | 1.2245 | 1.1653 | 1.1111 |
| 3 | 2.2459 | 2.1743 | 2.1065 | 2.0422 | 1.9813 | 1.9234 | 1.8684 | 1.8161 | 1.7663 | 1.7188 | 1.6735 | 1.6302 | 1.5889 | 1.4933 | 1.4074 |
| 4 | 2.7982 | 2.6901 | 2.5887 | 2.4936 | 2.4043 | 2.3202 | 2.2410 | 2.1662 | 2.0957 | 2.0290 | 1.9658 | 1.9060 | 1.8492 | 1.7195 | 1.6049 |
| 5 | 3.2743 | 3.1272 | 2.9906 | 2.8636 | 2.7454 | 2.6351 | 2.5320 | 2.4356 | 2.3452 | 2.2604 | 2.1807 | 2.1058 | 2.0352 | 1.8755 | 1.7366 |
| 6 | 3.6847 | 3.4976 | 3.3255 | 3.1669 | 3.0205 | 2.8850 | 2.7594 | 2.6427 | 2.5342 | 2.4331 | 2.3388 | 2.2506 | 2.1680 | 1.9831 | 1.8244 |
| 7 | 4.0386 | 3.8115 | 3.6046 | 3.4155 | 3.2423 | 3.0833 | 2.9370 | 2.8021 | 2.6775 | 2.5620 | 2.4550 | 2.3555 | 2.2628 | 2.0573 | 1.8829 |
| 8 | 4.3436 | 4.0776 | 3.8372 | 3.6193 | 3.4212 | 3.2407 | 3.0758 | 2.9247 | 2.7860 | 2.6582 | 2.5404 | 2.4315 | 2.3306 | 2.1085 | 1.9220 |
| 9 | 4.6065 | 4.3030 | 4.0310 | 3.7863 | 3.5655 | 3.3657 | 3.1842 | 3.0190 | 2.8681 | 2.7300 | 2.6033 | 2.4866 | 2.3790 | 2.1438 | 1.9480 |
| 10 | 4.8332 | 4.4941 | 4.1925 | 3.9232 | 3.6819 | 3.4648 | 3.2689 | 3.0915 | 2.9304 | 2.7836 | 2.6495 | 2.5265 | 2.4136 | 2.1681 | 1.9053 |
| 11 | 5.0286 | 4.6560 | 4.3271 | 4.0354 | 3.7757 | 3.5435 | 3.3351 | 3.1473 | 2.9776 | 2.8236 | 2.6834 | 2.5555 | 2.4383 | 2.1849 | 1.9769 |
| 12 | 5.1971 | 4.7932 | 4.4392 | 4.1274 | 3.8514 | 3.6059 | 3.3868 | 3.1903 | 3.0133 | 2.8534 | 2.7084 | 2.5764 | 2.4559 | 2.1965 | 1.9845 |
| 13 | 5.3423 | 4.9095 | 4.5327 | 4.2028 | 3.9124 | 3.6555 | 3.4272 | 3.2233 | 3.0404 | 2.8757 | 2.7268 | 2.5916 | 2.4685 | 2.2045 | 1.9897 |
| 14 | 5.4675 | 5.0081 | 4.6106 | 4.2646 | 3.9616 | 3.6949 | 3.4587 | 3.2487 | 3.0609 | 2.8923 | 2.7403 | 2.6026 | 2.4775 | 2.2100 | 1.9931 |
| 15 | 5.5755 | 5.0916 | 4.6755 | 4.3152 | 4.0013 | 3.7261 | 3.4834 | 3.2682 | 3.0764 | 2.9047 | 2.7502 | 2.6106 | 2.4839 | 2.2138 | 1.9954 |
| 16 | 5.6685 | 5.1624 | 4.7296 | 4.3567 | 4.0333 | 3.7509 | 3.5026 | 3.2832 | 3.0882 | 2.9140 | 2.7575 | 2.6164 | 2.4885 | 2.2164 | 1.9970 |
| 17 | 5.7487 | 5.2223 | 4.7746 | 4.3908 | 4.0591 | 3.7705 | 3.5177 | 3.2948 | 3.0971 | 2.9209 | 2.7629 | 2.6206 | 2.4918 | 2.2182 | 1.9980 |
| 18 | 5.8178 | 5.2732 | 4.8122 | 4.4187 | 4.0799 | 3.7861 | 3.5294 | 3.3037 | 3.1039 | 2.9260 | 2.7668 | 2.6236 | 2.4941 | 2.2195 | 1.9986 |
| 19 | 5.8775 | 5.3162 | 4.8435 | 4.4415 | 4.0967 | 3.7985 | 3.5386 | 3.3105 | 3.1090 | 2.9299 | 2.7697 | 2.6258 | 2.4958 | 2.2203 | 1.9991 |
| 20 | 5.9288 | 5.3527 | 4.8696 | 4.4603 | 4.1103 | 3.8083 | 3.5458 | 3.3158 | 3.1129 | 2.9327 | 2.7718 | 2.6274 | 2.4970 | 2.2209 | 1.9994 |

*(Continued)*

**Table B** (Continued)

| n/r | 16% | 18% | 20% | 22% | 24% | 26% | 28% | 30% | 32% | 34% | 36% | 38% | 40% | 45% | 50% |
|---|---|---|---|---|---|---|---|---|---|---|---|---|---|---|---|
| 21 | 5.9731 | 5.3837 | 4.8913 | 4.4756 | 4.1212 | 3.8161 | 3.5514 | 3.3198 | 3.1158 | 2.9349 | 2.7734 | 2.6285 | 2.4979 | 2.2213 | 1.9996 |
| 22 | 6.0113 | 5.4099 | 4.9094 | 4.4882 | 4.1300 | 3.8223 | 3.5558 | 3.3230 | 3.1180 | 2.9365 | 2.7746 | 2.6294 | 2.4985 | 2.2216 | 1.9997 |
| 23 | 6.0442 | 5.4321 | 4.9245 | 4.4985 | 4.1371 | 3.8273 | 3.5592 | 3.3253 | 3.1197 | 2.9377 | 2.7754 | 2.6300 | 2.4989 | 2.2218 | 1.9998 |
| 24 | 6.0726 | 5.4509 | 4.9371 | 4.5070 | 4.1428 | 3.8312 | 3.5619 | 3.3272 | 3.1210 | 2.9386 | 2.7760 | 2.6304 | 2.4992 | 2.2219 | 1.9999 |
| 25 | 6.0971 | 5.4669 | 4.9476 | 4.5139 | 4.1474 | 3.8342 | 3.5640 | 3.3286 | 3.1220 | 2.9392 | 2.7765 | 2.6307 | 2.4994 | 2.2220 | 1.9999 |
| 26 | 6.1182 | 5.4804 | 4.9563 | 4.5196 | 4.1511 | 3.8367 | 3.5656 | 3.3297 | 3.1227 | 2.9397 | 2.7768 | 2.6310 | 2.4996 | 2.2221 | 1.9999 |
| 27 | 6.1364 | 5.4919 | 4.9636 | 4.5243 | 4.1542 | 3.8387 | 3.5669 | 3.3305 | 3.1233 | 2.9401 | 2.7771 | 2.6311 | 2.4887 | 2.2221 | 2.0000 |
| 28 | 6.1520 | 5.5016 | 4.9697 | 4.5281 | 4.1566 | 3.8402 | 3.5679 | 3.3312 | 3.1237 | 2.9404 | 2.7773 | 2.6313 | 2.4998 | 2.2222 | 2.0000 |
| 29 | 6.1656 | 5.5098 | 4.9747 | 4.5312 | 4.1585 | 3.8414 | 3.5687 | 3.3316 | 3.1240 | 2.9406 | 2.7774 | 2.6313 | 2.4999 | 2.2222 | 2.0000 |
| 30 | 6.1772 | 5.5168 | 4.9789 | 4.5338 | 4.1601 | 3.8424 | 3.5693 | 3.3321 | 3.1242 | 2.9407 | 2.7775 | 2.6314 | 2.4999 | 2.2222 | 2.0000 |
| 31 | 6.1872 | 5.5227 | 4.9824 | 4.5359 | 4.1614 | 3.8432 | 3.5697 | 3.3324 | 3.1244 | 2.9408 | 2.7776 | 2.6315 | 2.4999 | 2.2222 | 2.0000 |
| 32 | 6.1959 | 5.5277 | 4.9854 | 4.5376 | 4.1624 | 3.8438 | 3.5701 | 3.3326 | 3.1246 | 2.9409 | 2.7776 | 2.6315 | 2.4999 | 2.2222 | 2.0000 |
| 33 | 6.2034 | 5.5320 | 4.9878 | 4.5390 | 4.1632 | 3.8443 | 3.5704 | 3.3328 | 3.1247 | 2.9410 | 2.7777 | 2.6215 | 2.5000 | 2.2222 | 2.0000 |
| 34 | 6.2098 | 5.5356 | 4.9898 | 4.5402 | 4.1639 | 3.8447 | 3.5706 | 3.3329 | 3.1248 | 2.9410 | 2.7777 | 2.6315 | 2.5000 | 2.2222 | 2.0000 |
| 35 | 6.2153 | 5.5386 | 4.9915 | 4.5411 | 4.1644 | 3.8450 | 3.5708 | 3.3330 | 3.1248 | 2.9411 | 2.7777 | 2.6215 | 2.5000 | 2.2222 | 2.0000 |
| 40 | 6.2335 | 5.5482 | 4.9966 | 4.5439 | 4.1659 | 3.8458 | 3.5712 | 3.3332 | 3.1250 | 2.9412 | 2.7778 | 2.6316 | 2.5000 | 2.2222 | 2.0000 |
| 45 | 6.2421 | 5.5523 | 4.9986 | 4.5449 | 4.1664 | 3.8460 | 3.5714 | 3.3333 | 3.1250 | 2.9412 | 2.7778 | 2.6316 | 2.5000 | 2.2222 | 2.0000 |
| 50 | 6.2463 | 5.5541 | 4.9995 | 4.5452 | 4.1666 | 3.8461 | 3.5714 | 3.3333 | 3.1250 | 2.9412 | 2.7778 | 2.6316 | 2.5000 | 2.2222 | 2.0000 |

Note: [a] r is the rate of discount and n is the number of time periods.

# About the Author

**Harold Bierman, Jr.** is the Nicholas H. Noyes Professor of Business Administration at the Johnson Graduate School of Management, Cornell University. A graduate of the U.S. Naval Academy, Annapolis, he received his MBA and his Ph.D. from the University of Michigan.

A Cornell faculty member since 1956, Professor Bierman formerly taught at Louisiana State University, the University of Michigan, and the University of Chicago. He has also taught at INSEAD in Fountainebleau, France, and at KUL in Belgium, and was a research fellow at Cambridge University (England).

He was a recipient of the Dow Jones Award from the American Assembly of Collegiate Schools of Business for his outstanding contributions to collegiate business education. He served as a financial consultant at Prudential Bache Securities in New York. His industrial experience includes consulting for Corning Glass Corporation, Eastman Kodak, Sun Oil Company, Exxon Oil Corporation, IBM, and Xerox Corporation. He has written numerous books, including *The Capital Budgeting Decision* (with Seymour Smidt), *Financial Accounting, Managerial Accounting*, and *Quantitative Analysis for Business Decisions*, as well as more than 170 journal articles.

# Index